PALMERSTON AND AFRICA

BOKÉ, RIO NUNEZ, March 24 1849

(Based on a sketch by Lt. de Kerhallet 1849, Centre des Archives d'Outre-Mer, Aix.)

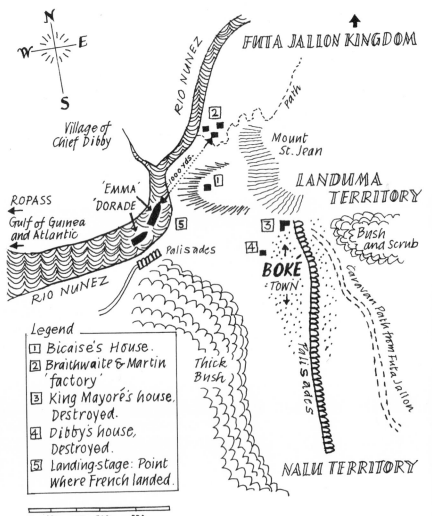

N W E S

RIO NUNEZ

FUTA JALLON KINGDOM

Path

Village of Chief Dibby

Mount St. Jean

LANDUMA TERRITORY

'EMMA' 'DORADE'

1000 yds.

ROPASS

Gulf of Guinea and Atlantic

Bush and Scrub

Palisades

BOKÉ TOWN

RIO NUNEZ

Thick Bush

Caravan Path from Futa Jallon

Palisades

NALU TERRITORY

Legend

1. Bicaise's House.
2. Braithwaite & Martin 'factory'
3. King Mayoré's house, Destroyed.
4. Dibby's house, Destroyed.
5. Landing-stage: Point where French landed.

0   100   200   300   500

scale in metres

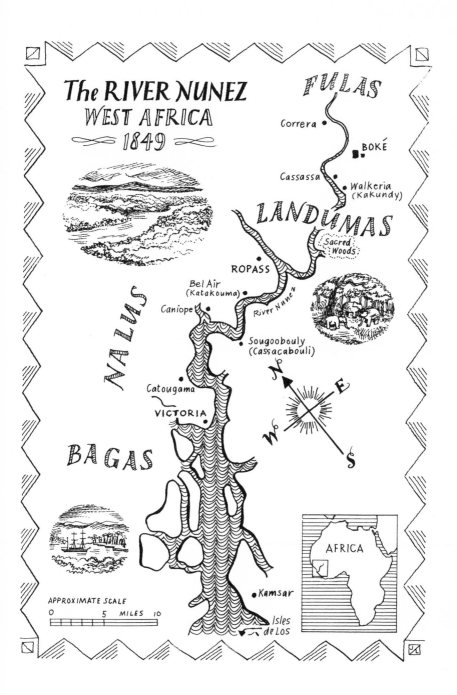

The RIVER NUNEZ
WEST AFRICA
⇒ 1849 ⇐

FULAS

Correra •

■ BOKÉ

Cassassa •

• Walkeria
(Kakundy)

LANDUMAS

Sacred
Woods

ROPASS •

Bel Air
(Katakouma) •

Caniope •

River Nunez

NALUS

• Sougoobouly
(Cassacabouli)

N

E

W

S

• Catougama

VICTORIA •

BAGAS

APPROXIMATE SCALE

0   5   MILES   10

AFRICA

• Kamsar

Isles
de Los

PALMERSTON AND AFRICA
The Rio Nunez Affair:
Competition, Diplomacy and Justice

RODERICK BRAITHWAITE

British Academic Press
London · New York

Published in 1996 by
British Academic Press
An imprint of I.B. Tauris & Co Ltd
Victoria House
Bloomsbury Square
London WC1B 4DZ

175 Fifth Avenue
New York
NY 10010

In the United States of America
and Canada distributed by
St Martin's Press
175 Fifth Avenue
New York
NY 10010

A full CIP record for this book is available from the British Library

Library of Congress catalog card number: available
A full CIP record is available from the Library of Congress

ISBN 1–86084–109–1

Copy-edited and laser-set by Selro Publishing Services, Oxford
Printed and bound in Great Britain by WBC Ltd, Bridgend,
Mid Glamorgan

Contents

'No age was quite so dull as the standard work upon it ... those stationary facts, that stiff procession of dead men are not the past. That was a living, shifting world, that once moved up and down, laughed, whispered, nodded.'

(Philip Guedalla, Introduction to *Palmerston and Gladstone*)

'As in the past, West Africa was not isolated from developments elsewhere in the world.'

(George E. Brooks, *Yankee Traders, Old Coasters and African Middlemen*)

'We must look again to Africa.'

(Palmerston)

Illustrations

Plates

1. J. Martin's drawing of scene of 'The Battle of Dubucca/ Dubucka/Boké' endorsed as correct by Captain Lysaght RN showing the Braithwaite and Martin 'House and Store' well out of the line of fire to the king's 'residence and town' from the *Emma* and the *Dorade*; from 'FO France, Messrs Braithwaite & Martins' Claims, 1849–1853'. By kind permission, the PRO, and Crown Copyright Unit.

2. Cartoon of a jaunty 'Pam', popular 'bottle-holder' between the European powers, 6 December 1851, just before his shock 'resignation', with the Palmerstonian 'signature tune' — the straw in the mouth, and holding his celebrated 'Protocols' — the allusions, and the humour, now obscured). By kind permission of the proprietors of *Punch*.

3. 'Winston', an early Low cartoon of 'Winnie', print from supplement of 1 May 1926, with the famous cigar, from the *New Statesman*, author's collection.

4. Belsize Court/House, Hampstead, nineteenth-century view from the south, family home of Matthew Forster. By kind permission, the Camden Local Studies and Archive Centre.

5. Captain Van Haverbeke of the *Louise-Marie*, Collections Musée royal de l'Armée, Brussels.

6. *The Battle of Boké* by J. P. Clays, Collections Musée royal de l'Armée, Brussels. The print (in P. Crokaert, *Brialmont*, p 407) identifies the Belgian three-masted barque *Emma* (left) and the French brick *Dorade* (right), '*le plus beau fait d'armes de la Marine royale militaire belge.*'

7. The Belgian 'ally', Lamina Towl, king of the Nalus, Rio Nunez, displaying the very European symbols of his authority on the river. Drawing based on that of Ensign Masui (Leconte, *Ancêtres*, p 164), Collections Musée royal de l'Armée, Brussels.

8. Bicaise's house, the Franco-Belgian dependant *comptoir*, Ropass, Rio Nunez. Litho by Jacottet from Leconte (*Ancêtres*, p 172), Collections Musée royal de l'Armée, Brussels.

Figures

1. The Sword of Honour, facing left, showing 'Rio Nunez 1849' on hilt, and *'Les négoçiants du Rio Nunez'* on upper blade, presented on behalf of King Leopold I by the Belgian foreign minister to Captain Van Haverbeke, December 1849. This was in recognition of his aggressive espousal of Belgian and French trading interests against the two British newcomers, Braithwaite and Martin, demonized here as a wicked serpent throttling the combined French and Belgian traders (symbolised by the defenceless naked maiden). By kind permission of Dr R. Boijen, Musée royal de l'Armée, Brussels.

2. West Coast of Africa, highlighting the position of the Nunez, and the 'Naloos' in *res nullius*, between the French to the north at Gorée and the Senegal, and the British to the south at Sierra Leone. From Captain Belcher's report 1830–2, *JRGS*, reproduced by kind permission of the Royal Geographical Society.

3. Routes by which Unilever and the United Africa Company evolved from a multiplicity of constituent firms in West Africa from the eighteenth century onwards, with acknowledgements to F. J. Pedler, *The Lion and the Unicorn in Africa* (London).

4. Letter on Palmerston's authority, from John Bidwell, senior clerk, Foreign Office, London, to HM Consuls at Ghent and Antwerp, July 1849, author's collection.

5. The Diplomatic Triangle, London–Paris–Brussels, October 1849–December 1850, by kind permission, the *Revue belge d'histoire militaire*.

6. Palmerston's memo on Bicaise's disputed nationality, sequel to his astonishingly detailed ten-page memorandum of 2 September 1850, to his Permanent Under-Secretary, Henry Addington, in his characteristically strong hand, and signed with the flowing intitial 'P' (FO France 97/198, by kind permission, the Public Record Office and Crown Copyright Unit.

7. Formal statement in Joseph Braithwaite's hand of the Braithwaite & Martin Claim to Viscount Palmerston, Foreign Office, January 1851, author's collection.

8 Palmerston's State of Current Business (handover) note for Earl Granville, December 1851, showing the high importance still attached to the Nunez Affair by the outgoing Foreign Secretary. By kind permission of the Trustees of the Palmerston

Archives, Hartley Library, Southampton University, and the Crown Copyright Unit.
9. Final letter on behalf of the then Foreign Secretary, the Earl of Clarendon, to Braithwaite and Martin, August 1853, author's collection.

Maps
1. Map of Battle of Boké, based on the drawing by Capitaine de Kerhallet, in Centre des archives d'outre-mer, Aix-en-Provence, by John Liddell.
2. *The Rio Nunez, Guinée, the West Coast of Africa*, drawing by John Liddell, a fellow descendant of the Braithwaite family.

Acronyms and Abbreviations

ADM	Admiralty
aet.	*anno aetatis suae*
B&M	Braithwaite and Martin
B-W	Captain Bouët-Willaumez
B/	Belgian archives
B/MAE	Belgian Ministry of Foreign Affairs
B/MRHA	Musée royal de l'histoire de l'Armée, Brussels
BARSOM	*Bulletin de l'Académie Royale des Sciences d'Outre-Mer*
BESBEC	*Bulletin de la Sociéte belge d'Etudes coloniales*
BL	British Library
BL SPIS	British Library Social Policy Information Service (formerly OPSS)
BL Add. MS	British Library, additional manuscripts, London
Bodl.	Bodleian Library, Oxford
CHR	*Camden History Review*
CO	Colonial Office
F&S	Forster & Smith
F/	French archives
F/CAOM	Centre des archives d'outre-mer, Aix-en-Provence (formerly, Rue Oudinot, Paris)
F/CARAN	Centre d'acceuil et de recherches des Archives nationales, Paris
F/MAE	Ministère des Affaires Etrangères, Paris
FO	Foreign Office
FS	Secretary of State for Foreign Affairs
GA	The Gambia
GC	Gold Coast (except in PBHA refs)
GL/A	Guildhall Library, City of London
HM	Her Majesty Queen Victoria

HoC	House of Commons
HoL	House of Lords
HRO/M	Hampshire Record Office, Malmesbury Papers
JAH	*Journal of African History*
JH/ML	Joan Heddle Papers, in custody of Dr M. Lynn, Belfast
JICH	*Journal of Imperial and Commonwealth History*
JRGS	*Journal of the Royal Geographical Society* (former title)
LJR	Lord John Russell
LR	La Royale (French equivalent of Royal Navy)
LSE	London School of Economics and Political Science
MS[S]	manuscript[s]
NMM	National Maritime Museum, Greenwich, London
NRA	National Register of Archives
P	Palmerston
PBHA	Palmerston Archive, Hartley Library, Southampton University, formerly at Broadlands, Romsey, Hants (BP)
PM	Prime Minister
PP	Parliamentary Papers, British Library, London
PPSC	Parliamentary Papers Select Committee 1842 (55), XI:1, XII:1
PRO	Public Record Office, London
PUS	Permanent Under-Secretary
Q	Questions asked in 1842 Select Committee
QVJ	Queen Victoria's Journal
RA	Royal Archives, Windsor Castle, Berks
RBHM	*Revue belge d'histoire militaire*
RFHOM	*Revue française d'histoire d'outre-mer*
RH/TFB	Buxton MS, Buxton Archive, Rhodes House Library, Oxford
SGA/B	Society of Genealogists Archive, Braithwaite Papers
SL	Sierra Leone
TFB	Thomas Fowell Buxton
TS	Treasury
UL/A	Unilever Archive, Blackfriars, London
VH	Van Haverbeke

Acknowledgements

This book draws from articles by the author which have appeared in the *Journal of Imperial and Commonwealth History* (vol.23, no. 3, September 1995); the *Revue belge d'histoire militaire* (vol.31, nos 1/2, mars–juin 1995); the *Revue française d'histoire d'outre-mer* (vol.83, no.311, 1996); and *Camden History Review 19*, to whose editors and, for *JICH*, Frank Cass Ltd, I am obliged for their permission to quote.

Throughout this research, the author has benefited from the guidance of a number of British authorities on West Africa, both topical — Professor Richard Rathbone (dean of postgraduate studies) and Barbara Turfan (librarian, Africa), School of Oriental and African Studies; and of the time and place — Dr Christopher Fyfe, former reader in African Studies, Edinburgh University; Professor John Hargreaves, emeritus professor of History, University of Aberdeen; and Dr Martin Lynn, School of Modern History, the Queen's University, Belfast. For expert advice on Palmerston and his contemporaries, I am ever in the debt of Jasper Ridley, the late Professor Kenneth Bourne, and Professor Peter Burroughs. I also wish to acknowledge the help of many other writers: Eva Haraszti-Taylor, Sir Robert Rhodes James DL, Philip Ziegler CVO, Lady Antonia Fraser, Rt Hon Kenneth Baker CH MP, Brian Connell, Thomas Pakenham, Ferdinand Mount, George Clare, Rudiger Goerner, and David Day. I owe a debt too, to so many good international historians, but particularly for the specialist knowledge of Professor George Brooks, University of Indiana; Professor Bruce Mouser, University of Wisconsin; Dr Anthony Howe, Department of International History, London School of Economics and Political Science; Dr Jonathan Parry, fellow of Pembroke College, Cambridge; Dr Robert Gavin, the University of Ulster; Professor Howard Temperley, University of East Anglia; and Dr Ray Jones, Carleton University, Ottawa. I also thank Chris De Wilde of Ghent University, for sharing his information about Bicaise, and his topical knowledge of the

Nunez. I would like to acknowledge the help and advice of Tony Cole, consultant archivist, Unilever plc; Dr Keith Hamilton, Foreign and Commonwealth Office; Peter Braithwaite, *The Good Book Guide*; Dr Richard Boijen, Brussels Royal Army Museum; and Professor Odile Goerg, University of Strasbourg. I would also like to express my thanks to Baron G. Dehennin, the Belgian ambassador, and his colleagues; Jenny Wraitt, the National Maritime Museum; M. Facinet Beavogui, University of Conakry; M. Mamadou Camara, the Commission nationale guinéenne pour l'Unesco; Professor Geoffrey Wilson, Department of Law, University of Warwick; Judge Neil Butter; Dr David Wetzel, University of California; Joanna Burch; Gillie de Haas and Dorothy Storr for facilitating the translation from the Flemish sources; Charles Walker; Terry Barringer, Royal Commonwealth Society Library; and John Richardson, chairman, Camden History Society.

For the use of material, I wish to acknowledge the gracious permission of Her Majesty the Queen for access to the Royal Archives, Windsor; also of the trustees of the Palmerston Archive, Dr Woolgar, Southampton University, and the Crown Copyright Unit, for permission to use and quote from the Broadlands collection; of Rosemary Dunhill, Hampshire Record Office and the Malmesbury Trustees; of the editor of the *Geographical Journal*, formerly the *JRGS*; of John Maclean for access to the Maclean/Forster correspondence; of Allan Lodge and Steven Tomlinson, assistant librarians of the Rhodes House and Bodleian libraries, Oxford; of Sarah Tyacke, chief executive, and her team at the Public Record Office; of the National Register of Archives, London; of the staff at the British Library, and the manuscripts department; of Dr Rabut and her staff at the French colonial archives in Aix, Dr Peemans and her staff at the archive of the Belgian Ministry of Foreign Affairs, Brussels; and to Ralph de Smet and his colleagues at the Bibliothèque Albert I, Brussels; my warm thanks also to Simon Blundell, librarian of Palmerston's and Matthew Forster's club, the Reform. For the use of visual material I am most grateful to Mrs E. Bourne, Dr R. Boijen, Messrs Heinemann, the *Illustrated London News*, the *New Statesman* and the proprietors of *Punch*. Nearly last but not least I am particularly appreciative of the support of Dr Lester Crook and his colleagues at I.B. Tauris & Co Ltd. Every attempt has been made to obtain clearance for copyright where needed: if, however, any such permission has been inadvertently omitted, sincere apologies are hereby expressed. Finally, I am warmly grateful to my daughter Clare for her editorial input, and to my wife Joanna for her unwavering belief in this book and for her forebearance with my four-year obsession with the word processor, for help in checking both the PRO and the CAOM papers at Aix, and in avoiding some at least of the more glaring stylistic errors.

For the two maps of the Nunez and Debucca (Boké), I am indebted to a fellow descendant of the Braithwaite family, the artist John Liddell. These are based on a number of sources, to be consulted for exact distances: (i) *Guinée, Carte genérale*, 3615 IGN (1992, 2nd edn), Institut de Topographie et de Cartographie, BP 4485, Conakry, Guinée (only shows present-day Boké, of all the villages mentioned in 1849, but now as a main communications centre, with its own prefecture and hospital); (ii) *Bartholomew's World Travel Map: Africa West 29* (1977 edn); (iii) detailed map by the Officiers du SG de l'AOF of the Boffa region of Guinée française, C.28, XVI, c. 1927 (still showing most of the old names) for a copy of which I am again indebted to C. De Wilde, of Ghent University; (iv) Bibliothèque nationale, Paris, *Cartes et Plans: Marine* 112/4/12(i), used in Everaert and De Wilde, '*Pindanoten*', *BARSOM* (vol.37, no. 3, pp 317–48); (v) Demougeot, *Histoire du Nunez* (p 287 from map of Rio de Nuno Tristao showing Rio Nunez villages, by Sr. d'Anville, the king's chief geographer, 1775); (vi) above all the CAOM, for the detailed sketch of Debucca by Captain de Kerhallet, 1849 (showing the B&M store and defences of Boké/Debucca).

Foreword
by Jasper Ridley

In 1849 the French and Belgian authorities on the West coast of Africa sent a punitive expedition to deal with a troublesome native king. They bombarded the village where he lived, and burned it. Two young Englishmen, Joseph Braithwaite and George Martin, had set up as traders in the village, and lived there in a house which they had furnished as a European residence, complete with silver cutlery on their dining table; and they had raised the Union Jack over the house. The French and Belgians tore down the Union Jack, stole the silver, and burned the house. Braithwaite and Martin asked the British Foreign Secretary, Lord Palmerston, to press the French and Belgian governments to compensate them; but France and Belgium refused to pay.

It was at the time when Palmerston was taking up the case of Don Pacifico with the Greek government, which led to the blockade of the Piraeus by the British navy and to Palmerston's '*civis Romanus*' speech and his political triumph in the House of Commons — the most famous incident in his career. The case of Braithwaite and Martin ended very differently. It has not even been mentioned in any of the biographies of Palmerston, and Roderick Braithwaite, in this erudite book, is the first writer to publish an account of the incident.

Palmerston was still pursuing the case with the French and Belgian governments in December 1851, when Queen Victoria forced him to resign as Foreign Secretary. His successors at the Foreign Office could not persuade the French and Belgians to pay up, and in 1853 Braithwaite and Martin were informed that the British government could do nothing for them. They never obtained any compensation.

What would have happened if Queen Victoria had not driven Palmerston from office? Would he eventually have succeeded where his successors failed? Palmerston did not always obtain compensation for British subjects who had suffered injury at the hands of foreign governments. When the offending country was a second-class maritime power, Palmerston could send the British navy to blockade or bombard its ports; but these vigorous measures, which he used against Portugal, Naples, Greece and China, could not be adopted when he was dealing with a Great Power. Palmerston was less successful in obtaining compensation for a British subject who was maltreated by Austrian troops in Frankfort or for British traders in Mexico whose property was damaged in military operations by the invading American army during the war between Mexico and the United States; but he tried his best to help them. Roderick Braithwaite believes that Braithwaite and Martin were abandoned by the British government, and that if Palmerston had remained at the Foreign Office he would not have abandoned them.

The question remains why Belgium and France refused so obstinately to compensate Braithwaite and Martin when they must have known how badly their forces had behaved. The answer probably lies in the great resentment that Palmerston's handling of the Don Pacifico case had aroused among the governments of Europe. Belgium and France thought it necessary for their prestige to show that Palmerston could not bully them as he had bullied the Greeks. Braithwaite and Martin were the unfortunate victims of the anti-Palmerston mood in Europe.

PALMERSTON AND AFRICA

Prelude: A 'Wanton Outrage' and the Battle of Debucca, 24 March 1849

At dawn on the morning of Saturday 24 March 1849, the Union Jack was flying defiantly at the four corners of the Braithwaite and Martin warehouses, to the north of the hillside at Debucca, a river village some 50 miles inland from the coast of West Africa. Debucca was the capital of the Landuma people, whose king, Margery, was now the 'landlord' to these two new English traders — his protected 'strangers', in the convention of the day. The Rio Nunez, whose upper reaches were dominated by Debucca, was itself the most important trading territory between the colonies of the Gambia and Sierra Leone — in the words of Britain's Foreign Secretary, Lord Palmerston, 'a great commercial highway open to the traders of all nations'.

By noon that day, the four proud flags would be hauled down contemptuously by a young ensign from Britain's ally, Belgium, part of a punitive expedition of French and Belgian sailors and disaffected Landuma mercenaries. Together with silverware laid out by their servant for the morning's breakfast, much of the Britons' trading stores would be taken back as booty on board one of the barques in the marauding force, which had been sent up-river to Debucca. The aim — to deliver a 'rude lesson' to Margery's Landumas — resulted in an incident unprecedented in the history of that time: an unprovoked attack by a foreign navy on traders peacefully engaged in the legitimate non-slaving trade. The British flags were to be burned unceremoniously, like the rest of the warehouse complex itself.

When Joseph Braithwaite and George Martin dared at last to creep out of hiding in the bush, and return through the smoke and the dust to the scene of what the same British Secretary of State was later to describe as 'this wanton outrage', nothing remained. In today's values, trade to the value of more than a quarter of a million pounds had been destroyed; this included the copies of correspondence in their letterbook which could prove their innocence in the whole business. They had been caught in the crossfire of a quarrel between their new 'landlord' and the protectionist Society of Traders further down the river at Ropass, whose interests, each for their own condign reasons, the Belgians and then the French decided to espouse by force.

Although this was the age of individual enterprise, these two young Englishmen, as their letters make clear, were very far from being mere adventurers, the 'dregs of European society', an epithet by which some of the founders of Britain's 'informal empire' have been described. They were patently upright, educated gentlemen, morally opposed to the 'abominable slave trade'. In trying to make some return from their modest capital, they, and many like them, faced conditions of appalling difficulty, danger and disease, with extraordinary optimism, despite only a 50 per cent chance of survival. Braithwaite and Martin were to spend the next four years of their lives struggling to achieve compensation under international law, for the loss of their livelihoods and their high hopes. They were backed by the indefatigable Matthew Forster, the colourful liberal MP for Berwick-upon-Tweed, and head of Forster & Smith, the London merchant house which had sponsored them. Forster, a friend of the great philanthropist, Sir Thomas Fowell Buxton, and the confidant of 'Maclean of the Gold Coast', was a well-seasoned political lobbyist; he became the enthusiastic catalyst for that struggle.

Palmerston and the 'Civis Romanus Sum' Doctrine: 25 June 1850

Just over a year later, the Liberal-radical Lord Palmerston, one of Britain's greatest Foreign Secretaries, would be defending his party, and his own political position, in a speech which was regarded then as one of the finest of his long career, and in the fullness of time as one of the most dramatic occasions that the House of Commons had ever experienced. He was answering accusations of gunboat diplomacy with the facts of a peaceful record: a policy of 'jaw-jaw, not war-war'.

From a position in which the court of a strong-willed young Queen, the Tory opposition, the House of Lords, and most of the absolutist thrones of Europe were all baying for his blood, and even his liberal friends at home and abroad, were predicting his fall, Palmerston — in the words of the wife of one of his own colleagues who had been intriguing with the court against him — 'utterly confounded his enemies'. The peroration of his great speech was the only part which was read out deliberately from notes by this highly accomplished player of roles upon the world stage. In it, he propounded the doctrine of *civis Romanus sum*: the quintessential mid-Victorian declaration that Britain's imperial strength should and would reach out to help any British citizen in any part of the world, like the citizens of ancient Rome, wherever they might be endangered. The speech lasted four and a half hours, about the same time that it had taken Captain Van Haverbeke, for Belgium, and Captains de la Tocnaye and de Kerhallet, for France, to destroy the village of Debucca, and with it the property of two innocent British traders.

It was not appreciated outside the confines of the Foreign Office that at the very time when Palmerston was delivering this thundering tirade against all who might dare to attack a *civis Britannicus*, he was at the height of a diplomatic battle which he had made very much his own — the fight for compensation for the two British citizens caught up in the Nunez adventure. All that was known publicly was the pretext for the speech, the case of Don Pacifico, and the burning of his rather more sophisticated house, three years previously, in Athens. The *cives* currently and unambiguously on his mind during those weeks, and on the desks of his embassies in Paris and Brussels, were Braithwaite and Martin.

'A Sword of Dishonour'

In December 1849 a Sword of Honour, designed by the jeweller of King Leopold of the Belgians, Queen Victoria's 'dear Uncle' and a regular correspondent of Palmerston himself, had been presented in Brussels by the traders of the Nunez. It was duly bestowed, clearly with the king's knowledge, on Captain Van Haverbeke, for his defence of French and Belgian interests in Africa earlier that year; the traders were represented as a beautiful defenceless maiden, forming the handle of the sword.

Viciously curled around her naked bosom was a powerful serpent, modelled on one of the giant pythons of the river, symbolizing the palpably wicked British traders, Joseph Braithwaite and

FIGURE 1 The Sword of Honour, facing left, showing 'Rio Nunez 1849' on hilt, and '*Les négoçiants du Rio Nunez*' on upper blade. Sword of Honour presented on behalf of King Leopold I by the Belgian foreign minister to Captain Van Haverbeke, December 1849. This was in recognition of his aggressive espousal of Belgian and French trading interests against the two British newcomers, Braithwaite and Martin, demonized here as a wicked serpent throttling the combined French and Belgian traders (symbolized by the defenceless naked maiden). By kind permission of Dr R. Boijen, Musée royal de l'Armée, Brussels.

George Martin, who were portrayed as threatening those interests. It might more correctly have been called a sword of dishonour. Someone, somewhere, was lying; the sword still lies, in both senses of the word, in the Brussels Army Museum.

An Unconstitutional Intervention: 19 December 1851

Victoria, still in her early thirties, and under the influence of her equally young husband, Prince Albert, and of the bizarre figure of their *éminence grise*, Baron Friedrich von Stockmar, finally succeeded in a personal aim from which she had been thwarted the year before. She did so through a series of actions whose doubtful constitutionality has not until now been fully explored; the cause of absolute monarchies appeared to be in the ascendant once more. On 19 December 1851, Palmerston, the Churchill of the nineteenth century, the popular 'Pam' beloved of the cartoonists and the people, was removed from the office he had held with success and distinction for most of the preceding 20 years. It must have seemed to him an equally 'wanton act of aggression', this time on the part of a monarchy clinging to an anachronistic concept of its royal prerogative. He signalled his anger by a misunderstanding; he failed to take the train to Slough, and thence to Windsor Castle, to hand over his seals of office. After waiting for him, disbelievingly, for several hours, the Prime Minister, Lord John Russell, with the Queen, decided that Russell could perform the ceremonial action on his behalf. The deed was done.

The private papers retained by Lord Palmerston include many that have still never seen the light of day — among them the generous diary references to the Prime Minister who had finally and so ignominiously failed to support him. There is one document of critical importance to the Nunez story, in what by now was evolving into 'an affair within an affair'. This was the 'State of Current Business' note prepared at feverish haste by his loyal Permanent Under-Secretary, Henry Addington, for the briefing of the first of the successors who would now step into Palmerston's well-worn shoes, Earl Granville. Under the heading of 'France', the country still of nearest interest to Britain, the second outstanding item of importance listed in the handover note is the Braithwaite and Martin claim, stating that the British case was once more in the hands of Palmerston's trusted legal adviser, the Queen's Advocate.

The implication is clear. Palmerston was fighting the Braith-waite and Martin cause with all the energy, authority and forensic skill at his command, and with whatever time he could spare from the other global matters that were then assailing him, up to the very moment of what he bitterly called his 'removal'. He was doing so imbued with the spirit of the patriotic doctrine whose colours he had nailed so prominently to his mast, before the eyes of the world, the previous year.

The truth about the central incident within what history calls 'the Rio Nunez Affair' is revealed not only in the personal papers of Joseph Braithwaite and George Martin, but in Foreign Office papers, none of which have previously been published. 'France: Messrs Braithwaite and Martin's claims 1849–1853' also under-lines the shamefully inadequate roles of the Colonial Office, and of the Royal Navy in the affair. The real facts behind that public ledger only start to emerge, however, from the confidential minis-terial letters in the French and Belgian naval and colonial archives, and from the story of one of the eyewitnesses to the attack; the outlines finally become crystal clear in the secret exchanges of the French and Belgian foreign ministers, working in collusion to safe-guard their national honour and the tissue of lies which had by then been created. Only in those records does the evidence at last come to light of an act of betrayal by a colonial governor against his two fellow countrymen, a covert momentary dereliction of duty that was to have disastrous consequences for them and to undermine all the Foreign Office's work on their behalf.

After the passage of nearly a century and a half, the story can now be told of an international affair, unique in itself, that linked the mightiest in the land in common cause with two young entre-preneurs of Victoria's Great Britain: Goliath siding with David in battle. It was an episode that could even be seen as marking an early moment of truth for Britain's imperial power, perhaps a premonition of what would be her long-term decline from the days of glory at Waterloo, at the very time when she was seen to be the mightiest nation in the world. The central thread linking these two worlds is Palmerston.

The Rio Nunez Affair is an episode of micro-history, exempli-fying Fisher's interplay of 'the contingent and the unforeseen' on six strands of interest — African, colonial, naval, commercial, diplomatic and constitutional — that are all too often seen in isolation: an entry point for a perspective on Britain's confused policy in Africa, the birthplace of commerce, at a time when Africa's confrontation with Europe, the free trade doctrine, gunboats and colonial rivalry all overlapped. It encapsulates a significant period along the path from informal empire to imperialism, poised between the anti-slave trade era, and the start of the process of the 'Scramble for Africa'.

PART I

PALMERSTON AND THE *CIVIS ROMANUS*

Britain in Mid-Century: The Political Setting for the Affair

Palmerston was in many ways the Churchill of the nineteenth century. Despite the points of difference, not least in their psychology, the areas of similarity in their lives are striking.[1] As with Churchill, there are many surprising and still under-chronicled aspects to his long career: his close and knowledgeable interest in Africa is one of them. This was all the more remarkable, given that it was his unrivalled understanding of Europe and its statesmen which made his name.[2]

Harry Temple, the third Viscount Palmerston, was born in 1784, and died, in harness, in 1865. Like Sir Winston Churchill, he inherited an aristocratic lifestyle, and was of an era that differed radically from the succeeding century in which he achieved fame and greatness. Both men only attained the ultimate honour of leading their country, in and out of a major war, at a late stage in their careers, when many men thought they were finished. Churchill's hour arrived in 1940, when he was 65: Palmerston's came at the age of 70, when in 1855 he led Great Britain out of the débâcle of the Crimean War.[3]

Both Palmerston and Churchill became men of the people — popular, beloved and the delight of the cartoonists of their day, each with his familiar visual 'signature' — for 'Winnie' the defiant cigar — for 'Pam' a straw chewed nonchalantly: it is an analogy unremarked by the historians, but assuredly a matter of deep psychological implication, that both men — alone in their respective centuries — became known by an affectionate feminine diminutive of their names. This analogy impacts on the story of the Rio Nunez Affair: it brings into even sharper relief the caring man behind the mask, a statesman who yet became personally

committed to prosecuting the claims of the two individuals who
suffered through it.

Besides the main popular issues of the day — anti-slavery, free
trade, reform, Ireland — on each of which Palmerston took up a
distinctive position — there are two broad themes, each relating to
a significant date in the annals, which form the British political
background to the story of the Rio Nunez Affair.[4] The first of
these themes focuses on a speech by the man who became the
political champion for the victims of the affair, the Secretary of
State for Foreign Affairs himself.

To understand Palmerston's complex, optimistic, evolving
character, and the ideas and ideals with which it was richly
endowed, is also to understand how this international incident
was first handled. Although he was not naturally an orator, these
Palmerstonian characteristics emerged most dramatically with the
opportunity he took to lay them before the people in the House of
Commons, one warm summer night in 1850; the language of this
great speech breathes the essential spirit of early Victorian
liberalism.[5]

A story was told later by Turgenev of the Russian peasant
whom he met, as he put it, emerging from 'the depth of the
Woodlands' asking earnestly: 'Is Palmistron alive?'[6] The inner
meaning of this story is clear: by the midpoint in the nineteenth
century, the name of Lord Palmerston, even if mispronounced —
the author of that famous speech which lasted from the late
evening of 25 June to the small hours of 26 June — had become a
household word in England, and much of the continent too.[7] That
particular judgement had been made of Palmerston's standing as
early on in his career as 1841; it was to become even more
impressed on the popular imagination right the way across Europe
— 'his name had become so familiar in Russia' — by the end of
the Crimean War in 1856. He was 'the defining political
personality of his age'.[8] In more insular terms, Palmerston has
been seen as one of the truly great parliamentarians in British
history, and 'perhaps the greatest ministerial figure of the nineteenth century'.[9]

'Household' did not automatically mean that Palmerston was a
welcome figure on every European doorstep. He was described by
some as being a liberal — or a radical — abroad but a conservative at home; Karl Marx, for one, disputed the first part of that

description.[10] By 1850, in his sixty-sixth year, one of his aims was undoubtedly to project himself as a kind of liberal citizen of Europe; by definition, those aims did not include international popularity among the absolutist powers. Palmerston has been held by some to be already the strongest man in the cabinet in Lord Melbourne's era, during the first three years of Victoria's reign, from 1837 to her marriage in 1840, when the young Queen was still finding her feet.[11] He continued to be seen as an indispensable cross-party member of administrations for most of the period from 1829 right the way through to his death in harness, on 18 October 1865, in his eighty-first year, after nearly a decade as Prime Minister.

If a key to Palmerston is to realize that there were at least three versions of him, it is clear that the three historical phases also showed three faces of Pam that were ongoing. Taking as read the patriotic, 'intermeddling', even 'irresponsible' statesman — the cold 'Lord Pumicestone' of the middle years, and the diplomatic files — the first necessity, apart from the comparison with Churchill, is to present Harry Temple the man, the enduring, basic warmer character which he had allowed to peep through again by the time of his 'good old Pam' years.[12]

Secondly, accepting the caveat in the view that 'speeches in Parliament ... will reveal something, but not all, of what was in the mind of the speaker', that speech of 1850 deserves to be studied even more closely than has been done up to now: for Palmerston's attributes — 'the character that breathes through the sentences', in Rosebery's phrase — were abundantly revealed in what was to prove one of the most triumphant solo performances in his long career as a performer upon the parliamentary, public, and European stage.[13]

The Hypothesis
It is around an insight into Palmerston's inner drives as an individual that one of the main hypotheses of this story revolves. The evidence about the antecedents, and the deliberate longer-term purpose of that brilliant speech reveal it to be on closer analysis a strategic, non-party proclamation of the deep-seated political and libertarian principles on which he sought to guide England's interests. He saw this declaration — before what his supporter Macaulay had called the most 'terrible audience in the world' —

as an opportunity for something very much more than merely the tactical, defensive — even desperate — fight to save his career, or the Lord John Russell government, by which history has tended to see it.[14]

The hypothesis is that, but for the resignation engineered by the court and implemented, but later regretted, by Russell in December 1851, Palmerston would have continued to conduct foreign affairs in the light of these aims; he would also have continued to bring Britain to focus on his vision of Africa too, and to fight for the representatives of Britain who sought to implement there that most sacred principle — 'free trade'.

One of the most significant unpublished documents at the Palmerston Broadlands archive is the 'State of Current Business' memorandum of 27 December 1851. This paper was prepared at the handover to the first of the four Foreign Secretaries who followed him in rapid succession, Earl Granville — a small piece of additional evidence as to how the epic speech of 1850 anticipated future happenings.[15]

The peroration to Palmerston's own speech on the second night reached a dramatic climax with its clarion call for the *civis Romanus sum* doctrine. That speech, and the debate as a whole about the right of one Signor Don David Pacifico to British protection and compensation, are now all but forgotten by history. The story of the Rio Nunez Affair will demonstrate the close conceptual relationship between the Foreign Secretary's thinking that night and the ten-page memorandum, another of the papers never before made public, which he wrote to the British embassy in Paris, three months later.

The common element was a liberal pursuit of justice, applied to a specific case then winning British diplomatic support against the French and Belgian governments — the Braithwaite and Martin claims.[16]

In the multiracial British society of the 1990s, the *civis Romanus* concept has acquired a new meaning — that non-white members of the British Commonwealth should have the same rights in Britain as the indigenous white majority: it was so depicted by Sir Edward Heath in a television series, *What Has Become of Us?*[17] It is interesting to speculate whether the pragmatic Palmerston would have understood that extension to his great doctrine.

Palmerston the Man

Palmerston was at first glance a complex and contradictory personality. There coexisted within him (as indeed within the make-up of Bismarck, the man who was to move into the gap he left on the European stage) both a basic directness, and at the same time a great capacity for role-playing.[18] Unlike the disturbed Bismarck, however (a product of a very different era), behind the style of Palmerston's regency mask was a secure, balanced, unexpectedly warm and generous man, committed from early on to put his own time and money into acts of kindness towards individuals in need. In the same vein, as a mature politician, he was later driven to put his energies behind some of the noblest humanitarian issues of his day, above all the abolition of the slave trade — provided, always, that Britain's 'eternal interests' were not thereby put at risk.[19]

A Small Problem

The distinguished army of Palmerstonian writers — from critics to hagiographers — starting with his son-in-law, Ashley in 1876, all paint a picture of a vivid political figure whose stature, save for a few troughs and plateaux along the way, grew larger right up to the time of his premiership. One of the problems facing researchers, however, in appraising any aspect of that long life's work is that he died in harness. A consequent difficulty encountered in the Broadlands archive, formerly held at the Palmerstons' Georgian family home near Romsey, is that some key material may well have been lost forever: 'the single most important factor was no doubt his death in office, involving as it must have done a hasty sorting of papers and considerable destruction'.[20]

Although this was the great age of writing, there is nevertheless another aspect of that problem referred to by the compiler of the Palmerston archive: unlike Churchill (or indeed once more, unlike Bismarck), there were no Palmerston memoirs to provide a subsequent commentary on motives, or an apologia for decisions: that is, if his brief early *Autobiographical Sketch* for his wife Emily is discounted. Instead there is a truly Churchillian 'faithfulness and fullness of narration' to all addressees and on all occasions, in which he sets out the logical arguments, or sometimes the agile *post hoc* rationalizations, for his instinctive views and actions.[21]

Only Queen Victoria, with the 60 million words she is reported to have put to paper during her reign — one million for each of her 60 glorious years — outpenned her egregious minister. The five years that are of most concern here are those from 1848 to the period preceding the onset of the Crimean conflict in 1853. For the first three of those years, much of the Queen's writing had the same objective as some of the 'interminable memoranda' of her equally assiduous consort: Victoria and Albert were trying to out-write and outmanœuvre 'that strong determined man, with so much worldly ambition' — their Secretary of State for Foreign Affairs.[22]

Palmerston was red-blooded and larger than life as a man, as well as in the world of statesmanship. The rumours about his rakish youth and even his middle years, before he finally — and very happily — married his stunningly beautiful mistress, Emily, Lady Cowper, in 1839, were one of the latent elements in the antipathy which Victoria, and even more so the unwaveringly moralistic Albert, were increasingly to bear towards him in his last phase as Foreign Secretary, from 1846 onwards.

There is a delightful irony in the tender invitation that the Queen will later extend from herself and Albert at Windsor Castle, on 4 March 1857, to her then gouty and no longer noticeably rakish Prime Minister, by now the renowned, if fortunate, hero of the Crimean War;[23] this was at a moment when it looked as if his popular government would have to resign after an adverse vote in the House: 'The Queen would be glad if Lord Palmerston would let her know by telegraph ... in order that she may be home at the right time, and if he will remain the night'?[24] A mere seven years earlier Prince Albert had felt it necessary to tell the Prime Minister, Lord John Russell, of a would-be scandalous incident at the same location — in Palmerston's 'extended bachelor' mode — which had been kept from the young Queen at the time. Lord Palmerston, fulfilling the earliest of his three sobriquets — that of 'Lord Cupid' — had been surprised one night in the room occupied by a lady of the Queen's bedchamber, Mrs Susan Brand (later Lady Dacre), where Palmerston was believed to be in the habit of visiting another complaisant gentlewoman when staying at Windsor; meanwhile, that lady was thought to be awaiting him in vain elsewhere in the castle.[25]

The Palmerston 'legend' is made up of a long list of character-istics — his courage, his energy, his foresight, his public toughness as a 'manager' of the army, his 'muscular authority', his resilience in adversity, his ability to empathize with what he called 'the man with the umbrella on the top of the omnibus' — that broad mass of the British people who 'were always more Palmerstonian than Palmerston' himself. Even more significantly, another cluster of qualities comes shining through. These are the hidden traits of private generosity and kindness, stemming from an aspect discerned in him from his youth onwards, and which later public actions and statements tend to conceal completely — 'his gentle and kind disposition'.[26] For Emily, he was ever her 'dearest kindest love' — that is when she could get him to herself with 'time to think of any thing but Red boxes'.[27]

These instances abound. For example, as a young man, newly orphaned, Harry Temple assisted a certain Ravizzotti family for many years with money and support, although the circumstances in no way required it of him.[28] Another random example is that of his unsought generosity towards Haydn, the publisher of *The Book of Dignities*. The Treasury would only offer him a pension of £25 a year, but Palmerston so valued his work that he not only increased 'this derisory stipend' out of his own pocket, but continued to pay it to his widow, when Haydn died suddenly only a few months later, in 1856.[29]

There were the actions too, that Palmerston took to improve the terrible lot of his Irish tenants, when he could find time for them; this was an experience that undoubtedly helped to form his ambivalent concern for Irish Catholics, and determined his part in the legislation which eventually emancipated them: 'Palmerston took up the Irish cause, not merely at the bidding of his strong humanitarian instinct and intuitive sympathy with the underdog.'[30] A less serious instance of that very human impulse came in 1839 when the rickety building that then housed the Foreign Office facing St James's Park, caught fire; Palmerston's first thought was to rush upstairs to the attic where the department's elderly German translator was working.[31]

In 1844, when out of office, there is a story of his belated realization of how hard young factory workers actually worked, with a demonstration by two trade unionists, Grant and Haworth (using the furniture on his floor at Carlton Gardens) provided on the spur of the moment; this insight, totally outside his experience, changed his whole attitude to the conditions in the factories.[32] His heart was certainly in the right place, once it could be reached and provided the whirling around on what he called the 'windmill' of his daily existence allowed him time to listen to it.[33]

There were inevitably some less appealing perceptions of him; Princess Lieven, the notorious wife of the Russian ambassador, was later to try to put him down as *un très petit esprit, lourd, obstiné*, but this view stemmed more from the fact that Palmerston had opposed her husband's accreditation, as Emily was quick to point out in his defence.[34] Many of these perceptions clearly derived, with the wisdom of hindsight and a century and a half of greater understanding of occupational stress, from the time pressures of his job as he chose to interpret it: what Emily called his 'hard work and unwholesome hours.'[35] They certainly do not justify an accusation which Victoria levels, at one point in her contest with him in 1848: 'The Queen is highly indignant . . . for vindictiveness is one of the main features in Lord Palmerston's character.'[36] This was in yet another of her many complaints to her Prime Minister during the nightmare years in the late 1840s, when Lord John Russell had to act, as he called it, as the harassed umpire between the court and its determined but idiosyncratic Foreign Secretary. Although Russell himself said that he 'had no military character', he actually agreed with most of his Foreign Secretary's tough policies and actions.[37] Lord John had declared at the start of his ministry in 1846, by which time his political career had, for the time being, overtaken that of his former senior colleague: 'I have the utmost satisfaction in constant cooperation with him upon all our foreign relations.'[38] He also understood, in a way that the court never did, the main reason for Palmerston's lack of advance consultation about dispatches, especially at the time of the European revolutions: 'the Queen's absence and mine, the constant flow of French, Danes, Germans, pressing for an immediate answer, may have made this difficult for the last month.'[39]

That tolerance foundered as the decade wore on, and Russell and some of his other colleagues became increasingly alienated from him, finally reaching the stage of working against him, in collusion with the court. Nevertheless, the Palmerston of the 1850s, with his natural goodwill towards colleagues, worked closely and harmoniously with the politicians who had actively opposed or connived against him during the fractious 1840s — including the cantankerous Earl Grey, who was to be his colleague as Colonial Secretary during the 'Rio Nunez' period. They also included the Earl of Clarendon, whom he was to support and from whom he subsequently obtained an enduring loyalty as his Foreign Secretary, as well as Russell himself.[40] A hitherto unpublished excerpt from his diary for 17 February 1852, only a few weeks after Russell's shabby revelation of the Queen's displeasure with Palmerston, reads: 'John Russell's speech very good.' The entry for 13 March shows him starting to bury the hatchet with this political rival who apparently had destroyed his career only four months before: 'Party in Evening... John Russell came ... first time we had met as Friends in private since he removed me.'[41] Many other such examples make it clear that that royal imputation of vindictiveness simply does not stick.

A few of the classic pen pictures — old and new — must suffice to bring Palmerston into a truer perspective, for example in this comparison with the Prime Minister of the 1830s, Lord Melbourne, his future brother-in-law, when he was serving his second term at the Foreign Office: 'Palmerston — jaunty, plain-spoken and unchaste — was also a survival from the Regency ... a man of adventurous and domineering temperament.... He and Melbourne were natives of the same fashionable Whig world, both talked the same blunt, flippant, male language.'[42] Another description recalls the early years at the War Office, when his amours were the talk of the town: 'Tall, dark and handsome ... about five feet ten, with a fresh complexion, dark hair, and magnificent blue eyes (though lacking a few teeth from hunting accidents), occasionally inclining to overweight ... a definitely receding hairline.'[43] The author of *Random Recollections of the House of Commons* records another facet in 1836, a characteristic he shared with the man whose career and relationships have tended up to now to outshine his own in the popular mind, Disraeli: 'his hair ... always exhibits proofs of the skill and attention of the perruquier. His clothes are in the extreme of fashion. He is very vain of his personal appearance.'[44] A concern with image, a 'hearty trencherman', eating 'like a vulture', giving rise later in life to the gout every winter: a fearless rider to hounds, a first class shot: a fluent speaker of several languages: the possessor of a sharp wit — all these comments touch different aspects of him.[45]

Palmerston was not merely a man with a great life force surging through his blood; he was also the possessor of a high intelligence

and a classically trained mind. He was well educated — initially in
the cold clear light of Edinburgh University — with respect for the
great liberal economist Adam Smith, through his disciple,
Professor Dugald Stewart; he used their ideas as his yardsticks,
and quoted consistently from them and from the classical sources
throughout his life. He had a capacity to see historical patterns in
current events, coupled with the ability to foresee possible outcomes to those events, thus enabling him to take precautionary
action to offset them. One such example was correctly ascribed by
one of the most perceptive of the major writers, and also by the
biographer of Leopold, King of the Belgians, to his usual 'far-
sightedness' (although Lord John's first biographer wrongly
credited it to the Prime Minister himself).[46] This was the nomination of his trusted boyhood friend (who was also John Russell's
father-in-law) Lord Minto, to take an investigative trip through
southern Europe in the spring of 1847, in the year before the
European-wide revolutions.

Underlying the capacity for vision, he had that other quality,
not always the lot of visionaries, a propensity for sustained hard
work, the tenacity to master the intricacies of a treaty, a negotiation, a long-term strategy — or an international claim. Above all,
he was blessed with the patience needed to research a detailed case
with the analytical skill of a barrister: 'Belying the blustering,
devil-may-care image, which he liked to project, Palmerston spent
the first years of his career as an official. . . . He remained, true to
his liberal Tory roots, as an immensely hard-working administrator. His tireless industry as Foreign Secretary and Home
Secretary was notorious.'[47] This attribute was as true of his
missives to his Permanent Under-Secretary, Henry Addington and
his overworked clerks, as to his sovereign and her spouse, or to
those he saw as 'his' agents — the Crown's ambassadors overseas.
The tortuous but successful resolution of the treaty establishing
the new Kingdom of Belgium, which took the best part of the
decade from 1830 to 1839, is one outstanding example of this
vital quality.[48] Another celebrated example was the 'Schleswig-
Holstein' question: it was one of most intractable diplomatic
issues of the century, yet Palmerston got his mind inside it.[49]

In the jargon of today, Palmerston was a natural 'role-player',
as the occasion demanded. This largely explains why the face he
portrayed towards the recurrently despotic regimes in Austria,

Russia, Spain, Portugal, and Greece, but also, most of all, to France, was intrusive, resented, hated, but, unquestionably, reckoned with and feared. 'To his great benefit, Palmerston appeared cosmopolitan and chauvinist at the same time. He set out an uplifting vision of national identity and purpose.'[50] Bullying, bluffs and threats — in a word, 'intermeddling' (the term he introduced and by which he was tagged, from the earliest of his major speeches, in June 1829) — these were the weapons he resorted to instinctively, if that appeared, with his vast experience of individual leaders, and the peoples they currently purported to lead, to be the best and most cost-effective way to secure Britain's immediate purposes. It was, however, always 'jaw-jaw' first, rather than 'war-war'; he did not invent 'gunboat diplomacy'.[51]

He was not so clearly driven by ambition to take power as his political competitor for the Whig Liberal leadership, Russell. 'Russell had a stronger sense of history, and hence of personal destiny.'[52] If Palmerston was certainly not blind to ambition, he only really bothered to explain himself when roused: 'Scarcely any thing calls him up except a regular attack on himself.'[53] He was so roused by another characteristically meticulous memorandum from Albert in 1847. In an unusually long riposte — its words anticipating the Pacifico speech — covering ten quarto pages, he described his foreign policy achievements from 1829 onwards, making the salient point that he had served Britain's interests throughout this time without recourse to war.[54]

One pattern that Palmerston discerned in the events of Europe was the ever present threat of a revanchist France, however 'good and kind' a man King Louis-Philippe might appear to be to the still susceptible Victoria and her Albert, on the occasions of their mutual visits to and from the French court in their early twenties, from 1843 to 1845. At one stage, in 1846, he decided to transmit his views direct to Albert, who was trying to impose, with the help of 'good Uncle Leopold' in Belgium, and their shared éminence grise, Baron Stockmar, what could be seen as either a 'Holland House' view or a precociously late twentieth-century continental angle on British affairs: 'Close to our shores [there was] a nation of 34 million people ... the leading portion ... is animated with a feeling of deep hatred to England ... the French nation remembers the Nile, Trafalgar, the Peninsula, Waterloo, and St Helena, and would gladly find an opportunity of taking revenge.'[55] He goes on to say, with a meaningful undertone for Anglo-French rivalries in Africa and elsewhere overseas: 'The two countries have in every part of the globe interests, commercial and political, which are continually clashing.'

That long memorandum provides striking additional continuity through to the *civis Romanus* speech itself, four years later, when once again, Palmerston was further roused, by a cumulative process of antagonism, to define himself and defend his policies. It also underlines the way that Palmerston arrived at clear principles and viewpoints: 'Palmerston was not to be deflected from his main line of policy.'[56]

That line of policy would be set out today, with a little hindsight, as a '12-point programme'[57]:

- Constitutional monarchy was the best form of government. Even though the Palmerstons were not members of one of the original Whig families, like the Russells, who regarded themselves as standard-bearers for the Glorious Revolution, Palmerston was brought up to espouse the same creed; he was a 'staunch believer in the principles of 1688' and carried his belief in constitutional monarchy to considerable lengths, especially at the time of his sacking.
- It was the best way to balance the objective of the freedom of the individual, with the residual interest of the state.
- The British system had evolved ahead of its time, it was the best possible form of that system of government and other major states ought to follow our example.
- Absolutist regimes would discover this fact to their cost; we had a duty to help those regimes towards the light.
- Such 'intermeddling' in the affairs of other countries was justified in terms of what it had peacefully achieved, in Palmerston's experience, in preserving Britain's interests.
- That justification certainly included the defence of legitimate British interests wherever they might arise.
- By reason of being the first over the industrial revolution hurdle, and through the fact of having beaten 'the great but bad' Napoleon, Britain enjoyed an extraordinarily powerful reputation abroad, which gave her more influence than she may have deserved, politically or militarily.
- The fact that his sovereign was related to half the crowned

heads of Europe, and corresponded with over 50 of them, did not come into the frame: the role of the elected member for Tiverton, now constitutionally appointed Foreign Secretary, and the master of the art of bluffs, was to play those stakes for all they were worth, short of war, whilst always holding that outcome open in the eyes of opponents.

- The British monarchy, from the Act of Settlement of 1688, was there to back the party currently and democratically placed in power; it was not to act, as even Melbourne feared it might, and as later Albert, with the help of the German-educated Stockmar thought it should, as 'a neutral moderating monarchy', a kind of 'permanent Prime Minister', which was likely 'to lead to the Crown taking an active line independent of the Government'.

- Britain's model of development from the seventeenth century, with its special mixture of economic liberty and gentlemanly paternalism, could be exported overseas, and needed to be, if it was to be preserved at home. At the end of the day the desire of the Crown for stability might well be identical with that of the Foreign Office; however, the government was there to decide the best means to that end.

- These beliefs and principles came together in 'Liberalism': 'Palmerston bound together the "great bundle of sticks" that comprised the Liberal Party and made it the supreme political force of the nineteenth century.'

- Perhaps, most influential of all Pam's beliefs, and the one which most infuriated those — above all the Queen and Prince Albert — who found themselves at variance with him: a conviction that he intuitively understood his country, 'a simple and practical nation, a commercial nation' — a belief that by now he knew what was best for Britain.[58]

The *Civis Romanus* Speech: 25–26 June 1850

This then was the man who people believed was fighting for his political future, in the bear-baiting atmosphere of the House of Commons, on the late evening of 25 June 1850 — his wife sitting loyally and anxiously throughout in the Ladies' Gallery.

The pretext was the Don Pacifico incident: the Athens home of a somewhat unsavoury character, the former Portuguese consul in the city but claiming British citizenship through his birth in

Gibraltar, had been the subject of an attack by an anti-Semitic mob at Easter time 1847, believing him to be responsible, as a Jew, for the ban imposed on their annual burning of the effigy of Judas. The fact that he was a Jew undoubtedly did not assist, in the climate of that time, an unprejudiced appraisal of the incident by many of the commentators. For example, Pam's trusted friend Lord Howard de Walden, now the minister to Brussels, had written on 4 February 1850: 'Pacifico is more difficult to deal with. His being a Jew — his dubious bona fide nationality ... set all against him.'[59] The address Palmerston then delivered was considered by many to be the greatest speech of his life, and one of the most notable parliamentary *tours de force* ever witnessed. It was all the more effective because it was a surprise: up to then Palmerston had been noted as an indifferent — as well as infrequent speaker in the House. Whatever the apparent ease of style with which it reads in print — and at that time Hansard was not the result of verbatim reporting, but was compiled from *The Times* — the speech was the cause of feverish activity by his clerks. They had to research with even more than the usual Palmerston-driven thoroughness; there were only five days between the laying down of the motion on Thursday 20 June, and the Tuesday 25 June, when the Cabinet evidently judged it would be the optimum time for the Foreign Secretary to enter the debate. The Foreign Office librarian recalled it through the perspective of 'the Office'; (it is necessary to aim off for his faulty memory about the role played by Roebuck, the radical MP for Sheffield, a former strong critic of the 'old Tory' Palmerston, and now brought in as an unwonted ally of the new 'radical' Palmerston, against the opposition of the Corn Law 'protectionists' and the 'Peelites'):

> During the sitting of Parliament in 1850 ... Mr Roebuck made a forceful attack [sic] ... against Lord Palmerston's foreign policy. The motion was divided into more than 40 headings, which occupied five pages of the 'Votes'. The period over which the attack ranged was from 1827 to 1847. ... To provide material for a complete answer to the various charges made in this 'monster motion', the librarian and his staff were sorely taxed, as the information sought was contained in between 2000 and 3000 MS volumes.[60]

Several parts of Roebuck's speech on the first evening, supporting Pam but 'from the opposition side of the House' — 'mine is not blind approbation' — bear quoting. First, he restated the constitutional position, unknowingly anticipating Palmerston's subsequent speech. 'No Administration is called upon to resign upon a resolution of the House of Lords ... our battle was fought in 1640.' However, the practicalities were much more important, with resonances for the politics of today. In default of a debate:

> This House ... would be almost impotent as regards the country at large, and they would be utterly impotent in reference to the governments of the world. ... If the matter be left there — uninquired into, the rights of Englishmen in their [foreign governments'] hands would be undefended ... the object of the noble Lord has been to extend the protection and shield of England to her wandering sons, who are carried by commerce, or by pleasure or by necessity, to the various regions of the world.

There were other weighty contributions both on the Monday and the Tuesday, before Palmerston rose to speak. It was just such an occasion with its unique 'sense of crowd and urgency' as Churchill, nearly a century later, was to proclaim as the essence of the House's character. The chamber of the old House of Commons was much smaller than the present one; it was absolutely packed, anticipating — with its normally unerring instinct — the blood of a senior figure. The atmosphere cannot have been very different from one of the classic descriptions:

> The packed benches and galleries, the members crouched in the gangways, massing around the Speaker's Chair, the phalanx at the bar, the almost tangible tension which manifests itself in gusts of excessive laughter at the most laboured jokes as the critical moment draws near, and then the tense and dangerous quietness, which can be changed into unbelievable tumult by a single injudicious phrase.[61]

Although some parts of Palmerston's speech involved reading out some key dispatches, eyewitness opinion confirms that the speech came mostly from a few notes, the peroration alone being deliberately written down, learned by heart as from a script. This was the moment when Palmerston quoted an analogy which the House could relate to the era of another famous British 'citizen', Oliver Cromwell, when he proclaimed that the arm of England, like that of the Roman republic of old, would reach out to protect its citizens wherever they might be. Fervent monarchist though he was, he chose to hang his Liberal-radical hat on this historical peg with intent: he could not have picked one which was more likely to make the incumbents of the English throne twitchy and defensive, given the very uneasy experience of the passing of the year of revolutions, 18 months previously.[62]

This indirect reference to Britain's brief but bloody experience of republicanism had in fact already been made in the House back in 1840, by the celebrated historian, Macaulay, then the holder of Palmerston's original ministerial job at the start of the century, 'Secretary at War'. 'The most eloquent talker in England' was then speaking in the context of another, unrelated, incident, in the Opium War with China.[63]

Palmerston at that time had complained that 'a representative of the Crown had been treated with violence and contempt, and that British subjects, innocent of any wrong, had been abused'. It is a reasonable assumption that Macaulay, speaking in the Foreign Secretary's defence, voiced what was in his heart: 'They belonged to a country which had made the farthest ends of the earth ring with the fame of her exploits in redressing the wrongs of her children; ... that had not degenerated since her great Protector vowed that he would make the name of Englishmen as respected as ever had been the name of the Roman citizen.' One historian has inferred that 'it is equally reasonable to suppose that Palmerston stored away Cromwell's and Macaulay's reference to the *civis Romanus* for his own use at some later day.' However, Palmerston himself had first spoken of Rome in one of his earlier speeches, but in a pejorative sense.[64]

This speech of June 1850 was conscious and deliberate, ordered to be printed as an official document, and meant to be studied by friend and foe, at home and abroad; it embodied Palmerston's essential credo. The defence of liberty, and of the Briton in foreign parts, even a Don Pacifico, were integral to it. The whole debate was the stuff of high parliamentary drama. The Lords had only shortly beforehand, on the previous Monday, crossed the constitutional Rubicon and passed a motion critical of the government's foreign policy; the Prime Minister, Russell, and his team were thus forced to defend Palmerston: 'It was decided by the ministry that the war should be carried into the protectionist and Peelite camp, and that the attack should be commenced by a radical, the famous Mr Roebuck.'[65] On the second night, a pointed speech by a lawyer, Sir Frederick Thesiger, quoted Roebuck as saying in a debate of 1843 that 'the noble Viscount has had a most pernicious influence on our foreign policy.' Talking of 'the Lucifer match at the Foreign Office again', he also quoted what were then the authorities for international law, first Vattel: 'The Prince ... ought not to interfere in the causes of his subjects in foreign countries ... to grant them his protection.' However, Thesiger attempted to assert from this venerable authority four exceptions to this purported rule: where justice might be refused, or there was palpable evidence of injustice, or rules or forms were openly violated, or finally where 'an odious distinction [be] made to the prejudice of his subjects, or of foreigners in general'. He also quoted Lord Mansfield that generally 'the law of nations ... does not allow of reprisals.' 'Palpable evidence of injustice' was the kind of gauntlet that Palmerston rejoiced to take up, and he duly did so, no doubt with recent events in Africa in mind.

In his response, Palmerston's prose reads impressively. His speech, 'in which exposition, invective, argument, declamation, plain talk and resounding eloquence were mingled together with consummate art and extraordinary felicity', had one overwhelming effect: it annihilated his enemies':

> The country is told that British subjects abroad must trust to that indifferent justice which they may happen to receive at the hands of the government and tribunals of the country in which they may be. ... Now, I say it is a doctrine ... on which the people of England never will suffer any British minister to act; ... in the first instance, British subjects ... [must] ... have recourse to the means which the law of the land affords them ... that is the opinion which the legal advisers of the Crown have given in numerous cases.[66]

He then asserted his own role in such matters: 'a man who aspires to govern mankind, ought to bring to the task, generous sentiments, compassionate sympathies, and noble and elevated thoughts.' Palmerston recited a long list of examples of Greek 'outrages' to British subjects abroad: these included the indignities meted out to the crew of HMS *Fantome*; the cases of some inhabitants of the Ionian Islands (at that time a British possession) being flogged in a police station at Salina; two other Ionians being paraded publicly at Patras; the incident of two other men being attacked while asleep in the street; the celebrated case of 'Mr Finlay's garden'; and finally the details of the case of Signor Pacifico himself.[67]

After that considerable recital, he continued, with references full of meaning for France, and Belgium, having regard to the 'Rio Nunez' diplomacy then currently on his desk, and with some surprising verbal resemblances to the currently ongoing diplomatic exchanges in that paper battle:[68]

> Is it to be held ... that if your subject suffers violence, outrage, plunder, in a country which is small and weak, you are to tell them ... that we cannot ask it for compensation? ... Many instances of such measures have been quoted in this debate as having been adopted by the governments of other countries, especially by the French government.

Palmerson had written in another context, in uncanny anticipation of the semantic political analyses of the next century, of the dangers of taking metaphors too far, and of applying to states the attributes of trees, crumbling buildings and sick men — he was thinking of the way politicians were then tending to 'write off' Turkey through such abuse of figures of speech: 'There cannot be a greater or more utterly unphilosophical mistake.'[69] There was no such abuse here. As Clarendon had implied in his eyewitness account, his figures of speech were restrained but strong enough to keep his narrative sweeping forwards: 'I leave the sunny plains of Castile and the gay vineyards of France, and now I am taken to the mountains of Switzerland, as the place where I am to render a stricter account' and then 'having crossed the rugged Alps into the smiling plains of Lombardy.'[70]

Among other remarkable aspects of the speech, he demonstrated a complete mastery, all from memory, of the geographical intricacies of the Turkish Dardanelles and the Bosphorus, including places that most of the House had not yet even heard of — Besica Bay, Barber's Bay and Buyukdere — which were relevant in his account of the earlier eruptions of the 'Eastern Question' in the 1830s and early 1840s. Before long, the Crimean War, and the dispatches of the world's first war correspondent in *The Times*, were to rectify that ignorance. The speech took up 64 columns of Hansard; he delivered over 30,000 words, before reaching a conclusion which still has valid overtones for the Britain of the 1990s:

> I believe that the principles on which we acted are those which are held by the great mass of the people of this country. I am convinced these principles are calculated ... [to promote] ... the welfare and happiness of mankind. ... For while we have seen ... the political earthquake rocking Europe from side to side ... this country has presented a spectacle honourable to the people of England ... that liberty is compatible with order, that individual freedom is reconcilable with obedience to the law. ... I fearlessly challenge the verdict which this House, as representing a political, a commercial, a constitutional country, is to give ... whether the principles on which the foreign policy of Her Majesty's Government has been conducted, and the sense of duty which has led us to think ourselves bound to afford protection to our fellow subjects abroad, are proper and fitting guides for those who are charged with the government of England; and whether, as the Roman, in days of old, held himself free from indignity when he could say '*civis Romanus sum*'; so also a British subject, in whatever land he may be, shall feel confident that the watchful eye and the strong arm of England, will protect him against injustice and wrong.

The first day of the debate, started on Monday 24 June, had adjourned at 1.00 a.m. on the second day; the critical day ended with Palmerston's key speech early in the hours of Wednesday the 26th; the third night, including attacks by Gladstone and Sidney Herbert, adjourned at 1.45 a.m. on Friday 28 June, to resume again later that evening, with further attacks by Sir Robert Peel, Cobden, and, winding up for the opposition, Disraeli.

Sidney Herbert, to be generously offered a ministerial post by Palmerston when Prime Minister — no vindictiveness there —

made a savage attack: 'I ask you to mark with your reprobation
that policy which ... has tended to lower the public character of
this country, and to produce alienation from, and an aversion to,
the British people and the British name.' Gladstone, whose
confrontations with Disraeli were later to overshadow Pam's with
Russell, and who was also to serve under him, and then carry
forward the emerging Liberal banner from him, added to the
attack: 'I say the policy of the noble Lord tends to encourage ...
our besetting fault and weakness — too great a tendency to self-
esteem ... this characteristic [is] too plainly legible in the policy of
the noble Lord.' The Tory Disraeli, perhaps by this time sensing
that the motion might be starting to move away from his party,
pleaded that the voting should at least show that the Parliament of
England 'is resolved that, in future, her policy shall be conducted
with due regard to the rights of nations'. This fourth and final
evening's debate ended at 2.00 a.m. The ayes totalled 310, a
majority of 46.[71] The four days had consumed 459 columns of
Hansard, and more than 220,000 often highly passionate words.
One description of the final scenes cannot be improved on:[72]

At last came the peroration ... with the resounding leitmotiv,
'*Civis Romanus sum*'. The House found itself cheering until
it seemed that the cheering would never stop. And Lady
Palmerston, who thought her husband had spoken for an
hour, discovered that it was after half-past two. It would be
difficult to exaggerate the effectiveness or the effects of this
amazing speech. Neither was to be measured by the government majority of 49 (*sic*). Among the superabundant testi-
monials to both which still survive, one may, almost at
random, select those of Lord and Lady Clarendon; [Claren-
don represented not only a source of wide knowledge about
foreign matters, having served Palmerston as an ambassador
in an earlier administration, but was also one of those who
had intrigued with the court against the anti-French stance of
his chief.] The former who, be it noted, was 'not disposed to
quarrel with the Lords for the result they arrived at' (the vote
against the Government of a week earlier) thought that the
Foreign Secretary's great effort 'for mastery of subject ...
order and lucid arrangement ... well-sustained interest ...
varied style ... and the good temper and good taste with

which he handled such a legion of bitter assailants', can never have been surpassed anywhere.

Like everyone else, Clarendon marvelled at the exhibition of 'physical and mental power almost incredible in a man of his age'.

As for the effect: 'It will place him on a pinnacle of popularity at home, whatever it may do abroad, and completely settle the question about which I never had a doubt, that no change at the FO is possible, and that Lord John must either go on with him or go out with him.' And Lady Clarendon, lamenting what she saw as 'the triumph of a wrong cause', wrote in her diary, 'He has triumphed over the great mass of educated public opinion, over that mighty potentate *The Times*, over two branches of the Legislature, over the Queen and Prince and most of the Cabinet he sits in, besides all foreign nations!'[73]

'The Minister whose downfall had been so carefully prepared had become, as Grey told Greville' (the clerk to the Privy Council and one of the great — if not always reliable — raconteurs of Victorian politics), 'the most popular man in the country'. Palmerston himself 'judged — and judged rightly — that he was the most popular man in England'. Lady Clarendon was wrong, however, about the impact on the court: 'Great was the indignation of Victoria ... : "The House of Commons is becoming very unmanageable and troublesome".'[74] The Queen, at least, was quite unconverted by the *civis Romanus* speech. Prince Albert confessed to his brother that the court was weakened by the turn of events. He wrote in gloomy terms: 'the unhappy combinations of circumstances that granted our immoral one for foreign affairs such a triumph in the Commons'.[75] The succession plan previously worked out between the court and Russell, seemingly with some knowledge on the part of Palmerston himself, was that he would indeed move or be moved from the Foreign Office later that year. He, however, was not going to let that happen without a fight; Don Pacifico effectively provided the catalyst for ending that machination.

The court was nonetheless resolved that the 'immoral one' should give up his portfolio. The public perception was all the other way, and the court showed itself once more out of touch with the country. To rub salt into the wound, the centre of all the hubbub started to be talked of in the same phraseology as he had used to portray the citizenry of Britain, coming to be referred to as himself the *civis Romanus*, the embodiment of all the supposedly sturdy English virtues. The writers, too, would catch the habit: thus later on, one American biographer was to write, apropos Palmerston's tasks as Prime Minister during the Crimean War: 'But surely, if popularity was to be the basis [of power], the *civis Romanus* could hope for some success.' With time, the emotional charge of that evening became attenuated, and in due course the debate and the speech, but not the phrase, became all but lost from view.[76]

Members of the upper House, in particular, were not yet fully used to the ways of the only chamber that now really mattered within 'the triumvirate — the Sovereign, the Lords and the Commons — which, together, form the British Parliament'.[77] Thus, for example, the very Conservative Lord Malmesbury was to recall Palmerston's speech, with regard to a similar case that came before him as Foreign Secretary on 28 May 1852; the attitude he then revealed forms another important factor in the Rio Nunez story. This case concerned a young man, Mather, and another English youth in Florence, at that stage still ruled by Austria, who became the victims of an unjustified attack by two officers of the occupying power, during a parade:

> The opposition [now, briefly, Palmerston and Russell's party] are making capital of this and other freaks of travelling Englishmen who put themselves into scrapes abroad, and, being often deservedly punished and arrested, call upon their government for protection. This conduct on their part is very much due to a blustering speech made some time ago by Lord Palmerston, declaring that John Bull, wherever he was, or whatever he did, was to be as sacred as the ancient *civis Romanus*.[78]

Yet another of the Palmerston successors, Earl Granville, 'Granville the Polite', reflected the quite different effect of the speech abroad: 'He had learned from an Englishman just returned from the continent that "the only chance one had to avoid being insulted was to say *civis Romanus* non *sum*".'[79] The press took up the cause in a big way, however, and 20 years before the jingo ditty was invented, waxed extremely — if anachronistically — 'jingoistic'. Palmerston's emerging relationship to what was to be called jingoism is now clear: his role 'was not to incite jingoism, as historians sometimes say; it was rather to rein in parliamentary pressures for low spending.'[80] Palmerston, already a celebrity, became overnight an established star.

The Reform Club had been formed, in 1836, 'to provide a common home for Whigs and radicals ... and 250 MPs and most Cabinet ministers joined that year, though it never supplanted more familiar meeting-places like Brook's'. It was the place where people met to find out what was really happening — for example to seek 'the best answer to the question whether Lord John Russell and Lord Palmerston could be induced to serve together'.[81] At a great dinner in July 1850, in the coffee room of that hallowed home of liberalism — all the more famous because public dinners were still a rarity in Victorian politics — Palmerston was fêted by his fellow men. It was a decisive step towards 'The Triumph of Lord Palmerston'.[82]

Two New *Cives Britannici*

With all these weighty matters on his mind, it might be thought that Palmerston could scarcely pay any attention to the other lesser things that Henry Addington and his clerks were bringing before him. Even less might it have seemed likely that the Secretary of State would give time to any issues that were not germane to the boiling cauldron of European and parliamentary politics, the area that was actually threatening to consume his career, as opposed to engaging his principles and his beliefs.

Yet that is indeed what he now did. With his capacity for 'generous impulses and of sympathy for the unfortunate', Palmerston was still able to put his energies behind the claims of two new *cives Britannici*, Joseph Braithwaite and George Martin, despite all the other pressures around him.[83] The credo enunciated in the Don Pacifico debate was in no way simply the empty 'bluster' of Malmesbury's metaphor.

The application of the policies might well fluctuate over time; indeed Lord John Manners was to assert in 1864, in connection with the case of the killing by the North American navy of a crew member of the British ship *Saxon*, that the House was 'assisting at the funeral rites and final interment of that celebrated historical personage, the *Civis Romanus*'.[84] Nevertheless, it is beyond doubt that this policy represented some of Palmerston's deep-seated beliefs, stemming from the fundamentally liberal stream in his thinking, and from his concern for the individual; they also stemmed from what by now had re-emerged as that essential 'warm-heartedness' which along with his 'high Honour, [and] noble-minded Independent policy', were the attributes cited by the House of Commons deputation when presenting him with his famous portrait, in 1849.[85] He would bring those qualities into play whenever, or wherever, the situation demanded it of him, provided that destiny gave him the opportunity to do so.

The second political theme underlying the Rio Nunez Affair, with a timing central to its outcome, will emerge more naturally within the story itself: the constitutional propriety of the dismissal of Queen Victoria's Foreign Secretary on 19 December 1851. It was an action influenced and precipitated by her still very Germanic court, the court of the House of Hanover. From the point of view of unwritten constitutional theory, the process leading up to the removal was at the very least questionable, even a scandal. Increasingly through the 1840s Victoria, encouraged by King Leopold and Prince Albert, had been working more as a member of Europe's 'union of Princes' — almost a reversion to a 'Legitimist' concept of monarchical power — than with the grain of British political evolution. This followed what has been characterized as the court's painful awareness of the degradation of that power signalled by the Reform Act of 1832.[86] The palace was trying to interfere to maintain its power 'against the tide which inexorably eroded it'.[87]

It was also questionable in terms of an equally grey area, that of constitutional practice. Only 20 months previously, in the period prior to the *civis Romanus* speech, Palmerston had had to set aside further precious time to send a letter to Russell after yet another broadside from Queen Victoria. His letter summed up both the unconstitutional nature of the court's intervention, and the danger that thereby the Queen was not acting in the true interests of the country. It indicates that at the same time Palmerston was philosophically resigned to the royal opposition, and that at this stage both he and his leader were shouldering this royal cross in partnership. Finally, it underlines Palmerston's conviction that the court's arguments were based on misunderstandings of the situation: they could be counteracted, if only he was not working — as he expressed it so vividly at various times — like a 'dray horse', or a 'Methodist minister', or like 'a man plumped into a mill race':

My dear John Russell,

It is extremely Embarrassing for a British Minister who is responsible to Parliament & to the Country for his Management of the affairs with which he is officially charged, to find his Sovereign becoming on every foreign Question a zealous Partisan of some particular foreign Power, without the slightest Reference to the Policy or Interests of England in regard to the Matters in Question. But in this world People cannot alter Things to Suit their own Convenience, & must take them & deal with them as they Exist. It would take a very long Letter to unravel & refute all the Sophistry and Misconceptions in the Queen's Memorandum but your proposed answer seems quite Sufficient.[88]

Palmerston's friend and colleague, Lord Howard de Walden, who would be playing a crucial role in the Rio Nunez Affair, was to write in horror from the British embassy at Brussels: 'Your giving up the seals of the Foreign Office is not merely a national but a European calamity.'[89] Another influence working on these events behind what Palmerston later called 'those people down at Osborne' had been revealed to Palmerston by this same faithful ally only a month earlier, when he reported, under the heading 'Most Private', the information passed to him by Seckendorff, the Austrian ambassador to Brussels. This conveyed Prince Schwarzenberg's determination, as the leader of another of the British court's favoured absolutist monarchies, Austria, to effect Palmerston's overthrow.[90]

The national hero became a national martyr. The subsequent failings of Palmerston's four successors at the Foreign Office, and the inability of that office to deal with the challenges that faced it in the period leading up to the outbreak of the Crimean War — almost a third underlying political theme in itself — form part of the penultimate chapter to the story.[91] This was the rich and complex political backdrop against which the drama of the Rio Nunez Affair was to be played out. Unlike its two unsuspecting British victims, and indeed unlike those who were to inherit his seals of office, Lord Palmerston, with his 'muscular authority', the leading political figure in the story, had been well prepared for his part.

Notes

1. The 'Pam/Winnie' analogy is examined further in Appendix 1. I am indebted here to the criticisms of Jasper Ridley, Sir Robert Rhodes James, Dr Anthony Howe, and Dr Jonathan Parry. I had researched the qualified Palmerston/ Churchill analogy before coming across the comment made by the late A. J. P. Taylor, in his introduction to Denis Judd, *Palmerston* (London, 1970), pp.vii–viii. Evidently Taylor did not 'rate' P, as he did not find him 'creative', although his comment that 'he was in politics for fun' suggests that he may not have quite got under P's skin. The analogy is nevertheless only offered here for consideration in the modified form he used: 'A sort of nineteenth century Churchill'. See A. J. P. Taylor, 'Lord Palmerston', *History Today*, vol.1, no.7 (July, 1952), pp.35–41. The secure and well-parented P would have been even less interested than the unloved and fiercely compensating Churchill was in his own 'psychology'; for an analysis of the latter see Anthony Storr, *Churchill's Black Dog and Other Phenomena of the Human Mind* (London, 1991), pp.5–51. The relationship of the B&M claims to the timing of the *civis Romanus* speech comes out most clearly in P's Letter-Books (correspondence with Lord H. de Walden at Brussels and Lord Normanby at Paris); BL Add. MSS 48,553, 48,557. See Part II, Chap.5 for data from the archives of the Belgian Ministry of Foreign Affairs, 'Correspondances/Légations: Grande Bretagne 1850'. A brief 'holistic' outline is set out in Appendix 2, Constitutional and Legal Factors. P's adherence to legal authority is touched on in Chap.5. Of the many judgements about P in Sir C. Webster, *The Foreign Policy of Palmerston* (London, 1951), he quotes Walter Bagehot, *Biographical Studies* (London, 1881), p.341 as saying, 'some people not unqualified to judge have said that his opinion on such matters was as good as any law officer's.'

2. 'The effort he put into extending Britain's trade and influence in the extra-European world needs to be emphasized because it is still underplayed by diplomatic historians' (P. J. Cain and A. G. Hopkins, *British Imperialism* (London, 1993) vol.1, p.99). The authors of this work single out R. J. Gavin's 'important and unfortunately still unpublished study' on 'Palmerston's Policy Towards East and West Africa 1830–1865' (Ph.D. thesis, Cambridge University, 1959), pp.16–48. Webster (*Foreign Policy*, vol.2, pp.750–1) cites P's belief that 'it is the business of government to open and secure the roads for the merchant'. For P's speeches against the slave trade — one of his abiding topics as a mature statesman — see J. Ridley, *Lord Palmerston* (London, 1970), p.297, citing Hansard, 16 July 1844, 8 July 1845. P's recent bibliographers, M. S. Partridge and K. E. Partridge, *Lord Palmerston 1784–1865: A Bibliography* (Greenwood, 1994) admit that P's 'career has not yet exhausted the attention of scholars'. This purportedly comprehensive work omits the PRO document, FO 97/198. For P's insights into the minds of European statesmen of his day, exceeding those of his premier, LJR, and those defended doggedly by the British court, see, for example, W. B. Pemberton, *Lord Palmerston* (London, 1954), pp.143–7.

3. Webster referred to P's seeming to belong to both the eighteenth and nineteenth centuries with his comments on 'The Two Views of Palmerston', *Foreign Policy*, p.793. Quick judgements, for example Roy Jenkins, *Gladstone* (London, 1995), p.xiii, can still fall into the trap of seeing P anachronistically, and not as a true 'mid-Victorian'. See Appendix 1; also H. W. Lucy, *Peeps at Parliament* (London, 1903), p.226, 'he was presented with a bit of straw. . . . This . . . had its origins in the jaunty Premier's love of horse-racing. At some time in the mid-century Leech or Doyle . . . placed the straw in Palmerston's mouth and there ever after it remained'; also Ridley, *Palmerston*, p.530. For Churchill, among the many legends, that of the removal of the famous cigar by Karsh, before taking the celebrated photograph bears repeating here. P born 20 October 1784; PM 15 February 1855, *aet.* 70 years 3 months; Churchill: born 30 November 1874; PM 10 May 1940, *aet.* 65 years 5 months.

4. Although P, with his then premier, LJR, was fervent on free trade and anti-slavery and, like many of his Cabinet colleagues, several of them Irish landowners, was unable to comprehend the nature of the fearful Irish situation, unlike LJR he was at best lukewarm on reform. See also Appendix 1. As the Nunez was first discovered by Portugal, the pronunciation is still in the Portuguese mode, not the Spanish — nearer to 'Noonyesh'.

5. For judgements about P's 'unfailing' optimism, and his oratory, see Webster, *Foreign Policy*, p.782. For the debate, see Hansard, V cxii 3rd ser 1850, 24 June col. 228+, 25–6 June col. 380+, 27 June col. 478+, 28 June col. 609+. See also H. Bell, *Lord Palmerston* (London, 1936), vol.2, pp.26–8.

6. Ridley, *Palmerston*, p.333; cf. D. Magarshack, *Turgenev* (London, 1954), pp.183–5. See also Bell, *Lord P*, vol.2, p.28.

7. Bell, *Lord P*, vol.1, p.256.

8. Jonathan Parry, *The Rise and Fall of Liberal Government in Victorian Britain* (New Haven, 1993), p.194.

9. Brian Connell, *Regina v. Palmerston* (London, 1962), p.2; also Judd, *Palmerston*, p.13, 'one of the most distinguished Parliamentarians of his age'.

10. Ridley, *Palmerston*, pp.423, 122–3, 173, 233. See also Bell, *Lord P*, p.31; Kenneth Bourne, *Palmerston: The Early Years, 1784–1841* (London, 1982), Chap.8, pp.332–407, 629.

11. Donald Southgate, *The Most English Minister: The Policies and Politics of Palmerston* (London, 1966), p.xviii; also Partridge, *Bibliography*, p.4. He was in the House for 58 years, and held office for 48 of the 61 years of his public life.

12. Ridley, *Palmerston*, p.1, and conversations with the author, 16 May 1994.

13. A. J. P. Taylor, *The Struggle for Mastery in Europe, 1848–1918* (Oxford, 1954), p.569; Sir Robert Rhodes James, *An Introduction to the House of Commons* (London, 1961), p.54; also B. Kingsley Martin, *The Triumph of Lord Palmerston: A Study of Public Opinion in England before the Crimean War* (London, 1924, rev. edn, 1963), *passim*. Bourne, *Early Years*, p.136. 'No man should be judged too readily on the evidence of his most private correspondence any more than on that of his public set performances. Each has its . . . quality of deception.'

14. Rhodes James, *House of Commons*, p.50, cf. Macaulay; Bell, *Lord P*, vol.2, p.26.

15. PBHA, 27 December 1851 FO/C/4; see Chap.5 *infra*. P was handing over to a protégé and Granville had learned his craft at the feet of his then master as his Under-Secretary in 1840 (Bell, *Lord P*, vol.1, pp.261, 295) 'He poured out his hopes and plans in a series of letters.'

16. FO 97/198, 'France: Messrs Braithwaite and Martin's Claims, 1849–1853. (I am grateful to Dr A. Howe for first bringing this document to my attention.)

17. Channel 4 TV programme, *What Has Become of Us?*, series by Professor Peter Hennessy, November–December 1994.

18. For Bismarck's mind, see Dr F. Post, *British Journal of Psychiatry*, review, *Guardian*, 30 June 1994: '17% of ... politicians suffer from severe psychopathology ... (including) Bismarck, Disraeli, Hitler.' I am also indebted here to conversations about Bismarck with Dr Rudiger Goerner. See Ridley, *Palmerston*, Chap.39, p.563 *et seq.*

19. Ridley, *Palmerston*, p.334; and Judd, *Palm*, pp.45, 88. P's speech in Commons, 1 May 1848, sets the scene for the Rio Nunez Affair a year later, and also raises some considerations for the Britain of the late twentieth century: 'The real policy of England, apart from questions which involve her own particular interests, political or commercial, is to be the champion of justice and right, pursuing that course with moderation and prudence, not becoming the Quixote of the world. . . . Our interests are eternal and perpetual'.

20. R. J. Olney, 'Introduction to Palmerston Papers', NRA, p.5, Broadlands Archive, Hartley Library, Southampton University.

21. BL Add. MS, 48,577 (unbound) P to Normanby, 10 May 1847, folio 148, imputing to the French view of the Greek situation a lack of 'that faithfulness and Fulness of Narration which is an essential Quality in a Government agent'. For *Autobiographical Sketch* of c.1839, see Bourne, *Early Years*, p.321; cf. E. Ashley (ed.) *The Life of Henry Temple, Viscount Palmerston by Sir Henry Lytton Bulwer (Lord Dalling)* (London, 1870–4), vol.1, p.383.

22. C. Hibbert, *Queen Victoria in her Letters and Journals* (London, 1984), p.1, says G. St Aubyn calculated that Victoria wrote c.2500 words a day throughout her working life. See also Connell, *Regina*, p.359; cf. RA QJ, 18 October 1865.

23. See also Hibbert, *Letters*, pp.129, 135: HM to P, 4 February 1855; also 27 June 1857; also K. Martin, *Triumph*, *passim*; also Ridley, *Palmerston*, pp. 433–5; cf. Duke of Argyll: 'I knew that he had been quite as unforeseeing as any of us. . . . But . . . the popular impression of Palmerston's powers as a War Minister, even though it was largely a delusion, was in itself a qualification for the moment.'

24. Connell, *Regina*, p.212 cf. BP, 4 March 1857.

25. I am grateful to J. Ridley, letter of 4 February 1995, for further advice on this incident. See C. C. F. Greville, *The Greville Diary* (Wilson edn, London, 1927), vol.2, p.88; RA A 79/10; Y53/99; Connell, *Regina*, pp.120–1; cf. RA A 79, 10 July 1850; Ridley, *Palmerston*, pp.275–6; also Philip Ziegler, *Melbourne: A Biography of William Lamb 2nd Viscount Melbourne* (London, 1976), p.270, quotes memo from Anson, 13 December 1841 (RA Y 54/99), with inference that this incident came after his marriage. However, as Ziegler himself points out, P's indiscretion cannot have been pursued with too much conviction, since the lady was able to escape and seek the help of Stockmar. A letter of apology from P to Mrs Dacre now appears lost.

26. Bourne, *Early Years*, p.20, quotes Lady Minto to Lord Minto, 29 May 1802 from Countess of Minto, *Life and Letters of Sir Gilbert Elliot* (London, 1874), vol.2. For other examples of private generosity, see Bourne, *Early Years*, pp.44–5, 160, 201, 207, 209, 255. Also, on 'his quiet and kind disposition, cheerfulness, pleasantness and perfect sweetness', see Judd, *Palm*, p.8. Also Bell, *Lord P*, vol.2, p.75, on 'Shaftesbury remembered no other Home Secretary' (P's role in the Aberdeen coalition cabinet, 1853) 'to undertake

every good work of kindness . . . especially to children and the working class'. Also Ridley, *Palmerston*, p.125.

27. BL Add. MS, 45,553, Lamb Papers 1840–9, Panshanger, *passim*, and 30 December 1848. Emily, Lady Palmerston to P, n.d. (1840?) folio 7. For this aspect of P's ability to understand the ordinary men and women of his time, and indeed for many other insights, see Pemberton, *Lord Palmerston*, pp.181, 195.

28. Bourne, *Early Years*, pp.38–9.

29. R. McWhirter's Preface to Joseph Haydn, *The Book of Dignities* (London, 1894, repr. Baltimore, 1970).

30. Bell, *Lord P*, vol.1, p.344; also conversation with Dr J. Parry of 27 January 1995.

31. Bourne, *Early Years*, p.408; also Sir Edward Hertslet, *Recollections of the Old Foreign Office* (London, 1901), p.45.

32. Ridley, *Palmerston*, pp.293–4; cf. C. Grant in Ashley, *Life*, vol.3, pp.127–9. See Bibliographical Summary.

33. Bourne, *Early Years*, p.221, n.69 quotes Webster, *Foreign Policy*, i, 58, reference to August 1834; but p.332, n.1, cf. P 'to one of his own neglected diplomats', reference to 23 November 1834. For other P similes for his chronic overworking, see Bourne, *Early Years*, pp.430–2, 551, who speaks of him having to cram 'six hours business into four hours time'.

34. H. Reeve (ed.) *The Greville Memoirs: A Journal of the Reigns of King George IV and King William IV* (London, 1875) vol.2, Chap.20, p.358, Princess Lieven to Greville.

35. BL Add. MS, 45,553, Emily to P, May–November 1840, folio 12. Also Bourne, *Early Years*, Chap.9.

36. Connell, *Regina*, p.92 quotes RA J 4, 11 August 1848.

37. S. Walpole, *Life of Lord John Russell* (London, 1889), p.67; also Bell, *Lord P*, vol.2, p.50, who quotes LJR saying to Clarendon, 'I have had for five years a most harassing warfare . . . as umpire between Windsor and Broadlands.'

38. Walpole, *LJR*, vol.2, p.5, LJR, 26 October 1846.

39. Walpole, *LJR*, vol.2, p.44, LJR to P, 1 October 1848.

40. For Clarendon's activity against P in the 1840s, see Bell, *Lord P*, vol.1, Chap.14. See Part II, Chap.4 *infra*, for further views of Grey.

41. PBHA, Palmerston Diaries, 19 February and 13 March 1852.

42. Lord David Cecil, *Lord M* (London, 1954), pp.114, 283.

43. Bourne, *Early Years*, p.185.

44. J. Grant (editor of the *Morning Advertiser*) *Random Recollections of the House of Commons 1830–1835 by One of No Party* (London, 1836), p.218.

45. Composite picture from the mainstream 'Palmerstonians' — Ridley, Bourne, Connell, Southgate, Bell, Judd, Pemberton, Ashley, Chamberlain q.v.; see Ridley, *Palmerston*, p.529.

46. Walpole, *LJR*, vol.2, p.30; for the value of this education in 'North Britain', see also Judd, *Palm*, p.6; Ridley, *Palmerston*, pp.15–17.

47. Parry, *Liberalism*, p.178; for P's industriousness, see Bourne, *Early Years*, pp.19, 103, 115, 134; also Judd, *Palm*, p.9: 'he always did his homework'.

48. Bell, *Lord P*, I, Chap.6, 'The Birth of Belgium'.

49. For Schleswig-Holstein question, see Part II, Chap.5, *infra*.

50. Parry, *Liberalism*, p.191.

51. For original 'intermeddling' speech, 1 June 1829, see Ridley, *Palmerston*, pp.100, 125; Bourne, *Early Years*, p.294. 'Nor did he invent gunboat diplomacy' (Judd, *Palm*, p.47) and 'he took risks but . . . these were calculated

risks' (p.72). For Churchill 'jaw/war' analogy, see K. O. Morgan's 'Introduction' to M. E. Chamberlain, Lord Palmerston (Swansea, 1987).

52. Parry, Liberalism, p.132.

53. Grant, Random Recollections, p.218.

54. Pacifico speech, see infra, n.59.

55. On 'Holland House' Europeanism, see L. Mitchell, Holland House (London,
     1980); Connell, Regina, p.45 cites RA E 42, 9 December 1846, P to Albert.
     See Chap.4 on Van de Weyer to d'Hoffschmidt's 'revenge for Waterloo'.

56. Connell, Regina, p.52; see Judd, Palm, p.110 for the compensating quality of
     flexibility: 'The great thing about Palmerston was that he had few absolute
     prejudices.'

57. These points are drawn from various sources, including Ridley, Palmerston,
     pp.138, 521; Parry, Liberalism, pp.130–1, 194 (the phrase was Clarendon's);
     also p.16: 'Liberalism was in fact profoundly chauvinistic, luxuriating in the
     sense of British superiority to European rivals.' See Cain and Hopkins,
     Imperialism, I, pp.99–104; also Bell, Lord P, vol.2, Chap.21; not all Bell's
     views on the British constitution are correct, see Appendix 2, especially for
     Jennings's critical opinion on Stockmar.

58. Ridley, Palmerston, p.145; cf. A. Czartoryski, Memoirs of Prince Adam
     Czartoryski (London, 1888), vol.2, pp.339–44.

59. For the Don Pacifico incident and the civis Romanus debate see Southgate,
     English Minister, pp.263–78; and Ridley, Palmerston, Chaps.26 and 27; also
     Bell, Lord P, vol.1, Chap.20. See PBHA, 4 February 1850, GC HO 719–39;
     also infra, Part II, Chap.4. For P was free of anti-Semitism, see Ridley,
     Palmerston, p.292.

60. Hertslet, Old Foreign Office, p.72.

61. Rhodes James, House of Commons, p.34.

62. Bell, Lord P, vol.2, p.20. P always had in mind that the royal family had been
     introduced constitutionally at the end of the seventeenth century by just such
     a revolution as he was accused of encouraging in Europe. His letter on this
     theme to LJR of 14 September 1849 managed to percolate to Windsor; Judd,
     Palmerston, Chap.5.

63. Ridley, Palmerston, p.255 cf. Macaulay, Hansard 7–9 April 1840.

64. For the Macaulay references see Bell, Lord P, I, p.276. See also influence of
     HM's 'dearest Uncle' Leopold ('One who has ever been a father to me'): M.
     Charlot, Victoria: The Young Queen (Oxford, 1991), pp.245, 200: 'He
     insisted that Cromwell had shown that the country could . . . flourish without
     a monarchy.' Bell adduces as his reference, Bishop Burnet's History of My
     Own Time (1724, repr. 1833), I, p.148; see first edn., vol.1, p.80, when
     Blake, off Malaga, declared that 'an Englishman was only to be punished by
     an Englishman . . . Cromwell . . . said he hoped he should make the name of
     an Englishman as great as ever that of a Roman had been.' (There is no
     reference to Rome or the civis Romanus in the index of W. C. Abbott, The
     Writings and Speeches of Oliver Cromwell (Harvard, 1937), or in T. Carlyle,
     Oliver Cromwell's Works and Speeches (London, 1895).) See Ridley, Palmer-
     ston, p.55; cf. Hansard, 8 March 1816: 'England was not a state like Ancient
     Rome'.

65. Bell, Lord P, vol.2, p.25.

66. Bell, Lord P, vol.2, pp.27–8.

67. Ridley, Palmerston, pp.370–2, 374–6. Judd, Palm, pp.91–2: 'Pacifico claimed
     £5000 . . . and £27,000. . . . Eventually [he] received £6400 for damages
     caused by fire, and, a year later, a paltry £150 for his missing documents.'
     The claim has significance for the Rio Nunez Affair. By comparison,

Melbourne's gross income of £21,000 p.a. in 1835 made him a very rich man: Cecil, *Lord M*, p.315.

68. See *infra*, Part II, Chap.5.
69. Bell, *Lord P*, vol.1, p.291; Ridley, *Palmerston*, pp.222–3; cf. P to Bulwer, 1 September 1839 in Ashley, *Life*, vol.2, pp.298–9.
70. Bell, *Lord P*, vol.2, pp.27–8.
71. Hansard, *supra*; note discrepancy of Bell's total, vol.2, p.27.
72. Bell, *Lord P*, vol.2, pp.27–8.
73. Bell, ibid, vol.2, p.28; also Judd, *Palm,* p.97; cf. *Reynolds Weekly*'s 'he's the people's darling.'
74. A. C. Benson and Viscount Esher (eds) *The Letters of Queen Victoria* (London, 1907), vol.2, p.253; cf. by G. Lytton Strachey, *Queen Victoria* (London, 1921), p.138.
75. Bell, *Lord P*, vol.2, p.29; also Ridley, *Palmerston*, p.519; cf. Albert to Ernst of Saxe-Coburg, 4 August 1850.
76. Bell, *Lord P*, vol.2, p.120. For a brilliant contemporary resuscitation of Don Pacifico 'Cupid' Temple and Lord Aberdeen, see F. Mount, *Umbrella* (London, 1994), p.213. Pacifico, the explicit pretext for the *Romanus* speech, died four months before the death of its implicit hero, Joseph Braithwaite, on 12 April 1854, at St Mary Axe, very close to the offices where Joseph's ship-broker father worked. To use Mount's idiom, their 'ghosts' might well have known one another.
77. Rhodes James, *House of Commons*, p.11.
78. James Harris (Earl of Malmesbury), *Memoirs of an ex-Minister* (London, 1885), vol.1, p.335. Malmesbury has this view despite help from P, his grandfather's ward; Judd, *Palm,* p.162; also Part II, Chap.5 *infra*. See Southgate, *English Minister,* Chap.17, pp.317–18 on 'the *civis Romanus* doctrine encouraged British people to behave irresponsibly.'
79. Bell, *Lord P*, vol.2, p.52.
80. Parry, *Liberalism*, p.184.
81. Parry, ibid., p.130; also G. Woodbridge, The Reform Club: 1836–1978 (London, 1978), pp.18, 25, 35.
82. Kingsley Martin, *Triumph, passim*.
83. In the wake of the year 1849 — 'a year of deepening discouragement' for P, 'some of the most trying circumstances of his public life' (Bell, *Lord P*, vol.1, p.431), the ensuing months of 1850 were as torrid a time as P had ever experienced (Ridley, *Palmerston*, pp.380–1 and PP, Greek Papers 1850, vol.1). Nevertheless, P saw B&M in person a few weeks after he had made the British fleet gather off Piraeus, and in the same week as Nesselrode delivered a strong Russian protest against the British action (*infra*, Part II, Chap.5). See Chamberlain, *Ld Palm*, p.1.
84. Ridley, *Palmerston*, p.561 cf. Lord J. Manners, Hansard, 12 February 1864.
85. PBHA, Palmerston Diaries, 1 August 1849.
86. Southgate, *English Minister,* p.250.
87. Southgate, *English Minister,* pp.248–251; also p.188.
88. Bodl., MS. Eng. lett. d.269, ff. 146–9: P to LJR, Carlton Gardens, 27 April 1850.
89. PBHA, 27 December 1851, GC/HO/740/1.
90. PBHA, 14 November 1851, GC/HO/740/1; see A. J. P. Taylor, Introduction to Judd, *Palm,* p.vii, for characteristic Taylorian touch, albeit his qualified view of P. 'Metternich hated him: there could be no finer testimonial.' (Pemberton, *Lord Palmerston*, pp.195–9).
91. See Cain and Hopkins, *Imperialism*, vol.1, p.104; also p.360. For judgements

about P's capacity to have averted the Crimean War, see Ridley, *Palmerston*, p.414. Also Southgate, *English Minister*, p.xxii, floating the idea of the P 'touch', with reference to post-Second World War crises of Berlin and Cuba, p.xv. See Part II, Chap.5 *infra*, for value of the P 'touch' in the Nunez Affair.

Part II

David and Goliath Together: Forsters, Braithwaite and Martin, and the Most English Minister, 1849–1853

1. Prologue: The *Cives Britannici*

On Sunday 17 December 1848, Britain was confronting the news of the triumphant return of a new Bonaparte — Louis Napoleon, the nephew of the great emperor — to the seat of power in France. Just before noon that day, a fine-looking schooner, rigged fore-and-aft and with a topsail, cast off at St Katharine's Dock in the port of London. Her destination was the River Gambia, on the far west coast of Africa. There did not seem to be any conceivable connection between the two events.[1]

For all those who loved sailing ships, a fore-and-after was one of 'the birds of the sea, whose swimming is like flying', unapproachable for the 'simplicity and the beauty of its aspect under every angle of vision'.[2] The *Princess Royal* was a seasoned vessel of 111 tons, strongly built by Irvines, a good Scottish yard, seven seasons ago, of American and British oak, elm, larch and red pine. She had been given the special 'yellow metal' treatment — a copper and zinc coating — for her current role in hot tropical waters, where the *Toredo navalis* worm could eat away into an untreated hull as it lay at anchor. Five years' service, first on the Malta run for her previous owners, and now since 1846 under the ownership of Forster & Company, on the West Africa route, had made this trim twin-master just slightly less seaworthy than would justify the full Al rating at Lloyds: she was currently 'AE', first class as ever, but just beginning to show her age.[3]

Standing at the prow beside Captain Venn, the ship's commander, were two young Englishmen, Joseph Braithwaite and his business colleague George Martin. The partnership of Braithwaite and Martin was not travelling this time, in the language of the Africa trade, as supercargoes responsible to a merchant in England for the shipload of trade goods now on board, and for its profitable exchange on the coast; this cargo was their own modest capital.[4]

FIGURE 2 West Coast of Africa, highlighting the position of the Nunez, and the 'Naloos' in *res nullius*, between the French to the north at Gorée and the Senegal, and the British to the south at Sierra Leone. From Captain Belcher's report 1830–2, *JRGS*, reproduced by kind permission of the Royal Geographical Society.

Trade goods could embrace many different kinds of lawful merchandise. A glimpse at the bill of lading, drawn up on 15 December, shows just what a colourful and varied consignment the *Princess Royal* was carrying on this voyage — rifles, cutlasses, iron bars, gunpowder, denim cloth, 'black felt hats (Negro)', 'blue diamond cut lapis' and amber, bottled ale and porter. Some of the contents read uncannily like the cosy list of items that a young undergraduate, Harry Temple, later destined to play a major role in their lives, had taken to Cambridge for his comfort nearly half a century earlier; the bedding, candles and soap, cutlery, crockery, cruet stands — not forgetting a water purifier and their medicine chest — were for their personal use too for their 'residence' over the next five months, the 'good' season. The objective was once more to set up a trading warehouse on shore, but now, at last, after years of service for the House of Forster, to do so on their own.[5]

There was enough food for them to live in some style. The list could almost be a foretaste of what was soon to become the archetypal Victorian cookbook, *Mrs Beeton* — pickled pork and beef, jellies, jams, raisins, flour, loaf sugar, cocoa, Heyson's tea, bottled fruit, as well as cigars, snuff boxes and 'Best Brandy'. One of their Belgian attackers would comment later: 'the Englishman exports his motherland with him ... abroad, he continues to lead that same domestic and family life on which his whole happiness depends.'[6]

Braithwaite, the elder, whose life is the better documented of the two, was not the first holder of that name to venture into Africa, nor would he be the last. Indeed, one of the melancholy comments of a previous 'Brathwayte' — John, in 1729 — 'Trade at a Stop by the Wars amongst the Natives' — was to have a sadly prophetic ring to it, as events unfolded.[7]

Unlike that early agent of the then Royal African Company, Braithwaite and Martin would not be engaged in what their foreign minister, Lord Palmerston, would characterize as the 'abominable crime of slave trade', but in 'legitimate' produce. As traders, they would be able to sell to the competitive complex of factors or middlemen — Africans, mulattos, Europeans and Americans — that had by now evolved on the west coast. They would get back in exchange, then or later, the 'returns', the indigenous products that Europe's industries and European consumers now demanded: groundnuts (peanuts), oils, coffee beans, ivory, gum, hides, or timber. Even though they might acquire some gold dust from the interior territories, little of their buying would be carried out in 'specie' — the Bank of England £5 notes or the gold sovereigns they carried with them, or the silver Spanish dollars and 'quarters' — a French piastre roughly cut into four — which also circulated on the coast.[8]

The era of free trade, beloved and proclaimed by Palmerston in the House of Commons and in his dispatches to his ambassadors, was at its height. In the glow of that doctrine, Braithwaite and Martin were setting forth once more, to brave the world, selling on credit provided by one of the most respected merchant houses in London. The merged 'commissioning house' of Forster & Smith, the sister trading company to Forster & Company, had been established on the Gambia under its present name for a quarter of a century; at that time it was the leading British firm all along the Guinea shore as far as Cape Coast.[9]

Joseph, at 32, was the moving spirit behind this very British enterprise; both men were in that age group that expert witnesses had signalled as the optimum age for men who decided to risk the rigours of the African life.[10] They were characteristic examples of that peculiar early Victorian compound of global optimism, moral precept, commercial instinct, and an unlimited and naïve faith in the simple fact of being British: an epitome of the Palmerstonian ideal. They themselves were very akin to the 'gentlemanly capitalists' who financed traders like them, in the image that a chronicler of the Rio Nunez, Ensign-Aspirant Delcourt, was to set down about the English traders of his day, through a flattering comparison with their French counterparts. 'The Englishman ... preserves his habits and his English customs ... and a thousand miles from home that same reserve and dignity, having the inner consciousness of his superiority over other people.'[11]

Joseph had been born in the year of Jane Austen's death, 1817; his birthplace, a narrow lane off Upper Street in Islington, then a leafy village just north of the City of London, was named, perhaps appropriately, Britannia Row; it is still there today. He grew up in the world of manners and morals that the great authoress had immortalized; pride and prejudice of many different kinds were to be the decisive elements in the life that lay ahead of him. The Christian name Joseph was part of a family tradition reaching back into the eighteenth century in Yorkshire. His father, also a Joseph, had been a ship broker, having migrated, like so many hardy and entrepreneurial Britons at the time of the industrial revolution, to seek his fortune in the booming metropolis, forsaking the Braithwaite farming lands at Buskey Fields, near Leeds.[12]

Both Joseph and the man later to become his friend and commercial partner, George Martin, hailing originally from Ipstones in Staffordshire, would have been indentured with Forster & Smith perhaps as early as the age of 13. The tang of the rapidly expanding 'Africa trade' had got into their nostrils early on. Each later must have come into money of his own: as the eldest son, Joseph had inherited initially from his father, when he died in February 1839, at the age of of 53. The cause of his death was described as 'inflammation of the lungs', brought about by one of London's chronic winter peasoupers — the 'smogs' which, as Home Secretary, Palmerston was later to be the first statesman to campaign against.[13]

In the passport that, despite Lord Palmerston's remonstrances with Belgium of a decade before, Joseph was to need for a critical visit to Ghent in the following year, his status is set down as *rentier*; in the same way, witnesses to a parliamentary committee would have had their 'condition' recorded as 'Esquire' — a man of independent means. That passport brings him to life vividly: 'five foot seven and a half inches tall, with hazel-coloured eyes, brown hair and beard [and brown eyebrows] — an aquiline nose, a high forehead, a mouth that was described as *moyenne*, and a rounded chin, all set within an oval face'. There were apparently no '*signes particuliers*' about him. Photographs of the family suggest that he was well-built; he may well have resembled his younger brother Charles, as he was painted by his daughter many years later. To survive in Africa, he certainly needed all the rude health he could muster; he could be grateful to the honest Yorkshire farming blood in his veins.[14]

There were no passports needed, of course, for the Gambia, one of Britain's oldest and most fertile — albeit least valued — colonies.[15] The territory was in any case very familiar to both Joseph and George. As they later intimated to Lord Palmerston, they had been making this voyage, once 'the rains' were over — usually by late November — almost as annual commuters, for the

best part of ten years.[16] The Gambia was by now home ground to
'Forsters', as the firm was still colloquially known in the City of
London. This highly-respected and many-sided firm had succeeded
in becoming all things to all men along the Guinea coast — by
turns shipowners, shippers, a commissioning house for other
traders, bankers and financiers to their competitors, and speculators on the future of commodities such as palm oil. Most
significantly, through their senior partner, the MP from the rugged
Scottish Borders, Matthew Forster, the house of Forster & Smith
had become the forceful Westminster voice for the 'legitimate'
merchants, as they slowly superseded the 'illegitimate' slave
trade.[17] Braithwaite and Martin could ride confidently on the crest
of this wave of success and commercial dominance.

The sky was clear, aided by a good easterly breeze, as the
Princess Royal cleared the London river at 10.30 that morning. By
later that afternoon, they were moving steadily past 'the Downs',
the stretch of water outside Deal, and veering into a favourable
northeast wind.[18] Joseph and George did some last-minute checking of their documentation — not that they needed to: Forsters
had two trusty clerks in their 'counting house' as they still quaintly
called it, in Mr Lintott and Mr Spink, who were totally reliable in
their calculations of price, quality and quantity.[19] They left what
were by now their accustomed cramped quarters on these voyages,
two bunks off the captain's cabin and map room in the stern, and
went up to join Captain Venn, by invitation, for the customary
start of voyage tot of rum.[20]

To two healthy, resourceful, well-educated bachelors in their
prime, with the spray of an unequivocally English Channel in their
face and hair, that was an exhilarating moment. They knew themselves to be citizens of young Victoria's Britain, manifestly by now
the greatest country in the world, with a monarchy and its patriotic government standing proud and secure, and its foreign policy
bold and defiant, while most of Europe was still reeling from its
year of revolutions.[21]

Life seemed, very simply, grand; it was good to be alive. The
two men who looked at the great protective cliffs of Dover passing
before them embodied the very spirit of Lord Palmerston's celebrated quip, which they often repeated to each other: to the
Frenchman who had said that if he were not a Frenchman he
would rather be an Englishman, 'Pam's' reply had come back

swiftly that 'if I were not an Englishman, I should wish to be an Englishman.'[22]

Later in the afternoon, as they moved out into mid-Channel, and the familiar coastline started to recede, their minds lingered for a while on the kith and kin they were once more leaving behind. First and foremost in Joseph's thoughts was his serious and dutiful younger brother Charles, just married, and the father of a one-year-old son, Charles John; Charles and his buxom Elizabeth lived nearby in Theberton Street, eking out a careful existence on £200 a year, Charles's starting wages as a clerk, 6th class, in the London docks.[23] For George his images were of his family in Staffordshire, and also of his eldest sister Catherine, and his younger brother, also a Joseph, a navy paymaster, who were still living near the family birthplace of Saltash, overlooking the Tamar and the great naval stronghold of Plymouth.[24]

Joseph pictured too his boisterous younger sisters, Sophie and Elizabeth, and little Rosie, and that rather prim and forbidding eldest sister Ann, two years his senior, teaching at her dame school in Camden. In a different compartment of his mind were images of his younger cousin William, with that very agreeable 26-year-old sister of his, Sarah, trying to make some sort of living together, with their youngest brother, out of old Badger Mill in faraway Shropshire; that was where his Uncle Stephen, now the head of the family, had migrated from Yorkshire, early in the century. Nevertheless those dear 'friends', as cousins sometimes called each other at that time, and even the comely Sarah, began to loom less strongly in his mind with every league that separated them. The wishes of a good few of the Braithwaite family went with him that day. Joseph's modest capital represented the greater part of the family wealth: his success, or failure, would be theirs too.

Ahead lay the bustle and colour and cut and thrust of the Africa trade that Joseph and George knew so well, a far cry from the dingy greyness of London's streets, let alone the rustic calm of Shropshire or Staffordshire, or the quietness of the Tamar hill-sides. The sense of excitement at finally making a bargain with the African middlemen, as a culmination to the elaborate negotiating sessions that were an essential part of the proceedings; the style and Regency elegance of Bathurst St Mary, now building steadily as the colony's capital; the thrill of outmanoeuvring their French competitors just a few miles up the Gambia at Albreda — these were the kind of exotic scenes that acted like a drug on those mid-century merchant adventurers, once they had tasted it. They flooded overpoweringly into Joseph's and George's inward eye again, as they always did once the voyage got under way.

Their course took them just about a month, the normal timing for that period of the year, allowing for some adverse winds across the Bay of Biscay and the Atlantic, and more of the same weather once they started to sail into African waters. The fare was sparse, with such foods as would last the end of the journey — their stocks were intended primarily for the months ahead. Even on this short voyage they sometimes had to throw food overboard as uneatable.[25] The arrival on the Gambia, with its plentiful supply of exotic local meat, fruit and vegetables could not come too soon.

They reached the mouth of the great river on 16 January 1849, and came alongside at Bathurst's tiny quay.[26] Their first visitor on board was Forsters' correspondent and resident agent, the experienced Richard Lloyd.[27] The first intimation of change from the accepted pattern of events came with his opening piece of news. It seemed that trading conditions on the Gambia were, as Joseph put it later, in his restrained wording, 'dull' — not so favourable as they had previously appeared back at New City Chambers. The gap of at least three months since the last dispatch via the mail boat could easily bring with it an alteration in the volatile movement of supply and demand along the river. Richard Lloyd's suggestion was that Braithwaite and Martin should alter their plans, reship some of their cargo, making a few substitutions to suit a new trading venue, and set off further down the coast; they could exploit what promised to be the currently more beneficial conditions in the 'Southern Rivers'; they had had previous dealings at Sedhiou, for example, on the nearby River Casamance, although not without some difficulties.

In particular, Richard emphasized the attractions of the Rio Nunez, where he and Forsters had for several years retained as their factor a long-established trader, a Mr John Nelson Bicaise. The company's judgement, however, was that Bicaise's performance had not proved satisfactory; they were not sure where his allegiances lay, although he had certainly been assiduous in warning them about aspects of the slave trading still being conducted on the river.[28] A little competition seemed to be called for.

The Nunez river had already been strongly recommended as

good for the legitimate trade by one of the Royal Naval squadron's officers, Captain Belcher, on the HMS *Aetna* survey expeditions in the 1830s.[29] The French were known to be particularly active there, as part of their apparently insatiable drive to grow and import more and more groundnuts; there was also a new type of mocha coffee being grown up-river in the wild, which looked interesting. Even the Belgians appeared to be developing links on that river: a Belgian warship, the *Louise-Marie*, was reported as having been exploring the area a year ago, and there were rumours that she was very shortly due back at Bathurst again, under the same commander, Captain Van Haverbeke.[30]

As a further indicator of opportunity, one of Forsters' Bathurst-based rivals, the Americans Pingree & Kimball, had now set up a factory on the lower river, and at least two other traders with English connections, Charles Heddle, and Nathaniel Isaacs, were also currently active in that part of the world.[31] There was a third well-known Englishman nearby — Benjamin Campbell — who had served his apprenticeship with one of Forsters's competitors, Macaulay & Babington, before it went bankrupt (as many did); he had later set up on his own at the appropriately-named 'Factory Island', on the Isles de Los.[32]

Finally — a crucial point for Joseph, as Richard knew — what he and the European world now called the legitimate trade seemed to have displaced the slave trade much more effectively along the Nunez, due to its configuration, than in the neighbouring river complex to the southeast; the Rio Pongas, the 'river of monkeys', with its many mouths and creeks, could much more easily conceal a slave trader from any prowling vessel of the British or French surveillance squadrons.[33] The upright Joseph, in common with the merchant house with which he was associated, would have none of that business.[34]

'The Rivers' did not have anything of the official colonial status of the Gambia, even if the local British traders there continued to try to assert something very like it. Ten years previously one of them, Michael Proctor, had petitioned the Colonial Office, arguing that the Rivers' proximity to the Sierra Leone border to the south made the area a virtual 'colonial dependency'.[35] Richard Lloyd could not remember what London's reaction had been to that request at the time; but he did recall that an earlier governor at Freetown — the entrepreneurial Cole — many years before the present somewhat lax incumbent, Macdonald, had tried to extend British power into what he saw as 'the Northern Rivers', when he occupied the Isles de Los.[36] In any case the squadron could theoretically always be on station there, within a few hours sailing, if the governor could be stirred, or despite London's critical eye, emboldened to authorize such an intervention.[37]

Joseph and George took an immediate decision. This was an opportunity not to be missed: the Nunez it was to be.

They both knew that there were risks in all aspects of the West African trade: that was something they had learned from their years in Forsters' service. Commercial life was full of challenge, from the French in particular, who seemed constantly to be trying to avenge Waterloo.[38] But this was part of the normal problem of trading in Africa, which they were accustomed to deal with and overcome by the traditional African techniques of 'palaber' and negotiation.[39]

If anyone could have warned Joseph at that moment that a mere five months later he would be returning to England's shores, having just escaped with his life from an African battlefield, possessing only the clothes he stood up in, and that he would be dropped by rowing boat onto a beach in Sussex, like a figure from one of the novels of that promising new writer, Charles Dickens, Joseph would have dismissed such a warning as preposterous.[40]

His disbelief would have been even greater if that same visionary had also predicted the events of the summer five years hence: that he — an experienced trader acclimatized to the diseases of the coast, and equipped with all the specifics medical science had yet come up with — would die of a fever in Bathurst, with no known grave; that at his death he would be destitute, broken and bankrupt; and that he would leave nothing behind from the earnings of all his years of exertion and privation — nothing, that is, save for his precious gold watch with the family crest on its fob, and the gold-headed cane bequeathed him by his father: that was unthinkable.

If, for good measure, this insight into the future were also to have revealed that Braithwaite and Martin's personal tragedy would become the subject of a unique international incident, an 'affair within an affair', that tested Britain's mettle to breaking point, neither of them would have credited it. If they had been told that this political affair would be linked to the highest in the land, above all to the passions and fortunes of Britain's world famous Foreign Secretary — that it would become another 'case for Lord Palmerston', and that their revered Queen herself would become the unwitting cause of their undoing, the bounds of credibility would finally have broken. They would have concluded that it was all just a very strange dream, and they would soon wake up to real life again.[41]

But it was no dream. It was to be a nightmare. The ensuing days of Joseph's and George's lives were to be lived at an intensity of despair that they had never before experienced, and for which nothing, other than some element in their blood and their upbringing, could have prepared them.

Death and destruction all around them: political scandals of which they were scarcely aware; French intrigue and jealousy; a well-crafted cover-up by Belgium; the undermining of their case and even the treachery of those who were apparently fellow citizens and allies; the incompetence and gullibility of the representatives of the British navy; an isolated but far-reaching dereliction of duty on the part of the governor's office at Sierra Leone, compounded by inertia at the Colonial Office; injustice, financial ruin, and ultimately, the harsh realities of European balance-of-power politics, as the 'Eastern Question' started to dominate the official mind in London: all this was to be their experience and their fate, in rich measure — an experience shared with Forsters, despite the presence of the great Lord Palmerston at their side, in the weeks, months and indeed years ahead.[42]

Notes

1. GL/A, Lloyds Lists, December 1848; *The Times*, 16 December 1848. See Kenneth Bourne, *Palmerston: The Early Years, 1784–1841* (London, 1982), p.339 on election of Louis Napoleon to President, 10 December 1848.
2. Joseph Conrad, *The Mirror of the Sea* (London, 1906), quoted in D. R. Macgregor, *Merchant Sailing Ships 1815–1850* (Conway, 1984). Some Conrad themes inform this story; he saw 'something odd and unnatural about Europeans being in Africa in the first place'. B. Pugh, in a review of A. White's 'Joseph Conrad and the Adventure Tradition' (*African Affairs*, 374, January 1995, p.148) said, 'Darkest Africa might well have originated out of geographical ignorance, but as Curtin argues it was adhered to out of cultural arrogance.'
3. GL/A, Lloyds Register; NMM; BL, Mercantile Navy Lists 1851. Schooners were by definition twin-masted, unless otherwise stated (Jenny Wraitt, NMM, to author).
4. 'Supercargoes', usually the ship's captain, went out on behalf of the owner of a cargo, for the four or five months of the 'good' season, returning to live off

their profits when the weather became inhospitable and trading ended for the season. (Contemporary comparisons are the commercial operators in Saudi Arabia and the Persian Gulf, also the world of the North Sea oil rig, and the merchant navy.) The 'good season' was December–April; see SGA/B, AP docs. Also George Brooks Jnr, *Yankee Traders, Old Coasters, African Middlemen* (Boston, 1970), pp.84–6, 103: 'Once his accounting was made, the master or supercargo could look forward to a month or two at home with his family while the cargo was put up for sale.'

5. Bill of lading, SGA/B doc. FP 7; also Brooks, *Yankee*, p.313 *et seq.* pp.368–70: list of 128 goods used in the Africa trade — guns and gunpowder were normal, if not the top priority, consignments. See also P. Manning, *Slavery and African Life* (Cambridge, 1990), p.100; see PRO FO97/198, Capt. J. Denman to George Martin, partner in B&M, 19 February 1851, 'Muskets were one of the principal objects of Trade in that River.' For the arrival of Harry Temple, the future Viscount P, at St John's College, Cambridge, 22 October 1803, see Bourne, *Early Years*, p.32.

6. See B/MRHA, Journal of Aspirant G. Delcourt, 'Relation du Voyage à la Côte d'Afrique avec la Goélette *Louise-Marie* 1848–9', p.3. See Chap.3, n.50, *infra*. Mrs 'Samuel' Beeton brought out, with her publisher husband, Part 1 of her *Book of Household Management* in 1859; see S. Freeman, *Isabella and Samuel: The Story of Mrs Beeton* (London, 1977).

7. PRO TS 70/7, 'The Royal African Company of England: From the West Coast of Africa, No. 3, 12 January 1719–26, August 1732, 7 October 1729; John Brathwayte to Royal African Company, London; Fyfe, *A History of Sierra Leone* (London, 1962), pp.564–71 mentions a Capt. C. Braithwaite Wallis, SL.

8. BL Add. MS, P's Letterbooks, P to W. D. Christie, HM envoy to the independent kingdom of Brazil, 8 July 1860. Although this phrase was used by P a decade later, it was characteristic of his views from the 1840s onwards. 'Specie' covered all coinage; Brooks, *Yankee*, p.114. (Dr C. Fyfe has pointed out that whereas at an earlier stage, by the 1840s, specie might only have been used by slave traders hurrying up their purchases, to avoid the 'squadron', as trade developed Europeans would have needed a supply for transactions with other Europeans.) The original currency had been the peculiar 'bar trade' — iron bars with a notional 'free market' unit of value for each commodity. For definition of 'factory' see Chap.2, n.21.

9. For definition of commissioning house, see F. Wolfson, 'British Relations with the Gold Coast, 1843–1880', (Ph.D. thesis, London University, 1950), p.L; *infra*, Chap.2, Redman's evidence, HoC, 'Report of the Select Committee appointed to inquire into the state of the British possessions on the West Coast of Africa', (55), XI:1, XII:1 (PPSC 1842). Also, Fyfe, *Leone* (London, 1962), p.203; A. McPhee, *The Economic Revolution in British West Africa* (London, 1926, repr. 1971), p.101.

10. For a judgement on 20–45 as the optimum age for Europeans trading in West Africa, see PPSC 1842, 27 May, Colonel Findlay (governor, GA, 1822–30) to Q 2412.

11. B/MRHA, Delcourt, 'Relation du Voyage', p.3. The significance of this slightly mocking tribute to the British by this junior Belgian naval officer becomes apparent in Chaps.4 and 5; he it was who alone noted that the B&M warehouse was sacked by Belgians, not primarily by a Fula mob, a fact asserted by the Britons, but hitherto unrevealed by any Belgian or French writer over the past 150 years. For the role of 'gentlemanly capitalists' in the

12.   development of Britain's 'informal empire', see P. J. Cain and A. G. Hopkins, *British Imperialism* (London, 1993); and Chap.6 *infra*.

12.   SGA/B docs Section II.

13.   Indentures assumed, from probably the age of 15 or even earlier as this would have been the logical career path for both traders, especially with Joseph Braithwaite's introduction to the world of City merchants by his shipbroker father.

14.   A question arises as to whether *rentier* was used instead of *commerçant* to conceal Joseph Braithwaite's identity from the Belgian authorities, ever suspicious of foreign entrants to their vulnerable little kingdom at that turbulent time (letter from Dr C. Fyfe to author, 17 December 1995). There is no evidence either way. For passports, see SGA/B docs Section II, and Braithwaite Papers in possession of the author. For P and passports, see J. Ridley, *Lord Palmerston* (London, 1970), p.362: 10 November 1835: 'The whole system ... is so repugnant to English usages that the Secretary of State could not propose to British subjects to submit additionally to the degrading and offensive Practice' (of giving particulars as to their personal appearance).

15.   See J. M. Gray, *A History of The Gambia* (Cambridge, 1940). GA was the most fertile of the British possessions on the West African coast. See also Brooks, *Yankee*, p.76.

16.   For details of PRO FO97/198, 'France: Messrs Braithwaite & Martin's Claim, 1849–1853, see Chaps.4, 5 *infra*. (This PRO document, fundamental to the Rio Nunez Affair, is the only individual claims ledger under 'France', in the category of supplements to General Correspondence, throughout 1782–1900.)

17.   UL/A; also F. J. Pedler, *The Lion and the Unicorn in Africa* (London, 1973), despite inaccuracies in the evolution of Forsters into Unilever. See *infra* Chap. 2, for the wider relationship of Forster to public life.

18.   GL/A, Lloyds List, National Meteorological Archive, Bracknell.

19.   For the central place of Messrs Lintott and Spink in the firm of Forsters, for which they did a 'management buy-out' in 1873, see GL/A docs, Chap.2 *infra*.

20.   NMM, advice by Jenny Wraitt, archivist.

21.   1848, the year of revolutions in Europe. See Part I, *supra*; also Part III, Appendices, *infra*.

22.   Ridley, *Palmerston*, p.589; and Bourne, *Early Years*, p.349. For quotation on Lord Rendel, see F. E. Hamer (ed.) *The Personal Papers of Lord Rendel* (London, 1931), p.60. According to Gladstone, who, not surprisingly, did not think highly of P, this was one of his rare, but good jokes — there is no context for the origin of this remark; J. Ridley, letter to author, 15 July 1995, states 'There is no indication as to the date on which Palmerston made the remark, nor of the identity of the Frenchman to whom he made it.' It is assumed here that it was made long enough before 1848, since it embodies all the bouncy patriotism of P's middle years for Joseph Braithwaite and George Martin to be familiar with and delight in quoting it.

23.   SGA/B doc. EP20.

24.   Saltash Heritage Society, letter to author, 17 November 1994; also letters in PRO FO97/198; see Chap.5, n.101.

25.   PRO ADM53/2594, log of the *Grappler*, 1848.

26.   W. E. F. Ward, *The Royal Navy and the Slavers* (London, 1969). Voyages from London or Ostend to the West African coast usually encountered light but persistent northeast winds, interspersed with frequent calms, and perhaps two or three days of rain. Off Portugal they would sometimes experience

heavy winds, but generally the weather was fine. Also P. Lefevre, 'Les Voyages de la Marine royale belge en Sénégal', *RBHM*, vol.21, no.23, (Brussels, 1972–80), journals of Dr Celarier, 1850 and 1856, pp.40, 144 *et seq.*

27. For probable background of Major Richard Lloyd, 'the new British commandant [at Gorée] ... in the Gambia' in 1804, see Brooks, *Yankee*, pp.44–7, 166; also CO267/83 1827, Goderich. For incidents at Sedhiou, see *infra*, Chaps.2 and 5; Gray, *Gambia*, pp.202, 309, 316, 332, 402.

28. CO267/205, Addington, FO, to B. Hawes, CO, 24 February 1848, enclosure on F&S to FO, and on Bicaise to F&S, of 18 December 1847. For volatility of trade, see Brooks, *Yankee*, p.28. The description 'dull' is Joseph Braithwaite's, SGA/B doc. AP 20. For Bicaise, see Chaps.3 and 5 *infra*. This is the only hypothesis that fits the case.

29. Capt. Belcher RN, 'Extracts from Observations on Various Points of the West Coast of Africa Surveyed by HM Ship *Aetna* in 1830–32', *JRGS*, vol.2, 1832, pp.278–304.

30. 'Voyages', *RBHM*, 8 December 1978, Dr Durant; also B/MAE dossiers, see Chap.3, *infra*. Cohen seems to have been the victim of a partly justified campaign of mistrust, based presumably on jealousy, and on doubts as to his motivations, but partly on anti-Semitism: he is constantly referred to as '*le juif* Cohen'.

31. For traders on 'the Rivers', see Fyfe, *Leone*, pp.66, 203, 226, 239, 255–6; also Brooks, *Yankee*, pp.176, 180, 190.

32. Brooks, *Yankee*, p.176. See Chap.2, n.123 *infra* (reputedly the inspiration for R. L. Stevenson's *Treasure Island*). See also references to 'Combeel' and his establishment, in Dr Durant's first report, 1847–8, *RBHM*, 7, pp.572–3.

33. The author is greatly indebted for much of the historical background to the Rio Nunez wars to Bruce Mouser, 'Trade and Politics in the Nunez and Pongo [*sic*] Rivers, 1790–1865' (Ph.D. thesis, Indiana University, 1971); see also Bruce Mouser's article, 'The Nunez Affair', *BARSOM* (Brussels, 1973–4), pp.697–742. Despite limitations inherent in that study not having had access to some of the original British and Belgian official sources, and to subsequent original Belgian and English material, this work nevertheless provides the best historical background to the Rio Nunez incident. For translation of 'Pongas' see the author's article, 'Sabre d'Honneur?', *RBHM*, vol.31, nos.1/2, mars–juin, 1995. 'Pongas' is the name used in PPSC 1842.

34. There is no doubt where B&M stood on the slave trade issue. Joseph Braithwaite is later recorded as highly censorious of Tay for 'trafficking' in slave dealing, Chap.4, n.23 *infra*, SGA/B doc FP 17. For the attitude of Forster to what Brooks calls the 'symbiotic relationship' between the legitimate and slave trades, see SGA/B doc. AP 30; also Chap.2 *infra*; Brooks, *Yankee*, p.116; see too Chap.4, n.16 *infra*.

35. PPSC 1842, see Chap.2 *infra*; also Brooks, *Yankee*, p.203.

36. Gov. Cole's attempts to bring the 'Northern Rivers' into SL's sphere of influence were rebuffed by the CO; see CO267/47, 2 January 1818. This remained British policy right the way through the period of the Rio Nunez Affair, conditioning much, but not all, the behaviour of Acting Gov. Pine in 1849–50. (His culpable 'derelictions' were not to lie in his refusal to step outside these parameters, but in a very simple act of disloyalty to his fellow countrymen, see Chap.5 *infra*.)

37. CO368, SL Registers, 1849–53. Gov. Macdonald, appointed 1847, was to be replaced on 12 October 1852, by Gov. Kennedy, having incurred the displeasure of the PUS, H. Merivale, for his 'serious responsibility in proposing

. to call troops out of the colony (SL); the Under-Secretary, Hawes, called his actions 'censurable' (CO267/213, Macdonald to Grey, 3 March, 2 May 1850). See Ward, *Royal Navy* and Chap.2, *infra* for the practical limits to the coverage of the squadron; also CO267/211, Hotham to ADM, ADM to CO, 12 December 1849, 17 February 1849 on 'It is possible that the visits of the French Men of War may have been more frequent than ours but': see *infra* Chap.4.

38. B/MAE, General de la Hitte, French foreign minister, specifically threatened retaliation for Waterloo in connection with the Don Pacifico affair, according to the Belgian archives, 1850. The French sense of burning resentment was no imaginary thing, see Chap.3.

39. F/CAOM, Sénégal et Dépendances, IV, 1838–50, dossier 26 (a) to (e), see Chap.3 *infra*. Also views of the senior French officer on the West African coast, Capt. Bouët-Willaumez (henceforth B-W), Chap.3. 'Palaver' was the wise, accepted African way to try to resolve problems; see also Gov. Maclean's adjudications in G. Metcalfe, *Maclean of the Gold Coast* (London, 1962).

40. SGA/B doc, FP 17, Report to P, January 1851; there is no extant Braithwaite grave in the Banjul graveyard: thanks to Dr C. Fyfe for this information from his research *in situ*. See *infra* Chap.5, n.14.

41. Ridley, *Palmerston*, p.390. P met Joseph Braithwaite and George Martin at his home, Carlton Gardens, on Saturday 23 February. See Part I, *supra*, for the relevance of this date in terms of the other pressures on P at that time. See SGA/B docs EP20, 21.

42. These events form the 'scandalous' aspects of the Rio Nunez Affair, set out in Chaps.5 and 6 *infra*. The impact of the Eastern Question, of the inadequacies of P's successors in office, and of the inability of the FO machinery to cope with this sharp increase in its work load from 1852 onwards, are set out as a working hypothesis in Part III, Appendix 3. Most authorities now take it as read that if P had been allowed to remain in office, he would have 'coped' with Russia, and yet again caused 'jaw-jaw' to prevent 'war-war'. See Ridley, *Palmerston*, p.123. It is a comparable postulate in this study, based on close examination of his character and his behaviour that he would also have managed, whirling around on what he called the fearsome 'windmill' of his daily round, to get satisfaction out of both the Belgian and French governments, despite their stone-walling. He would have done so for the sake of his two *cives Romani*, whose cause he had clearly espoused; see Chap.5 *infra*. For the evolving character of P, see Part I, *supra*. For coverage of the affair hitherto in the classic British works of time and place, see Fyfe, *Leone*, p.255, and J. D. Hargreaves, *Prelude to the Partition of West Africa* (London, 1963), p.94.

2. Matthew Forster MP: Champion of the Legitimate Trade

L ord Palmerston had said, 'We must look again to Africa.' In allying themselves with the City merchants Forster & Smith for this first trading venture on their own, Joseph Braithwaite and George Martin had chosen their 'agents' (in effect their commercial sponsors) more opportunely than they realized. The firm's senior partner, Matthew Forster, was to became their 'white knight'. The story of the Rio Nunez Affair cannot be told without first looking at his rise to power, his influence with Lord Palmerston, and of the early nineteenth-century colonial background against which he achieved them.[1]

After 30 years of peace in Europe, a good part of whose benefits could be attributed — directly or indirectly — to the policies of Palmerston, the only British presence in many parts of West Africa was still merely a business presence: within that context, the house of Forster & Smith was at the very height of its wealth and influence. As it approached the midpoint in the century, it had become the acknowledged leader in the West African trade, from the Gambia to the Gold Coast; the firm's senior partner could publicly claim that it was 'the only house that has connections through the whole coast'. Later, after the advent of MacGregor Laird's monthly mail steamer run from Fernando Po to Plymouth in 1852 — which they actively encouraged but which ironically had the effect of undermining their financial strength — and after an ill-judged extension of their sway as far as Lagos, Forsters' fortunes were to begin their gradual decline.[2]

In the 1990s, when the focus is again turning to Africa, the great continent is at last being recognized for what it is — the 'birthplace of commerce'.[3] By the end of the eighteenth century,

Forsters had been 'looking to Africa', some 50 years before Lord Palmerston, with his geopolitical breadth of vision, started to advise the nation to do likewise.[4] The firm had not merely survived the vicissitudes of the competitive years following the end of the American and Napoleonic wars; they had gone on to exploit to the full the opportunities that Africa was now unfolding for the Western world. In parallel with this success, the head of the firm, Matthew Forster, came to be the accepted communicator with government about West African trading interests, and one of the most forceful 'spokesmen' that Westminster had yet seen. He had the good fortune to be operating in that increasingly liberal period leading up to and flowing from the 1832 Reform Act, when the House of Commons was becoming more open to what the Whig Prime Minister, Lord Grey, complained of as 'constant and active pressure from without'.[5]

Through their connection with Forsters, Braithwaite and Martin's brave little enterprise was also to play its part as one of the myriad commercial threads that were to lead — first through a 'management buy-out' and then absorption by the River Gambia Trading Company — to the United Africa Company of the twentieth century; the 'UAC' was to become in its turn a central element in one of the world's largest multinationals, the Unilever corporation. Great oaks and little acorns. . . .[6]

Postwar Challenges to the West Africa Trade

After 'The Great War', as the early Victorians — like their Edwardian successors a century later — called the major conditioning event of their lifetime, Forsters faced challenges on every level. In the first place, there was a renewal of foreign competition, with the inevitable problems resulting from the resumption of traditional rivalries. Due to their enforced move from the former French settlement on the Senegal, this meant a 'start-up' situation for them on the Gambia.[7] Over and above the endemic problems of the climate for all Europeans, 'seasoned' or unseasoned, there was the need to come to terms with the changing patterns of African commerce in the light of the anti-slave trade campaign.[8]

To cap it all, they were shortly to become directly dependent, from 1821 onwards, on 'a department of inertia', where 'originality and initiative were not required'.[9] 'Downing Street', the then preferred synonym for the British Colonial Office, gave scant

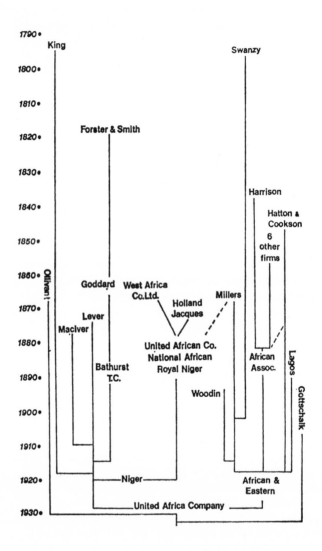

FIGURE 3 Routes by which Unilever and the United Africa Company evolved from a multiplicity of constituent firms in West Africa from the eighteenth century onwards, with acknowledgements to F. J. Pedler, *The Lion and the Unicorn in Africa* (Heinemann).

support to what was in any case a fragile British political presence on the coast; it operated a policy which has been described as 'wavering, indecisive ... seeming to contradict itself at every turn'.[10]

The two Treaties of Paris of 1815, whilst cutting France back to size in Europe, depriving her of her conquests in Belgium and Holland, and of a goodly proportion of her fleet too, were crucially generous in one particular respect: the French regained control — once more — of St Louis, on the Senegal, their former colony within the wider Senegambia region. They were also given back the strategically related fort to the south, the island of Gorée (today's Dakar), and their tiny but disproportionately contentious enclave on the Gambia, Albréda. These were the tiny seeds from which France's dominance in the French West Africa of the coming century was to germinate and flourish. The British traders who had been encouraged to take over French settlements during the war were not best pleased: William, Matthew's younger brother, was among them; if Forsters' pleadings with the government to hang on to these spoils of war had been acceded to, the whole history of West Africa could well have been very different.[11]

The trading pattern which had already developed on the Senegal River was unlike that of the aptly-named Windward Coast — the stretch of mainland starting 100 miles to the south, off which the prevailing southeasterly winds favoured sail departing 'windward' for the Americas and Europe. It was the first, western, section of the longer Gulf of Guinea, extending 1200 miles southeastwards round the western extremity of the African continent, from the 'green cape', Cape Verde, to Cape Palmas, off the American-inspired independent republic of Liberia. The Windward Coast was regarded by Forsters and its fellow traders as a single interlocking trading complex, not, as some politicians did, in terms of a set of dissociated posts and settlements.[12]

The Senegal had once been conjectured as a possible mouth of the Niger; together these two noble rivers cradled and fed the broad area of the 'Sudan', the great sub-Saharan landmass of West Africa, from the northwest and the southeast respectively.[13] A traveller making his way upstream on the Senegal or the Niger (and no one had yet succeeded in reaching the source of either) would have followed a course which initially reached to the north; he would have then turned southwards again to their common source in the Futa Jallon massif. This was the mountain range climbing to over 4000 feet, north of both Sierra Leone and the Rio Nunez. From its accessibility to the upper reaches of both rivers, the Rio Nunez derived its special influence as a trading route to the coast, via the centres of Fula power at Labe and Timbo. The embracing outlines of the two rivers on the map could resemble the mask of some primitive watchful deity — perhaps even *le génie des eaux* of West African legend: it would not be an inappropriate metaphor for the blessings which these two waterways bestowed on the interior. The commercial opportunities they offered had become a natural lodestar for European traders and explorers since 1788.[14]

On the Senegal, the French succeeded in forging trading relationships several hundreds of miles up-river. In addition to commodities that were typical of much of the West African trade, it also yielded two particular products of high value. The first was 'Senegal gum', derived from the acacia trees that grew at this latitude — vital to the printing of cotton fabric, as well as being a constituent needed for the manufacture of silks. The second was the fine 'furniture timber' growing in the forests of Senegambia, which compared with the teaks of east India and the mahogany of Honduras. Matthew Forster was proud to demonstrate to Thomas Fowell Buxton MP, the famous brewer-philanthropist, and his anti-slavery committee, when they met at Forster's offices at 121 Bishopsgate, in London, the elegant desk and chair which he had had made from a consignment of that timber, imported from the Gambia.[15]

Along the rest of the coast, the pattern of legitimate trade which emerged over the next three decades, was cut-throat and cosmopolitan. No country achieved overall ascendancy, despite the undeclared paramountcy flowing from Britain's naval strength at its main base at Freetown, in the so-called 'white man's grave', the province of freedom, Sierra Leone; 'the mid-Victorians . . . attempted to bring about . . . a system of informal commercial influence . . . a flimsy structure of order.'[16] A surprising number of legitimate 'Yankee traders', from Massachusetts and Rhode Island, still traded vigorously despite efforts to exclude them — by the British through the Navigation Acts, and by the French through their *exclusif* system.[17] Competition was fierce: English merchants from London, like Forsters, and others from Bristol,

Manchester and Liverpool;[18] traders based in Freetown, like
Macaulay & Babington; an increasing influx of French merchants
from Marseilles, Nantes, Rouen and Bordeaux; a few isolated
Dutch, Danish, and even German and Belgian traders and
outposts; and a final hard core of morally 'unreconstructed'
Portuguese and Spanish merchants, still involved in slave dealing,
the pale shadows of the former masters of these seas. This was the
texture of the non-African trade; they brought goods to the
coastal traders, who then fed the highly developed African commercial networks, through credit and barter, into the interior.[19]

Despite mercantilist restrictive practices aimed at monopolizing
trade and shipping, Americans could still offer rum and tobacco at
highly competitive prices. The Europeans brought various kinds of
specially manufactured 'trade goods', including cloths from
around the world. The British excelled in providing metalware
from Manchester and Sheffield, iron bars for fabrication in the
African forges, cutlasses, better-quality rifles from Birmingham,
and gunpowder; the French had found a particular market for
their established spirit and brandy trade, and — before Belgium
was separated from her in 1815 — had been the means of bringing
in Flemish textiles.[20] The factors on the coast — the African,
mulatto and European middlemen — made available in their factories the produce and products that the Old and New Worlds
could not get as economically elsewhere — or at all. Merchants
like Forsters had long made it their business to follow the trends in
produce and products; as early as as 1792, another Forster, T. F.,
and his colleagues of the Sierra Leone Company had commissioned a famous botanist, Afzelius, to report to London and to
Freetown on the produce that was already freely growing along
the coast, or could be developed for sale to Europe.[21] From 1835,
in the northwest territories, they were to develop the trade in
groundnuts, whose oil was much in demand in France: a vege-
table, it had been introduced by the Portuguese from Brazil. Then
came a rapid development in the tropical southeast latitudes of the
older trade in palm oil, including the new use of palm 'kernels'.
These products were now directed not only to the European soap
industry as a whole, but also as lubricants for the European rail-
way boom of the 1840s.[22] There were all the traditional products
too — cinnamon, rice, beeswax, Indian corn, and exotic dye
woods such as indigo, 'fustick', 'tulip wood', and camphor; this

was in addition to the produce from which sections of the coast had been given their original names — the Gold Coast, the Ivory Coast, the Grain or 'Malaguetta Pepper' Coast (today's Liberia), as well as the Gum Coast itself. Hides were also a key product: from the earliest days, the Rio Nunez stood out as a vital source for the best that the Fula tribes of Futa Jallon could produce. 'Nunez' hides were highly prized for the leather trade, not least in New England. For France's Captain Bouët-Willaumez — author of a contemporary study on trade on the coast, and destined to become a key figure in the Nunez Affair — their hides were 'perfectly prepared and of first-class quality'.[23]

More significant than any of these, Africa had yielded over the preceding two centuries a traffic in one commodity that no other continent offered: what Palmerston would typically describe as 'the abominable crime of Slave Trade'.[24] It too had given rise to a named section of the Guinea, although the 'Slave Coast', stretching eastwards through several warlike kingdoms (including one still reported to be cannibalistic), was never the sole source of this trade in raw humanity.[25] For many African rulers, the trade in slaves was still — even by the mid-century — as 'legitimate' a part of their commerce as those new kinds of produce, such as cotton, which 'metropolitan humanitarians', particularly in Britain, were trying to promote to replace it. The two trades continued to coexist in a kind of mutually reinforcing vicious circle; it has been authoritatively defined as a state of 'symbiosis'.[26]

Britain had outlawed its own slave trade at the start of the century, in 1807, when Matthew Forster was just starting his career — 15 years after the Danes passed a similar law to take effect in 1802, and almost 20 years after two of the main American trading states banned it. For a brief moment, in 1794, revolutionary France had also declared against it, but the French imputed more self-interest than pure humanitarianism to Britain's motives. They stayed with Napoleon's reversal of the revolutionary decree until 1815, and with the Spaniards and the Portuguese, and most of America they continued to turn a blind eye to *la traite*; the plantations of Brazil and Cuba, as well as the Deep South, continued to absorb Africa's enslaved workforce eagerly and without too much scruple.[27] Slavery itself had remained a much more deep-seated issue; it was declared unlawful in all British territories from 1833, but was not totally eradicated. It is still to be found, in different forms, in other parts of Africa to this day.[28]

The traffic in slaves not only remained in being from the 1820s onwards, but indeed Forster's friend, Buxton, asserted that it had actually doubled in volume in the 30 years after 1807.[29] This was the case, despite the growing moral opposition which it engendered on both sides of the Atlantic; even more to the point, it continued in the face of the increasing interceptions on the high seas above the equator, led by the still inadequate British naval squadron, with its 'superannuated tubs', commanded by some of 'its most drunken captains'.[30] As deeply integrated within the whole African economic system as ever, it was even more profitable to the slavers than it was to the 'primary producers', the inland and coastal chiefs, who took part in it. Moreover, as Forsters knew only too well through the dispatches received from their factors on the ground, it inhibited the growth of that same legitimate trade which they would argue was the best and most permanent antidote to it.[31]

The slave trade was partly able to survive the British naval patrols due to the nature and the occupancy of the coastal terrain. To an extent that is almost unimaginable today, West Africa, for at least the first half of the century, presented an extraordinarily contrasted pattern of activity. Along the coastal belt, at the mouths of the countless creeks and rivers, the European trading posts remained small and scattered, with here and there a few fortified positions, such as the two dozen or so on either side of Cape Coast Castle.[32]

After the war, building on the basis of the seven scientific exploration missions financed by the Africa Association up to 1815, and spurred on by the publication of Mungo Park's report on the course of the Niger, a new impetus was given to the exploration of what was still described in ignorance as 'the dark continent'. Encouraged by governments, and sometimes materially helped, for good commercial reasons, by the merchants — including Forsters — a handful of intrepid but often ill-fated explorers started to try to break out of the stranglehold of this coastal zone.[33] These explorations included two missions setting off from the Nunez itself, and making it famous: René Caillié's successful solo journey to Timbuktu and beyond in 1828, following the doomed venture inland of Majors Peddie and Campbell in 1817, in which William Forster had assisted.[34] Other exploratory projects followed, including the failed Niger expedition of 1832; its would-be commercial successor, promoted by Buxton and his society, in 1841/2, was to prove an even greater failure.[35] The culmination of these government-sponsored attempts during the first half of the nineteenth century was to be the great Anglo-Prussian expedition of Barth and Overweg to the Niger in November 1849, later in the same year as the battle of Debucca.

Palmerston's enthusiastic and well-informed endorsement of the project came as a surprise to those who thought — wrongly — that he did not care about Africa. His instructions to the British organizer, James Richardson, in 1849, would be characteristically practical; Matthew Forster might well have mused that some of the objectives then pronounced by Palmerston, now entering his 'good old Pam' period, were ones that Matthew himself had been pleading for many years. They also cast light on the kinds of issues that were simultaneously making Palmerston interest himself in the Nunez Affair:[36]

> The countries you are about to visit are as yet so little known to the nations of Europe that every information of every kind respecting them will be interesting and useful, but ... it is the wish of Her Majesty's Government that you should specially endeavour to ascertain by what means the Commercial intercourse between Great Britain and Africa might be extended and developed; what are the European Commodities which are most sought after by the Natives, and what are the main articles of African produce which could best be obtained in payment for the productions of Europe?

Progress was uneven; the interior was reluctant to yield up its secrets to Europe. On the map, if the fragility of a foreign presence along a continental rim might at first glance resemble today's Antarctica, the comparison falters immediately. Inland from the trading posts there was no *tabula rasa*, no undiscovered unpopulated wilderness, but a continuous and well-established tracery of trading paths and markets, fully 'discovered' for centuries by the peoples who occupied them.[37] In the 'birthplace of commerce', trade was balanced — albeit imperfectly — between the territorial network of one chieftain, or king, and the next; goods, including enslaved prisoners, were bargained for in marketplaces, forward-traded, and passed on along the trails by the infamous slave-driven 'coffles'.[38]

The enormous stretch of country covered in order to carry heavy produce to its markets was no object. As Captain Broadhead of the Royal Navy was to report to a House of Commons select committee in 1842, with regard to one of the most important products to emerge: 'The palm oil is brought down to the coast on the heads of the natives, from a great distance, each native carrying a calabash which is a pumpkin hollowed out, which perhaps holds a couple of gallons.' Bouët-Willaumez reported to the French marine ministry that in the salt trade with the Futa Jallon kingdom, 'each man carries 50 kilogrammes weight on his head.'[39]

Intricate forms of credit existed, with each party to the transaction having a subtle knowledge of relative pricing, currency, and the current state of supply and demand. Another witness to the 1842 select committee, Mr Wood told them, 'The natives understand the value of dollars, as well as of everything else ... quite as well as the Europeans.'[40]

Colonial Policy: 'Inns on the North Road'

Within this context, after 1817, the British were still able to counter the growing importance of Senegal, St Louis and Gorée with their 'three tiny poverty-stricken colonies', which France eyed with increasing jealousy, and sought to outwit wherever possible. The oldest was the historic settlement on the Gambia, dating originally from 1618, but now in 1817 effectively in the process of being re-created — the next riverine trading point 200 miles to the south. Some 500 miles further to the southeast was the major colonial focal point — the British forerunner and equivalent of Liberia — the colony of Sierra Leone, founded for 'African settlers' in 1787. Finally, another 1000 miles eastwards, were the fortified posts on the future Gold Coast, with its four main constituent forts of Cape Coast, Dixcove, Anamaboe and Accra.

Traders like Forsters had to adapt to whatever was the prevailing organizational ethos emanating from the Colonial Office. For 20 years, from 1821, all three colonies were united under the control of the senior governor at Freetown. In 1843, first in the Gambia, and then in 1850, after pressure by Forster and others, on the Gold Coast, the two colonies once more became separate entities, responsible not to the Sierra Leone administration but, like Britain's other colonies round the world, to London. However, the difference in scale between the British political commitment and presence in West Africa at this period, compared with her massive imperial activity in India, Canada, and Australia, was huge, and explains in part the later course of events on the Nunez. Even by 1861, when Lagos, the germ of the future Nigeria, was finally annexed, the four British colonial territories could still only merit the description of 'pinpricks along the coast'. For Forsters, one result of that thin presence was what they were to continually complain of as 'the lawless state of things and the lack of facilities for obtaining redress from debtors'; (this problem drove them to withdraw from Lagos in 1857).[41]

By contrast with the period of the Napoleonic Wars, when 17 new colonies were acquired by Britain, in the following quarter of a century colonization was a policy that no major European power, least of all Britain under Palmerston, applied to the west coast of Africa.[42] Nor did British traders such as Forsters necessarily wish it to be so either, provided that other benefits, principally naval protection, but also including favourable legal and excise arrangements, could still be obtained. There were continual tensions; governmental perceived shortcomings in both respects were to be a constant theme of Forsters' letters from as early as 1814 onwards.[43]

Penned in the insular security of London government offices, the comments of civil servants as to the traders' expectations, were equally pointed; whilst correctly interpreting government policy, they also reflected an innate attitude towards mere 'trade'.[44] In order to make commonsense prevail, as they saw it, Forsters had had to put plenty of backs up, both administrative and military. James Stephen, the celebrated permanent head of the Colonial Office, stung by the criticisms of the action — or rather, inaction, of his team of governors and officials, minuted cynically in 1842: 'Nothing is less wonderful than the affected ignorance of commercial men of any rule of law which interferes with their gains.'[45]

Stephen, a former lawyer, hailed as an outstanding Under-Secretary, was not without his defects, and his *bêtes noires*. That same year, another of his comments speaks volumes: 'If some 50 or 60 of the Queen's subjects will settle themselves as a distinct

Community in a settlement some 100s of miles distant from any other British Colony, they have no fair right to expect the advantages of the Institutions ... of other parts of the British dominions.'[46]

Matthew Forster became one of those *bêtes noires*. There had been one long and particularly perceptive letter from Matthew Forster, at the peak of his influence, in 1846, to the colonial Under-Secretary, about the need in any government 'for an intimate knowledge of the immemorial customs and usages of the natives ... nothing but gentle measures accompanied by firmness and justice can ensure their attachment and respect.'[47]

Such a thinly-veiled criticism of Colonial Office policy earned this defensive, potentially libellous rebuke, penned by Stephen on the end of the letter, for advice to his new master, Earl Grey:

> It is nothing more than the advocacy by a merchant of a scheme of local government ... having for its end his own personal interest ... [a previous decision] has probably diminished the influence and the profits of Mr Forster, but it has not increased the habitual acrimony of his language. ... Earl Grey should be fully aware that it is the language of a writer ... who is unsparing in his criticisms of every person employed on the Africa Coast who is exempt from a pecuniary dependence on himself.[48]

Matthew Forster's criticisms might well seem today to have had some justification but, regardless of the sensitivity of his insights into the best ways to win 'the natives' over peacefully, there was to be — on principle — no aggrandisement and no going back to the days of rule by merchant councils. What Britain had, she held; British political eyes and Colonial Office priorities were turned to broader horizons in other continents. New territories were only acquired at this time with extreme reluctance, usually for *ad hoc* tactical reasons.

For Palmerston, in one of those down-to-earth metaphors which he was wont to come out with — despite his celebrated semantic warnings about abusing figures of speech — the very idea of possessing more territory at this period was unnecessary. When questioned later by Emperor Napoleon III, in the context of partitioning Egypt, he wrote to Lord Cowley in Paris: 'Who could want such a burden ... any more than a rational man with an estate in the North [Europe, Canada, India?] and a Residence in the South [Australia, South Africa?] would wish to possess the Inns on the North Road?'[49]

What British policy did favour, however, was the great shibboleth of 'free trade'. This policy rested on the sound basis that Britain, having been the first country over the hurdle of industrial revolution, stood to benefit most from a freedom to exploit the fruits that it offered in terms of manufactures. If his metaphor were to have been extended to cover West Africa, any 'Inns on the North Road' there were justified only to the extent that British traders could make them profitable; there was no official presumption in favour of total ownership. Successive Colonial Secretaries and their civil servants purported to encourage traders, as their French counterparts did once again after 1817, despite a general public indifference as strong in London as in Paris; this too in the face of a European and Mediterranean orientation on the part of their monarchies, and above all against the resistance of a taxation-conscious postwar exchequer in both countries.

These were early days in the opening up of Africa, whatever the reputed lure of profitability rates of 50 per cent, 100 per cent or more on trading itself.[50] The actual returns for the knowledgeable merchant houses that decided to invest capital in the West African trade were seen as longer term, spanning several seasons and market fluctuations, rather than short term: this was not the kind of investment that, for example, a trustee could happily recommend, even in a leading firm like Forsters.[51]

Forsters had chosen the Gambia as its base in West Africa, and this remained so. It was the nearest British port to London, and the British presence was long established; perhaps the fresh Atlantic breezes and the great river itself, combining with centuries of tradition, calmed the temperament of the local peoples and made them more amenable to European rule. Nevertheless, life on the Gambia, as on the rest of the coast, was far from easy and enough to daunt the faint hearted. Some additional insights into conditions on the coast come from the writings of a man whose son was later to be an administrator of Joseph's estate, J. A. Boocock:[52] 'If it be of importance not to have Public accounts in arrear in Europe, of how much more consequence is it to have them closely kept up in such a frightful climate where illness is almost always fatal, and where disease most commonly commences and terminates in 2 or 3 days.'[53]

Two years later, in January 1817 and now at St Louis on the Senegal, he was speaking with some resignation of 'the privations to which every individual must be subject in the first establishment of a Colony in Africa'.[54] This was at the time of his role in overseeing the removal of the troops and stores from Senegal and Gorée, with some help from Forsters, in advance of the French return under General Schmalz. What made it even more difficult was the fact of 'almost every disposable vessel having proceeded to the Rio Nunes [*sic*] with the Expedition under Major Peddie'.[55]

The Growing Influence of the House of Forster

It was against this bleak, competitive and uncertain background that the Forsters had begun to develop their new commercial trade on the West African coast. There were many strands in the influence they were to bring to bear on public life. The four most positive elements were, first, their commercial success and the wealth that flowed from their strength in the legitimate trade, coupled with their representative role on behalf of trade as a whole. They did so where possible in combination with other merchants, as witness their joint association to develop cotton.[56]

Complementing this purely commercial activity was a strong commitment to help the anti-slave trade campaign under Buxton; and the final flowering of its influence through the person of Matthew Forster as an MP. There were, however, two negative aspects to its reputation. The first was the impact of the criticisms contained in the notorious Madden Report of 1842, a fifth and unwelcome wheel to the otherwise smooth-running Forster coach. There then came the effects of the reversal in the commercial fortunes of the firm in the 1850s, which coincided with Matthew's departure, in contentious circumstances, from the House of Commons in April 1853.[57]

The Scots border name of Forster crops up in many spheres of nineteenth-century activity — the Russia trade, the anti-slavery campaign, commercial banking, the Charles Dickens biographies, and the Gladstonian drive for better education. This particular and highly entrepreneurial branch of the far-flung clan hailed in the eighteenth-century from the raw, rich, windswept county of Durham, with its proximity to the Tyne and an age-old familiarity with seaborne commerce.[58] By the early nineteenth century Matthew's father, John, was supervising the Forster businesses from London, trading timber and ships' goods from the Baltic, feeding shipments into the new docks that were now springing up within call of the City. The Russia Dock in Rotherhithe, designed in 1809 to handle timber, was one of the earliest to be built.[59] Napoleon's continental blockade forced traders to look elsewhere than Europe; as the chronicler of the United Africa Company surmises, 'What more natural for the Forsters ... in such circumstances than to send their ships to West Africa?'[60]

John was able to turn over the daily running of affairs very early on to his capable son Matthew, later to be commended to a fellow MP as 'of good abilities and a perfect man of business'.[61] By the time of Matthew's twenty-third birthday in 1809, he was recorded as a 'shipowner' and living at 31 Cannon Street, St George's, on the Ratcliffe Highway, conveniently near to the docks. Matthew and his family finally 'arrived' in grand style in the hilly splendour of Belsize Villa, Hampstead, with cattle grazing on its 16 acres of ground, leading down to a tree-fringed lakeside. Here he continued to live, as the archetypal self-made man of George Eliot's *Middlemarch* era, through the ensuing 30 eventful years, which included the tragic events associated with 'Maclean of the Gold Coast' and the mysterious death of the beautiful poetess, 'LEL', whom he met at the Forsters' home.[62]

Meanwhile, Matthew's brother William had been sent out to manage the trade from the African end at Gorée. His focal point was then moved to the original Gambian settlement of Banjul, which now became renamed — sycophantically — Bathurst St Mary, to please the then Colonial Secretary , Lord Bathurst.[63] At first the traders had to satisfy themselves with building 'wattled houses thatched with grass', not exactly suited to the harmattan winds, which blew strongly in the Gambia, 'like the breath of a hot furnace', or to the southeasterly tornadoes which sprang up from time to time.[64] By 1818 he had bought property at 3 Wellington Street; in 1823, there was still 'only one stone house built'. By the 1830s, the governor of Sierra Leone, Colonel Findlay, saw Bathurst as 'a very pretty little town'; William stayed on there, and in 1838 added to the house in the wake of the growth of their business.[65]

He reported assiduously on the inroads of the French against their commerce, and warned about the problems posed by the French enclave within the Gambia, still plying its trade to their disadvantage — and cocking snooks at the British flag — a little way up-river at Albréda.[66] At least as early as 1817, 25 years before the Madden Report was to cast its negative spell over perceptions of the firm, the Forsters were unequivocally putting their considerable weight behind the campaign against the slave trade. William made one of his periodic return trips to London; his purpose was to assist with evidence as to the slaving activity on the river by the French, which persisted in defiance of the Allies' prohibition. Matthew reported on his behalf to the Secretary of State for Colonies and War: 'The Slave Trade is reviving under the French in a surprising and serious manner. He [William] saw many slaves confined in the yards of the merchants' premises at Gorée and while they were lying off Senegal a vessel came out with 240 slaves on board and passed close by a French vessel of war unmolested!'[67]

Government interest in both West African trade and exploration reached its lowest point by the early 1830s. As the Forsters discovered continuously, remedies for problems were still sought in outdated eighteenth-century practice rather than in nineteenth-century reality, and this made the life of traders even more difficult that it otherwise would have been.

By the end of the 1830s, however, a corner was being turned; 'decisions taken then ended the indifference of the previous decade to the inheritance of the eighteenth century on the coast.' The five years from 1839 to 1844 came to be seen as a 'watershed' for the colonial administrators, as well as for trade and for Forsters.[68] Matthew Forster, with the instinct of the political animal that he was, had been preparing himself for the wider role which this situation made possible. It would certainly have been at this period that Palmerston became aware of Matthew Forster, not merely as a new fellow 'Liberal' in the House, but more usefully as someone who could assist with expertise, and perhaps put new life into the anti-slave trade campaign.

Matthew's proclivity for the forceful pleading of causes with the mightiest in the land, from which Joseph Braithwaite and George Martin were later to benefit, started to enter the public records as early as 1814.[69] Already on 17 May 1817, from his new offices at 8 New City Chambers, he was writing to Lord

Bathurst about the plight of the merchants on the Gambia, deprived of their revenue from the gum trade, as a result of the return of the French to the Senegal.[70] In 1826 he had moved to larger offices at 5 New City Chambers, by which time Forsters had merged their trading arm with fellow Africa merchants, Smith & Sons. Whilst Forster & Smith looked after the Africa trade, shipping remained a separate entity, retaining the name Forster & Company; it was to become the major shipowner of its time, with a fleet of 14 vessels trading, including the *Princess Royal*.[71]

The objects and subjects of Matthew's correspondence over the next 25 years were many and various. Five recurrent themes emerge. First and foremost, he sought to force an unthinking insular government to correct stupidities in the customs and excise regulations, to enable his various businesses to survive at all.[72] The second theme, evident from the outset, was to warn government about the increasing threat to British interests offered by the resurgent French administrators and traders, backed, as time went on, by a strongly revanchist navy. Forsters' fears compare with Palmerston's constant preoccupation about the danger inherent in a resurgently patriotic but politically unstable France.[73]

A third and very essential function was the provision of basic information about what was going on *in situ*.[74] There was a practical aspect too: the local colonial power was only too grateful for any help it could get from anywhere at this time. Forsters' own schooner, named after brother William, was hired in 1828 by the governor of the Gambia to convey troops to help merchants plundered by a native attack.[75] A fifth theme was exemplified in the six-page 'Memorial' to a new Colonial Secretary , in Grey's Whig Ministry — Viscount Goderich — on 9 January 1832. A printed memorial was the vehicle used by campaigners outside Parliament to present their views to ministers — in this case to drive the economic facts of life home to the desk-bound civil servants in Downing Street. Forster's prose has a certain proto-Palmerstonian ring to it. The newly-appointed Foreign Secretary would soon become aware of this fresh adherent to the twin aims of his policy as it unfolded for Africa: facilitating legitimate free trade and eradicating the illegitimate slave trade. Palmerston's famous phrase — full of meaning for later events — declared that 'it was the business of the government to open and secure the roads for the merchant.'[76]

The nub of Matthew's approach was its basic arithmetic:

> My Lord ... the total gain to the industry and revenues of
> the Mother Country (from our Settlement on the West Coast
> of Africa) cannot be less than £600,000 p.a. ... in the last 20
> years the trade in Palm Oil, Timber and Bees Wax has been
> very great. ... It should also be borne in mind that every
> article imported from Africa is in exchange for goods, and
> that consequently it is one of the very few legitimate trades
> remaining to this country. ... Let those who undervalue the
> importance of Colonies [realize] that they return to the
> nation directly or indirectly more than ten-fold the annual
> cost of their defence. ... [The aim should be the] foundation
> of a new system under which war and treachery should give
> place to the regenerating influence of peaceful industry.[77]

An additional undercurrent to be picked out from Matthew's
communications is one that links through to his non-political
interests — his adherence to the widely-held self-imposed task of
the British to 'redeem Africa'. His letter of 3 May 1826 to the
Secretary of State included an assertion of his 'feeling a lively
interest in the honour of the British name and influence on the
Coast of Africa, and for the promotion of English commerce as
the greatest medium of civilizing the Natives and destroying the
slave trade.'[78]

As the 1830s unfolded, Matthew Forster's stance was becoming
more and more politically aware. He realized that unless the
Atlantic naval squadron was brought even further into play,
Britain would not only be outwitted in trade, but its campaign
against the slave trade would be undermined. He was about to
move up a gear.

In parallel with this communication with government, Forster
was also identifying with the continuation of the humanitarian
campaign to try finally to supersede the slave trade, now being
championed by the third successor in the William Wilberforce and
Thomas Clarkson tradition — Thomas Fowell Buxton. The
Buxton archives reveal that Matthew Forster was far from being
merely a politician with a taint of slaving, as suggested subsequently by the Madden Report and the electoral records, and by
some commentators. He was certainly a strong personality and a

pragmatist, like Palmerston himself, whose illustrious path his own was to cross, advantageously for Braithwaite and Martin, by the end of the decade. Although the word 'bluster' was to be used of both of them by their respective adversaries, he was certainly not just another 'palm oil ruffian'. Perhaps he was to be 'too unbending and vehement to be a good advocate', but he was a competitive, practical businessman, living within the African context as it was, in its slow, uneasy 'symbiotic' transition from the illegitimate to the legitimate mode.[79] It was a situation which in the short term neither he nor his agents could transform.

However, again like Palmerston — by now, the early 1840s, out of office although never out of public affairs — his heart was in the right place. He was a committed confidant of Buxton's during much of the 1830s, the period when the movement against the slave trade was in danger of running out of steam and support; they were almost exact contemporaries, thus in some degree having the same perception of a shared generation about the war and its aftermath.[80] Forster had clearly made it his business to assist the campaign being waged inside and outside the House, during the time that Buxton sat as MP for Weymouth, from 1818. Forster fuelled him with all the direct evidence that came into his hands, seeing himself as the fount of wisdom for any matter affecting the west coast. Buxton asserted in his 1840 treatise, 'Central Africa possesses within itself everything from which commerce springs. No country [sic] in the world has nobler rivers or more fertile soils.'[81]

One writer has questioned the validity of those views: 'No one in England knew anything about West African soils and crops.' Matthew Forster was the answer to that conundrum. By 1840, three years after Buxton had ceased to be an MP, Forster was still continuing his support for the cause as an 'expert witness'. In a letter about a scheme being put forward for the Royal African Company, he claimed for himself that 'his long and intimate connections with the Coast of Africa and with its people, its soil, its climate and productions, has naturally afforded him opportunities for information.'[82]

One particular paper among the voluminous Buxton archives sums up Matthew's purposes, and indicates beyond doubt where his sympathies had always lain, and what kind of man he was. This was in the same Memorial to the Colonial Office of 1832. He wrote in terms that commended him to Buxton's notice. He looked forward to a time when 'the effect of the Slave Trade shall have ceased to exercise its baleful influence over the native population. ... Europe owes to Africa a heavy debt for the crimes that have been committed.'[83]

In his 'Observations' on a plan of 1840 for the Royal African Company, Matthew presented this argument in straight commercial terms with regard to the yield that the new company should be expected to achieve on the moneys to be invested in it: 'The public and the Government must prove the sincerity of their benevolence by paying the Debt they owe to Africa, without looking for any other return at present.'[84]

Matthew was also able to act as an intermediary for Buxton, putting the great crusader in touch with commercial men who could assist their common cause; it is evident that he went to considerable trouble to do so, and also put his own name on the line, in recommending such contacts.[85]

On 11 November 1839, he relayed to Buxton a quaint letter he had earlier received from Mrs Elizabeth Proctor, then still the wife of one of his agents on the coast, Michael Proctor.[86] This tells of the supply of palm oil on a river next to the Nunez, and also points up the purely practical problems, shorn of any moral flavouring, flowing from the continuance of slaving:

> Since my last respects I have to inform you of the arrival of two more slavers in the Rio Pongas under American Colours, which I am sorry to say interrupt very much our operations; as the natives neglect the produce trade to attend to the Slave Trade, which is generally the author of wars and disturbances as the stronger tribe generally falls on the weaker one in order to seize and sell them as Slaves.[87]

Forster also showed his increasing confidence in dealing with government, laced with a potential backbencher's cynicism, when he colluded with Buxton to prevent political appointments to the West African colonies by an insensitive Whitehall.[88]

The spokesman-cum-'poacher', James Stephen's 'unsparing critic' of the Colonial Office, eventually realized that he could best promote the interests of the legitimate trade, which he fervently believed in, by becoming one of the elected Westminster 'gamekeepers': a pocket borough was to hand. When the time came for the Whig government of Victoria's beloved Lord Melbourne to resign, Matthew Forster sought nomination for one of the two Reform-cum-Liberal seats in his native constituency of Berwick-upon-Tweed, where the family was still very much a power in the land. He was elected on 3 July 1841, at the ripe age of 55, one of that small but welcome minority of 29 per cent of the MPs of the 1841–47 intake, who were not descendants of peers, baronets or the gentry.[89] He won by a show of hands recorded as 394, a relatively good margin of 51 more than his nearest rival, one of Peel's Tories, who gained 343 votes. By way of a twentieth-century perspective, this was out of a constituency vote of no more than 1072, set in a total English and Welsh electorate of 825,000, not much more than the conjectured size of British public opinion at that time — a mere three-quarters of a million people.[90]

Notwithstanding the initial reforms of 1832, this was still very much a transition period in England, between the old ways and the new ways, in politics as in all other spheres. These continued to be rough and ready times as far as elections were concerned, with the local agents often a law unto themselves, and secret ballots still more then a decade away; Forster's estimable son, John, his successor in the seat in 1853, was to be one of the MPs to vote for this reform.[91] In the light of later events, the report in the *Newcastle Journal* about Matthew's election — already suggesting a hint of shenanigans, needs to be read in the context of its time, and not judged by later standards:

> The election for the Borough of Berwick on Tweed took place on Tuesday ... the Whig candidate ... is a Mr Forster, a merchant connected with the Africa trade, a shipowner and a considerable partner in the South Hetton Colliery, and also a shareholder in the Hartlepool Docks. It is not stated what particular form of the 'Africa Trade' Mr Forster is connected with, but it is supposed he is not a stranger to the 'gold dust' traffic, as this material has been very unblushingly thrown into the eyes of the electors, and the grossest system of bribery and corruption practised by the liberal agents. It is openly stated that the price of Whig Votes ranged during the day from £20–£30 each.[92]

It is at first sight difficult to reconcile the implication of this report with the character of Forster as set out in his long correspondence with government and with Buxton. However, local politics at Berwick, as elsewhere, were still a fairly crude business, with no holds asked for or given; there was to be a continuous story of challenged results at Berwick over a period of 20 years. Nationally, the total of elections called into question at this period was extensive; 69 election results were invalidated between 1832 and 1850.[93] Possible warts and all, this was the man who now entered the privileged lists of MPs. He thereby marked himself down to enter 'lists' of a very different kind at the end of the decade, fighting unremittingly, like a medieval champion, on behalf of two of his luckless associates, Braithwaite and Martin.

Within months of his election, Matthew began to play a full part in the work of the House as it impinged on the African trade. His sentiments about the slave trade must have been known to Palmerston, who was later to set out his convictions in one of his greatest and most evocative speeches: 'Let anyone imagine 150,000 human beings drawn up on a great plain and that he was told as they marched past him that they were all travelling to the same doom ... not a single or an accidental calamity, but that every succeeding year the same ground would again be trodden by the same number of victims.'[94]

Muddying the Waters: The Madden Episode of 1841/2

Matthew Forster's big moment appeared to arrive with his appointment, under the Tory administration of Sir Robert Peel, as a member of a select committee of the lower House, following the controversial report of Dr Robert Madden, 'a fiery Irish abolitionist', in 1841. This report, based partly on Madden's own prejudices, was to become an element in the events leading up to the Rio Nunez Affair.[95] The stated remit, framed by its progenitor in the outgoing ministry, the Colonial Secretary, Lord John Russell, was 'to inquire into the state of the British possessions on the West Coast of Africa, most especially with reference to the present relations with the neighbouring tribes'. Heavyweight fellow members included two former Colonial Secretaries and future Prime Ministers, Russell himself, together with Lord Stanley, later to be Earl of Derby, and Mr William Hutt, MP.[96] The committee sat from 12 April until 8 August 1842. The

elaborate maps produced for the public document included the
section of the coast attributed meaningfully — not to nearby
Sierra Leone's but to the much more remote Gambian sphere of
influence; they showed the Rio Nunez, alongside the description
'slave trading', and a certain small town — the later Boké —
rendered as 'Robugga' or 'Debucko'.[97]

Matthew Forster stands out in the voluminous pages of the
published select committee report for several good objective
reasons. He was the only experienced specialist present, and was
the sole member to be called before his fellow committee men as a
witness; he called six expert witnesses in his own right, more than
any other member, including the chairman, Viscount Sandon, and
he attended more sittings than anyone else; above all it his questioning of witnesses which comes through as the most incisive and
knowledgeable of all the committee. He was prominent too in
calling for motions in connection with various equitable decisions,
designed not to expose unheard the reputations of people out on
the west coast who had had no chance to defend themselves in
public.[98] Characteristically, he was often — undismayed — in a
minority of one. He contrived to have literally the last word; this
was a written answer in his fourth examination as a witness, to
question 10,880, about future sites for a settlement between the
Gold Coast and the much maligned colony of Sierra Leone. The
judgements and views emerging in the five months and nearly
11,000 questions of the committee's sessions serve to present a
comprehensive picture of activity on the West African coast at that
time. The format was at best quasi-judicial, and there were some
very leading questions from all sides, including Matthew Forster
himself: answers must be read in that light. Several topics emerged
which bore directly on later happenings, embracing insights which
clearly would be influencing Forsters in a favourable attitude to
future trading on the Nunez.

Most of the witnesses and questioners between them presented
a commonsense understanding of the intricate way in which the
legitimate trade and the slave trade were interrelated, with Forster
in particular bringing out the practical limits to the trader's
responbility for the onward destination of the goods he sold. He
tried to offset, as far as possible, the insinuations of the idealistic
but emotional Dr Madden, contained in his report of the previous
year, that the trader was almost by definition 'the helpmate to the

slave dealer'.[99] One of the Royal Navy witnesses — and not one called by Matthew himself — was Captain Broadhead, who made the key point: 'The lawful trade is so mixed up with the slave trade that it is impossible for any merchant to trade to the coast without being indirectly mixed up with it.'[100]

The same witness reminded the committee, in response to a question from Matthew, that if English goods were in some way banned from being sold to potential slavers, as Madden seemed to be implying, there would be a looming commercial danger of the resultant gap being simply and immediately filled by 'in particular the French, the use of whose vessels all over the coast is very remarkable'. Another witness, James Bannerman, also not one of those called by Matthew and thus equally free from any possible accusation of bias in his favour, echoed this realistic fear: 'The French are making great exertions to obtain a footing in every hole and corner.'[101]

Against the popular tide, and in a way guaranteed to heap coals of fire on his head from another direction — the armed forces — Forster cast doubts on the value of the celebrated attack by Captain Denman on the slave barracoons at the Gallinas River two years earlier, citing the subsequent opinion of the Queen's Advocate (no doubt to the legally-minded Palmerston's satisfaction) in support of his criticisms.[102] Knowing that these buildings could be rebuilt in a matter of days, he elicited this answer from Captain Courtland RN about the short-term effect of Denman's actions. 'He destroyed a Spanish factory ... burnt the houses ... and about six weeks afterwards there was a slaver there again.'[103] The Gallinas slave trade lasted another nine years.

Above all, Forster seized the opportunity to undermine the credibility of the very report which had given rise to the select committee, not least because among the wild and largely unsubstantiated accusations and assertions set out by Dr Madden, there were several imputations of impropriety, and of guilt by association, against the house of Forster and its agents on the coast. He asked one of the main witnesses: 'Then you think that a stranger visiting the Gold Coast for six weeks, and being ill the greater part of that time could acquire ... knowledge of the character of traders or the system of government?' The anticipated answer came back: 'There are ... many misstatements in Dr Madden's Report.'[104]

Forster was also able to bring out from the same admirably sensible Captain Broadhead one of the main arguments for believing that the legitimate trade would in the long run drive out the illegitimate — its very permanence and durability: 'One [the legitimate trade] being a steady commerce, the other only a chance thing.'[105]

The committee's proceedings also brought into the public arena a new international contender for commercial advantage on the coast, in the context of the widespread assumption that there were easy pickings to be had. Earlier on, an MP, Mr Redman, had told the committee that in addition to the Dutch, and the 'Hamburghers' as suppliers of goods to the slave trade, the Belgians were now involved too.[106] In his own later evidence, Forster said 'I know of no trade in which there have been so many adventurers for the last thirty years ... it appears to be a trade peculiarly attractive to speculators, who fancy the natives do not know the value of gold, ivory etc.'[107]

The outcomes of the report are of relevance for the Rio Nunez Affair. On the political front, while the effect was considerable, it was slow burning: the Gold Coast did get its separate government again, nearly a decade later, but not in the locally-influenced form that Forster wanted.[108] The report made the home government uncomfortably aware that the slave trade and the basic forms of slavery might well now be officially illegal under the Union Jack, but nevertheless there was a long way yet to go. Various forms of domestic servitude still continued throughout Africa, including the 'pawn' system, which did not automatically appear to all British officials to come within the Act prohibiting slavery. As amply described by Dr Madden in different contexts, this was the ancient system, comparable to the Spanish *cohortados*, whereby an African was retained, chiefly in domestic labour, on account of debts incurred, until he or she could buy themselves out from their master.[109] Most importantly, having regard to Forster's standing with government, he clearly established himself in the eyes of his new fellow politicians as a man of authority in his field, and as a strong 'media' character to be reckoned with. He also gave some public validity to his view that there was no reason to ask traders to make sacrifices in order to defeat the slave trade, let alone to end slavery itself. Publicly as well as privately, as the Maclean correspondence makes clear, he showed himself resolute in defending honourable causes, both those of his friend, George Maclean, and of other Gold Coast men who had been impugned in the evidence, but who were unable to get to England to defend themselves.[110]

Had it not been for the flawed nature of Madden's evidence, his non sequiturs, and his wild generalizations — however well meaning — and indeed for the almost plaintive manner in which he gave way under some of the questioning, more damage would have been done to the house of Forster. In one of his subsequent letters Madden wrote, in phraseology worthy of Dickens's Uriah Heep, and designed to undermine the man he chose to regard as his so-called 'calumniator', Forster: 'I am fully sensible of the superior sharpness and shrewdness of the intellectual power of Mr Forster over any mental dexterity of mine. ... I freely admit the advantages of a magnificent abode over a humble lodging.'[111]

For all his good arguments — and there was no doubt that the 'pawn' system was a shameful anachronism needing to be pilloried — Madden certainly muddied the waters; the suspicion remained that those with whom the Forsters dealt on the Gold Coast knew more about such practices than was good and right. Madden's report must also have influenced the minds of colonial administrators like Governor Macdonald and the naval officers in the squadron at Freetown, in making them less sympathetic to the problems of traders in places remote from the colony, such as the Nunez, which might still have a 'slaving' aura to them.

However, even if the imputation of guilt by association did not enhance Matthew's reputation, nothing was proved. Matthew was free to continue his career and to seek the right of audience with government when the need arose. Above all, the report did nothing to clarify the ambiguous relationship between the two fields of trade: it underlined the obvious — that no hands could be totally clean. This truism was, however, counterproductive to the important, and entirely plausible, Forster argument that the development of the legitimate trade would, ineluctably and little by little, by its greater permanence and reliability, make the slave trade redundant; it would achieve this for reasons that African dealers would come to see as in their longer commercial interests. The later judgement — that the legitimate trade actually increased the incidence of internal slavery in the short term — could not have been reasonably foreseen by anyone at the time.[112] This was only one part of what was evolving as the tripartite Palmerston doctrine, complementing the power of the naval blockades, and the policy of 'treaty'-making with the chiefs: the later appointment of consuls would form a fourth part of this approach. If Russell had been Foreign Secretary, and not Palmerston, in 1849, Forster's influence would undoubtedly have been reduced.[113] As it was, the aristocratic but normally fair-minded Lord John, now in the early 1840s the leader of the Liberal Party, and a Prime Minister-in-waiting, had seen 'his' Madden Report severely mauled by this new upstart MP and businessman. Also he had been forced to sit through five months of criticism of the policy of his recent portfolio, the Colonial Office. This cannot have endeared Forster to him. By 1846, a potential ally had been lost. As a first sign of that future trend, Forster's name was conspicuously absent from the next select committee of the House, which began sitting in 1847, under Russell's ministry, to investigate the slave trade yet again.[114]

For the longer term, it is evident that Madden had his knife into the likes of the Forsters, perhaps prejudiced by his previous encounters with the 'plantocracy', as the superficially comparable 'aristocrats' of the plantations in the West Indies were called. As his memoirs, were to make clear, he continued to muddy the waters well into the future, casting Forster, without any proof, as a merchant 'largely implicated in the slave trade'.[115] In an attempt to counter the alleged influence of Matthew's wealth in certain areas of the press, an edition of the Saturday *Leeds Mercury*, ascribed to 'February 13th' (*sic*) 1843, had contained reports that were intended to put Forster and his friends in the dock again.

The *United Service Gazette and Military Chronicle* had loyally taken up the cudgels on behalf of Captain Denman and any other naval officers caught up in the criticisms expressed by Forster about the Gallinas exploit of 1840. A long letter from Madden on 14 January 1843 had as its sequel a wild editorial in the next Saturday's edition, in which 'Forster & Company' were accused of being 'the gentlemen who got up a late committee of the House ... explaining to the world ... that British merchants ought to be permitted to trade with slave dealers *ad libitum*.' Lord John must have been interested to read this attribution.

At the time, Forster had answered Madden's further accusations of 1843 with a studied silence, wisely choosing not to keep them alive by refutation. Forster had such good contacts with the press that he could have waged the paper war further; (this was a potential strength of his, whose later absence from the annals of the Rio Nunez Affair will need consideration).[116] The Madden versus Forster issue receded from the public gaze, but not from the eye of history; it can at last be laid to rest.

Braithwaite & Martin and Forster & Smith

The Nunez, whither Braithwaite and Martin were to be bound in December 1848, had literally been put on the map by the Madden Report as a focus for the legitimate trade. The picture painted in the evidence as to its possibilities, and its inherent problems, was to be reflected in the events of 1849.

It was a normal development for future independent traders to start off their careers in the employ of one of the established merchant houses, or as their 'agent' — a term used loosely, to describe various commercial relationships. James and Charles Heddle, as well as their cousin, Dr Frank Dind, were three such men who began with Forsters in this way.[117] They later branched out into partnerships on their own, probably with financial support from the sponsoring company. Forsters would of course continue to benefit from that sponsorship, in its role as a supplier and shipper of goods to its former agents, to and from Europe: all part of the Forster magic, which had given it its position of many-sided dominance in the Africa trade. This is undoubtedly how Joseph Braithwaite and George Martin started too; they were to claim in their later submissions to Palmerston at the Foreign Office that by 1850 they had been active in the trade for 'ten years'.[118] Joseph's father, the ship broker, had died in 1839, and his redoubtable farming grandmother had died six years later. Thus, by this time Joseph, as the eldest son, would have amassed enough capital to take the necessary first steps as a *rentier*; they were typical of that other 'informal' Victorian army, proclaimed a few years earlier by the future Colonial Office chief who would help to decide their fate, the 'British adventurers now so widely scattering themselves over the surface of the earth'.[119]

As they continued their work on the coast during the 1840s, Joseph and George witnessed a disjointed process of evolution. The official news, which Matthew would certainly have pointed out to them, as he read widely, both in Europe and America, included the over-optimistic 1842 report by James Bandinel, head of the Foreign Office's slave department:

> Her Majesty's naval forces have recently followed up with
> much success a system of constantly stationing cruisers at the
> principal mouths of rivers ... this measure has proved [*sic*]
> ruinous to the slave-dealers ... and many of them ... have
> been induced to ... turn their attention to some more inno-
> cent commerce. ... The Rio Nunez, once the great resort of
> slave-dealers, is no longer visited by them.[120]

After 1846, the French came fully into line with the British
policy of using naval strength to help stop the slave trade at the
point of departure. From being the pre-eminent slaving nation in
the eighteenth century, Britain was now, 50 short years later, the
world's 'crusading abolitionist'.[121] The Royal Navy's West Africa
squadron — its lords and masters at the Admiralty acting under
Foreign Office instructions — were there, in theory, to patrol a
coastline that stretched from 12° north of the equator, to 15°
south — with orders 'diligently to look into the several bays and
creeks.'[122] In practice, there had to be a concentration of effort,
and this focused on the 2000 miles between the Isles de Los, just
100 miles south of the Nunez, and the island of St Thomas, off the
Gabon River.[123] Significantly, this implied that the Rio Nunez and
to a lesser extent its neighbouring river, the Rio Pongas, both
above the ten degrees north latitude, received less attention from
the squadron than they might have deserved or expected. Many of
the comments made in the 1842 committee's hearings confirmed
this perception of neglect. Forster quoted a letter from Benjamin
Campbell, then trading at Kacundy on the Nunez, and later British
consul at Lagos, which had implications for later events on the
river. He complained: 'Unless we very shortly receive some protection from our naval squadron, it will be impossible to remain here,
and we must abandon this important trading station to the
French.' 'The commanders of the cruisers are so engrossed in the
more profitable employment of searching for slaves and slaving
vessels, that it is no difficult matter for them to get up some plea
for not having visited the British factories in this river.'[124]

Forsters and their associates along the coast had every interest
in the success of the anti-slave trade movement, but Matthew must
have been aware that there were forces at work to mitigate its

effectiveness — above all the fact that British public opinion was starting to flag.[125] Nevertheless, from 1839 onwards, the 'Equipment clause' of the earlier Anglo-Dutch agreement of 1822 started to have its full effect, once it was accepted by Portugal — and only after much needed Palmerstonian pressure, castigated, from an American perspective, as a 'characteristic act of wilfulness'. A captain found to have on board any evidence that indicated that slaves were intended, even extra eating utensils (not just the grisly equipment — manacles and chains) was henceforth deemed to be automatically suspect of slaving, and thus liable to the confiscation of the ship, and personal trial at an appropriate location. There was at last a sense of momentum towards a better future for free commerce, as well as for the eventual winning of the protracted war against the slavers.[126]

Making 'agreements' with the African chiefs (as Palmerston, for somewhat discreditable discriminatory reasons insisted should be the phraseology for 'second-class treaties') came to be seen as the new way ahead; it would be the means of legalizing and facilitating the ending of the formation of the barracoons, as opposed to the illusory short-term effectiveness of Commander Denman's controversial attack on the Gallinas in 1840.[127] Palmerston's influence on these matters was pervasive even when not involved and out of office: his successor in 1841, Lord Aberdeen, sought the view of the law officers about the legitimacy of such direct action; the answer, which Matthew used in the 1842 committee, was deliberately misinterpreted by the coastal slavers as implying that there had been a revolution in England, and that the Queen had sacked Palmerston — a prophetic thought — and that Britain now sanctioned the resumption of the infamous trade.[128]

However, the Royal Navy recovered its purpose, and treaty-making started to regain its momentum. There was strong pressure by MPs (including the same William Hutt of select committee fame) to cut down the squadron's costs — now absorbing one-fifth of the navy's strength; nevertheless, Lord John Russell's new 1846 government, with Palmerston back at the Foreign Office for his third term, supported the efforts of the squadron.[129] Forsters must have been encouraged to sharpen its interest in the opportunities that once more seemed to open up on the southern rivers, and particularly on the Nunez.

* * *

The recommendation by Richard Lloyd to Braithwaite and Martin in February 1849 to 'try the Nunez' seemed on the face of it to be valid. By now the equally sensitive French and Americans were at last cooperating with their former victor, and supplying their own patrols, partly in joint cruises with the British. French self-esteem had matured to the point where they would in due course feel able to approve purely British achievements, such as Sir Charles Hotham's follow-up action to Denman's 1840 intervention on the Gallinas.[130] The time seemed propitious.

Richard had also put them in touch with a source of local help and guidance, Thomas Jackson, and under his guidance the *Princess Royal* sailed on from the Gambia, for the next phase of its voyage in February 1849. Jackson would also be in a position from his knowledge of the coast and its traders to introduce them to John Bicaise, the uncrowned 'king' of the Nunez; this would enable them to get to Debucca 'where we intended residing'.[131] As they sailed smoothly on, past the coast of Senegambia, with its innumerable inlets and swamps, the atmosphere would have resembled the account provided by the former commander of the brig *Rolla*, almost exactly six years earlier, 18 February 1843, 'the weather being generally thick and hazy, with light breezes and smooth water.'[132] The lack of differentiation in the landscape must have appeared to Captain Venn and his two passengers much as it was to be described a century later:

> The coast is generally flat, a ribbon of dull green scrub or forest ... and few conspicuous landmarks ... one river mouth is much like another: most of them are muffled in mangroves. ... The monotony deepens as one enters the mangrove creeks. ... They are all formidable; one has the feeling of being constantly watched by hundreds of invisible eyes.[133]

Just as that bland sameness of the shoreline militated against the success of the squadron's crews, adding to the langourous effect of the climate, so too it could be said to have acted against the chances of success for the two blandly optimistic English traders, obscuring the realities that lay behind it. The identity and the malevolence of some of those invisible eyes behind and beyond the Guinea shore would soon be made only too manifest to Joseph Braithwaite and George Martin.

Notes

1. The origins of the joining of the Forster name with that of Smith remain debatable, despite the assumptions put forward by Pedler that it was the fellow MP, William Smith, son of Samuel Smith, merchant, friend of Clarkson; the Joan Heddle/Martin Lynn Papers include correspondence of 8 and 23 March 1975 between her (a great-granddaughter of Robert Heddle, 'a prosperous merchant in Senegal until 1817') and Pedler, where they are revealed to be conjectural. James and Charles Heddle, Robert's sons, also became rich merchants. I am grateful to Dr M. Lynn for access to these papers — originally passed to Dr C. Fyfe — and for their guidance on F&S. Joan Heddle's unawareness of the papers of Sir Thomas Fowell Buxton (henceforth TFB) (RH/TFB Mss. Brit. Emp. s.444), *infra*, led her to doubt Forster's anti-slave trade sympathies, although she does add: 'To be fair to the man, he does seem to have been a loyal and punctilious curator to Robert Heddle's orphaned children.' For F&S refs in the central documentary work, see C. W. Newbury, *British Policy Towards West Africa: Selected Documents* (Oxford, 1965), pp. 86–7, n.2, 96, 300. In evidence to the select committee of the HoC Parliamentary Papers (PPSC) HC, 1842, Forster's declared but unreliable adversary, Dr R. R. Madden, asserted, to Q 9021, that 'a Mr Smith, the brother of the late partner, I believe, of Mr Forster in London' acted as auctioneer of 'pawn slaves' on behalf of Gov. Maclean in Accra (GC). This was neither confirmed nor denied in the subsequent evidence.

2. For definition of 'West Africa', see Newbury, *Policy*, p.4: 'the general rubric "West Africa" may mean a region from Morocco to the Cape or from the Gambia to the Cameroons.' Here, narrow definition is used. PPSC 1842, Forster to Q 10662, 27 July 1842; F. J. Pedler, *The Lion and the Unicorn in Africa* (London, 1973), p.58; C. Fyfe, *A History of Sierra Leone* (London, 1962), *passim*; M. Lynn, 'British Business Archives and the History of Business in Nineteenth Century West Africa', *Business Archives*, vol.7, no.62, 1991, p.1, *passim*; Newbury, *Policy*, Doc 9, 25 March 1851. For Lagos, see J. Gordon, 'The Development of the Legal System in the Colony of Lagos 1862–1905' (Ph.D. thesis, London University, 1967), p.51; also George Brooks Jnr, *Yankee Traders, Old Coasters, African Middlemen* (Boston, 1970), pp.115, 142, 153, 183, 251–2, 262, 267–9. See the author's article, 'Matthew Forster of Bellsise', *Camden History Review* 19, 1995; C. Wain (ed.) *The Streets of Belsize* (Camden History Society, 1991), pp.76–7.

3. See BBC2 TV programme series *Africa*, 19 July 1995, and events in the nationwide 'Africa 1995' campaign.

4. R. J. Gavin, 'Palmerston's Policy Towards East and West Africa 1830–1865' (Ph.D. thesis, Cambridge University, 1959), pp.10, 20. Gavin's phrase, the speech was P's, 6 July 1842, Hansard, Ser 3 V64, cols 1073,4. 'He looked particularly to the teeming millions in the great landmasses in the tropics to provide in future the markets for British manufactured goods.' The concentration of many writers on P's European interests is understandable, although not the whole story. For example, Ridley's and Southgate's excellent works (q.v.) make no reference to Africa anywhere in their extensive contents pages or indices; in Bourne's biography, q.v., of ten page references to 'Africa', only

two, pp.626 and 633, refer to West Africa, while p.178 refers to P's War Office period.

5. Jonathan Parry, *The Rise and Fall of Liberal Government in Victorian Britain* (New Haven, 1993) n.41, p.104; also P. Hollis, *Pressure from Without in Early Victorian England* (London, 1974), p.25.

6. Fyfe, *Leone*, p.239; C. W. Newbury, *The Western Slave Coast and its Rulers* (Oxford, 1966), p.38; Pedler, *Lion*, pp.19,33, Chap.4, pp.50–65; J. M. Gray, *A History of The Gambia* (Cambridge, 1940), p.309. See GL/A, for Lintott and Spink era 1869–73, absent from Pedler diagram, Docs 10,624, 10,625, 10,626, 10,626a; also J. D. Hargreaves, *Prelude to the Partition of West Africa* (London, 1963), pp.153, 176, 184. Also British Library of Political and Economic Science, for River Gambia Trading Company papers — gloves/ overalls advisable — these papers are in the same state as the TFB MSS (P. Pugh, Introduction, 8 October 1979) are reported to have been when first discovered in a Norfolk apple loft. The original documents consulted by Pedler are now in the UL/A, Blackfriars, (not at Port Sunlight, see Lynn, 'Business Archives', p.25). For later history, see D. K. Fieldhouse, *Unilever Overseas: The Anatomy of a Multi-National, 1895–1965* (London, 1978).

7. See Donald Southgate, *The Most English Minister: The Policies and Politics of Palmerston* (London, 1966), pp.139, 548.

8. Brooks, *Yankee*, p.24 *et seq.*

9. See W. H. Scotter, 'International Rivalry in the Bights of Benin and Biafra, 1815–1885', (Ph.D. thesis, London University, 1933), p.v; also H. L. Hall, *The Colonial Office: A History* (London, 1937), and Fyfe, *Leone*, p.336. For an analysis of the unchanged position in subsequent years, see C. Gertzel 'Imperial Policy Towards the British Settlements in West Africa: 1860–75', (B. Litt. thesis, Oxford University, 1953), p.229, also p.232: 'The dominant note is vacillation, the dominant mood boredom, with settlements which only seemed a drag-chain around the Colonial Office neck.'

10. For role of CO staff, despite their political masters, see D. M. Young, *The Colonial Office in the Early Nineteenth Century* (London, 1961), Chap.1; Newbury, *Policy*, see n.108 *infra*.

11. A. A. Boahen, *Britain, the Sahara and the Western Sudan* (Oxford, 1964), p.37; also B. Schnapper, *La politique et le commerce français dans le Golfe de Guinée de 1838 à 1871* (Paris, 1962), pp.28–9, Chap.3 *infra*. CO267/80, 14 November 1817, Goulburn to Forster. Also P. Marty, 'Le Comptoir français d'Albréda en Gambie: 1817–1826', [*RFHOM*], vol.17, 1942, p.242. For overview of an earlier phase, see E. Martin, *The British West African Settlements: A Study in Local Administration, 1750–1821* (London, 1927), pp.17–29.

12. D. McCall, N. R. Bennett and J. Butler (eds) *West African History* (New York, 1969), p.2, Chap.6 and G. E. Brooks, 'American Trade as a Factor in West African History in the Early Nineteenth Century: Senegal and the Gambia, 1815–1835', in ibid. pp.132–53.

13. R. Oliver and J. D. Fage, *A Short History of Africa* (London, 1974), p.142 *et seq.*; Newbury, *Policy*, p.44 *et seq.*

14. B. Appia, 'Notes sur le Génie des Eaux en Guinée', *Journal de la Société des Africains*, vols 14–17 (Paris, 1944–7).

15. P. E. Lovejoy, *Transformations in Slavery: A History of Slavery in Africa* (Cambridge, 1983), p.210. This work provides the essential overview for slavery in Africa, up to the 1960s; Hargreaves, *Prelude*, pp.23–4, 108; RH/TFB, v31, n.6, Note by TFB re Forster, 24 April 1838.

16. J. Gallagher, R. E. Robinson, and A. Denny, *Africa and the Victorians: The*

Official Mind of Imperialism (Cambridge, 1961), pp.34, 41; Fyfe, *Leone*, p.16. For correctives to the notorious West African epithet, see Howard Temperley, *White Dreams, Black Africa* (New York, 1991), p.175: 'Instead of being a white man's grave, it became a place where stirring deeds were performed.' For a later view, see J. Harris, *Annexations to Sierra Leone and their Influence on British Trade in West Africa* (Freetown, 1883), p.44.

17. McCall et al., *History*, p.146; Brooks, *Yankee*, pp.26, 32, 97, 116–7, 124, 180, 196, 206.

18. Lynn, 'Business Archives', p.36 n.31; also Newbury, *Policy*, p.38.

19. The author has amalgamated an overview of the African trading system from a number of authorities, in particular from P. Curtin, *The Image of Africa: British Ideas and Action, 1780–1850* (London, 1965); Oliver and Fage, *Short History*; Lovejoy, *Slavery*; and P. Manning, *Slavery and African Life* (Cambridge, 1990).

20. Brooks, *Yankee*, p.116. For summary of American trade, see McCall et al., *History*, Chap.6; for French and Belgian trade, see Chap.3 *infra*; also Newbury, *Policy*, pp.79–80.

21. Oliver and Fage, *Short History*, p.123: 'the original use of the word factory (namely a "merchant company's foreign trading station, where their factors (i.e. merchants) did business".' BL Add. MS, 12131, Adam Afzelius to T. Forster, 16 March 1798.

22. Pedler, *Lion*, p.54; McCall et al., *History*, p.146, for American interest in the peanut trade, 'that barely adequate economic life-preserver'; Gray, *Gambia*, p.379; Fyfe, *Leone*, pp.239, 258; also see C. Fyfe, 'Charles Heddle: An African Merchant Prince', in Alain Forest (ed.) *Entreprises et Entrepreneurs en Afrique* (Paris, 1983), p.239; R. Clarke, *Sketches of the Colony of Sierra Leone and its Inhabitants* (London, 1863), p.42.

23. Brooks, *Yankee*, p.97; E. Bouët-Willaumez, *Commerce et traite des noirs aux Côtes occidentales d'Afrique* (Paris, 1848), p.71. For American trade in hides, see McCall et al., *History*, p.139; Scotter, 'Rivalry', p.2.

24. See R. Hyam, *Britain's Imperial Century: 1815–1914* (London, 1976), p.264, 'the Slave Trade was the one subject he never joked about'. See Ridley, *Palmerston*, p.79, for P's evolving attitude to slavery and the slave trade from the days of his 'Tory' opposition in 1806. 'In 1820 he had become a supporter of the Anti-Slavery Society which Wilberforce, Brougham and Buxton had formed.' He was inspired more by 'a theoretical belief in freedom'. Also Ridley, *Palmerston*, p.297–8, [n.94 *infra*] for his speech on the slave trade (competing with his *civis Romanus* speech for the role as his greatest). Also Southgate, *English Minister,* pp.144, 157, 181: 'In terms of man-hours the suppression of the Slave Trade was the principal occupation of the FO under Palmerston.' The slave trade was not a direct aspect of the Nunez Affair, although it is impossible to consider any transaction at that time without being aware of the indirect links between the legitimate and illegitimate trades, see n.115 *infra*. See P. Tindall, 'Race Relations in West Africa in the Slave Trade Era', *Central African History Association* (Salisbury, 1975): also Epilogue *infra*, for a twentieth-century perspective.

25. PPSC 1842, Maps in Appendix to vol.2.

26. J. Walvin, *England, Slaves and Freedom: 1776–1838* (London, 1986), p.129; Brooks, *Yankee*, pp.4, 105, 125.

27. See W. E. F. Ward, *The Royal Navy and the Slavers* (London, 1969), p.229, for chronology of anti-slave trade measures, 1792–1852; Lovejoy, *Slavery*, pp.283–7 for comprehensive list, 1772–1962.

28. Lovejoy, *Slavery, passim*; also Dr C. Fyfe, discussions with author re

Mauritania, 22 July 1995; see also P. E. Lovejoy and J. S. Hogendorn, *Slow Death for Slavery: The Course of Abolition in Northern Nigeria, 1897–1936* (Cambridge, 1993), *passim*.

29. Scotter, 'Rivalry', p.44, n.8; cf. T. F. Buxton, *The African Slave Trade and its Remedy* (London, 1840).
30. Brooks, *Yankee*, pp.108–11; Hyam, *Century*, p.267.
31. Ward, *Royal Navy*, p.185.
32. Hargreaves, *Prelude*, p.23.
33. Newbury, *Policy*, pp.44–79. Also Bourne, *Early Years*, p.16. It is of interest in relation to P's intellectual involvement with Africa that he met Mungo Park during his educative years in Scotland, in 1800; see n.36 *infra* for his continued focus on African exploration; Oliver and Fage, *Short History*, *passim*.
34. R. Caillié, *Travels through Central Africa to Timbuctoo: 1824–1828* (London, repr. 1992), vol.1, p.182; also JH/ML, AO16/47, Corr. Boocock at Senegal, 25, 30 March 1817. The graves of both these explorers are still to be found at Boké on the Nunez. Lovejoy, *Slavery*, pp.190, 193–5, 210.
35. Temperley, *White Dreams, passim*; Newbury, *Policy*, pp.161, 374. It was the Niger expedition that Dickens caricatured through Mrs Jellaby and the natives of Borioboola-Ga.
36. Gavin, *Africa, passim*; Newbury, *Policy*, pp.70–1, Doc 11, Draft Instrs, P to Richardson, November 1849; cf. in FO 101/26, 34. Also Lovejoy, *Slavery*, p.195.
37. 'The European adminstrator was not dealing with a *tabula rasa*, but with an Africa whose past impinged on his day to day decisions' (M. Crowder, *West Africa under Colonial Rule* (London, 1968), p.16).
38. Lovejoy, *Slavery, passim*, but see pp.135–40, 159–61; Hargreaves, *Prelude*, pp.14–15.
39. PPSC 1842, Capt. Broadhead to Q 2455; Bouët-Willaumez, *Commerce*, p.72.
40. PPSC 1842, Wood to Q 10606.
41. Gordon, 'Lagos', p.51. Gallagher et al., *Victorians*, p.14; Gertzel, 'Imperial Policy', pp.1–2; PPSC 1845, J. Carr to Q 7179, 'Out of the colony . . . in a lawless state of things'.
42. 'These mid-Victorian years are not an exciting period in the history of British colonial policy' (W. P. Morrell, *British Colonial Policy in the Age of Peel and Russell* (London, 1930, repr. 1966), p.478). This was a 'period of restraint', with regard to the acquisition of territory, *c.*1827–48. After first being opposed to the idea in 1848, Grey agreed to buy the Danish forts on the GC, in 1850 (Newbury, *Policy*, pp.29, 406). For CO refusal to allow Acting Gov. Carr to exercise sovereignty over the Nunez, see Newbury, *Policy*, p.419 on CO268/38 ff 1131–15, Stanley to Carr, 8 November 1841.
43. Hall, *Colonial Office*, pp.24–8: 'For a long time, the Office had to fight hard [for] its claim that, save in matters of weighty foreign or financial policy, its decisions were final.' CO267/38, 17 May 1814, Forster to Gov. C. MacCarthy, SL: the earliest instance of Forster's lobbying against government shortcomings; see also author's article, 'Palmerston and the Nunez', *JICH*, vol.23, no.3, pp.411 n.194, 425.
44. Gallagher et al., *Victorians*, p.20.
45. See Metcalfe, *Maclean*, p.204: 'Stephen, not perhaps at his best on African questions, was not above talking about the Congo (instead of the Niger)'; also pp.249–50. Metcalfe gives a full account of Forster's activities in relationship to the GC, and Maclean. Gallagher et al., *Victorians*, p.20 n.1; cf. CO267/162, Minute by Stephen, 2 April 1840, on Maclean to LJR, 27

January 1840. Newbury, *Policy*, p.17: 'Stephen played a less constructive part than is sometimes assumed'. Also T. J. Barron, 'James Stephen, the Black Race, and British Colonial Administration 1813–47', *JICH*, vol.5, no.2, January 1977, p.134: 'Stephen's superciliousness towards the Blacks was offset by his suspiciousness towards the colonists'.

46. Newbury, *Policy*, p.508, Doc 23; cf. CO87/28.

47. CO267/196, Forster to CO, 10 December 1846.

48. CO267/196, 10 December 1846, Note by Stephen for Grey, on Forster to CO; the bitterness of this comment can only be fully appreciated in the light of the interactions flowing from the Madden Report of 1841 and the HoC Special Committee proceedings of 1842. See also author's article in *JICH*, vol.23, no.3, 1995. See also Wolfson, 'Gold Coast', pp.19, 20, for Grey's dry comment that 'Mr Forster, like all other merchants, has no objection to encouraging warlike operations in their own interests, so long as they did not have to bear the cost'; cf. CO96/13 Min. on Note 1485, 20 July 1848.

49. Ridley, *Palmerston*, p.542; cf. BL Add. MS 48581, P to Cowley, 25 November 1859. While the context was neither West Africa nor colonialism, the sentiment is still relevant.

50. McCall et al., *History*, p.133; also Madden's 'Profits on the [slave] trade had risen to 180 per cent in 1840' (Wolfson, 'Gold Coast', p.xlvii, n.1.

51. JH/ML, Scottish Records Office, GD 263/63/3 66, W. H. Fotheringham, Edinburgh, to W. Traill RN, 16 November 1843.

52. SGA/B doc. EP20, 1854. See Epilogue. Joseph Braithwaite died on 18 August 1854, at Bathurst, GA, after an attack of 'fever' unspecified. Charles Boocock JP, son of J. A. Boocock, the Army commissary, became one of the administrators of his bankrupt estate (see Chap.6, n.14). Through the intervention of Thomas Chown, a trader in the GA, featured in the River Gambia Trading Company papers, Joseph's personal effects, his gold watch and his goldheaded cane, bearing the family crest, were saved from the creditors, and returned to his brother Charles in England. The crest, 'a greyhound, with three spots gules, sejant (not couchant — the Ambleside branch's crest) upon a mound vert, was the means of linking the family back to Buskey Fields, Leeds and thence eventually to the Braithwaites who crossed over from Cumbria in the sixteenth century. Thanks here to genealogists J. Derriman and C. Chapple, SGA/B EP20, 21.

53. JH/ML, WO 57/91, Senegal, 29 August 1815, Boocock to Herries, commissary in chief, London.

54. JH/ML, AO16/47, Senegal, Boocock to G. Harrison, 31 January 1817.

55. Ibid.

56. UL/A, Memorandum on behalf of Forster MP, William Hutton, and two others (Manchester) as trustees for an association to grow cotton at Cape Coast, as an alternative to imports from the USA. Forster is the major shareholder with £200. The document, undated, must be *c*.1849, as a letter of 26 November 1849 from F. Swanzy to his son Andrew at the GC refers to the scheme 'with a capital of £8000'. It also notes the 48-day delay in post reaching London, i.e. a minimum of over three months between correspondents. He also sympathizes that 'trade is so bad' there, and comments on a meeting organized with Earl Grey by Forster, on 20 November, to progress a Legislative Council for the GC. He also asks his son to bring home 'two or three parrots'!

57. For Madden/Forster confrontation, see n.115 *infra*.

58. JH/ML, *passim*. See also author's 'Matthew', *CHR*.

59. JH/ML, GL/A and Post Office Directories 1832, 1839; Middlesex Land Tax

Assessments, MR/PLT, 5472–5490, 5508–5524; John Pudney, *London's Docks* (London, 1975), p.58.

60. Pedler, *Lion*, p.50.
61. The education of Forster is unknown: almost certainly he was educated at one of the many first-class private 'academies' in Hackney, possibly New-comes, or nearby Sutton House. See T. F. T. Baker (ed.) *Victoria: History of the Counties of England* (vol.10, Oxford, 1995), pp.161–4. I am grateful to John Richardson, chairman, Camden History Society, for this source, letter, 20 November 1995. Re evaluation of John Forster, see JH/ML, SRO GD 262/63 3/9, Fotheringham to J. Loch MP, 10 August 1841.
62. JH/ML *passim*; G. Metcalfe, *Maclean of the Gold Coast* (London, 1962), pp.204–8, 234, for 'LEL'; also Maclean family papers. I am indebted to John Maclean for access to the Maclean–Forster correspondence, 1835–48, although the Maclean story is only tangential to this narrative. However, see author's 'Matthew', *CHR*. (Also L. Blanchard, *Life and Literary Remains of LEL* (London, 1841); Joanna Burch's unpubl Ph.D. thesis (Cambridge University, 1991) on 'LEL'; Wain, *Belsize*; W. Robinson, *History of Hackney*, vol.1. (George Eliot, *Middlemarch*).)
63. RH/TFB, v33, U2, P. Pugh re William Forster to TFB, 26 July 1838, 'a merchant who lived at Bathurst, GA, for 20 years'. Pedler, *Lion*, p.50; Newbury, *Policy*, pp.86–7.
64. E. Melville, *A Residence at Sierra Leone* (London, 1849), p.15; Brooks, *Yankee*, p.81; PPSC 1842, Findlay, to Qs 2847, 2860.
65. GL/A doc. 10,626a, 18 January 1838. Sale to William Forster of properties of William Goddard; further sale on 25 March 1847 to R. Lloyd; PPSC 1842, Findlay. Also, re Lloyd's reference to Forster as a witness, read R. Lloyd's letter, '11 May last' enclosing letter from 'his cousin Edward Lloyd at the Casamanza River'.
66. Newbury, *Policy*, p.96; JH/ML, CO267/80, 4, 31 October 1817, Forster, London, to Goulburn, CO.
67. JH/ML, CO267/46, 30 September 1817, Forster to Lord Bathurst, CO.
68. Newbury, *Policy*, pp.5, 43.
69. CO267/38, Letter from Gov. MacCarthy to CO, 17 May 1814; see author's paper, 'Palmerston and the Nunez', *JICH*, n.100–2, 104. For a wide-ranging view of Forster's letters to the CO, see P. G. James, 'British Policy in Relation to the Gold Coast, 1815–50', (Ph.D. thesis, London University, 1935). See also FO 97/185, 186, 187, 189, the only other comparable claims, from Portendic, 1834–8. In 1837 WF was quoted as having 'twenty years experience on the West African Coast'.
70. JH/ML, CO267/46, 17 May 1817, Forster London, to Bathurst, CO.
71. Pedler, *Lion*, p.19; see n.1 *supra*; also Lloyds Register and Mercantile Navy Lists 1850; Chap.1, *supra*.
72. JH/ML, CO267/28, 16 April 1847, Treasury to CO, enclosing Forster to CO; also for example BT3/18, Fol 100, Lords of the Committee of the Privy Council for Trade to Forster, 25 October 1824.
73. Newbury, *Policy*, p.96; for example BT 3/23, 31 March 1823, Forster to Bathurst, CO, encl WF to Forster.
74. For example, CO267/46, 4 October 1817, WF to Bathurst; also CO267/59, 3 December 1823, Forster to Bathurst.
75. JH/ML, AO3/211, p.166; also Newbury, *Policy*, pp.298–301; on Gov. Winniett chartering a brig, *Governor Maclean* from F&S, in struggle with the chief of Appolonia, docs 13, 14.
76. This declaration is also found, in the context of the China debates of 1840, in

the form: 'It is the business of the Government to open and to secure the roads for the market.' See Ridley, *Palmerston*, p.260; cf. Sir C. Webster, *The Foreign Policy of Palmerston* (London, 1951), pp.750–1. RH/TFB v29, F12, Forster to TFB, 9 June 1838: 'To send a man out as governor who cannot write his name or a word of English is too much even for Downing Street.'

77. RH/TFB, v29, E 49, pp.313–4; cf. CO267/117, Forster 'Memorial' to Viscount Goderich, CO, 9 January 1832.
78. CO267/78, SL and African Forts, Misc A–G, Forster to CO, 3 May 1826. F&S is given a separate entry, not subsumed under 'F'; see Heddle/Pedler correspondence, n.1 *supra*.
79. Metcalfe, *Maclean*, p.281; Malmesbury archive, HRO, Earl of Malmesbury, Diary, 28 May 1852, vi, p.335; *United Service Gazette*, Saturday 14 January 1843, No. 552, p.7, 'The Pawning System ... Dr Madden, and Messrs Forster and Maclean'; Letter from Dr R.Madden, 'All the sophistry of Maclean or the bluster of his friend cannot get rid of the preceding references.' (See n.95, n.115, *infra*.) See Gallagher et al., *Victorians*, pp.34–5, 'The palm oil ruffians disliked state intervention on the Coast'.
80. For further data on the Forster/TFB relationship, see the author's article in 'Matthew', *CHR*. See n.77 *supra*. Birth years, P 1784, Forster 1786, TFB 1786.
81. See n.82.
82. Ward, *Royal Navy*, p.192, apropos TFB's assertion (p.190); 'Central Africa'; RH/TFB, v30, I8.
83. RH/TFB, v30, E 49; cf. CO267/117, Forster to Goderich, 9 January 1832.
84. RH/TFB, v30, I8, Forster to TFB, Observations on a scheme for the Royal African Company.
85. RH/TFB, v31, N6, Forster to TFB, 26 May 1838, with reference to Mr Turner of Manchester, 'every syllable may be relied on as correct'.
86. Capt. Belcher RN, 'Extracts from Observations on Various Points of the West Coast of Africa Surveyed by HM Ship *Aetna* in 1830–32', *JRGS*, vol.2, 1832, p.288, Proctor/'Proggot'; also Brooks, *Yankee*, pp.202–3.
87. RH/TFB, v32, S23, Forster to TFB, 11 November 1839, on Mrs Procter [*sic*] to Forster, 12 July 1839; follows Proctor to F&S, 5 November 1838.
88. RH/TFB, v29, F12, Forster at New City Chambers, to TFB, 9 June 1838, re appointment of Hawkins as governor of GA.
89. Parry, *Liberalism*, p.99; M. Stenton (ed.) *Who's Who of British Members of Parliament, 1832–1885* (London, repr. 1976).
90. Stenton, *Who's Who*; Parry, *Liberalism*, p.335. cf. PPSC 1844, XXXVIII, p.427 (1839–1840).
91. Stenton, *Who's Who*. 'For many of these commercial middle-class MPs, Parliament was often a diverting sideshow, not the central historic theatre that political historians are wont to imagine'; H. L. Malchow, *Gentleman Capitalists: The Social and Political World of the Victorian Businessman* (Manchester, 1991), p.9.
92. JH/ML, *Newcastle Journal*, 3 July 1841; *The Times*, 25 April 1853.
93. Stenton, *Who's Who*.
94. Hansard, 16 July 1844; R. Coupland, *The British Anti-Slavery Movement* (London, repr. 1964), pp.179–82.
95. Fyfe, *Leone*, pp.47–8.
96. PPSC 1842, pp.xxiv, xxv.
97. PPSC 1842, II, App. Q 7295. 'The Nunez is navigable to Debucca for vessels drawing 10 feet of water.'
98. Metcalfe, *Maclean*, p.281 n.3.

99. PPSC 1842, Capt. J. A. Clegg, supercargo to Q 1671. 'In selling goods to the same parties who dealt in slaves, you consider yourself as being as a "helpmate to the slave dealers"?' Answer: 'Not in the least: the slavers bring their own cargoes out.'

100. PPSC 1842, Broadhead to Q 2663.

101. PPSC 1842, Forster quotes letter of Jas Bannerman, 19 March 1842.

102. Newbury, *Policy*, pp.18, 539 *et seq.*; Ridley, *Palmerston*, pp.276–7; also PPSC 1842, 25 July, Forster as witness, to Q 10642. The antipathy shown by Forster to Denman's actions at the River Gallinas makes Denman's later helpful letter to B&M re normality of selling guns, all the more surprising.

103. PPSC 1842, 10 May, Courtland to Q 2309 *et seq.* by Forster. See also Ward, *Royal Navy*, p.170, 'A warehouse could be rebuilt in a week, a barracoon in a day.'

104. PPSC 1842, Broadhead to Q 2332.

105. PPSC 1842, Broadhead to Q 1518.

106. PPSC 1842, Answer to questions 3452, 3453 by G. C. Redman MP, also 'Brandenburghers' and Danes; Lovejoy, *Slavery*, p.250.

107. PPSC 1842, Forster to Q 10879.

108. Newbury, *Policy*, pp.2, 16, 17, 407. The vacillation of CO policy in relation to West Africa is demonstrated by the sequence of government responsibilities; 1821 GA, GC, and SL controlled from Freetown; 1830 from GA: first Lieut. Gov. (Findlay); 1843 Crown Control over GC; 1850 GC, separate government, plus Lagos; 1864 separate governments for all four colonies; 1866 overall government at Freetown; Lieutenant governors in GA, GC. For analysis of sovereignty, see W. C. E. Daniels, 'English Law in West Africa' (Ph.D. thesis, London University, 1962). Also W. E. F. Ward, *A History of the Gold Coast* (London, 1949), p.28.

109. 'If the slave pays his master the price fixed on, the slave is said to be *cohortado*, or in a condition to be freed.' (*United Service Gazette*); 'The distinction between a Slave and a Pawn . . . selling a Slave and binding him over to a new master . . . was too subtle for most English observers.' (Metcalfe, *Maclean*, pp.24, 259).

110. However, see Fyfe, *Leone*, pp.223, 338, who says that traders like Forsters nevertheless preached the government's duty to protect them!

111. *United Service Gazette*, 21 January 1843, letter, Dr Madden.

112. J. Grace, *Domestic Slavery in West Africa during the Nineteenth Century* (London, 1975), p.32. See D. Northrup, 'The Compatibility of the Slave Trade and the Palm Oil Trade in the Bight of Biafra', *JAH*, vol.17, no.3, 1976.

113. The appointment of consuls (including Hanson, with responsibility for the Nunez area) was to become a fourth element in this particular Palmerstonian policy. See D. C. M. Platt, *The Cinderella Service: British Consuls since 1825* (London, 1971), p.56, notwithstanding the nineteenth century 'was a self-reliant age, in which government intervention was treated with suspicion' (ibid., p.20).

114. J. Prest, *Lord John Russell* (London, 1972), pp.152–6; PPSC of the HoC, four reports on the slave trade, 1847–8.

115. R. R. Madden, *The Memoirs 1798–1886* (edited by his son, London, 1891), p.113, writes 'On this Committee a seat was given to an affluent West African merchant, largely implicated in the Slave Trade'; Ward, *Royal Navy*, p.73 writes, 'Slave dealers aspired to live the life of autocratic Southern planters on their . . . estates with huge slave households.' Newbury, *Policy*, p.111. 'Madden v. Forster': apart from *The Times* and the *Morning Chronicle*, the

main sources for this bitter public battle are the *Morning Herald*, 29 November and 1, 6, 17, 26, 27 December 1842; *United Service Gazette*, 29 October, 19 November, 3, 17 December 1842, 14, 21 January and 18 February 1843; *Leeds Mercury and Intelligencer*, 14, 21 January 1843; *Berwick Advertiser* and *Berwick and Kelso Warder*, 7 and 12 January, 4 and 8 February 1843; *Freeman's Journal*, 1842/3. The effects of this smear on Forster reach out over the next 100 years; Scotter, *International*, p.59. Forster 'the head of one of the principal firms implicated in dealings with slavers'.

116. *United Service Gazette*, 21 January 1843, editorial; Madden, *Memoirs*, p.114; cf. Madden's pamphlet, 'Mr Forster has wealth. He has the columns of a morning newspaper at his command.' attributed to *Leeds Mercury*, 13 February (*sic*) (not published on this date); see Chap.5 *infra* for Forster and the press.

117. JH/ML, J. Heddle/F. Pedler correspondence, 8, 23 March 1975. See *Leone*, p.239; also Fyfe, 'Charles Heddle', *passim*.

118. B&M statement to P, 27 February 1850; also Chap.1.

119. H. Merivale, *Lectures on Colonies and Colonization* (Oxford, 1841), vol.1, p.vi; these lectures by the Oxford professor of political economy led him to follow Stephen's 16 years at the CO for his 12-year stint as PUS in 1848; Hall, *Colonial Office*, p.22. For Forsters, see also RH/TFB, *passim*. There are two different branches of the Forster 'clan' involved with TFB, not directly related. To make the Forster/Braithwaite tangle more confused, the Anna Braithwaite (NRA, Pugh, Intro, reference pp.224, 236, 248) is not directly related to the Joseph Braithwaite of this narrative; she is a member of the Quaker branch of the Braithwaite clan. This puzzle awaits the attention of a dedicated genealogist (see n.52). On Joseph Braithwaite passport, see SGA/B doc. FP 5.

120. J. Bandinel, *Some Account of the Trade in Slaves from Africa* (London, 1842), pp.294–302.

121. Walvin, *Freedom*, p.14.

122. 'These Orders existed from 1816 onwards' (Ward, *Royal Navy*, p.49). Also Newbury, *Policy*, p.170, doc. 23. 'The boats are never to be detached between Cape Palmas and the River Gambia except to pursue suspect vessels' (extracts from the Slave Trade Order Book to the West Africa Squadron of 3 November 1846 and 21 January 1848).

123. Ward, *Royal Navy*, p.44. Also reputed as source of R. L. Stevenson's *Treasure Island*. See T. O'Toole, *Historical Dictionary of Guinea* (New York and London, 1978), Introduction.

124. CO267/146, 24 April 1838, Forster to CO, with encl. on Campbell to Forster. Also PPSC 1842, p.736, Forster written evidence to Q 10873; cf. letter from B. Campbell of 20 April 1842.

125. Newbury, *Policy*, p.38; Ward, *Royal Navy*, p.229.

126. Brooks, *Yankee*, p.112; Ward, *Royal Navy*, p.121.

127. Newbury, *Policy*, pp.3, 21, 226, doc. 7; also pp.8, 172. P's dispassionate approach to Africans in general, as opposed to his passionate attitude to the slave trade, and in contrast to the humanitarian approach of the abolitionists, is reflected in his comment, 'To mark the distinction between Agreements with barbarous Chiefs and the international Compacts of Civilized States'. Also Newbury, *Policy*, p.269; cf. CO267/225, Grey to Macdonald, 28 June 1851. 'Treaties would be agreed with Tougoh [*sic*] King of the Upper Nunez . . . and with Lamina Towle [*sic*]'. See Epilogue *infra*.

128. 'Aberdeen's letter to ADM, 20 May 1842. 'The navy staggered under the blow' (Ward, *Royal Navy*, p.170); Fyfe, *Leone*, p.224.

129. Prest, *Russell*, Chap.12; Ward, *Royal Navy*, p.190.
130. Newbury, *Policy*, p.132 *et seq.*
131. RH/TFB, v29, Bicaise to F&S, 2 August 1839. For further background see also C. Lannoy/T. du Colombier, 'Une Expédition franco-belge en Guinée: La Campagne de la Goélette de guerre *Louise-Marie* dans la Colonie belge du Rio-Nunez (1849)', *BESBEC*, (Brussels, mai–juin 1920). Chap.3, *infra*. For B&M's plan to settle in Debucca [Boké], see SGA/B doc. FP 17, and Chap.4, *infra*.
132. *United Service Gazette*, 18 February 1843, p.5, letter from Capt. Hall, of HM brig *Rolla*.
133. Ward, *Royal Navy*, pp.99–100.

3. Focus on the Nunez: 1847

At the midpoint in the 1840s, a crucible of national elements was simmering away on the Nunez. There were tensions and rivalries between the Landumas and the Nalus, the established black-skinned peoples of the river, and the reddish-brown skinned Fulas, the dominant nation state of Futa Jallon in the interior. As was soon to become clear, this was only one aspect of the alchemy which was then at work in that area of 'the Rivers'. Whether they would crystallize through a distant French perspective, seen from the Senegal as the Rivières du Sud, or as a 'Northern Rivers' extension of the adjacent British colony at Sierra Leone, a mere 150 miles to the southeast — or whether the final distillation would form without a European flavour of any kind — all that lay in the future.

However, as with the indigenous peoples of the Nunez, there was a marked instability about all the elements interacting in that crucible: none was quite what it seemed. The British still appeared to dominate the Guinea coast at this stage, with their three settlements and their naval power. Several of their traders had established themselves in the Nunez area; and Freetown was a good 700 kilometres nearer than St Louis and Gorée. Yet the British strength and proximity were to prove illusory when the Nunez Affair arose.

This sense of things not being as they looked was even more true of the French presence on the Nunez. The small group of French traders, now, by 1847, clustered at the market centre of what may now be more conveniently called by its later French name, Boké, could not know it, but they were to prove to be the first but not yet very visible sign of a wider strategy: a process whereby France would in due course pre-empt the British presence throughout this part of Africa, and indeed across the whole of the southern Sudan.[1]

Despite the observations of the 1842 select committee, the third force, Belgium, had not yet threatened this hegemony. American merchants were there once more in strength, now that the Anglo-French maritime regime was eased, but they posed no political threat to anyone. Apart from a few traders from Hamburg, a fourth power, Germany, by the 1880s the most menacing future participant in Africa — had not yet started to reassert its ancient historical role: the interest once shown by Prussian explorers from Kurland.[2]

Although older colonies already existed here and there, this was still the precolonial era in Africa: the tentative first notes in the 'Prelude to the Partition' of the African continent were only just beginning to be heard. It was to burst out into a full-scale — though badly improvised — battle symphony, the Scramble for Africa, by the last quarter of the century.[3]

France

'La France est comme un poème magnifique ... qui a pour titre la colonisation de l'Afrique.'

Victor Hugo (*L'Emancipation*, 1849)

In the years following the covenanted French reoccupation of their former possessions in the north, in 1817, the *caboteurs de Gorée* had started to extend the French presence down the coast.[4] These ventures succeeded despite the still impoverished state of their merchant navy. By 1828 France only had 2297 ships of more than 100 tons, whilst the British lorded it through their comparable fleet of 25,000, with the United States also commanding a significant strength of 14,000 vessels.[5]

French traders and merchants started to venture further and further away from their main base at Gorée, towards the opposing British commercial and naval strong point at Freetown. Behind them, with an increasing boldness and sense of purpose as the years proceeded, but still spread too thinly to be effective, had come the French naval squadron, also based at Gorée. Commercial *comptoirs* sprang up wherever there was a toehold not already under the influence of any of the other European or American interests seeking a share in the West Africa trade — always provided that the tax-conscious colonial and naval ministry in Paris sanctioned them.[6]

Two particular French naval officers destined to play a special part in this process, were to feature prominently in the battle of Boké of 1849. A Breton *capitaine de frégate*, Charles-Marie Philippe de Kerhallet, later of *La Prudente*, and *capitaine de frégate* Henri-Marie Bougrenet de la Tocnaye, of *La Recherche*, had a common agenda.[7] The fact that they both boasted a particule in their surnames — along with a small but significant minority of the executive class of officers in *La Royale* — was no automatic sign of blue blood; however it was a sign of the increasing gentrification of the French navy after 1815.[8] Both officers were products of the same school of strongly patriotic thinking which came increasingly to epitomize the French navy, as it slowly but steadily recovered from the cataclysms and humiliations of the Napoleonic Wars.

Their combined actions on that day in March 1849 were to rank as a small stanza in the 'magnificent poem', Victor Hugo's metaphor for what was to prove to be a triumphant expansion of French control in West Africa. Those actions, building on the two phases of the bloody conquest of the pirates' haven, Algeria, in the two preceding decades, cannot be understood without placing them in the wider context of the French national experience over the preceding quarter of a century, which coloured the early years of their careers.[9] It was above all the officers of *La Royale* which embodied the French 'psychological complex of the defeated'. They carried a considerable weight of intellectual baggage around with them.

A background to their thinking was the newly-disciplined training of the French Navy School, refounded at Brest in 1827. Infinitely more powerful than that formal teaching, however, was the collective conditioning which they shared with millions of their fellow countrymen — the heavy consciousness of how much France had lost in the world, compared with the days of her greatness. In the short term, French military circles continued to remember the final carnage and collapse at Waterloo. Their counterparts in the naval establishment recalled not only the defeats of Alexandria in 1801 and Trafalgar in 1805, which were, at the end of the day, fair battles in the open seas, but more bitterly the subsequent reduction of the French navy by the victorious allies. They were deprived of 50 vessels of the line, leaving them with a total of 70 — in theory — although their quality was poor.[10]

But for the generation of de Kerhallet and de la Tocnaye, the bitterness went further back, beyond the decade of their birth at the turn of the century to the days of the old monarchy when the flag of France, that *pavillon* that meant every bit as much to Frenchmen as the Union Jack did to the British, could be struck as far afield as Canada, Louisiana, India or Indo-China, to say nothing of the *vieilles colonies*, such as the Île de France — Madagascar — and the island of Réunion in the Indian Ocean, or the Antilles, the once highly profitable French West Indies. For the present, Frenchmen had meekly to endure this sadly reduced 'confetti' of the former French empire, *les miettes* of a once grand feast.[11]

However, the negatives of this history would tend to get forgotten in the mind of a determinedly patriotic French naval officer, faced with any affront to his 'conception of national honour', thousands of miles away from the *métropole*,[12] all the more so, if he found himself facing, in one form or another, the old *'tyran de la mer . . . le séducteur des vagues'*, Great Britain: the incident of the Englishman, Pritchard, in Tahiti in 1844, had been a striking illustration of this problem.[13] Between 1830 and 1870 there was a marked Anglophobia in the minds at least of *La Royale*, even if the Quai d'Orsay seemed to be trying to observe British interests where it could. The frequent experience of defeat by the British meant that 'Anglophobia was the only rational prejudice', long after 'Francophobia' had given pride of place to 'Russophobia' on the other side of the Channel. However, this prejudice was not to be compared with the Germanophobia that was to ensue a mere two decades later, after the defeat in the Franco-Prussian War of 1870, and the loss of Alsace-Lorraine: 'fear and hate' would be 'reserved for Germany'.[14]

The return of the French to the Senegal, which William Forster had witnessed, was the start of a long process of recolonization. In parallel, there was a greater degree of 'intellectual assertiveness' among the officer corps of *La Royale*.[15] The small but growing cohort of well-trained naval officers carried this spirit with them whenever they patrolled the waters of the Atlantic during the 1840s. These qualities were not only of the mind and heart. De la Tocnaye had already won special acclaim for his performance in the joint Franco–British action off Argentina in 1844/5: from their service together at the River Parana, his dashing white-haired commander, nicknamed *il pelo blanco* — Capitaine Tréhouart — had commented that he was one of the navy's best young officers.[16]

The eyes of the merchants of Bordeaux, Nantes and Le Havre were increasingly focused on Gorée, and the fort of Saint Louis at the mouth of the Senegal, for here, regardless of politics, they were steadily rebuilding a strong trade. This was predominantly in legitimate produce, but as the Forsters had emphasized to their officials in London, quietly illegitimate too.[17] This was the continuation of the infamous triangular flow composed of the export of slaves to the Americas, the import of European manufactured goods, and the carriage of African staple produce — principally oil and groundnuts — back to Europe. The French talked of Senegal at that time as the *clef de voûte*, the mainspring to their trading activity. By 1847, French eyes were looking with increasing keenness for commercial opportunities further down the Guinea coastline — the *glissement vers le sud*.[18]

During the 1830s and 1840s, at least in the mind and memory of Britain's main foreign policy exponent, Palmerston — and despite the apparent spirit of the recent and expedient Quadruple Alliance — France remained the country to worry about. By the early 1840s, two disparate events, the advent of steam warships, and the Mehmet Ali crisis in the Levant, had affected policies on both sides of the Channel.[19] The recurrent British fear of losing their insular uniqueness became loudly proclaimed by Palmerston, the main claimant to the invention of the populist phrase 'the steam bridge'. On 30 June 1845, he warned the Commons: 'Steam navigation has rendered that which was before impassable by a military force nothing more than a river passable by a steam bridge'.[20]

On the political plane, French support for Mehmet Ali had seemed to vindicate Palmerston's innate distrust of France, and his confident belief that he could act in the Near East without consulting her. In Paris, for the Soult–Guizot ministry, this crisis underlined the relative impotence of their navy, and the fact that 'everywhere in the entire world, we found England confronting us.'[21] A major speech by Guizot of 3 March 1842 had begun to signal some changes, including the policy of the *points d'appui*; it was meant to bring France the 'bases of assistance' which its ships, and above all the new coal-burning steamships, needed along the world's trading routes, without the expense of full colonies. Although it upset the oversensitive British *en route*, the overriding aim was summed up in the freshly-minted, almost accidental, phrase of a new *entente cordiale* between France and Britain. This phase of their recurrent relationship lasted four short years.[22]

The commandant of the French naval station for West Africa, Captain Bouët, was asked in 1837–39 to undertake a programme of exploration and settlement, both in advance, and in subsequent fulfilment of the *points d'appui* doctrine, planting the tricolour as far afield as Gabon, 4000 kilometres away, on the equator. The role of the ambitious Louis-Edouard Bouët is as central to later events on the Nunez as it was critical to the development of France's future empire in West Africa.[23] Perhaps the most forceful French naval officer of his day, he was born in the heart of French maritime country, the son of the mayor of Lambezellac in Brittany, in 1808. Bouët was a *capitaine de frégate* (equivalent to the English rank of commander) at 32, in 1840, and only three years later he was appointed governor of Senegal; he was promoted *capitaine de vaisseau* (captain) in 1844. At the end of that year he was adopted by his guardian and uncle, the celebrated veteran, Vice-Admiral Comte Willaumez, whose name he then attached to his own, before his uncle died the following year. The career of the future Admiral Bouët-Willaumez seems to have been well planned.

In a later book, the man whom he commissioned with others to explore the Senegal River, M. Anne Raffinel, picked two words to describe him: 'active and enterprising'.[24] Certainly, Bouët-Willaumez had a vision. His instructions from the Minister of the Marine and the Colonies on 12 December 1842 were short-term and specific: 'to strike a decisive blow' for France, and make 'an indelible impression on the minds of the peoples of Senegambia'.[25] He proceeded, however, to unfold for the first time a strategy whereby France's influence should be extended throughout the territories of West Africa. His order of 1 April 1843 included an unequivocal aim — 'to increase our territorial domination'. For the past 25 years, France had lacked 'a grand and well-conceived strategy ... towards an agreed goal'.[26] In a memorable dispatch of 6 November 1844, he painted new horizons for France: peace, and what he called her 'civilizing role' would, if necessary, be imposed. She could fill for France what he rightly perceived as a vacuum in

European ambition, 'in a land which at the end of the day belonged to her because no other foreign power was competing with her for its possession'.[27]

Guizot's eventual anti-slave trade treaty with the British, of 29 May 1845, covered the main part of the coast from Cape Verde southwards, to run for ten years.[28] Article 6 stated: 'And if it should be deemed necessary for the attainment of the objects of this Convention that posts should be occupied on that part of the Coast above described, this shall be done only with the consent of the two High Contracting Parties.'

Bouët-Willaumez was well seized of the significance of this agreement, having been a member of the diplomatic team which brought it about.[29] It meant that Britain, hitherto the stronger, could not do as she pleased, at least on this part of the coast. In the true spirit of the paradoxical love-hate relationship of the two ancient rivals, Bouët both resented and admired the British: he dreamed of founding great companies for France like that of Forster & Smith. In the second of his two important treatises about the west coast of Africa, he wrote of his task — 'whilst actively pursuing the watch over the abuses exercised on board our ships of commerce by the English squadron, under the pretext of the Right of Search ... this continuing source of annoying procedures on the part of the British cruisers'.[30] The treaty bound France too: he was already aware of the need to keep Britain sweet, through his involvement in disputes about the French post at Albréda.

With the help of his writings, he always kept *La Métropole* well informed of his views and activities. As is inevitable for anyone who sticks his head 'above the parapet', he attracted adverse comment. For the officer Ernest Souville, with a particular 'insider's view', in a phrase which defies literal translation, his characteristics were '*un air tapageur, son intempérance de parole, son Charlatanism [sic] ... un Breton non pas bretonnant mais gasconnant.*'[31]

Bouët-Willaumez is rightly seen as the instigator of the policies for France's later dominion over much of West and Equatorial Africa, for which the legendary General Faidherbe was to win the military credit from the 1860s onwards.[32] He was not a man to be deflected, nor to be trifled with by anyone, let alone by his own officers, as the Nunez adventure was to demonstrate. Much practical work was done; some of his subordinate officers were sent to carry out mapping missions from as early as 1842. One of these, the then Lieutenant de Kerhallet, was thus the first to chart the waters of the future French colony of the Ivory Coast; his sketches and detailed maps of the Nunez, all the way up to Boké, were to form an important background to the Rio Nunez Affair. Bouët-Willaumez publicly acknowledged, however, one especial characteristic of the Nunez: its 'use belongs to all the nations'.[33]

The year 1847 was a turning point for the French. France's July Monarchy had brought prosperity: by the end of that year, a level of foreign exchange of 988 million francs in 1830 had grown to 1867 million francs. France was emerging from the state of semi-subjection which she had had to accept for half a century.[34] In consequence of this newly-regained economic strength, from 1847 onwards, a year before the return of a Bonaparte could conceivably have been dreamed of by anyone other than Louis Napoleon himself, a new naval strategy began to be implemented. It had about it the flavour of things to come. That year also saw the launching, under the hand of King Louis-Philippe's son — the still influential Prince de Joinville — of a plan to build a totally new type of steam-driven warship, whose successive names over the three years of her construction were to reflect France's political destiny: the *24 février* (of 1848), the *Président*, and the *Napoléon*.[35] The French pulse was quickening; with that change there were beginning to be signs that the enforced French deference to Britain was at long last starting to evolve into something closer to the *pied d'égalité* now more befitting two senior powers, with the major conflict of their generation already 30 years behind them. That sense made itself felt throughout the French navy, and not least among Bouët-Willaumez's officers, as the decade moved forward; an entrepreneurial mood was abroad, well before Louis Napoleon came to power to give it full and flamboyant expression.

The French had long had their eyes on the Nunez. In 1842 there had come a decisive report from Lieutenant Fleuriot de Langle, on the *Malouine*, to Gorée, and thence as always on to Paris, with frequent comments on the situation *jusqu'ici*, implying that it might well be time for a change:

The Rio Nunez is very rich in products of all kinds: gold, raw

ivory, palm oil. ... Access is open to all flags. ... Like the
Americans, we have only one commercial house there — the
English, encouraged by the proximity of Sierra Leone, total
three or four which have, up to now, absorbed most of the
trade in the river. ... Coffee and hides are the most sought
after ... above all a kind of wild mocha which is beginning
to find great favour in Europe.[36]

De Langle went on to make two points, as familiar to the British
as to the French, to ask for a scarce commidity (more protection
for their traders) and to recognize that official neglect of opportunities was costing them dear: 'This naval protection would in consequence be one of the most effective supports for the extension of
our trade in the Rio Nunez which we have too much neglected up
to now.' De Langle's report also pointed out what were then ongoing British doubts about Sierra Leone's viability, not least due to
its 'incessant mortality'; however, he judged, with notable foresight, that the British would have to stay on 'despite everything'.

Meanwhile, at St Louis, both the possibilities of the Rio Nunez
and the perception of the British as a continuing thorn in the
French flesh had become part of the governors' regular agenda. In
a memorandum of 18 May 1841, M. de la Roque had recorded a
note from his predecessor, M. Charmasson: 'Our trade with the
lower coast seems in need of extension. ... The few merchants
that have established themselves there have complained frequently
about the trouble which the English Houses were giving them:
they demanded protection.'[37]

Only a year later, de Langle had drawn up a new treaty, but
this time with the Nalus only, cutting out the Landumas
altogether, and thus further codifying the rivalry between the two
peoples. The treaty was on behalf of the French traders alone,
with no mention of free trade for all — the French traders at that
earlier moment choosing to concentrate at Kacundy. In addition to
the three Nalu signatures, among the seven signatories on behalf
of *'tous les français présents au Nunez'*, was the name of J.
Bicaise. The middle name of 'Nelson', which he later affected, was
conspicuous by its absence; a Nelsonian blind eye seemed to be
conveniently turned by him and by the French, to any question of
his Englishness.[38]

The situation started to become edgy. On 27 July 1847 de

Kerhallet reported in *La Flotte* that a British ship had fired at some French sailors; Britain was accused of sabre-rattling.[39] On the 5th of that month events had moved on: a critical step was taken by de Kerhallet, and another name of importance for the Rio Nunez Affair — Ismail Tay, described as a French trader — entered the story. After four months' delay, Margery, now appearing, as Mayoré, to speak as between one king and another, with no mention of Tongo, but clearly under pressure, ceded land at Boké to France. The document was addressed impressively to '*Sa Majesté Louis-Philippe, premier Roy des Français, à Paris*':

> Sire ... the undermentioned Mayoré *Roi des Landoumans* assisted by the principal chiefs of his nation, found himself constrained to refuse [previous demands] through lack of time to reflect, and due to the advice of the English. ... Today I am deciding to make the said concession ... [he] has come to the house of the aforementioned Ismail Tay, French trader, to help him convey the attached.[40]

'Ishmael Tall', was also described as an agent of the house of d'Erneville in the Nunez in 1844, and by 1849 was spokesman for a number of Senegalese Wolof traders on the River.[41] Six months later, on 29 February 1848, just a year prior to the battle that was to erupt at Boké, the next officer to take up the Nunez duty, Ducrest de Villeneuve, son of a famous admiral, and captain of *L'Amarante*, sent to his chief — at this time Admiral Montagnies de la Roque — a document which sets out the antecedents of later events with great clarity. With Mayoré having taken the kingship by force of arms, and sending his brother Tongo fleeing into the forest, he retraced the story of how a Belgian yacht, the *Louise-Marie*, under a Captain 'Vanhaver Beke' had now become involved; he was there on behalf of a Belgian company seeking a *comptoir* on the river. However, de Villeneuve could only discern a very tentative stance in all this on the part of the British navy, in the person of Captain Lysaght of the *Grappler*.[42] Significantly, de Villeneuve underlined how, after the movements in the decisive year of 1847, two nationally-based camps had now developed on the upper river: 'Commercial jealousies and rivalries had already thrown a little discord between the French and British traders ... the events that were evolving divided them completely.'

Two months later Baudin, the governor of Senegal, wrote to his minister at Paris, re-emphasizing the value of the Nunez, but sounding the alarm for its defence: 'We must preserve our influence by every means ... on the whole coast of Africa there is not a more beautiful river nor one more useful from the point of view of navigation.'[43]

Before further developments could unfold, there was a brief break for a restatement of France's libertarian credo. The 1848 Parisian revolution of Lamartine and his *quarante-huitards*, which so alarmed the British court, was too short-lived to dislocate all the institutions of the ousted monarchy, although on the new notepaper for the ministry, the republican slogan was once more in evidence, and officials again wrote to each other as *Citoyen Ministre*.[44] In the earlier political upheaval, after the defeat of Napoleon I, 400 naval officers, a whole generation of valuable naval and colonial experience, had been retired, because in the previous regime they had been on the wrong side — that of *l'Usurpateur*. It was not to happen this time; Lamartine had after all voted, with all his poetic eloquence, for the new navy a few years before.[45]

The French West African naval squadron, strengthening all the time, continued its patrols along the Guinea coast. Ostensibly by law they at last fully shared with the British squadron the task of searching for the continuing flow of slave-carrying ships of all flags, bound for the plantations of Brazil or Cuba. In fact, Bourbon France took this duty less seriously than did the British, who after 1846 had been acting once more under the impact of Palmerston's return to the Foreign Office, with his all-powerful anti-slave trade policies and passions. Palmerston could treat most topics with a light touch, even in the most august company: the stories abound, for example his explanation to Queen Victoria, when later reviewing troops who were noticeably perspiring in their hot uniforms, that this was what was meant by *esprit de corps*. The slave trade was the one topic he never joked about.[46]

Despite the fact that it was eventually to triple the extent of France's territorial possessions, the accession of a Napoleon to power, initially as an elected president, in December 1848, with the short revolution over and done with, did not change matters for the immediate future. However, this beginning of the restoration of a new empire led to a rekindling of the French imperial spirit. The ability to think big, and the change of direction and momentum implied in that new vision was to have profound consequences for the pattern of European and world developments for at least the next 20 years. It was also, inevitably, reflected in such closely-juxtaposed events as the battle of Boké, to erupt in the spring of 1849.

Reports were now passing to and fro through the seaborne mails up and down the coast between Gorée and the growing number of French traders currently at Boké; messages were also passing between Freetown and the British traders now predominant upriver at Kacundy; seemingly at this stage they were counting J. Nelson Bicaise among their number. Mayoré, backed by the Nalus, was claiming the kingship at Boké; Tongo opposed his claim but at Kacundy — backed by Bonchevy. The Fula's representative, Madhi, was in the middle of the fray, with the peripatetic French and British naval captains attempting to identify a common cause with him and his influence, hoping to find an agreement which would get them out of their impasse, without needing to have too much regard for how individual traders fared as a result. It was difficult to see who could emerge as a winner in what was now a 'cockpit of competition and strife between French and British trading interests'.[47]

De Kerhallet and de la Tocnaye had been taught that France's future colonial destiny, her duty even, lay in Africa; the French navy was the essential partner in that process — they were two sides of the same coin. The subtleties of African traditions, and the sense of identity that distinguished an apparently primitive people such as the Landumas, were not uppermost in their minds. They needed to be controlled for their own good, and for the good of honest French traders whose only wish was to do business on their shores and rivers, for the greater glory of France. In so far as they considered the interests of the other European powers along the coast, they would certainly place any Belgians who might hove into view, in a different category to the Dutch or the Americans, let alone the English. Whilst they had to ensure that no one infringed French trading interests, the Belgians were, after all, only fellow patriots of the old French empire. They had been separated from *la mère-patrie* in 1815 and in 1830 by France's inveterate enemy, which had also robbed France of the Americas, and reduced their proud navy to ignominy. They had firmly in their

minds the precepts of their commander, Bouët-Willaumez, about
the 'vacuum' on the coast. If, once again, some undoubtedly
perfidious Englishmen were to be found interfering in what was, if
not actually French — or even Belgian — territory, certainly not
the exclusive concern of the British, then it was not their responsibility. If they were to align with a Belgian force in such an event,
notwithstanding this strange *entente* invented in Paris, and
endorsed officially at Gorée, so be it. Another revolution had
come and gone in the distant *hexagone* of continental France, and
now the new age of a revitalized French empire seemed to be
dawning; the name of a Napoleon was once more implicit on the
mastheads of *La Prudente* and *La Recherche*. There was now
abroad what a famous Frenchman later described as 'that delicate
vessel, beflagged with brilliant generalities, which people call the
"French spirit"'.[48] History, past and future, demanded that the
French navy, through its sole available representatives, captains de
la Tocnaye and de Kerhallet, should show what they were made
of.

Belgium
                    'Pour rehausser le nom belge'
                         (*Journal du Commerce d'Anvers*)

Contrary to a mutually-cherished tradition, relations between
Britain and Belgium, two intensely proud monarchies, have not
always been fraternal. That Belgian pride is still to be traced in
Brussels, despite its reincarnation as an international city, very
much in the spirit of the father of the new Europe, Robert
Schuman; it is also a city associated at every turn with the memory
of the small kingdom's first and intensely political and, by adop-
tion, patriotic monarch, Leopold I. Nowhere is that patriotism
more evident than in the Royal Army History Museum, one of
those white stone buildings, with its huge triumphal arch, that
dominates the skyline eastwards from the old Berlaymont, and the
new parliament of Europe, beyond the Rond-Pont Schuman itself.
One section of that museum — Marine Royale 1831–1862 —
symbolizes many of the newly discovered aspects of the Nunez
Affair, shorn at last of its mythology.[49]
    Prominent on one of the walls is the *Prise et Destruction de
Boké*, J. P. Clays's oil painting celebrating an imagined scene in

that distant little war, only the second call to battle for Belgian armed forces in their own name, since their creation, and the last for more than 60 years, before the onslaught of 1914. In contrast, tucked away in an obscure corner, one small, faded and anonymous photograph of Captain Joseph P. Van Haverbeke is still visible, the uniforms which he bequeathed now entirely absent from view, and without any mention of his leading part in that battle; it is hard to find the picture of the *Louise-Marie*, one of only two major vessels in the Royal Belgian Navy between 1848 and 1854, which carried him and his crew many times to the coast of West Africa during the 1840s and 1850s. As if to rub salt into that wound, pride of place is given to the high-buttoned, dark blue uniforms of one of his most junior officers at that period, Aspirant Delcourt — one being the early uniform he wore at the time of the Rio Nunez incident, the other his splendid full dress kit as *ingénieur en chef* from the final stage of his career.[50]

In the reserve collection of that museum lies the sword that was presented to Van Haverbeke by the grateful traders of the Nunez in 1849. It was conceived as a Sword of Honour, its bejewelled handle being designed by the king's jeweller. The extent and quality of the honour — or dishonour — that lay behind that award are questions that can at last be assessed.[51] There is no memorial of any kind, anywhere, to Abraham Cohen, the French-born merchant from Antwerp, who went out to the Nunez in a three-masted brig, the *Emma*, at the same time as the *Louise-Marie*.[52] Yet for a brief moment in time, these three disparate men — a very anglicized German prince, a refugee Frenchman, and Van Haverbeke, a true son of Flanders and only the eleventh officer to be commissioned into the Belgian navy, all three in a strangely informal combination — very nearly created Belgium's first African colony. They were given critical assistance in this undertaking by a colourful 'fourth man', described as a 'pasha from Trinidad', who claimed British or French nationality according to circumstances — John Nelson Bicaise.[53] The internationalism which underlay the nation's first real attempt at colonization was of a different order from that which was to characterize Belgium's later destiny.

This early essay at becoming a colonial power was set up through the medium of the first two of a series of naval expeditions, carried out with the knowledge — but under the guard —

of the British and the French. That endeavour exemplified some essential differences between the approach of this new small European state, as compared with the two nations that were — in principle — her big brothers. The sovereign whom Van Haverbeke served, and whom Cohen desperately sought to serve, reigned from 1831 until his death in 1865, when he was succeeded by his son, Leopold II, notorious for the Congo and the H. M. Stanley connection.[54] The main feature that distinguished the success of the son compared with the relative colonial failure of the father, was that the young Leopold had learned to 'manage' his kingdom's democratic institutions, in order to secure the funds needed for colonization.

The major difference between the policies that Leopold I was able to bring to bear, as compared with those of France or Britain, was not the obvious one of scale, but that of purpose. Modern Flemish historians have clarified that here was a case not just of exploration in the spirit of free trade, as the outside world was told; it was in fact 'a limited involvement in colonial penetration along the west coast of the African continent, before the phase of the Congo Free State'.[55]

The salient point was that, despite their limited funds, there was a clear aspiration on the part of Van Haverbeke's political masters in Brussels to become involved not merely in the commercial development but in the armed possession and colonization of some part of the coast of West Africa. Certainly Britain and — officially — France were, on the contrary, resisting further formal colonization on the west coast of Africa, albeit from the vastly different basis of 'what we have, we try to hold'.

A second area of contrast, painfully obvious to Van Haverbeke and his crew, lay in their naval power itself. In 1845 'the Belgian navy was still of little importance'.[56] Over and above a dozen *cannonières*, the whole fleet consisted of only two small vessels: the *Louise-Marie* — a *goélette de guerre* displacing 200 tons, with a crew of 70; and a 300-ton brig, the *Duc de Brabant*.[57] Claims were of course advanced that this force made up in quality what it lacked in quantity, with voyages to Mexico and Chile, and to the fishing grounds off the Shetlands, to its credit, not forgetting the exploits in China in 1848 of the same commandant, Van Haverbeke, who was to feature in the Nunez Affair. The military prowess of its crew too would later be claimed to be of a 'high professional calibre', largely on the basis of their performance in that same incident.[58] Even this slender force was to be cut back in an economy drive later in 1849, at the time when the German confederation was making tentative steps towards creating its own naval presence; many officers were allowed to transfer to the even more embryonic German force, including the *enseigne de vaisseau*, Themistocle du Colombier, one of Haverbeke's promising young officers.[59]

The third and most significant area of difference was the simple fact of the extreme brevity of Belgium's history. Compared with the over-long memories that France and Britain preserved of each other, the folk-memory that moved the Belgium of 1849 *vis-à-vis* other powers was, in one sense, blessedly short, pragmatically rooted in the present, not the past. There were no old scores to be settled by the king or his politicians, nor by the country's traders or its armed forces. Belgium did not exist before 1815, when the first and only Belgian republic was brought into being. There was no Belgian monarchy until, with the revolution of 1830, the processes of the Concert of Europe placed a king onto the throne of the new kingdom. They achieved this with the considerable help of Lord Palmerston, once more a connecting thread in the story of the Rio Nunez Affair; that first king was the 'beloved Uncle' of Victoria and Albert — Leopold of Saxe-Coburg.[60] It was the long period of conditioning in England of this former 'Consort Presumptive' to the English throne, which was to play its part in the overseas policy of the new kingdom.

At the start of this era, however, the only scores were new ones: there was no inherited European agenda, let alone any extra-European score to be settled. All lay in the future. An article in the *Journal du Commerce d'Anvers* of 6 July 1849, part of the Nunez evidence, would be seen to express the country's underlying theme — a common enthusiasm to build up an identity and a reputation for Belgium in her own terms.[61] In the case of the Nunez incident, even that noble idea, however, could conceal other less patriotic motives.[62]

For most of the first two decades of Leopold's new monarchy, the 1830s and the 1840s, Belgium had needed all its energies to stay afloat economically. The victorious Allies of 1814 had been focused on cutting a defeated France down to size, and had given little thought to what was implied when the industrial strength of

the northern part of the erstwhile Dutch provinces was cut off, at
the stroke of a pen, from the Belgian territory to the south:

> The situation at that moment in Belgium was very pre-
> carious. Our national economy was reacting acutely to the
> effects of the separation from the provinces of the north,
> caused by the revolution of 1830; moreover the introduction
> of machines into the textile industries brought a large part of
> the working population onto the dole. Wages had fallen
> considerably. From 1840 to 1850, 500,000 of the poorest
> classes had been added to the 400,000 already registered for
> public assistance. And that in a country whose population
> scarcely exceeded seven million. In Flanders, where the crisis
> raged with particular severity, one person in every three lived
> on charity. Such a situation required an energetic solution, a
> rapid intervention which the king, from his intimate
> knowledge of political methods in England, sought in colon-
> ization.[63]

In parallel with this economic vulnerability, a militarily fragile
Belgium still had to keep a wary eye on France, as well as to her
'other half' to the north. Palmerston was not alone in Britain in
fearing that King Louis-Philippe in France might at some stage
decide to renege on the 1815 settlements, and repartition Belgium
with — or without — the assistance of William of Orange.[64] The
Dutch king still resented the loss of his greater kingdom, and was
also looking for ways to 'raise the profile' of his country. He had
hoped to attain this end by marrying one of his sons to Victoria,
so that the Prince of Orange might accede to the English throne, as
Victoria's consort. Victoria, however, had found them 'very
plain ... and not at all prepossessing': so much for the
'Oranges'.[65]

When the then Belgian republic was briefly invaded from both
sides in 1830, only Palmerstonian diplomacy had sent the invading
French and Dutch back inside their post-1815 borders once
more.[66] *Vis-à-vis* Britain the relationship was both deeper and
simpler. For centuries the geographical distance between the great
port of Antwerp and the Thames estuary had caused English eyes
to regard developments there with a keen interest: a friendly
presence in the Low Countries was vital to Britain.

With Queen Victoria's 'Dear Uncle Leopold' now installed at Brussels, a new age of mutuality beckoned. There was a continuing and intimate correspondence between Palmerston and the Belgian king, dating from the period of his inauguration during the first of Palmerston's three long stints as Foreign Secretary. This went in parallel with the incessant courier service running between the English and Belgian courts. The resolution of nine years of protracted negotiations between Britain, France and Holland, about the future, but often over the head, of Belgium, culminated within the processes of the Concert of Europe in 1839 in one of Palmerston's earliest diplomatic triumphs; it also provided the occasion for one of his major speeches in the House of Commons.[67]

Not for nothing were their respective ambassadors, both of them old friends of Palmerston, *persona grata* at their respective capitals, and secure in their offices — by contemporary standards — for extraordinarily long periods: Sylvain Van de Weyer at London from 1831 to 1867, and Lord Howard de Walden at Brussels from 1846 to 1868.[68] When Palmerston was first, for any length of time, freed from the crushing workload of the Foreign Office, with the fall of the Melbourne administration, he undertook a European tour with his family; Brussels and Leopold were his natural first port of call.[69] The close relationship was further strengthened during the year of revolutions, 1848, when the Belgian monarchy remained firm. Palmerston's letters to Leopold of 1848 echo this.[70] Sylvain Van de Weyer reported with great satisfaction to Brussels on Palmerston's eulogistic references to Belgium's survival intact in 1848, and as to how his 'experimental little monarchy' had been laughed at by the Commons when he first mooted the idea.[71]

With France, Belgian royal relationships were for a considerable period of time strengthened through Leopold's second marriage to Louis-Philippe's sister Louise-Marie, just as political in intent as his first to George IV's daughter, Caroline, who had died in childbirth. In later years, when arguably the connection with France was still just as critical, Leopold developed affections for a Madame St Herbert, and his frequent absences to visit her in the Ardennes, hunting — as he put it, and as the British ambassador, Lord Howard de Walden, crudely reported to Palmerston — '*gros gibier*', cannot have enhanced that fragile relationship between

what were then still two French-speaking courts and governments.[72]

For the Anglo-Belgian connection, it appeared so important to
Britain, that one of her ongoing aims during the 1840s had been
to try to secure a tripartite treaty between Belgium, Holland and
Britain.[73] It might be supposed that Britain would not allow minor
matters to cut across these special relationships. However, this
was not the view that was to emerge from Palmerston's communications with the British envoy, for representations to the Belgian
foreign minister, d'Hoffschmidt de Resteigne, apropos the
Braithwaite and Martin claim in 1849–50; for Palmerston at least,
broad policy was one thing: the interests of a *civis Britannicus*
were something apart.[74] Indeed, such intra-European relationships
took on entirely different aspects when extra-European matters
were the focus. Britain and France were each pursuing their different overseas priorities around the globe at this precolonial period,
only very loosely constrained by the embryonic *entente cordiale*.
That tenuous relationship was even more pronounced where their
interests overlapped in Africa; the same policy would apply to
Belgium in due course.

Leopold: The Strategist of Colonization

In three territorial ventures — Mexico, Guatemala and the Rio
Nunez — there emerged what seemed to be clear-cut examples of
the personal involvement of the Belgian sovereign himself in a
colonial entreprise.[75] Not that such royal backing ensured success:
the fact was that at the end of Leopold's reign, Belgium possessed
no more overseas territory than she had at the start of it. In the
1840s, however, that simple fact of royal interest in colonization
represented another significant difference between Belgium and
her neighbours: the French and British courts were much more
focused on Europe than on extra-European matters. Although no
actual evidence has emerged that the king was allowed publicly by
his foreign minister to put the royal authority behind the Nunez
expeditions that took place in 1848 and 1849, he had been at the
very least the prime mover for a favourable view being taken of
commercial developments there during the two preceding years.[76]

In late 1847, the first of Van Haverbeke's voyages to the west
coast took place: from Belgium's point of view, as for all the other
participants, 1847, not 1848, is the year in which the broader Rio

Nunez 'decade' can be said to have begun.[77] For the French as for
the British there was the 1845 agreement to divide and rule along
this part of what the Belgians still preferred to call by its wider
geographical title, 'Senegambia'. In areas that lay between their
colonial territories, such as the Nunez, where neither a *Pax
Britannica* nor a *Code français* could be said to hold sway, they
were careful not to tread on each other's toes. The British and the
French each had quite enough African worries and expenses,
without gratuitously adding to them; they were emphatic in
formalizing that understanding. The representative of the governor
of Sierra Leone declared — and Admiral Sir Charles Hotham was
to confirm — that there was 'a treaty concluded between France
and England by which the two governments agreed not to take
possession of any river or portion of territory situated between the
Gambia and Sierra Leone which they did not occupy at the time of
the treaty.'[78]

The 1840s had seen first the British, and then on the same
model the French, seeking to draw up treaties with various native
rulers along the coast, whilst the successive governors of Sierra
Leone and Bouët, the French naval commander at Gorée, each
kept as watchful an eye on the scene as their resources, and several
days sailing time, would allow: this was their 'patch', and they
each operated a kind of unspoken 'balance of power' policy over
it. Any intervention by a *tierce puissance*, as the governor of Sierra
Leone was said to have put it, would be looked on initially with
suspicion, whatever might have been the preamble to it in London,
Paris, and in this case, Brussels.[79]

It is clear that in the case of the Belgian project for the Nunez,
the Belgian foreign minister, d'Hoffschmidt, had been at pains to
get a formal clearance for his West African plans with both the
French and British governments, without making those plans too
specific.[80] The British Foreign Office, either generously — which
seems out of character — or negligently, under the pressure of
business, had expressed no opposition at the time — 1847 — and
Van de Weyer was to report a satisfactory approval by London, in
a dispatch of 27 September 1849. Subsequent correspondence
between Palmerston, Howard de Walden and Van de Weyer
suggests a belated awakening, with alarm, to the implications.[81]
The French foreign minister in Paris had even gone so far as to
welcome the Belgian initiative, provided that free trade was

preserved.[82] That policy was not echoed by Bouët at Gorée. For him the Belgians threatened relationships which he had been carefully building up all along the coast as far as Libreville, the township for freed slaves which he himself had founded in equatorial Gabon back in 1839 — modelling it on the British Freetown experience. As for the vision of this particular river in Guinea, with its untapped commercial possibilities, 'le rio Nunez était son rêve'.[83]

This was an age of economic individualism. A significant and long-undetected role was played in the Rio Nunez ventures from as early as 1845 by another individual, a French-born merchant and reputed shipowner in Antwerp, who had left his native Marseilles under circumstances that have been in dispute: this was Abraham Cohen.[84] Cohen conceived the grand idea of a Belgian *comptoir* somewhere on the 'Senegambian' coast, which could then play a decisive part in providing a much needed new market for Belgian manufacturers of what they understood as 'African trade goods'. There was an assumption by some merchants new to the trade that such goods did not need to be of high quality; however, it was clear to those more experienced, such as Matthew Forster, that the African and mulatto trading community had a very considerable commercial awareness of quality and value, and simply did not accept inferior merchandise into their warehouses. This *comptoir* would offer 'a regular and productive outlet for Belgian industry'. It would bring with it above all an income for Belgian importers of the groundnuts and other produce of the rich and fertile upper Guinea coast, as well as the products brought down the caravan routes from the interior. Cohen also had in mind the possibility of starting a cotton plantation at Victoria, which would have minimized Belgian dependence on the expensive American version. Much of Cohen's grandiose thinking is preserved in the Belgian archives. On 25 May 1848, from 14 Rue du Meridien, he wrote to the government about his initial findings from the crucial year, 1847, and the long-term value of the Rio Nunez as the key objective for Belgium:

In the plan about the west coast of Africa which I sent you on May 17th 1847, I concluded: that Belgium could take a very active part: because the advantages which certain of her products gave her put her in a superior position to those of several nations which exploit it. ... The Rio Nunez only needing a few years of peace and security to raise it to great commercial prosperity and probably reaching the importance of the Senegal and Gambia rivers. ... I am assured of the ease of founding a permanent depot, [and] even the possession in perpetuity of the greater part of the river.[85]

Cohen's ultimate problem lay not so much with his commercial counterparts and backers, as with the cautious *bourgeois bruxellois* in power in the democratically-elected *Chambre des Députés*.[86] In the face of attempts by their navy and at least one of their traders to colonize, they were to evince as great a degree of the kind of 'metropolitan' distrust of open-ended colonial disbursements of hard-taxed public moneys, as could be heard in the similar parliamentary debates in Paris or London.

As with the French, however, the main support for his ideas came from Belgium's eyes and ears to the outside world, her naval forces. That navy could also overplay its external role, and it was to be the short-termist and intemperate actions of the respective senior French and Belgian naval commanders on the spot, which were to transform what was meant to be a peaceful Rio Nunez expedition into an international incident.

At the departure of the *Louise-Marie* from Antwerp on 28 December 1848, a fortnight after the departure of the *Princess Royal* from London, Captain Van Haverbeke had with him in his crew no less than five of the writers of contemporary accounts of the battle. Themistocle du Colombier, an *enseigne de vaisseau*, wrote the most frequently quoted account, which lay forgotten until 1920; as the story of the battle will reveal, he incorporated into it, uncritically or deliberately, an eyewitness account of a key part of the battle itself, that by Ensign Dufour. Constant Dossche was another of the writers; he was a leading citizen of Ghent, a former estate agent, and assistant to Cohen in his role as agent to the shipowner, J.-L. Decoster, Cohen's initial backer.[87] It is a nice coincidence that their vessel was named after Leopold's French Queen, thus symbolically linking the two royal houses which were soon to become, if only briefly, brothers in arms: the battle of Boké would be described quixotically as 'the finest feat of arms by the Belgian Royal military navy'.[88]

However, the prime causative element in the situation from the

Belgian point of view was not the patriotism of the Belgian and French sailors who would certainly be risking death and mutilation on the plateau and the heights of Boké: the underlying driving force was commercial and individual, not military, nor political. Cohen the merchant was not merely 'the hub of the wheel', and the driving force of the whole expedition and its accompanying naval support; he was actually using the Belgian cause to further a deeper ambition: 'Belgium appeared through its economic potential, its small size, and its lack of a vigorous colonial tradition, to be the most suitable field where he could play a first-class role without competition.'[89]

In this sense a completely different pattern can be discerned to that being simultaneously pursued by the ambitious Bouët on behalf of France. In Belgium's case, an equally ambitious and clearly influential figure, adept at working the corridors of power, a wilier counterpart to England's Matthew Forster, was succeeding in manipulating the state to achieve end purposes that were personal rather than patriotic. His letter to d'Hoffschmidt, written two years later, seemed to say it all:

> It is impossible that Belgium should not be grateful to me, despite my status as a foreigner, for what I have done and continue to do for her: she and I, I may say, will harvest the fruits, and my children will soon find themselves at the head of an establishment the more honourable in that it is all the creation of their father.[90]

At the same time, Cohen embodied a more worldly-wise, unmoralizing, purely commercially based approach to trading, which seemed to pay off later, in competition with Braithwaite and Martin. When he finally returned to Belgium in the summer of 1847, after a protracted stay at Gorée, he began to campaign with the Belgian foreign ministry to set up a fort, a trading port and a company on the Senegambian coast. Cohen's demands were nevertheless rejected. The expedition of 1847/8, escorted by the Belgian navy, and during which Captain Van Haverbeke, in the name of the Belgian king, entered into the first — and in fact highly provisional — concession with the king of the Nalus on 4 March 1848, led to the fateful voyage of 1848/9.[91]

The Flemish writers conclude on this note — aiming off for

their narrower definition of the extent of the Rio Nunez 'affair': 'Our research has proved that the whole Belgian Rio Nunez episode was essentially the life's work of one man ... he pursued his plans by a well-considered strategy ... the top events and decisions — even at governmental level — had their origin ... in his inspiration. ... There remains the basic historical question, why was Belgium chosen?'[92] Their answer lay in Cohen's need to regain his self-respect after his bankruptcy, not in the motive which Palmerston, among many others, believed was the sole force driving any trader — namely financial gain: 'He places the concept 'Belgium' ... at the same level as his own person and obstinately seeks to identify with it.'

Where does Joseph Edouard Van Haverbeke, the one-time hero of his tiny nation, fit into this new picture? Born in Antwerp in 1812, he entered the merchant navy at the age of 14, and the Dutch navy in 1826, transferring to the Belgian service on 18 August 1832.[93] Cohen praised this self-made man for having evinced on the Africa run 'such an enthusiasm for getting back debts ... he has done it with much perseverance'[94] He was later painted in glowing colours as a 'splendid type of sailor, with the head of a bird of prey, prominent cheekbones, deep-set eyes, a square jaw — a solid man, who will lay his fist down on the Nunez, and cover our flag with glory'.[95]

However, if this was, for Belgium, as it was later described, 'an expedition without a tomorrow', were those first-hand accounts of the battle of Boké simply patriotic self-delusions — or as the later Flemish writers themselves characterized them, 'popularizations impregnated with patriotism'?[96] Clearly, that would be too dismissive a judgement of the participants, although it may have some justice with regard to some of their subsequent historians. The Belgian naval forces sincerely believed that their valour was put to the test 'to enhance the name of Belgium', whatever the cost might be in terms of the blood shed by Africans, Belgians, Frenchmen, and, for all they knew or cared, two British traders as well, who happened to get in the way. Van Haverbeke's original assignment in the *Louise-Marie* had been to survey the Windward coast, not to acquire concessions: this followed Cohen's recommendation that two factories should be established, one in the Bissagos Islands a few miles to the north, and one in the River Nunez.

In the spring of 1848, Van Haverbeke did an astute appreciation of the situation on the river. He identified the facts that neither the French nor the British appeared to be in full control of anyone, anywhere, and that from the point of view of a possible new European allegiance the most vulnerable African peoples appeared to be the Nalus; Lamina Towl, their chief, was dissatisfied with the treaty that had been drawn up, and even more so with the French refusal to reward him for his earlier support against Tongo. He therefore managed to secure what seemed to be a firm agreement with Lamina Towl for the cession of a one-mile strip on both sides of the river between Victoria and Ropass; to his government in his report of 21 May 1848, he implied that the idea came not from him — that would have exceeded his remit — but from Lamina, who, he said, was under British influence and apparently advised by his trading partner, a certain Bicaise.[97]

John Nelson Bicaise

'Un homme à ménager'
(Ministère de la Marine et des Colonies)[98]

At this point the role, power and subtle machinations of John Nelson Bicaise start to become clearer. He was a colourful figure; his domain at Ropass makes an impressive picture. He was seen as a kind of pasha, surrounded by 12 slaves and many women, 'a jolly, cheerful, likeable host ... the true king in the river, being moreover of no country nor of any religion'.[99]

Bicaise seemed to be adamant that no further French territorial gains should be yielded, and had put Lamina up to this new ploy. There were certainly several British traders on the river by this time, but they did not appear to be in a position of great influence with their own government, let alone with the naval squadron or with the governor at Freetown; any earlier evidence of British governors seeking to extend their sway into the adjacent Northern Rivers territory seemed to be a thing of the past, firmly squashed by 'Downing Street'.

The French might appear to be poised to gain some commercial advantage, but it was not inevitable. Belgium could provide a useful counterweight to either of the main nations, and be manipulated in due course by Bicaise to his benefit. Not for nothing was the French colonial ministry to state subsequently, attributing, like du Colombier, a British nationality to him:

M. Bicaise — a rich Englishman resident at Ropass ... he it is who is the provisioner of all our warships in the Rio Nunez and indeed for several years now. He is for the French a sort of consul, a representative, a *grand Seigneur*, who receives them and assists them, in whatever and wherever, with magnificent generosity: he has rendered us good service. It is he who does three-quarters of the trade in the river, he is a man to be looked after — *un homme à ménager*.[100]

Clearly, neither the British government nor Forster & Smith were 'looking after' this influential trader, the *de facto* head of the community at Ropass. He it was who finally pulled the strings as far as trade on the river was concerned. Van Haverbeke was allowed to believe the unlikely scenario that he and Towl had achieved their apparently secret agreement at the expense of, and behind the backs of Bicaise himself and the ever-vigilant resident foreign trading community. In fact Bicaise had a dominant hold over the Nalus, and particularly Lamina: the word 'Towl' meant 'servant' — a word full of meaning for Bicaise who called him his *gendarme*. By the time Van Haverbeke weighed anchor at Caniope on his return to the Rio Nunez after a year's absence on 13 February 1849, the stage was set. He believed that he had manœuvred his country into the leading position on this deep, navigable and under-developed river, and that his accustomed smartness and enterprise could win huge prizes for his beloved Belgium.

The Nunez Affair was in essence a struggle for commercial ascendancy and territory, but that struggle was not limited to Europeans. If the two years from 1847 to 1848 can be seen as its opening round, a second phase was about to open, with the deft self-preservative touch of John a.k.a. Nelson Bicaise detectable at every turn.[101] Even if he could assert British nationality when it seemed propitious, from his birth in Trinidad, he had become to all intents and purposes an 'African' in the way he operated politically. He could make himself *persona grata* with whichever power appeared to be winning the day in his 'fiefdom'. If he could have spoken Flemish as well, his cup would have overflowed.

The Landumas, the Nalus and Futa Jallon
'The blood of kings and the tears of the canoe-makers are sacred things that must not touch the ground.' [102]

All unknown to Joseph Braithwaite and George Martin, as well as to Joseph Van Haverbeke, Abraham Cohen, and de la Tocnaye, the invisible eyes that watched out for European arrivals along the Guinea coast were those of the peoples at the real heart of the affair — the Africans themselves.[103] The still evolving situation on the Nunez needs constantly to be borne in mind: the autochthonous peoples had been described as 'aborigines' only a few years earlier, when Captain Belcher RN made his exploratory visits in HMS *Aetna*, in the 1830s. They were unable to see themselves as part of a continent of Africa, simply as 'the land', as opposed to the territory of the Europeans, 'the sea'. Although they were cast in the role of having to defend rights which they saw as immemorially theirs, against changes being imposed from outside, the Landumas and their fellow Africans were to prove to be the eyes of the only ultimate victors in a greater centuries-old struggle — the fight for the soul of Africa itself.[104]

Although at that time some of the indigenous inhabitants still called it by its traditional Soussou name, 'Kakundy', the name Nunez had become, and has remained, the accepted title for the broad and beautiful river which perpetuated the name of its original Portuguese 'discoverer', Señor Nuñao Tristao.[105] Its life and trade had been scarred by decades of civil war between three of the groups concerned. The Landumas were seen in 1848 as 'a quiet people, the original possessors of the Karcandy country', whose power was 'fast passing away under the pressure of their more warlike neighbours the Nelloes' and the 'Foulahs' — the Fula theocracy of the Futa Jallon hinterlands, 'the Indians of Africa'. The Nalus were 'a proud intelligent but unprincipled race which has emigrated from the northeastwards'. The Fula were different: 'decidedly handsome, many are considerably darker. Their features are regular, and good, and unlike the Mandingoes and Yoloffs … tall, well-proportioned and of erect and graceful figure.' The coastal peoples, the rice-growing Bagas, 'a retiring people, of pastoral habits', kept well clear of this power-play.[106] Even allowing for the fact that 'most European traders to West Africa never realized the complexity and richness of its culture', the well-nigh 'Lilliputian' complexities of the African background to the Nunez story are daunting.[107] As one British naval officer, Commander Lysaght — to feature later in the affair — wrote to the Admiralty, with some understatement, after his first visit to the

Nunez in 1848, these particular disputes 'were not very easy for Europeans to understand'.[108]

The role of the river itself, flowing into its rich alluvial plain, was central to an understanding of the quarrels and intrigues that continued to rage around it. The rivers of Africa have been likened to its primitive *Autobahnen*;[109] they were the commercial lifelines for the kings and their peoples; the canoe makers revered in the old west coast proverb were the essential facilitators of that traffic. On the Rio Nunez, the small town of Boké held the key position. It was set in the higher grasslands that characterized, and still characterize today, the Upper Nunez. It was the point where the caravan trails bringing valuable hides and other produce from the interior met the river, and the coastal peoples who related with the outside world; its possessor could therefore determine the whole pattern of trade down to the coast. At the twice-daily high tides, many craft could get so far, but no further; there were rapids further upstream. Boké itself was on a hillside looking down towards the river; it was capable of being well-fortified with the traditional African system of palisading, with good lines of fire for its defending riflemen, a feature of much importance for the events of the spring of 1849.[110] Between it and the Nalu territory to the south and southeast, lay a further supposed source of defensive strength, the sacred woods, where the Landumas' secret society, the Simo, guarded its mysteries; it was thought to be impregnable to outside attack.[111]

The Nalus held an equally strong card in their hands: from their territory at and below Ropass, they could blockade all traffic coming up or down-stream, and also had the advantage of being the first people that any visiting trader would encounter, giving their astute European-oriented, English-speaking leader, Lamina Towl, the opportunity to define the context for any new relationship. In the Belgian literature of the Nunez, Lamina (in distinction to the people he ruled) with his white top hat, his blue ex-footman's frock coat with its gold epaulettes, and the ever-present umbrella and sandals, has become the archetypal supposedly 'Europeanized' African.[112]

In one sense, this was in modern terms a battle for 'market share'; yet it also smacked of the Europe of the Middle Ages. It threw up a pattern which nineteenth-century Europeans hoped they had left behind, but were exasperated to rediscover in full swing on the Nunez: petty kingdoms warring for transient and marginal advantage, when all that really mattered, from any perspective, was that the trade of the river as a whole should flourish, in competition with other riverine avenues to the coast and sea.

The Landumas' ability to compete was made more fragile by virtue of their tribal convention: that kingship had to alternate between two branches of the ruling family: Mandialé Coumbassa, the grandfather of the warrior King S'ahara, had set up his capital downriver at the village still carrying the traditional generic name, Kakundy; his brother, Modiéré, had succeeded him but moved his centre to Boké. The right of succession went first to the brothers and then to the eldest son of the current ruler's sister. This gave to the female children an importance entirely underestimated by most of those 'ugly men with red faces and long hair', the Europeans.[113] This ignorance would be even greater in the minds of newcomers such as Van Haverbeke, who had not cared to investigate these cultural niceties; it gave rise to continual tension and acrimony, and was to prove a fundamental cause, in fact the flash point, of the affair.[114]

The French and the British had severally tried to back each of these two dominant peoples in turn, first the Nalus, then the Landumas, and after S'aharah's death in 1844, first his elder son, Tongo, then his younger son Mayoré. Tongo had forfeited popular support among the younger Landumas by choosing to live away from Boké, which he later described poignantly as 'my father's house'.[115] He was a heavy, robust figure, impassive and immobile of features, dressed normally in a simple blue cotton *pagne* cloth, with the characteristic slippers and tattered umbrella, and sporting a red fez, with tassels. Mayoré was the more excitable of the two, given to alcohol, and an inheritor of his father's bellicosity. He would even be described by another European trader, as 'half an idiot'.[116] The superficial judgement that here was a strange, savage older world was deepened for fresh European eyes by the fact that Landuma men and women had little copper bells around their necks and knees, and had their teeth chiselled into sharp points, as a sign of beauty and style; many were festooned with *gris-gris*, would-be magic ornaments — Koranic if they were within the growing Muslim tradition, multifarious and secular if they were still leaning towards the original pagan fetishistic culture.[117]

One of the most recent over-optimistic attempts to impose peace between these alien and alienated factions had been made a year previously, in February 1848; when Captain Thomas Lysaght of HM steam vessel *Grappler*, a future stalwart ally of Braithwaite and Martin, had called on the newly victorious King Mayoré, 'the whole of the chiefs expressed their determination to protect British traders as long as they remained neutral' — a vital pointer for the future.[118]

As both Braithwaite and Martin, and Van Haverbeke's expedition, were arriving on the Nunez, exactly a year later, in February 1849, this was the rich concoction of elements and sharp cultural differences that was bubbling away in the Nunez crucible. The Rio Nunez, the 'cockpit of competition and strife',[119] had now become a mixture fit for an explosion, a fuse waiting to be lit. The next phase in the decade of troubles that constituted the affair of the Rio Nunez — the clash of arms and the European diplomatic battle which was to form 'the affair within the affair' — was about to begin.[120]

Notes

1. For sources on France, see G. D. Westfall, *French Colonial Africa: A Guide to Official Sources* (London, 1992); IDC, *Guide des Sources de l'Histoire de l'Afrique au Sud du Sahara: Archives et Bibliothèques Françaises* (Zug, 1970), vol 1, *Archives*, p.253. For descriptions of the Nunez peoples, see *infra*. From this chapter onwards, the anglicized name Debucca, a.k.a. Debouka or Debucko, is replaced in the text by the shorter form of the French name, Deboqué — Boké, since this is the name that has been handed down and is used today. (See note on Maps, in Acknowledgements, *supra*.) It was also called Rebecca by R. Caillié, *Travels through Central Africa to Timbuctoo: 1824–1828* (London, repr. 1992), p.150. Similarly, the anglicized 'Margery' now becomes known under his gallicized name of Mayoré or Madioré (B. Schnapper, *La politique et le commerce français dans le Golfe de Guinée de 1838 à 1871* (Paris, 1962), p.233. He also thought that Tongo and Mayoré were Sarah's nephews. For further background on 'The Rivers', see George Brooks Jnr, *Yankee Traders, Old Coasters, African Middlemen* (Boston, 1970), *passim*; J. Martin, *L'Aventure coloniale de la France: L'Empire renaissant, 1789–1871* (Paris, 1987), p.232. See also W. B. Cohen, *The French Encounter with Africans: White Response to Blacks, 1530–1880* (Indiana, 1986), *passim*; L. Marfaing, *L'Evolution du commerce au Sénégal, 1830–1930* (Paris, 1991), p.49 *et seq*.

2. Schnapper, *Golfe de Guinée*, pp.9, 239; Martin, *Aventure*, p.261; A. Arcin, *Histoire de la Guinée française* (Paris, 1911), pp.257, 419, Preface, p.vi. For 'C'est nous qui avons triomphé', see W. Eckert, *Kurland unter dem Einfluss des Merkantilismus* (Riga, 1927).

3. J. D. Hargreaves, *Prelude to the Partition of West Africa* (London, 1963), p.14; also J. D. Hargreaves, *France and West Africa: An Anthology of*

Historical Documents (London, 1969), *passim*; T. Pakenham, *The Scramble for Africa* (London, 1991), p.360.

4. D. McCall, N. R. Bennett and J. Butler (eds) *West African History* (New York, 1969), pp.146–7. 'L'Angleterre s'était montrée assez généreuse' (Martin, *Aventure*, p.80).

5. Arcin, *Guinée française*, p.251, refers to the British attitude as *'un sable excellent où le coq français pourrait gratter'*. See also Martin, *Aventure*, pp. 92–5; J. Tramond and A. Reussner, *Eléments d'histoire maritime et coloniale contemporaine* (Paris, 1947), p.3; P. Masson, *Marseilles et la colonisation française* (Marseilles, 1907), *passim*.

6. H. Priestley, *France Overseas: A Study of Modern Imperialism* (American Historical Association, Harvard, 1938), p.91 *et seq.*

7. E. Taillemitte, *Dictionnaire de la Marine* (Paris, 1962); CARAN, Service Historique de la Marine, LH/2142/3, LH/312, Marine CC7 alpha 1975 and 283. For equivalent naval ranks, see C. I. Hamilton, *Anglo-French Naval Rivalry: 1840–1870* (Oxford, 1993), p.181. NB a point of importance where the Rio Nunez Affair belies Hamilton's account (p.309), 'the narrow-focused rivalry of the two decades after 1840, narrow in . . . geographical concentration' (Schnapper, *Golfe de Guinée*, pp.32, 231).

8. Hamilton, *Rivalry*, pp.189–90.

9. P. Leroy-Beaulieu, *De la Colonisation chez les peuples modernes* (Paris, 1886), p.273; cf. Victor Hugo, *L'Emancipation* (Paris, 1849); C. Schefer, *Sénégal et Dependances: Instructions aux gouverneurs* (Paris, 1927), pp.594–5.

10. Martin, *Aventure*, pp.87–91.

11. R. Aldrich and J. Connell, *France's Overseas Frontier* (Cambridge, 1992), pp.12, 280; Tramond and Reussner, *Eléments*, p.70; Martin, *Aventure*, pp.9–12, 14, 92; F. Mauro, *L'Expansion européenne: 1600–1870* (Paris, 1964), p.99.

12. Hamilton, *Rivalry*, p.17; Martin, *Aventure*, p.61.

13. Hamilton, *Rivalry*, p.1; cf. Chateaubriand's *le séducteur des vagues*; J. Ridley, *Lord Palmerston* (London, 1970), pp.289, 338; Martin, *Aventure*, p.118.

14. For deeper examination of these pan-European phobias, see Henri Brunschwig, 'Anglophobia and French African Policy' in P. Gifford and W. R. Louis, *France and Britain in Africa: Imperial Rivalry and Colonial Rule* (Yale, 1971), pp.6, 23, who claims that 'Anglophobia developed at the same time as the navy, and remained until 1870 the navy's prerogative.' See also J. H. Gleason, *The Genesis of Russophobia in Great Britain: A Study of the Interaction of Policy and Opinion* (Cambridge, Mass., 1950), Chaps.1 and 10, pp.272–90; Hamilton, *Rivalry*, pp.31, 289 and *passim*; also F. Furet, *Revolutionary France: 1770–1880* (Paris, 1988), pp.359–60.

15. Hamilton, *Rivalry*, p.199.

16. F/CAOM dossier 26.d, Admiral Tréhouart to Ministère de la Marine et des Colonies, 8 June 1849, 'un des meilleurs officiers de la marine'. Also Hamilton, *Rivalry*, p.33; Taillemitte, *Dictionnaire*, q.v.

17. Gifford and Louis, *France and Britain*, p.6. The French did not get as worked up as the British about the slave trade until V. Schoelcher in the Lamartine government abolished it finally in 1848, one clear action of the revolutionary government. See also R. Pasquier, 'A Propos de l'Emancipation des Esclaves au Sénégal en 1848', *RFHOM*, 54, 1967, pp.188–208.

18. On 'triangular trade' see Brooks, *Yankee*, pp.11–6; Schefer, *Instructions*, p.587 (*'Notre sphere d'intérêts subissait une sorte de glissement vers le sud'*); Martin, *Aventure*, p.229; Schnapper, *Golfe de Guinée*, p.229; E. Bouët-

Willaumez, *Commerce et traite des noirs aux Côtes occidentales d'Afrique* (Paris, 1848), p.53.

19. Ridley, *Palmerston*, pp.225–41; Hamilton, *Rivalry*, p.20; Kenneth Bourne, *Palmerston: The Early Years, 1784–1841* (London, 1982), pp.375–84, 589–620. Tramond and Reussner, *Eléments*, pp.36, 71–2.

20. Hansard, HoC debates, ser 3 v.lxxxii, cols 1223–8, P speech, 30 July 1845, in opposition; also Tramond and Reussner, *Eléments*, pp.71–2: '*La vapeur* [Peel] *a fait perdre la qualité d'île à notre pays.*' Hamilton, *Rivalry*, p.20.

21. Martin, *Aventure*, p.86. See A. de Vigny, *Servitude et Grandeur Militaires* (Paris, London, repr. 1966). '*L'Océan n'entendait plus une parole qui ne fut anglaise*' (Arcin, *Guinée française*, p.257).

22. Hamilton, *Rivalry*, p.19; Tramond and Reussner, *Eléments*, p.38; Gleason, *Russophobia*, pp.133, 140, 175; Martin, *Aventure*, pp.86–8.

23. Hamilton, *Rivalry*, pp.31, 58, 112–16, 133, 199; Schnapper, *Golfe de Guinée*, pp.16–19, 26–7, 30–1, 45–6; also Brunschwig, 'Anglophobia, p.15 (despite the mispelling, Willaumetz); Martin, *Aventure*, pp.107–8; Tramond and Reussner, *Eléments*, p.25; Taillemitte, *Dictionnaire*, q.v.; Schefer, *Instructions*, pp.105–48, 166, 194, 567–73, 594–5, 635.

24. M. Anne Raffinel, *Nouveau Voyage dans les Pays des Nègres* (Paris, 1846), vol.2, pp.123–4; cf. George Brooks, 'Peanuts and Colonialism: Consequences of the Commercialization of Peanuts in West Africa 1830–1870', *JAH*, vol.16, no.1, 1975, p.50 (peanuts = groundnuts = *arachides*).

25. Schefer, *Instructions*, p.107; Ministère de la Marine et des Colonies to B-W, 12 December 1842.

26. Schefer, *Instructions*, p.146, 171, B-W's order of day, 1 April 1843.

27. Schefer, *Instructions*, pp.168, 569–71; Schefer, *Instructions*, p.166: B-W to Ollivier, 6 November 1844; Ministère de la Marine et des Colonies to Ollivier, 21 November 1844.

28. E. Hertslet, *Index of British Treaties* (HMSO), vol.1, Convention signed (London, 29 May 1845) 'with France for the suppression of the traffic in slaves' (vol.2, p.57) by Lord Aberdeen, M. Aulaire, French Ambassador for HM King of France (five years after P had sought it) 'to station in the West Coast of Africa from Cape Verde to 16° 30' south latitude, a naval force of at least 26 cruisers' (Art. 1). See Schnapper, *Golfe de Guinée*, pp.78, 82–5; also reference in CO267/272, 1861, Hammond to Sir F. Rogers.

29. Schefer, *Instructions*, pp.3, 573; Schnapper, *Golfe de Guinée*, pp.76–8; also Hamilton, *Rivalry*, p.127.

30. B–W to Ministère de la Marine et des Colonies, 6 November 1844, in Schnapper, *Golfe de Guinée*, pp.27, 171. See also Bouët-Willaumez, *Commerce*, p.vi.

31. Hamilton, *Rivalry*, p.199, quotes E. Souville, *Mes Souvenirs Maritimes*, p.444. The nearest English translation would be: 'With his dashing manner, and intemperate way of speaking, a real charlatan . . . a son of Brittany, but with the personality of a gascon, a musketeer'.

32. G. Hardy, *La mise en valeur du Sénégal de 1817 à 54* (Paris, 1921), pp.301–8, 320–1, 348–9, 358–9; L. Faidherbe, *Le Sénégal: La France dans l'Afrique Occidentale* (Paris, 1889), p.158 *et seq.*

33. Schnapper, *Golfe de Guinée*, pp.32, 331. Cf. Charles de Kerhallet, *capitaine de corvette, commandant la goélette* L'Amarante, report of 4 May 1847 in *Annales Maritimes et Coloniales* (Paris, 1847), pp.196–201, 199. '*Le frère cadet, Majoré, le plus energique, le plus capable, . . . maître du Boqué . . . en mars 1847 . . . a fait avec son frère une paix que je crois peu durable*' (for

map, see F/CAOM); Bouët-Willaumez, *Commerce*, p.71; Martin, *Aventure*, p.231; Schnapper, *Golfe de Guinée*, p.32.

34. For the reasoning behind the redesignation of 1847–57 as the 'decade' of the Rio Nunez Affair, see n.77 *infra*.; Tramond and Reussner, *Eléments*, p.71. For France, '*la fin du pénible éffacement auquel elle avait du se résister depuis 1815*', see Southgate, *English Minister*, pp.188–9. For parallels between the roles of King Louis Philippe and Konrad Adenauer in West Germany, 1945–53, where both leaders succesfully sought to recover a due measure of self-esteem for a vanquished nation, whilst still placating their former victors, see Beate Buhm von Oppen (ed.) *Konrad Adenauer, 1945–53: Memoirs* (London, 1966), p.395.

35. Tramond and Reussner, *Eléments*, pp.20–1. Joinville had accelerated the process with a famous article, 'Nous étions inférieurs aux Anglais ... Américains ... Hollandais ... Napolitains ... Russes'. Hamilton, *Rivalry*, pp.18–19, 58.

36. Taillemitte, *Dictionnaire*, q.v.; F/CAOM, de Langle [a.k.a. de l'Angle] to Gorée, 9 August 1839.

37. F/CAOM, Charmasson to de la Roque, 18 May 1841.

38. Arcin, *Guinée française*, pp.284–9; Schnapper, *Golfe de Guinée*, p.238: 'Un métis de Barbade, autrefois lié au commerçants de Sierra Leone, et devenu pro-français'.

39. F/CAOM dossier 26.c, letter from de Kerhallet, *La Flotte*, 27 July 1847.

40. See F/CAOM reference in Chap.5 *infra*, n.5.

41. F/CAOM dossier 26.e, undated note for Ministère de la Marine et des Colonies, Paris, p.17.

42. F/CAOM 26.c, Lieutenant Ducrest de Villeneuve, commander of the schooner *L'Amarante*, to Amiral Montagnies de la Roque, *chef de station des Côtes occidentales d'Afrique*, 29 February 1848. This was the son of the celebrated eponymous admiral of Trafalgar fame; Taillemitte, *Dictionnaire*, q.v.

43. F/CAOM, Baudin, Governor, Senegal to Ministère de la Marine et des Colonies, 17 April 1848. For the names of French governors see Schefer, *Instructions, passim*; also D. P. Henege, *Colonial Governors from the Fifteenth Century to the Present* (Madison, 1970), *passim*.

44. F/CAOM, for example dossier 26.c, 27 July 1848, Baudin to 'Citoyen Ministre'; see G. J. Billy, *Palmerston's Foreign Policy 1848* (New York, 1993), Chap.7, p.137 *et seq.*; Hamilton, *Rivalry*, pp.240, 289. Southgate, *English Minister*, p.207.

45. Tramond and Reussner, *Eléments*, p.39.

46. 1848 saw the final act in the prolonged French dalliance with anti-slavery. See n.17 *supra*; Judd, *Palm*; see Chap.2, *supra*; Ridley, *Palmerston*, pp.192–4, 265–7, 281–2, 297 (HoC debate, 16 July 1844), 484.

47. Brooks, 'Peanuts', p.50.

48. K. Hamilton, 'The Historical Diplomacy of the Third Republic', *Diplomacy and Statecraft*, vol.4, No 2, July 1993, pp.175–209, cites (n.19) E. Boutmy's 1872 reference to the adventurism of Napoleon III: 'Cet esquif pavoisé de généralités brillantes qu'on appelle l'esprit français'.

49. For an overview of this section, see Patricia Carson, *Materials for West African History in the Archives of Belgium and Holland* (18 docs, London, 1968), pp.189–95; also A. Duchesne, 'Bibliographie: Rio Nunez', *BARSOM* (Brussels, 1958), no 68, new series IV2, pp.783–5. I am grateful for help provided by the Belgian ambassador, Baron H. Dehennin and his staff during the early stages of this research. See also author's article, 'Le Nunez: Sabre d'Honneur?', *RBHM*, vol.31, nos 1/2, mars–juin 1995, pp.85–116.

50. B/MRA, Aspirant Guillaume Delcourt, 'Journal de Mer: Relation du Voyage à la Côte d'Afrique avec la Goélette *Louise-Marie* 1848–49', page references are taken from the original typescript of his daughter Françoise Delcourt, Anvers. This unedited journal was noted by O. Petitjean in 1930; also by Louis Leconte, *Les Ancêtres de Notre Force navale* (Brussels, 1952), pp.161 n.1, 191, 165, 180, 191, but solely for his account of the Belgian naval exploits (which he wrongly says agrees with that of Dufour), not for their significance for B&M's story; Delcourt gives the lie to d'Hoffschmidt's claim (FO 123/64, 3 September 1850) that *'aucun marin belge n'a participé au pillage'*; see also Chap.1, *supra*. Leconte also includes pictures of three of the Belgian naval officers — VH, Delcourt and Dufour. See P. Lefevre, 'Les Voyages de la Marine royale belge en Senegal', *Revue belge d'histoire militaire*, vol.22, p.560 n.4. For details of Risquons-Tout, see Chap.6 *infra*, n.26.
51. B/MRA reserve collection, formerly at the Musée de la Porte de Hall, Brussels; Leconte, *Les Ancêtres*, p.190. G. Macoir, 'Note sur un Sabre d'Honneur décerné à Capt [VH]', *Bull. des Musées royaux des Arts décoratifs et industriels* (Brussels, 1907), p.93, *Directeur général de la marine* to VH, 6 December 1849, says 'le ministre des Affaires étrangères, mercredi prochain, 12 de ce mois, . . . vous fera la remise du sabre d'honneuer.'
52. J. Everaert and C. De Wilde, 'Pindanoten voor de eerste ontluikende industriële revolutie: Een alternative kijk op de Belgische commerciële expansie in West-Afrika, 1844–1861', *BARSOM* (Brussels, 1992), vol.37, no.3, 1991 (page references from author's translation, SGA/B).
53. For role of Bicaise, see *infra*.
54. For the importance in trying to develop colonies, on the British model, of Belgium's first two monarchs in what P's critics derided as his *'petite monarchie expérimentale'* — Leopold I and his son Leopold II (and the H. M. Stanley connection) — see E. Corti, *Leopold I: Oracle politique de l'Europe* (Brussels, 1927), *passim*; E. Cammaerts, *The Keystone of Europe: History of the Belgian Dynasty, 1830–1939* (London, 1939), p.104.
55. Everaert and De Wilde, 'Pindanoten', p.1: *'Bettrokenheid . . . in de koloniale penetratie langs de westlijke flanken van het Afrikaanse continent voor de faze van de Kongo-Vriejstaat'*.
56. C. de Lannoy, 'Une Expédition Franco-Belge en Guinée . . . d'après le Rapport de l'Enseigne de Vaisseau Themistocle du Colombier', *BESBEC* (Brussels, mai–juin 1920), pp.178–210. Colombier was born on 2 March 1818 and died on 31 July 1892 (ibid., p.179).
57. Ibid.
58. Ibid.
59. Ibid., pp.179–80.
60. For the best account of the close relationship between Victoria and Leopold, see J. Richardson, *My Dearest Uncle: A Life of Leopold, First King of the Belgians* (London, 1961), *passim*; also correspondence in Royal Archives, Windsor.
61. See Chaps.4 and 5 *infra*.
62. Everaert and De Wilde, 'Pindanoten', pp.5–6.
63. Leconte, *Les Ancêtres*, p.163.
64. See Ridley, *Palmerston*, pp.122–37; Bourne, *Early Years*, pp.333–49.
65. Bourne, *Early Years*, p.336. For hopes for Prince of Orange as the Belgian king, see Cecil Woodham-Smith, *Queen Victoria: Her Life and Times, 1819–1861* (London, 1972), p.119 n.25; cf. RA Y88/11, Princess Victoria to King Leopold, 17 May 1836; also Ridley, *Palmerston*, pp.133–5.
66. See *supra* Part I.

67. Ridley, *Palmerston*, pp.136–7; Donald Southgate, *The Most English Minister: The Policies and Politics of Palmerston* (London, 1966), pp.38–9.

68. B/MAE 'Correspondance diplomatique: Légations: Grande Bretagne' vols 25–7, *passim*.

69. Ridley, *Palmerston*, p.301 on European tour in 1844.

70. PBHA, RC MM, 114–24, P to Leopold, 15 June 1848, 'the continued Tranquillity and Stability of your kingdom'.

71. B/MAE, v26, 104, 26 June 1850, Van de Weyer to d'Hoffschmidt. See *infra*, Chap.5.

72. PBHA, GC HO 719–39, 24 July 1850, de Walden, private, to P.

73. BL Add. MS, 48,499, P Letterbooks, P to Sir J. Seymour, 26 August 1840, re French efforts to set up a Franco-Belgian commercial treaty.

74. For P's pursuit of these two seemingly conflicting aims see FO97/198 *passim*. For consideration of the ebb and flow in the *entente cordiale* with France from as early as the 1830s onwards, see *supra*.

75. R. Massinon, *L'Entreprise du Rio Nunez: Mémoire de Licence inédit ULB* (Brussels, 1965), pp.311–60; also J-R Leconte, *Les Tentatives d'Expansion coloniale sous le Règne de Leopold 1er* (Anvers, 1946), pp.141–2.

76. Georges-H. Dumont, *150 Ans d'Expansion et de Colonisation* (Brussels, 1956), p.24. '*Tant d'efforts ... furent-ils ... inutiles? En apparence, oui, puisque la Belgique ne disposait d'aucun territoire d'outre-mer, à la mort du souverain.*' See author's article, 'Sabre', p.85; and Massinon, *Entreprise*. It is a fact that Leopold's royal jeweller had been used to design two Swords of Honour, one presented to VH by Leopold's senior and trusted foreign minister, d'Hoffschmidt, in December 1849, the other presented in Paris to de la Tocnaye.

77. For the re-evaluation of the so-called 'decade' of the Nunez Affair, see Chap.3, *supra*, n.34. Decisive factors for placing it as starting in 1847, not 1848, and ending in 1857, not 1858, are the defeat by the *de facto* if not yet *de jure* king of the Landumas, Mayoré, of his brother Tongo, during 1847. This enforced change of leadership, coupled with the increased influence, thus ushered in, of the powerful Fula peoples inland, set off a chain reaction in the area. Externally, this was the year in which the relations between the two main trading communities, British and French, started to move apart, as against the pattern of relatively peaceful European relations hitherto, whatever the anarchic state of the ongoing civil war then in progress, between the Nalus, the Landumas, and the Fula. It was also the year in which, with P back in the British FO from 1846 onwards, a new energy was given to the achievement of treaties with the native chiefs along the coast: the total of what he insisted on calling merely 'agreements' doubled within the year. Above all, this was the year in which Cohen besought the Belgian foreign ministry, with the patriotic d'Hoffschmidt now succeeding Dechamps, to spread its wings in West Africa. At the end of that year the first official Belgian expedition under VH set sail for Africa. By 1857, the last Belgian expedition had set out, with the purpose of renouncing all the previous attempts at colonization. By then French influence was manifestly winning ground, as Britain ceased to contest the territory with any degree of seriousness. This was signalled in the decisive victory by General Faidherbe over Umar Tal at Medina, which marked the beginning of the drive to create French West Africa. (See Lefevre, 'Voyages', vol.22, p.560;) also *infra*, Epilogue, and Bibliographical Summary.

78. For 1845 treaty, see Chap.3, *supra*, n.28.

79. See Chap.4 *infra*, n.20.

80. C. Lannoy/T. du Colombier, 'Une Expédition franco-belge en Guinée: La Campagne de la goélette de guerre *Louise-Marie* dans la Colonie belge du Rio-Nunez (1849)', *BESBEC* (Brussels, mai–juin 1920), p.183; Massinon, *Entreprise*, pp.330, 335.

81. FO 125/2, Belgium 1836–57, FO to Brussels Embassy, 15 July 1850, P to de Walden.

82. B/MAE.

83. B/MRA, Delcourt, 'Relation du Voyage', pp.30–3; also Lannoy/Colombier, 'Expédition', pp.181–2, 201, 217: see *infra* Chaps.4 and 5.

84. Delcourt, 'Relation du Voyage', p.2; Everaert and De Wilde, 'Pindanoten', p.2.

85. B/MAE, dossier AF7, B2019, 'Colonies Françaises [*sic*] 1840 July 1853, 29 May 1848', Cohen to Ministry of Foreign Affairs, Brussels.

86. Massinon, *Entreprise*, pp.323–4, 330, 343–5.

87. Everaert and De Wilde, 'Pindanoten', p.3.

88. Lieut. Collignon, 'A la Découverte de Van Haverbeke', *La Gazette du Soldat* (Brussels, December 1956).

89. Everaert and De Wilde, 'Pindanoten', p.6.

90. Ibid. and n.35, Cohen to d'Hoffschmidt, 21 December 1851.

91. Lefevre, 'Voyages', pp.559–62; Leconte, *Les Ancêtres*, pp.161–2.

92. Everaert and De Wilde, 'Pindanoten', p.6.

93. B/MRA archive, R. Boijen, 'Inventaris van het Archieffonds, Belgische Marine 1809–1845/6', p.8, 292. VH was born on 22 October 1812 and died on 7 September 1907. See also Delcourt, 'Relation du Voyage', pp.35–6.

94. B/MAE, AF7, B2019, 29 May 1848, Cohen to Ministry.

95. B/MRA, Sec B34 Marine, VII, II, 593–7, H. de Vos, *La Revue catholique des Idées et des Faits* (Brussels, 1954), p.6.

96. P. Crokaert, *Brialmont, Eloge et Mémoires* (Brussels, 1925), p.407. 'L'expédition fut sans lendemain pour nous. Le pays du Rio-Nunez devint colonie française en 1865.' Everaert and De Wilde, 'Pindanoten', p.1 (p.319 in original) 'een patriottische vulgarisatie'.

97. J-R Leconte, *Tentatives*, pp.142–5, on orders of VH to *enseignes de vaisseau* du Colombier, Tratsaert, and Dufour, 14 February 1849. It is clear that he knew more than he divulged to his subordinates, and that he anticipated a Belgian military occupation: 'Quoique j'ignore entièrement les intentions du ... le gouvernement lorsqu'il se décidera à occuper militairement la rivière' (Everaert and De Wilde, 'Pindanoten', pp.10–11).

98. For views about Bicaise, see Delcourt, 'Relation du Voyage', pp.13–16, 26, 28; C. De Wilde has generously made available his researches into Bicaise, including insights into his very 'African' way of doing business. See also Leconte, *Les Ancêtres*, p.167, n.1: 'le capt ... de la Tocnaye dit qu'il était Anglais, ce que nous ne croyons pas.'

99. B/MRA, Boijen, 'Inventaris', B34 Marine VII, 1850, Journal, p.3. '*Bicaise ... gai, rond et aimable hôte ... sorte de pacha, 12 esclaves, nombreuses femmes ... au reste n'étant d'aucun pays ... comme il dit*'.

100. F/MAE, see n.98.

101. See Chap.5 and Epilogue *infra*. Bicaise is still being described as British by the British ten years later; CO267/257, Gov Hill 87, 14 May 1857; Dr C. Fyfe to author, letter, 16 January 1996.

102. This study does not permit longer analysis of the role of the indigenous Nunez peoples in the affair. See N. Matthews, *Materials for West African History in the Archives of the United Kingdom* (London, 1973); however, see n.104 *infra*. For quotation, see W. Rodney, *A History of the Upper Guinea Coast, 1545–1800* (Oxford, 1970), p.18.

103. The metaphor of 'invisible eyes' links back to Chap.2, *supra*. Alone among the main participants in the Nunez Affair, the French naval officer, Capt. de Kerhallet, (from his earlier hydrographic visits for Capt. Bouët) and of course Bicaise himself, may be assumed to have had a deeper knowledge of the political state of things; to the other characters in this story, it must all have come as a surprise, both welcome and unwelcome, according to their situation.

104. The status of the Landumas is most probably that of one of the *refoulés* of the Upper Guinea coast, driven from the interior; they were an *envahisseur* of the Middle Ages, along with other 'pre-Mandingo' peoples, such as the Nalus and the Bagas. They drove out the previous autochthonous peoples, the 'primitives'. See Rodney, *Upper Guinea*, pp.1–39; also Thierno Diallo, 'Les Institutions Politiques du Fouta Djalon au XIXème Siècle' (Ph.D. thesis, University of Paris, 1924); W. F. McGowan, 'The Development of European Relations with Fouta Jallon and the Foundations of French Colonial Rule: 1794–1897' (Ph.D. thesis, London University, 1979), Chap.4, pp.165–210, and *passim*. An alternative explanation by Figarol, that they only arrived in Guinea in the eighteenth century, has been pointed out by F. Beavogui, Conakry University, letter to author, June 1994. There is as yet no single account of the Landumas on record, and given the centralizing nation-building policies of modern Guinea, the prospect is not promising. Today this former distinct ethnic group has been absorbed into the Soussou peoples, part of the populations of the republics of Guinea, and SL. See Lefevre, 'Voyages', vol.22, p.573, n.17. See also *Grand Larousse encyclopédique* (Paris, 1962), vol.5, p.717. Also, J. Suret-Canale, *La République de Guinée* (Paris, 1970), *passim* and p.14, 'un pays carrefour'. Linguistically they are, in Hargreaves's analogy, part of Africa's *Völkerwanderungen* of centuries producing a 'baffling mosaic . . . a historical palimpsest awaiting decipherment'. See Hargreaves, *Prelude*, p.14. See also J. H. Greenberg, 'The Languages of Africa', *International Journal of American Linguistics*, vol.29, no 1, January 1963, p.167. For wider perspectives on Africanist history of West Africa, see O. Davies, *West Africa Before the Europeans* (London, 1967); A. J. Ajayi and M. Crowder, *History of West Africa* (London, 1971); A. G. Hopkins, *An Economic History of West Africa* (London, 1973); M. Priestley, *West African Trade and Coast Society* (London, 1969); R. Oliver and J. D. Fage, *A Short History of Africa* (London, 1974); and R. Oliver, *The African Experience* (London, 1991); J. Flint, *Cambridge History of Africa* (Cambridge, 1976), vol.5, 1790–1870, Chap.5, p.170, *et seq.* Chap.6. See Epilogue for the European legacy in Africa.

105. Rodney, *Upper Guinea*, p.111.

106. Rodney, *Upper Guinea*, *passim* for overview; Capt. Belcher RN, 'Extracts from Observations on Various Points of the West Coast of Africa Surveyed by HM Ship *Aetna* in 1830–32', *JRGS*, vol.2, 1832, p.283; also Lieut.-Com. Thomas Lysaght, 'Report on the Rio Nunez, its Trade and Resources', *JRGS*, vol.19, 1849, pp.29–31. For civil wars, see Bruce Mouser, 'Trade and Politics in the Nunez and Pongo [*sic*] Rivers, 1790–1865' (Ph.D. thesis, Indiana University, 1971), and Bruce Mouser, 'The Nunez Affair', *BARSOM* (Brussels, 1973–4), p.739, n.53; also the author's condensed version of 'Sabre'; also Gov. Ingram, 'Expedition up the Gambia', *JRGS*, vol.17, 1847, p.574.

107. J. Grace, *Domestic Slavery in West Africa* (London, 1975), p.20 quotes M. Crowder, *West Africa under Colonial Rule* (London, 1968), pp.16–17. For analogy, see Jonathan Swift's *Gulliver's Travels*.

108. Lysaght, 'Rio Nunez'.

109. Rodney, *Upper Guinea*, p.17.
110. Lannoy/Colombier, 'Expédition', pp.184–5.
111. Mouser, 'Trade and Politics', pp.11, 31. The use of masks and stilts by the traditional Simo is still in evidence in current books about Guinea's rich folklore, which has obstinately survived the brief but would-be ultimate Marxist interventions — the social 'demystification' campaigns — of the Sékou Touré years from 1959 to 1980. See D. Cruise O'Brien, J. Dunn and R. Rathbone (eds) *Contemporary West African States* (Cambridge, 1989), pp.1–11 and *passim*: 'The West African States . . . an allegedly artifical entity, the creation of European colonial rule'. See also Claude Rivière, *Mutations Sociales en Guinée* (Paris, 1971), pp.26, 31, 232–8; and Claude Rivière, *The Mobilization of a People* (Cornell, 1977), p.14 for explanation of term 'Guinea', the Berber *aginau*: a person whose language is incomprehensible. The Portuguese applied it to all the southern region, between Senegal and Gabon. It extended to cover the piece of cloth used as money by the early English traders and thus to the gold coin for the value of the piece of cloth.
112. Lannoy/Colombier, 'Expédition'.
113. Mouser, 'Trade and Politics', p.304; T. Howard, *Eye-Witness Accounts of the Atlantic Slave Trade* (Boston, 1971), p.25.
114. See Chap.4 *infra*, and particularly the statements and unsubtle colonialist language of VH.
115. CO267/217, Tongo to Campbell, for Gov. SL, 21 October 1850; see Chap.5 *infra*; also Mouser, 'Nunez Affair' article for ingenious analysis of the filial relationship between Tongo, his younger half-brother, Mayoré, and the former king, Sarah.
116. Delcourt, 'Relation du Voyage', pp.18–9. '*Homme assez grand et qui avait l'air robuste; sa physionomie était impassable et ne décelait aucun sentiment de plaisir ou de crainte; il portait des souliers et s'abritait du soleil avec un méchant parapluie, comme insigne de sa dignité il avait le chef couvert d'un chapeau à forme conique à fond rouge avec festons.*' Also FO 123/69, Whitchurch, 28 Somerset Street, Portman Square, to Forster, 28 December 1850.
117. For comparable observations, see also Ingram, 'Gambia', pp.150–1. *Gris-gris* — collections of all kinds of 'small objects of desire' to which were attributed magic protective properties — included penknives and teeth. Devout Muslims would incorporate quotations from the Koran in their 'gris-gris'. 'I have seen men and women so laden with their *Gris-Gris* that the shape of their persons was not discernible, and were apparently as destitute of symmetry as a rum puncheon.' For description of the appearance of the peoples of the Nunez, see Lefevre, 'Voyages', vol.22, pp.574–8.
118. Lysaght, 'Rio Nunez', 1848 visit.
119. Brooks, 'Peanuts', p.50. This article by the authority on the history of this part of Africa throws valuable light on the reasons behind the development of groundnuts at this time, as well as on the roles played therein by both F&S and Senegalese, French, and African traders. For French aspects, see Hargreaves, *Prelude*, pp.50, 94–5.
120. For phrase 'The affair within the affair', see the author's 'Sabre', and 'Palmerston and the Nunez: The Affair Within the Affair, 1849–53', *JICH*, vol.23, no.3, 1995, pp.395–426. As will have become apparent, the 'Rio Nunez Affair' meant very different things according to varying national viewpoints.

4. The Clash of Arms, the Quest for Truth, the Veils of Deception: Actions in Africa and the Return to Europe, Spring 1849

Shortly after dawn on Tuesday, 13 February 1849, eight days sailing from the Gambia, Joseph Braithwaite and George Martin watched with interest as their captain skilfully engineered the *Princess Royal* away from the sand bars of Sandy Island on their port side, and approached the mouth of the Nunez. The sharks and flying fish and dolphins of the open sea were left astern. At the suggestion of Thomas Jackson, the pilot they had recruited at Bathurst, Captain Venn had handed over the wheel to him as they approached the estuary. Backed by a light sea breeze, they sailed slowly past the dangerous-looking rocky flats of Young Gonzalez Island to the starboard, with its distinctive coarse red sandstone, just visible above the waterline. They emerged into a broad, calm basin, some three miles wide. It seemed as is they were entering some innocent primeval world, still blanketed in the dawn mist: a peaceful green paradise. There was no hint of the inferno that was later to be unleashed.[1]

On either side of the river was a pleasant curtain of greenery — mangrove trees with their octopus-like roots, huge bulbous baobabs, coconut palms and oil palms, with little villages of round thatched huts on stilts, scattered along the banks. This, Joseph and George learned, was the territory of the Baga peoples, the rice-growers of the river, who still went around 'in a state of nature', as Captain Belcher had described them some years before. As they sailed slowly upstream with the tide over the next few hours,

Joseph, armed as usual with his eyeglass, could see vistas through clearings in the thicket, and picked out plantations and small settlements. Antelope, deer, wild oxen and other animals grazed by the water's edge. He caught glimpses of half-submerged alligators in the swampy mud at the river bank, and the sinewy shape of a python between the tall rushes; every so often the outlines of some of the river's predators — a pair of tiger cats, a pack of hyena, and even at one moment, a leopard, could also fleetingly be seen. Occasional groups of monkeys swung noisily through the branches, disturbing the sea eagles, herons, spoonbills and bengalis — a kind of waxbill — as they went along. Further inland they could see and hear guinea fowl and doves above the trees; now and then a vulture would rise menacingly into the air, and then suddenly swoop down again out of sight, seeing or scenting the fresh carcass of some dead or wounded gazelle.[2]

To their port side, some five miles up-river, they passed the higher ground of Victoria, with its groundnut plantations and orchards of pineapple, oranges and mangoes. With a population of some 200, this was the property of the widow of the former American trader and slave-dealer, Skelton.

A hippo wallowed quietly in the mud at the mouth of the small river that flowed into the Nunez a little further upstream. The air here was still freshened by the winds blowing in from the open sea, although the river was now beginning to narrow slightly. They scarcely noticed the smell of the mud and rotting vegetation at the mouths of the many streams where swamps were created at high tide. They were now moving into the middle river, the territory of the Nalus; they drew past the villages of Caniope and Cassacabouli, where the three chiefs lived: Lamina Towl, the worldly-wise head of the group, Carimon the devout marabout, and Joura, the fighter. A little further inland they saw the first of the French factories, that of Monsieur Santon, at Katekouma. No hippo, let alone elephant, were to be seen here: the industrious and commercial Nalus hunted both species for their ivory. It was said that not so long ago, one elephant was killed in an average day.[3]

Although it was the village of Debucca further upstream where they now 'contemplated residing', their first landing point was to be the little port of Ropass, lying on its own broad creek, some 30 miles inland, where they hoped — through Jackson's introduction — at least to make contact with Forsters' former agent and factor,

John Bicaise. Ropass was known to have developed rapidly, almost to becoming Bicaise's fiefdom — it was not even mapped by the celebrated Captain Belcher back in 1832; now its 500 inhabitants were all involved in one way or another with the Bicaise *comptoir* and its economy. There was uncertainty in this, however: Forsters had stopped supplying Bicaise with goods because they had found him an unsatisfactory debtor. At the outset, therefore, his attitude and his allegiance were in question; with hindsight he was seen to be 'anti-British', but this was not known at the time.[4]

On the opposite side of the river from Ropass, to the northeast, the land started to rise above the plains, in a series of terraces; far away, a small herd of elephant came into view. The rich red iron-bearing soil was very little cultivated, as far as they could judge from on board. In the main stream, beyond Ropass, the river's banks rose above the high-water level, its course lost to view as it curved and twisted out of sight. The high country of Futa Jallon dominated the skyline to the north, swathed in a grey haze.

The clusters of round mud and thatch huts were becoming more numerous; the first sight of Ropass on the port side, set in its own inlet, half a mile wide, still came as a surprise. Here was a small but well-established factory compound, Gambian in its style and purposefulness, fortified with cannon at strategic points, with locked warehouses, and dominated by an elegant little stone-built two-storey building to the northeast of the central clearing, complete with a piazza, an echo of the house of William Forster at Bathurst.[5] Instead of a few fruit trees, here in the flat rich country that stretched out to the west were orange trees, lemon, lime, pineapple and mango growing in ordered abundance. On the starboard shore there were taller trees in the forest beyond the huts that housed the inhabitants; from their experience on the Gambia, Joseph could pick out some superb mahogany, and the African oak which passed as 'teak'.[6]

Their ship's boat brought them to the landing stage, alongside several other ships lying at anchor. The change of air became apparent immediately; it was thicker and more humid here, as the green walls closed in on them, blocking off the breath of wind from the estuary. The smell of the swampy muddy shore assailed their senses. They rapidly realized that there were mosquitoes and other insects all about them; large black cockroaches flew onto the

deck, sunned themselves briefly and flew off again. Kingfishers of
a rainbow of hues darted through the air, close to the water. This
was new ground, carrying a new message, which needed to be
taken seriously.

Their initial encounter with Bicaise was short and sour. This
was anything but the 'jovial and hospitable host' that other
visitors to Ropass were to record. Although this was indeed a
'man of colour', in the phrase of the day, and with the familiar
dark sallow skin tone of the established African trader, born of
exposure to the dry harmattan wind, this was not a man of the
Nunez.[7] They were not welcome here, that much was obvious;
Bicaise was not prepared to lease any of his warehouses to them.
The reasons for this frosty reception from what was, by hearsay at
least, a fellow British citizen, were less obvious, other than that
Bicaise seemed to have no time for anything that had to do with
Forsters. It became clear that there was now nothing for it but to
go further up river to their destination of Boké, where previous
British traders had done good business in an earlier generation.
Bicaise also seemed to be very preoccupied with the visitors
already ashore who had preceded them from the Gambia, the
officers of the armed Belgian schooner, the *Louise-Marie*;[8] they
spoke French with a thicker sound than Joseph was used to from
his time on the Gambia, evidently a Flemish accent.

Jackson found a Susu interpreter for them, and some local
Krumen Grumettas and a new pilot who were willing to go up-
river with them to Cassassa, where they would help tranship their
cargo and provide a fleet of canoes to transport their stores to
Boké; the deeper draught of the *Princess Royal* would prevent her
from taking them further. Once more, this time with a small
armada, they cast off, the tide carrying them upstream from
Ropass for Cassassa; from there, Captain Venn would then sail
down-river again and on to Freetown to pick up a further cargo of
goods for them, and also to seek a return shipment to London, via
the Rio Pongas. The captain of the *Louise-Marie* watched the
proceedings with more than a little interest.[9]

The river above Ropass at once took on a new and more
dangerous character, as it serpentined its way sinuously between
riverbanks, hollowed out from the enclosing forest, which came
nearer and nearer to each other as they worked their way
upstream; the sharp bends and elbows made navigation hazard-

ous, even for their new pilot, one of the highly skilled group of
Kru seamen who specialized in this service to traders. The signs of
habitation became much less frequent. They were now moving
into the lands of the Landumas. Although Bicaise had said nothing
about it to them, there were reports of trouble: Captain Thomas
Lysaght of HM Steam Vessel *Grappler* had been investigating the
scene again recently.[10]

Soon, on their port side, Kandouma, the village of one of the
senior Landuma chiefs, Dibby, was pointed out to them; on the
opposite bank was the first of the two 'sacred woods' of this still
pagan people — or aborigines, as others called them. After moving
by under the lee of a high hill, Bancafelt (or 'Bancoflette'), and still
on their port side, the pilot pointed out the former factory site of a
British slave-trader of earlier in the century, Dr Walker, although
they learned that the old title on the maps, Walkeria, had been
superseded by the name of the local Landuma country, Kacundy.[11]
Down in Ropass earlier in the day, the temperature had been just
bearable at 33 °C. Now their thermometer registered 38 °C, and
still rising; the thought of an equivalent humid heat of more than
100 °F in England did not bear thinking about. There was no air,
scarcely a breath of wind, and no sound except for the echoes of
the paddles and of the Krumen's rythmical singing reflected from
the trunks of the massive boabab trees at the water's edge. It was
particularly dense and oppressive at this point; even the monkeys
were unaccountably quiet. Their pilot put his finger to his lips,
and whispered that the dark forest to starboard was the second of
the sacred groves, where the Landumas' secret society, the Simo, a
kind of 'druidic' priesthood, created their *gris-gris*, and practised
their rites.[12] All kinds of 'magic' went on, ostensibly protecting the
Landuma territory. Erring strangers would be immediately cap-
tured, and circumcized, even put to death; there was talk of
human sacrifice. No one dared to go there; the Kruman was
uncomfortable even to talk about it. An unaccustomed feeling
came over both Englishmen, something quite new and outside
their previous experience of Africa, for all their familiarity with its
differences and challenges. It was if they were suddenly moving
back in time, and leaving all known landmarks and signposts
behind them.

Towards evening, they pulled in by a small clearing at the
former small village of Cassassa; they noticed the ruins of an old

warehouse there. Here they started the laborious process of unloading, while constantly guarding, their complicated consignment of crated merchandise. They spent the night there on board ship, under the canvas across the deck. Next morning, at sunrise, leaving their Krumen behind, Joseph and George took a canoe party further upstream. Rocks of closely-grained basalt closed in on them as they steered through a narrow gorge. Four miles above Cassassa, they arrived at the first real opening in the forest. Joseph started to revert to the country ways of thinking that he and Cousin William had followed in the days of their youth, when they would go out wildfowling together in the Shropshire countryside — the only time he had carried arms: 'we go left here' still came more naturally to him than 'starboard', 'port' and 'forrard'.[13]

To their right, round a bend in the river, rose the gentle wooded hillside of Boké. Open ground reached up to the king's village, with its traditional rounded huts, on the crown of the hill, to the northeast. There were some trading factory buildings, but they looked uninhabited. Word must have preceded them: they had seen many young men running in and out of the trees along the river path, keeping pace with them as they worked their way northwards. An excited crowd of Landuma men, women and children gathered at the landing stage, as their canoes started to draw towards the shore and tie up; they seemed friendly enough.

The Calm Before the Storm
The traders' first task was to climb the hill to the Landuma village, said to comprise some 2000 people. They needed the permission of King Mayoré and his elders to hire a factory on his land, to get a store built at Cassassa, and to establish the traditional 'landlord and stranger' relationship. This was accomplished with the usual ceremonies and the giving of payments and 'custom' — presents of various kinds, including alcohol.[14]

There was a vacant site lower down by the river, to the north of the small ravine which divided the hillside, later described as being between 500 and 1000 yards to the left of the landing stage. Previously it had been the factory of an English trader, the late Samuel Daniel Ellam the elder. His son, Samuel Daniel the younger, was available to work for them as their clerk, and the business was concluded. They took on a cook, John Farmer, and

Samuel Johnson and young Billy Ellam as their servants. The two traders went back with the canoe party to Cassassa to start the next stage, the laborious process of hauling up part of their off-loaded and unwieldy stores by canoe to Boké; it was to take more than a week to get them even that short final leg of the distance. The minute their new trading station was functioning, the news was passed by word of mouth along the Fula coffle trail to the interior, and they began to trade. The formation by Bicaise of a purported 'closed shop' of traders, his Chambre de Commerce, had led to an evacuation of the other traders from Boké; there had been a complete cessation of activity, and a brisk unsupplied demand had built up. Even over the next few weeks, and despite attacks of sickness, Braithwaite and Martin would trade some £200-worth of produce, exchanging 500 hides, some beeswax, ivory and five ounces of gold dust, for their trade goods.[15]

There is no evidence as to when Braithwaite or Martin sized up to the situation in which they now found themselves. There must nevertheless at the very least have been a degree of naïvety about their reaction. It would have been quickly made clear to them that Mayoré was on bad terms with the traders down-river, that he cannot have been blameless for this state of affairs, and that there had to be something opportunistic about the warm welcome that he gave them. Yet 'free trade' was the watchword of the day, at least for Europe's dominant nation, Britain. Moreover, the Nunez was, in principle, covered by that Franco-British Convention of 1845, not a territory that either of the main competitive European powers could stake claim to without the agreement of the other. One of the reasons for Richard Lloyd recommending the Nunez was that it was, theoretically, in Palmerston's later words 'a great highway of Commerce open to the traders of all Nations'; in practice it had become an Anglo-French preserve, with an occasional American presence as well.[16] There was certainly a measure of unthinking British optimism, even pride — in the way that the two traders set to, and pragmatically made the best of what chance seemed to have placed in their way: the possibility of doing immediate business, with no other traders on the spot to undercut their prices. They were not to know that they had in fact entered a veritable lion's den of complexity, menace, and indeed prejudice; Joseph and George would have needed the divine intervention enjoyed by a Daniel to emerge unscathed.

A lot happened on 27 February; it was a key date in the Nunez Affair. One event with an unforeseen outcome had been the arrival of HMS *Favorite*. The commander of the British West Africa squadron, Admiral Hotham, had been caused by the Admiralty to send one of his infrequent missions to the Nunez.[17] Visits to what he called these 'pestilential rivers' had never been popular, even less so after the lessons at last being learned from the disasters of the Niger expedition seven years previously.[18] There would later be an enquiry into the protection that the navy provided on the Nunez, following a complaint by Forsters; Herman Merivale, Earl Grey's new Permanent Under-Secretary, concealed the evidence.[19]

The British representative, Captain Murray, arrived with a haughty request to Captain Van Haverbeke, on board the *Louise-Marie* — this irritating 'third party' — to caution him against infringing the rights of British traders, but in effect to warn him off the river. Murray was unaware that the Belgians had covered their tracks carefully beforehand, through the diplomatic channels. This fact had not yet been communicated by the Foreign Office to the Royal Navy.[20] The Belgian captain declined to accept the warning, saying that the legal agreement at issue was only struck between the French and the British, and therefore did not bind the actions of any third party. Considering the superior strength of the British navy, this was bold stuff. However, the British accepted his logic, apparently glad for an excuse to get back on board.[21]

There was a nice irony in this development, totally unappreciated by those concerned. The Belgians, who were to be one of the main factors in the calamities about to befall Braithwaite and Martin, had as much right to intervene in this territory of Anglo-French dominance, however inconvenient to those established powers, as the two Britons had to set up in competition with the Chambre de Commerce which had been formed by Bicaise, in order to outwit Mayoré.[22]

Meanwhile, Bicaise and his fellow traders now gathered at Ropass were concerting their actions with the Belgian party, in order to put an end, once and supposedly for all, to Mayoré's increasingly intemperate demands and actions against them, as well as to get these troublesome newcomers out of the running. Matters had been boiling up for some time. It all finally came to a head over what was in fact a side issue, that of the still covertly slave-dealing Ishmael Tay, and the woman, who according to

Lamina Towl, was (together with his bought slave Sally) one of his three wives — Mayoré's sister Massoonkung, and her little son, 'still at the breast'.[23]

King Mayoré, understandably pleading that his sister was vital to the succession traditions of the Landumas, and should therefore never leave the Boké territory, had first tried to keep her there; then when she and the child managed to escape to Ropass, he had sent down the man who had acted as her guarantor at their wedding, John Bateman, on pain of forfeiture of his goods at Boké: he brought them both back by force to the Landuma capital again on 27 February.[24] Their protector at the Santon residence, Monsieur Avril, later declared: 'They violated my home ... uttering furious cries, their swords raised against me'.[25]

This abduction had nothing directly to do with the established traders' legitimate commercial grievances against the unpredictable king. However, it certainly entailed a forcible entry onto the property of a French trader, and it infringed the respectful relationship that traders then expected from the indigenous peoples of their adopted territories. Also, since Ishmael Tay came from Senegal, French citizenship became a factor. Although Van Haverbeke had been instituting arms drill and firing practice from 20 February onwards, this was now intensified — a daily routine up to at least 6 March. The abduction was the final straw: it provided the *casus belli*. The 27 February was the turning point.

At this precise moment Bicaise could claim that he had had no other European military force but Van Haverbeke to appeal to: this he had duly done, through one of the procedures of the Code Napoléon, a *procès-verbal*.[26] Belgium's real interests were not merely commercial but colonial; Van Haverbeke rapidly concluded that these fundamental purposes of what he had secretly described to d'Hoffschmidt in January as the Belgian *campagne*, could suddenly be unexpectedly furthered by lending his support, particularly now in the absence of either of the two protecting powers. The Britons later surmised that Bicaise carefully waited until the *Princess Royal* had set sail for Freetown on 24 February before acting.[27]

On 26 February an ostensibly peaceful visit to Mayoré at Boké had been envisaged, to seek Belgian treaty rights for the upper river, to complete those now ratified with the Nalus for the river banks between Ropass and Victoria. Now the plan changed. Van

Haverbeke set off instead with a well-armed collection of vessels, including Bicaise and his sloop. As they reached Cassassa, Bicaise was incensed to notice that Mayoré and his men were building a warehouse on property that Bicaise purported to believe was his; Mayoré told him that he was doing it for his new 'strangers', and that the ground had only been lent to Bicaise. This was all the pretext that Bicaise needed in order to open his own private war on these two British intruders into his domain, whose competition he so evidently feared and resented; Mayoré was later to declare that Bicaise had started this process of exclusion right after their arrival, with an attempt to bribe Mayoré with a gift of 2000 dollars if he would refuse to deal with them. Mayoré had apparently replied that he would not do so even for 100,000 dollars, since Bicaise had never previously asked him to do anything for him.[28]

There was still nobody else around to guide Van Haverbeke's hand politically, or contain the increasingly militaristic spirit of his officers and men.[29] Right on cue, the French presence reasserted itself that same day, in the person of Captain de la Tocnaye, at the bridge of *La Recherche*, dispatched to the Nunez by Bouët-Willaumez, after he had learned on 23 January of the Belgians' arrival on the scene; the future admiral was determined to ensure that the Belgians did not interfere with his personal ambitions, which coincided with his longer-term strategy for France in West Africa. To the surprise of de la Tocnaye and his officers, he further reinforced the French naval strength with the arrival on 12 March of Captain de Kerhallet on *La Prudente*, an officer familiar with the history of the Nunez civil wars of the past few years, and also the trusted confidant of his powerful squadron commander.[30]

Meanwhile, the first armed expedition to Mayoré at Boké was followed by a lower-key visit on 3 March, headed by one of the later chroniclers of the Boké battle, Themistocle du Colombier. On 5 March, Van Haverbeke sent a note to de la Tocnaye asserting both that the Nunez was a Belgian possession, and that its neutrality was guaranteed by France and Britain. He claimed he owed a duty of protection *'aux commerçans des nations amies'* (a description that might be thought to include Britain). He concluded, in terms that, under the actual words, suggest some uncertainty: 'I am certain ... that you will approve the measures which I took in the interests of all.'[31]

There was a second fully-armed expedition on 11–12 March, led this time by the commander who had now at last managed to wrest back the initiative from the Belgians, Captain de la Tocnaye. Thus, within three and a half weeks of their arrival, the two British 'strangers' would have become aware on at least three occasions, from the comings and goings over at Monsieur Bicaise's landing stage, and from their contact with their new 'landlord', that things were taking a new turn.

As the diplomatic tussle of the next four years bore directly on the timing of the events of the next two weeks, it is necessary to record exactly what happened and was communicated, and what the practical, and geographical, implications were. Several factors need to be kept in mind. First, however reprehensible to a twentieth-century perspective, it was a normal, legitimate aspect of European trade on the coast at this period to sell arms to the Africans: no moral stigma was attached to it. Braithwaite and Martin were even subsequently to obtain a letter from Captain Denman, of Gallinas fame, to this effect.[32]

In parallel, however unwise it might appear in hindsight in the particular circumstances of the Nunez situation, there was also nothing untoward in supplying alcohol to the Africans: everyone did it, as a normal part of their trade; the Africans not only demanded it, but would not have traded without it. The gift of 25 litres of Geneva gin on 23 March to the less than battle-hungry Landumas, assembled under the red flags of Mayoré's elder brother, Tongo, was to feature as a very straightforward part of the pre-attack plans of the French and Belgians — 'to encourage them to fight'.[33]

Third, it was not the mere distance from Ropass that was significant in the events about to unfold; it was the tortuous nature of that stretch of river. It was difficult to navigate it with any vessel, let alone a collection of canoes laden with cumbersome merchandise, designed for conveyance in the hold of a merchant schooner. Much more to the point, as anyone would realize, by the time of the events of 16 March these goods had been unpacked and broken out. Even messengers running along the shore path needed four hours to reach Boké.

Furthermore, European concepts of ownership were not common ground. What Bicaise might at least plausibly have argued to be a cession of freehold title, could well be held by

Mayoré to be merely a temporary lease; in any case, he manifestly could not own all the land at Cassassa. Later on, what the Belgians firmly claimed were binding contracts of land transfer with Mayoré's half-brother, Tongo, did not apparently have anything like that sense of finality with him. As tradition put it, 'the water was the Europeans': the land belonged to the Africans.'[34]

Last, it was a normal part of the life of African peoples to defend their villages with stockades; this tradition was well-established at Boké. However, such matters were entirely outside the knowledge of two purely commercial men, each brought up in the English countryside, and with no known army experience. They declared later to Palmerston that they would swear on oath that they had had nothing to do with it all.[35] Uncorroborated hearsay — what Joseph called 'presumptions' abound in this story; it can be safely assumed that Bicaise, advised by Cohen, pounced on anything to implicate his two new rivals. A blatant example was the later 'canard' that the Britons were the masterminds in the defences that Mayoré was about to build for the protection of Boké. De la Tocnaye was later to describe to Acting Governor Pine 'formidable defensive preparations, better thought through than those normally erected by the blacks'.[36] Another significant factor that later investigations did not pick up was why, in such an implausible scenario, the two traders had not embraced their own buildings within such a fiendishly European-inspired defence system. It was all to turn on the hearsay evidence of the opinion attributed to one man, Lamina Towl, who played an equivocal and fluctuating role in the proceedings, seeking always the best advantage for the Nalus, depending on who seemed to be winning. His white top hat and his umbrella were not merely objects of curiosity: they were the outward symbols of his position of authority on the river, a role that was to be executed relentlessly to the advantage of his people.[37]

Critical to an understanding of the time factor, it was not until 15 March that the two commanders sent their ultimatum of war to Mayoré. It was only the day previously that they sent the first of the two written messages to the two beleaguered British traders: their wording and timing are vital. One initial message was never sent: this was to have warned them of a potential state of war. Against expectations, du Colombier could report of his 3 March visit to Mayoré, 'My mission had been peacefully concluded . . . therefore I did not declare war.'[38]

The first message, delivered not directly, but via the house of Mayoré, dated 14 March, stated baldly:

> We reserve the right to take the most energetic measures, inviting you to leave the village of Boké immediately . . . placed this day under a threat of war, which might break out from one moment to another. It is up to you to take advantage of this notice, you will become personally responsible for the damaging consequences which your stay in this enemy village may entail.[39]

Critically, war was not yet declared, only threatened — no 'rules of war' yet. This message did not reach them until the following day. Contrary to their own over-generous recollection of this first message, even then there was no mention of how they might deal with their merchandise. There was no offer of transport; no hint of assistance. They replied with a short letter using the same formula, saying that it was they who would hold the French and Belgians responsible for any acts committed against them, relying on the threat of the protection implicit — as they patriotically believed — in the British flag.

Braithwaite and Martin translated their recollection of the second equally uncompromising message, which as they later pointed out to Palmerston, reached them only eight days before the expedition against Boké. It was untempered with any suggestion of practical concern about what was at stake for them, and sent jointly as from de Kerhallet, on behalf of de la Tocnaye, and from Van Haverbeke.[40] Although dated 15 March, a Thursday, Cubely, the messenger from Bicaise, did not leave Ropass until 9.00 a.m. on the 16th, and did not get to their house until 1.00 p.m. Their remembered understanding of its contents was as follows — and what they were enabled to understand was what mattered, not what the commanders might have wished to imply: even the gullible naval officer who was later to come and investigate — Monypenny — was to concede that there could have been misunderstanding about the warning:

> The River will be blockaded on Friday next [i.e. on the day

of its receipt], after which day no communication will be allowed between Ropass and Debucca. We give you 48 hours from this day [i.e. the 15th, by which time three-quarters of the warning period had elapsed] to come down the River with your goods and place them in a place of safety [despite the fact that within six daylight hours the river would be impassable]. No transport will be allowed either by land or water for any Arms.[41]

As they were later to write, in desperation, to the governor of the Gambia, on 9 May, the British traders' available transport was nil, and their stores were considerable — 400 to 500 guns, 22 barrels of gunpowder and much else besides.[42] They were caught, as indeed it now has to be assumed they were intended to be, as the purported collaborators and master military strategists of the tiny Landuma army: the timing and language leave no other interpretation, whatever the subsequent efforts of the French and the Belgians were to the contrary.

The two Britons could only reply with their normal precision, at 1.30 p.m., returning it by the same messenger that very day:

To the commanders of the French Corvette *La Recherche* and the Belgian Schooner of War *Louise-Marie* off Ropass: We have this moment received your letter dated Ropass the 15th Instant. ... In reply we have only to repeat that we shall hold you personally as well as your respective governments responsible for any loss or injury to our Property in the Nunez that may arise from whatever measures you may think proper to adopt towards King Moyra.

We have not interfered, nor do we intend to interfere in the quarrel between King Moyra and Ishmael: we came to the Nunez for the purpose of carrying on a legal Trade and we rely on the British Government of whom we are subjects for protection in carrying on the same.

Were we even disposed to go down from Debucca, the time given is not sufficient as more than a week was occupied in bringing our Goods from Cassassa to this Town.[43]

Palmerston ought, in principle, to have been proud of these two *cives Britannici*, defiantly manning the frontier of the Queen's informal empire. He most certainly would have applauded their pluck, when he read the papers subsequently, in particular their detailed statement of January 1851. Whether this was the wisest stand to take, under the darkening cicumstances, is open to debate. Braithwaite and Martin were in 'frontier territory' in more ways than one. Not only was the Nunez a significant geographical and linguistic dividing line between the peoples and terrain to its northwest and southeast, but Boké itself was the frictional meeting point of the Islamic Fula presence to the northeast, with their tributary, the still unconverted Landumas. In European legal terms, it was no man's land — *res nullius* — halfway between the nearest seats of British colonial jurisdiction, Sierra Leone and the Gambia. However, they were unquestionably within such rights as could be asserted by two lone traders, 50 miles up a remote African river, with no defence other than their trust in the omnipotence of the Union Jack, and in the traditional protection of an African landlord for his strangers. Their bold but gentlemanly response was to be castigated by the French as 'insolent' in the later diplomatic exchanges.[44]

The Battle of Boké

As a setting for a melodrama, the battle of Boké had many of the essential ingredients: a heroine and an infant heir to a disputed throne, at least one plausible and cunning villain, two innocent if misguided strangers, a bibulous king imbued with fraternal if not quite fratricidal hatred for a half-brother: Tongo was King Sarah's son by another wife, possibly even a slave girl. In addition, there were multiple misunderstandings, jealousy and ambition, heroism and cowardice, patriotic pride, and challenges to the courage and honour of several naval commanders — all set against a background of European and African cultural tensions. A combination of a totally false reliance on old superstitions, a defensive outlook, and raw numbers, was pitted against an admittedly smaller force of some 200 well-trained and by now highly motivated men, blessed with the absolute advantage of superior technology. Practically every wrong imaginable would be perpetrated: murder, abduction, arson, pillage, burglary. What the situation did not have was the redeeming quality of a fair contest; the Landumas were 'panic struck' from the first. As the two traders were later to assert to Palmerston, 'What resistance could a small village composed of Mud Huts offer with a few Muskets against round shot and shells from two vessels armed as Men of War?'.

No account of a battle can be impartial. The battle of Boké, however, was the subject of several eyewitness accounts. The best known up to now has been that of Lieutenant du Colombier, who had to rely on the story of his colleague, Ensign Dufour, for the narrative of the actual fighting, since he himself was not in the attacking party; that simple fact gave rise to many of the distortions that history has handed down.[45] Du Colombier's 'journal' is also remarkable for its visual sense, both in words and in line; his descriptions of many of the figures in the incident read as freshly now as in 1849. At the back of his rough notebook are the drawings he did of the faces he observed on the Nunez, another singular record of that time, showing an ambivalent attitude, part benign, part prejudiced.[46]

For a recreation in words, however, it was the leader of the attacking force, Captain de la Tocnaye, who most vividly conjured up the atmosphere of that morning, comparing the strangely deserted scene with that which had met his astonished eyes on the occasion of his first visit: 'A mournful silence ... no cries, no pantomimes or warlike dances, no war-drums or trumpets, no *griot*s with their piercing shrieks and their grotesque movements, no threats or gestures.'[47]

For a colourful, albeit incomplete and inevitably one-sided story of the six days from 22 to 27 March, the account published in the *Journal du Commerce d'Anvers*, of 6 July 1849, which Joseph Braithwaite translated, copied out in his neat hand, and carefully preserved, provides as good a picture as any; Lord Howard de Walden was to send the original back to Lord Palmerston on the same day, for study.[48]

This was the letter which one of Abraham Cohen's civilian colleagues in the Belgian barque *Emma*, Constant Dossche, sent back ahead of him to his brother Leon, at Antwerp. It was the truth as it had been vouchsafed to him and was only one of several newspaper stories of the exploits of Belgium's sons in distant waters; it does not appear in the British official account of the affair.[49]

Belgium's free and independent press, with its anti-French tone, was later to become a key aspect of the outcome of the Rio Nunez Affair. Its purely pro-Belgian coverage of the Nunez battle helped in the short term to create a climate of patriotic opinion which was to prove a determining factor in the way in which matters developed. This article was notable for the minimal attention paid to the Landuma's side of the story, and to the complete absence of any reference to two British traders and the damage that was known to have been inflicted on their property amidst all the carnage. For this reason it would have undoubtedly made its point with Palmerston, suggesting some kind of bias in the Belgian approach, or even grounds for suspicion, as his later comments were to underline.[50]

Journal du Commerce d'Anvers

The article opens with two paragraphs which give the full flavour of the chauvinism with which the news of 'the battle of Boké' was heralded, and of the wave of emotion that then began to pressurize the official mind. Apart from the incident at Risquons-Tout in the heady libertarian spring of 1848, when an insurgent Paris-led attack was repulsed on the French border, this was Belgium's first clash of arms as a nation.[51]

> We believe ourselves to be pleasing our subscribers in communicating the extract of a letter from one of the actors, M. Constant Dossche of Ghent, in the naval battle which has taken place on the African coast at Rio Nunez. It is with a lively satisfaction that we observe the honourable conduct maintained by the country's navy in these circumstances, under the command of its captain, Van Haverbeeck. [sic] We also record with pleasure the courage and intrepidity of Merchant Marine Captain Witteveen, one of our fellow citizens. The report made by the French commanders to their government speaks of this sailor with the highest praise. It is to be hoped that the government, in its sollicitude for all that can contribute 'pour rehausser le nom belge', will worthily reward those who have contributed so well to this end.
>
> Rio-Nunez, Rospas

> Mon Cher Léon, I confirm the letter I wrote you at Gorée which place we left the 28th January; we staid [sic] successively at Bathurst, Albréda, Cacheo, Birrao [sic for Bissao], and we arrived here on the 11th of this month, at the extreme position of the states of King Lamina.

I shall pass over what I could write to you concerning the places we have visited, and the sickness of nature; my next letter will make you fully acquainted therewith.

On our arrival we found here Commander Van Haverbeeck and his Schooner of War, the *Louise-Marie*. Seven or Eight leagues higher up the river is the Town where King Majoré, the Chief of the Landoumas resides — This King particularly befriending the English, wished to hinder the French and Belgian traders from making Trade in the Upper part of the River. After many interruptions previously, King Majoré had insulted the French traders and had without cause driven away his half Brother Ishmail Say, depriving him of his wife and son aged Four years. (The loss of the child is of this importance, the son of the king does not succeed his father here, it is the Eldest son of the king's Eldest Sister who is the presumptive heir to the Crown.)

The insulted French complained to Mr Van Haverbeck, the only Man of War Commander then in these parts. He went into the lower part of the River where he fell in [sic] with two French Frigates, *La Prudente*, Commander De Querrellay, and *La Recherche*, Commander De la Tocquenay. These commanders arrived at Ropass with their Boats.

The three Commanders having resolved on going to demand satisfaction from King Majoré for his conduct towards the French and Belgian Traders, and Ishmail Say being with them to make his just complaint, many large Long Boats conveying the two French commanders with 85 men, with whom were joined — equally well-armed — 30 Men commanded by M. Van Haverbeck, and accompanied by Messrs Bicaise (the Principal Trader of the Country), Cohen, Brisart and Bols, my travelling companions, and many other persons, merchants of the Country, proceeded to Debucca. I was prevented by illness from making one of the party.

The king in Council with his Ministers received the deputation very well when he saw it so numerous and so well-armed: he made all sorts of promises, even that of sending his Sister and her Child to Ropass the following day. Two days after, the party returned, filled with joy and happiness. The Captains were however much disappointed when on the following day they received a very cavalier letter from the King, in which he announced that he would have nothing more to do with them, and begged them to leave him alone. Indignant at such conduct, the Commanders resolved to give King Majoré a severe lesson. By a requisition dated the 18th, Captain Witteveen, of the Belgian Barque *Emma*, was required in the name of his Government to place his Vessel at their disposal from the 20th for an armed expedition. The 19th we landed, opened the remainder of our goods in M. Bicaise's Stores, and the 20th we responded to the requisition. This day Captain Witteveen assembled his Crew, and informed them what was going to happen, and what was required of him; he added that each man was at liberty to accompany the expedition or to go ashore, where the Board and lodging would be excellent, seeing that the expedition would present perhaps the greatest dangers. Not one of the crew would leave the Vessel — I was the only one of us four who joined the expedition: M. Brisart who was in the lower part of the River knew nothing of it — M. Cohen being very busy ashore remained there, and M. Bols was obliged to remain to assist him, notwithstanding his desire to accompany us.

In the night of 20th to 21st we received on board 182 armed sailors and twenty officers and Midshipmen, and then the day following our Vessel was if by enchantment transformed into a Vessel of War. The two Cannon we had on board were increased by Eight more.

On the 22nd at 2 p.m., three vessels left for Boké (Debucca); these were the *Emma*, the *Louise-Marie*, and the *Dorade*, a French Schooner which like our Vessel they had transformed into a Vessel of War, putting on board her Six Cannons and Fifty Men. At Landouma [*sic*] the *Louise-Marie* was compelled to anchor as she drew too much water to proceed any higher up the River. Commander M. Van Haverbeck, his officer M. Dufour, and twenty men then came on board the *Emma*.

The next day at 7.00 a.m. Captain Witteveen, who manoeuvered his Vessel himself, anchored her, one anchor forward and one aft, presenting the Starboard side to the Town of Debucca, in such a manner that the artillery could attack the most prominent points of the place, so that afterwards the landing could be effected with more ease and more security. The *Dorade* took her position behind us, making fast with a Rope to our Stern, and carrying out an anchor astern of her. When the two vessels were well moored, the three Commanders took their measures for commencing the attack. The Black people are in the habit in like cases (Case of War) of beating the tom-tom and making an infernal noise; this time the most sullen silence reigned all over the town: this derogation from the manners of the Natives we considered the presage of an obstinate resistance on their part.

Boké extends from the river just to the top of a steep Hill of about 300 metres [325 yards] in height; the town is protected on the right and left by very high and wooded hills, the River before the town is not more than 50 metres [54 yards] wide. At a league distant we saw numerous groups of armed men, ready to fight, unusual preparation in this country having been made. Seven Cannons, among others a 24-pounder, were pointed upon the Vessel, at thirty paces from which were raised strong barricades for protecting men armed with Muskets, who opened fire on us through innumerable loop-holes.

Towards 8.30 a.m., when the Tide was sufficiently high, Commander De la Toquenay gave orders to fire and at the same instant we were answered by a discharge of grape shot and well aimed fire of musketry. You know, Leo, that I have no more fear than others, but I can tell you that I saluted the first shots (that is, I bowed my head). This first discharge wounded some of us; in an instant the deck was covered in blood — from the middle of the deck two howitzers played continually under the practised hand of Commandr Van Haverbeke — M. de la Toquenay managed the cannon — Captain Witteveen managed the Vessel. I kept my place for a quarter of an hour on the Poop, with Commander De Querrelay [*sic*] and M. Witteveen, when we received a discharge from the larboard side; we soon commenced with grape shot from both sides with the 10 Guns at a time, as did also the *Dorade* — I now quitted the poop and took a place on the main deck; the action had lasted 42 minutes when we were enabled to go ashore. A Shell fired by Commander Van Haverbeck decided the business.

King Majoré was in Council with his Ministers, in his house situated behind a barricade; the shell fell in the midst of the Council, killed two Ministers and wounded three others. The King thought it was most prudent to leave the place, those who were at the Guns followed him. We then effected a landing. Commander de la Toquenay took the centre, M. Dufour, officer of the *Louise-Marie* the right, Commanders De Querrellay and Van Haverbeck, as well as myself, the left. Although the enemy had discontinued firing their Cannons, our landing cost us dear; every moment the wounded were being taken on board. Captain Van Haverbeck, having posted himself on a hill, fired his shells, which could not fail of making great ravages among the enemy. (He knew so well the management of these projectiles that he seldom missed his aim.) In an hour afterwards we were masters of the town and its environs within a circumference of more than a league.

Then commenced the Pillage by the Black People. The Commanders had strictly forbidden their Sailors to carry anything no matter what it might be on board. After the Pillage succeeded conflagration. The Town was set on fire and destroyed from the bottom to the top, more than 500 houses in the suburbs [*sic!*] were served in the same manner.

Towards five o'clock in the evening we returned on board after the Carpenter of our Vessel had spiked four of the enemies' Guns; one of them went off during the operation, and if it had not been for the experience of this old soldier,* five or six of our men would have then lost their lives; the fifth Gun, which was smaller than the others, was dragged down and carried on board, and Commander Van Haverbecke ordered six of his men to go to set fire to the 60 or 75 houses on the other side of the River, because we had also been fired at from that side: they were not pillaged as there were no Black people among the men sent, but the whole of the houses became a prey to the flames.

The French and Belgians being all returned on board, the Black People went ashore a second time, and destroyed what remained of the Town.

---

* 'A veteran of Waterloo!'

At 11 p.m. the two dead men we had on board were
consigned to awaiting graves with all the Ceremonies usual
aboard a Man of War. Commander De la Toquenay
delivered a Funeral Oration to the Sailors during a mournful
and solemn silence, interrupted at intervals by the reports of
Musketry and Cannon, communicating to the country round
the melancholy news aboard the Vessel. After the ceremony
the wounded were conveyed in large boats down to the
Louise-Marie.

The following day at 10 a.m., we departed for Ropass. We
were fired upon all the way down, and the situation of the
commanders became most critical. Captain Van Haverbeck
placed himself on the bowsprit in order to point out to
Captain Witteveen — the place being very shallow — the
direction the Vessel should proceed, for in the Upper part of
the River, the navigation is excessively difficult. This was the
first [*sic*] Vessel that had been seen at Boké. Notwithstanding
the dangerous spot in which these two people were standing,
they saw all the manœuvres executed with admirable
coolness, regardless of the showers of bullets whistling about
their ears. They were the targets for the enemy who knew
that our welfare depended on them. Commander Van Haverbecke only left the bowsprit to fire the Shells at the enemy,
Captain Witteveen continued to manœuvre his Vessel notwithstanding the danger to which he was exposed where he
had placed himself.

We reached the Belgian Schooner at 3.00 p.m., when we
anchored, as did the *Dorade*, until the following day at
Noon. The *Louise-Marie* had a quarter of an hour's start of
us when we suddenly heard a brisk fire of musketry.
Commander replied to it by means of his Cannon, and the
firing became so astonishingly energetic that we supposed,
and that correctly, that Captain Van Haverbeck was
experiencing a severe attack; we used every exertion to rejoin
the *Louise-Marie*. In a quarter of an hour we found that
Vessel aground abreast of a thick wood, situated on a hill,
and called the Sacred Wood. We placed our Vessel before
and the *Dorade* behind the stranded Vessel, and our guns
loaded with grape shot answered the vigorous fire of
musketry from the Shore. The natives were most advan-

tageously placed, protected as they were upon the ridge of a Hill by trees of gigantic size.

During this time Captain Witteveen exhibited heroic courage; wishing to convey assistance to the stranded Vessel, he proceded on board the *Louise-Marie* in a small boat in the midst of the briskest firing of musketry; he returned on board the *Emma* and left a second time for the *Louise-Marie* to convey to Commander Van Haverbeck something he was in need of. His noble conduct received on his return the eager congratulations of the two French Captains, admirers of his coolness and bravery.

One of the Landouma Chiefs had placed himself near the water's edge behind a large Tree, from which position he had fired for two hours, with impunity, on us [*sic*]. More than twenty-five Cannon Balls fired at the tree could not force him to quit his post, and to the cannon he replied with his musket. Commander De La Toquenay pointed five cannon against the tree loaded with bullets; at the first fire the wood shook again. I placed myself then behind the bulwark waiting for our enemy, leaving his position, to make him acquainted with my carbine. At the second firing of the cannon, our land lord [*hôte*, host] left the tree to conceal himself in the wood, but had scarcely gone ten steps when my ball overtook him and stretched him on the ground, amidst the acclamations of all who witnessed it.

Commander De Quelleray came and congratulated me on my good shot, and while we were together, a ball passed between us, grazing the epaulette of the Commander, and lodged in the bulwark against which I was standing.

The firing lasted until 7 p.m., and again we had the victory, but not without paying dear enough for it, for it was there that our countryman, M. Dufour, officer of the *Louise-Marie* who had exhibited much bravery and energy, received a shot in the head which wounded him dangerously and disabled him. We had two killed and twenty wounded, of which a dozen were seriously so; but I have the satisfaction to be able to inform you that the doctors have assured us that our worthy friend M. Dufour is out of danger, and he will not be disfigured.* Towards 9.00 p.m. the *Louise-Marie* floated off without any damage; the *Emma* took the lead, the *Louise-Marie* followed, then came the *Dorade*, and towards midnight we arrived safely at Ropass without any other accident, after a furious fight of three days.

The Natives, after the terrible lesson which they have received, seeing that they cannot insult the Whites with impunity, we notice already the respect they have for us. We can be certain henceforth that trade will not be any longer shackled by these men who require force to make them let it exist.[52]

This is, my dear Leo, the accurate and veracious recital of the war in which I have taken part.

Au revoir, Mon Cher Léon. Je te serre amicalement la main.

Signed — Constant Dossche.

The Second Battle: Deception and Truth

When the two traders at last dared to come out of hiding in the surrounding bush later in the day, and survey the smouldering scene of crime, the stark horror of what they had experienced, and miraculously escaped from with their lives, began to sink in. Practically nothing remained of the warehouse and stores, save for a set of scales, some iron bars, and some hides: even though all the goods in which their savings had been invested were now destroyed, with hindsight the even more damaging fact was that none of their papers had survived the burning and looting.

With extraordinary resilience, Joseph Braithwaite and George Martin resolved there and then to start to do something about it. Who would believe such an unbelievable story? They would clearly need to prove the truth to others — to the nearest British authorities, at Freetown, or the Gambia, or to any known — and as they now needed to qualify it — trustworthy British presence they could identify; they could only think of the JP, Mr Campbell, down at the Isles de Los.[53]

---

* Postscript at end of column. 'Late news informs us that the hopes of the doctors have been realized and that in fact M. Dufour has been spared.' It is another of the ironies of the Nunez story that Ensign Dufour was saved, to then become the vehicle for distorting the subsequent understanding of these events.

King Mayoré, with his senior chief, Dibby, was still alive, though shaken by the attack and the loss of many of his warriors, most still lying where they fell in the forest, in pools of blood.[54] He returned to Boké once the attacking forces were safely back at Ropass, short-sightedly secure in their victory, and believing that their 'rude leçon' had been decisively delivered, once and for all. With great sang-froid, and despite their state of shock and outrage — helped by their loyal servants, Samuel Ellam, John Farmer and Samuel Johnson — Joseph and George began to take statements, with formal witnesses, from anyone who might bear testimony for them. They did this working from the relative safety first of Samuel Ellam's home at Correra, two miles above Boké, and later from John Holman's factory 24 miles downstream at the village of Catougama, ten miles upstream from Victoria: they had to get there all the way on foot.[55] Martin in particular, his fever beginning to abate, was still in need of rest and medication.

A start was made. By 30 March, three tenuous depositions were in their hands, from Mayoré and John Bateman, the first of 50 pieces of paper, the beginning of a year-long crusade of evidence-gathering, which was to take them to the highest councils in the land, and be copied and argued over between three of Europe's leading foreign ministries.[56] On 2 April, not knowing that their addressee was away in England, they sent a bold but correctly-phrased request to 'His Excellency the Governor of Sierra Leone or the officer Administering the government'; (legally there was always a second in line). They asked for nothing less than the provision of a 'man of war' to get them to the Gambia, to start to seek redress for what they, and later Palmerston after them, called this 'outrage'.[57]

At first the French, the Belgians and the traders under Bicaise's wily hand thought they would get away with it. They acted as if they really believed the 'bad rumours' reputed to be circulating along the river about Braithwaite and Martin's complicity and aspirations, as well as about their capacities as planners of African defence systems. Over the next three months, seven veils, each serving in its own way to obscure the truth, were spun by different actors in the drama, some by now familiar, some new to the story. This is not counting the two different deceptions that Van Haverbeke himself was also pulling off, with some success, both against his new French ally and against his apparent protégé, Tongo.

The first and perhaps most effective of these concealing effects was the letter from Bicaise, Cohen and four of the French traders, as early as 30 March — writing this time in French — proposing the award of Swords of Honour, at a cost of 19,000 francs, to the two naval commanders, de la Tocnaye, and Van Haverbeke. The two Britons were to be immortalized in the design as a wicked serpent, throttling Bicaise and company.[58]

Next came an action by de la Tocnaye which was clearly his top priority, even taking precedence over the duty to report to his superiors. On 2 April he wrote a politically astute three-page letter — interestingly and perhaps apprehensively, addressed to 'M. le Gouverneur de Sierra Leone et ses dépendances' — (these included the Isles de Los) — in which he set out the post hoc justification for his actions, and sought to establish his bona fides vis-à-vis Great Britain.[59] He at least conceded one point that was later to get buried under the sandbanks of claim and counterclaim: 'For a long time, serious differences had existed between King Mayoré and all the traders.'

However, he then asserted that Bicaise was (at least in this context) British, and that the expulsion of Ishmael Tay was 'motiveless', ignoring the point about the Landuma traditions for the heir to the throne. He purported that the two traders were warned on 11 and 12 March of the 'possible eventuality of a battle'. As to the morning of the attack of 24 March, he portrayed Braithwaite and Martin as being 'in the midst of the enemy', and accused them, incredibly, of not sending anyone out from their warehouse 'for any kind of explanation': this was presumably supposed to take place in the face of the assembled Franco-Belgian fire power. He concluded most plausibly, but as it transpired mistakenly, 'I come to ask you most respectfully for justice in respect of this behaviour which could renew the irritating debates between two countries ... whose people live in such a good entente despite the current state of things in Europe.'

In fact, following the heady days of the outbreak of France's Second Republic in March 1848, and the decoding by Palmerston of the real meaning behind Lamartine's libertarian messages, relations between the two Foreign Offices were surprisingly good: 'Vive Lamartine!', had been Palmerston's reaction.

De la Tocnaye followed this clever letter with two long reports on 15 and 28 April, one 'circumstantial', and one on the political and commercial considerations that caused him to act as he did, this time to his own commanding officer, the head of the French west Atlantic station at Gorée, Bouët-Willaumez. In this letter he tried to establish that everything they had done was within the framework of the commander's own orders, 'with the aim of worthily upholding the honour of our flag, our influence on the coast of Africa, and the integrity of everything which pertains to our nationality and to the advantages of a well-ordered commercial activity'.[60]

From the point of view of the affair as it developed, what makes these reports of de la Tocnaye's so revealing is not simply the self-justification of their every line, but a new admission that does not appear elsewhere. The two Britons are not mentioned anywhere. It was not they who advised Mayoré, but his own people from the nearby river. 'Some miserable strangers from the Rio Pongas, his habitual advisers, had persuaded him that the moment had arrived to finish with the whites once and for all.'

Even more significant were his commandant's subsequent sceptical comments in the margins, and the underlinings of passages that he seemingly found hard to swallow. On the claims that the attacks of their enemy at one point called for great heroism on their part, Bouët-Willaumez made the acid aside, 'moreover this fusillade was not at all dangerous'. In apparent irony, borne out by the Britons' later comments, the commandant scored de la Tocnaye's phrase, 'but it was very fortunate that the [people] of Debucca had not put up a greater resistance.'[61]

The other piece of evidence that has now surfaced after 150 years is that of the dereliction of duty of the gubernatorial command at Freetown. This lay not merely in the failure of the acting governor, Benjamin Pine QC, to espouse the cause of his two countrymen in distress, who were technically outside the Sierra Leone jurisdiction, although in common decency he could have done more than he did. Colonial governors on the west coast of Africa had to fight with most of the Colonial Office cards stacked against them — particularly Pine's boss, Macdonald, then in England on leave, in whom the censorious Earl Grey had little confidence.[62] There was an ever-present danger of rebuke, or even formal censure, awaiting them if they incurred unapproved costs or undertook military action, especially beyond their boundaries. The history of the settlements throughout the first half of the nineteenth century is littered with examples of governors — including Forster's friend, Maclean of the Gold Coast — who fell into this 'catch-22' trap. If they acted out of moral or practical conviction, they risked criticism in London; if they refrained from acting on the spot — and in time to achieve anything — they risked censure from those around him.

Acting Governor Pine had had to do something in response to the message of 27 March which had been passed on to him by Benjamin Campbell. On 18 April, he instructed a naval officer on HMS *Sealark*, Captain William Monypenny, to sail to the Nunez to investigate, possibly in line with where he thought his absent governor's own sympathies might have lain; he also carried back, two weeks after the event, the acting governor's inadequate reply of 18 April to the traders' cry for help of 2 April.[63] This was the same luckless Monypenny who earlier in the previous decade had already blotted his copybook: 'he accidentally lost sight' of his parent ship, Captain Belcher's *Aetna*, while in charge of a small boat, 'with four hands . . . off the Straits of Gibralter'. Having lost his way, he 'providentially succeeded in reaching Plymouth in his flimsy tenement after a passage of 19 days.'[64] As events were to prove, Monypenny lost his way again, but this time morally, rather than physically. On arrival at Victoria, on 22 April, Mony-penny received word that Braithwaite and Martin were now at Catougama. He sailed on up to Ropass where he was welcomed by — who else — John Bicaise, no doubt this time with his 'Nelsonian' persona well to the fore. Moneypenny was accommo-dated in Bicaise's comfortable house, and treated assuredly to the traditional Bicaise hospitality. In the words of the Englishmen's statement two years later, they questioned whether 'these Gentle-men impartially performed the important duty in which they were ordered'. Of Bicaise they wrote of the 'anti-English feeling of this man'. The British captain duly took a deceptively short deposition from Bicaise himself on 25 April. In this Bicaise blatantly lied that the two traders had arrived on the river about 'three or four months ago' — whereas he knew that it was only two and a half months previously.[65] The longer they were thought to have been on the river, the more they might be expected to understand what was happening, on behalf of their brother 'whites'. Disin-genuously, he also said that he had warned them to move down to Ropass on about 15 March: 'I knew from experience that there would be some disturbances.' Indeed he did: he had instigated them.

Monypenny then took a detailed six-page statement from Braithwaite and Martin, and from two independent traders, John Holman and William Miller, who were taken into custody by the attacking force on 23 March, ostensibly asking them to act as interpreters with Mayoré, but actually professing to suspect them of spying for the king.

There was to be much lofty reference by the French and the Belgian commanders to 'the rules of war', as if this was some mighty conflict, in which events assumed an unstoppable momentum. Such was the whipped-up state of martial spirit among the forces, that later, in a statement in 1850, Captain de Kerhallet was even to declare that within the rules of war, Holman and Miller could have been shot on this suspicion. Given that these two traders 'were fully Cognizant of the whole of the misunderstanding between Mayoré and the French', they were lucky to escape: they knew too much.[66] One principle of war which the evidence of both Holman and Miller underlined was the basic rule of taking every last chance to avoid the bloodshed of your own or your opponent's men. Both traders offered to go up to Mayoré's house on the very morning of the battle, when they arrived under guard at Boké, but were told that it was too late. The same answer had been returned to Mayoré when he sent a last-minute offer of compromise to Ropass about Ishmael Tay and his wife and baby. For the intemperate and increasingly impatient French and Belgian commanders, only force could now avail. Another Frenchman has pointed out the problem of 'staying seated on a throne of bayonets' — 'on peut tout faire avec les baïonnettes sauf s'asseoir là-dessus.'[67]

Monypenny made his report to the governor on 1 May in which he did at least volunteer the view that there had been no a priori need to endanger the Braithwaite and Martin warehouse, as it was completely out of the line of fire from the river to the king's village on the crown of the hill. 'We are quite of the view that the town itself might have been totally destroyed without the slightest necessity for injuring the stores.'[68]

However, that concession made, he went on to make a range of arbitrary judgements which undermined the Britons' case. There was hearsay evidence that 'natives' had gathered on the hill behind

the store, and even that Mayoré had been seen to go there for
succour, only to be turned away by the traders, who were determined to stay neutral, however ungrateful it might appear, in the
appalling dilemma now facing them. This fact caused Monypenny
to fall into the trap of raising matters to the plane of a full-scale
war and advance the opinion that 'the attacking force had been
quite justified by all the usages of war in directing their fire
towards that locality.'

That assertion would be parroted later by Palmerston's own
Permanent Under-Secretary, Addington, as if it were the final
word on the matter.[69] Thus the main thrust of Monypenny's
report, made on the limited basis of such evidence as he had
bothered to unearth — which even Bicaise castigated as merely
'curiosity' — was that it was all the fault, not of the aggressors,
but of the victims: this is an accusation that has a disturbingly
familiar historical ring to it.[70] No doubt the acting governor was
satisfied. He was glad to be able to get rid of the report by the
next mail packet to Earl Grey at Downing Street, lending weight,
by subtle semantics, to the reliability of Monypenny's report. In
this dispatch, de la Tocnaye's letter of 2 April was classified as
'explaining the circumstances'. Monypenny's report is predicated
on the need for 'accurate information'. Pine made no comment on
the documents, in the light of 'the departure of the mail . . . nor do
I think that they require any. The report is clearly written and
would appear to show that Messrs Braithwaite and Martin have
themselves to blame for the disasters which have overtaken
them.'[71] An effectively deceptive framework was already being
built around the truth.

Pine's real failings, however, were covert and, in the end, even
more destructive of the interests of the two citizens of his Queen
and country than his overt statements. He allowed his private and
unsubstantiated view that the two Britons 'only had themselves to
blame' to circulate within the apparent confines of his office. On
23 May, that view percolated secretly to the French consul at
Freetown, Guillaumard d'Aragon, who promptly winged this
important item of espionage back to the commandant at Gorée.[72]

That single act, buttressed by Monypenny's cursory judgements
and despite Palmerston's later and characteristically perceptive
repudiation of the captain's superficial contribution, was to have
immense consequences for the outcome of the affair.[73] It was

further reinforced by a similarly treacherous breach of confidence by Monypenny himself a month later, to a French naval officer at Freetown, Capitaine Villemain, of the *Espradon*, who reported him as saying 'the French are not to blame'.[74]

This falsehood was echoed throughout the next four years, as indicating, in de la Tocnaye's words, that the British, as personified in this *haut fonctionnaire* did not believe in their own case.[75] Although the French could not have realized just how little the evidence of Captain Monypenny was to count for in Lord Palmerston's eyes, the damage was done.

Colonial Office Inertia and Prejudice

Between 1846 and 1852 the Colonial Office was not only overstretched and unappreciated as usual, but was in addition under constant criticism from various political factions, each sniping at Lord John Russell's minority government.[76] Its Secretary of State, the third Earl Grey, sat remotely in the House of Lords, and did not attend many Cabinet meetings; his department was represented — inadequately — in the lower House by Benjamin Hawes MP, 'a dull party hack, and owner of a Lambeth soap factory'. Grey had learned his departmental craft, and his attitude towards overseas governors and traders, at the hands of the celebrated James Stephen, when he first took office as colonial Under-Secretary in 1830. He has been described as 'an incubus on unfortunate colonialists' and 'crotchety and disputatious' — 'a lone figure occupying the second rank among Victorian politicians'. As far as West Africa was concerned, he was not well informed, and gave scant attention to it in his later writings.[77]

He was not expansionist, believing that ultimately the Africans would govern themselves. He had opposed Palmerston, and had actually prevented Lord John Russell from forming a government, in 1845, by virtue of his refusal to serve in the same administration as this 'blustering' Foreign Secretary. The two other members of his team were a former professor from Oxford, Herman Merivale — and Sir George Barrow, a 'baronet relic of the Old Corruption'.[78] The Colonial Office records suggest that neither was likely to bother to go out of his way to oppose their master's line of sentiment, let alone stick up for two tiresome traders out of sight and out of mind in 'no man's land', unless there were very good cause to do so.[79]

In that atmosphere so pleasantly removed from the hurly-burly of benighted 'commercial men' overseas, to use James Stephen's derogatory phrase, the most significant comment on the papers that were, after a month and half's delay, presented to the office, was that of the clerk, Sir George Barrow. He employed the hallowed phrase used to pigeonhole matters that looked like causing trouble with those superior brethren of theirs at the Foreign Office, led by his political master's senior but hitherto least favourite colleague, Lord Palmerston. He minuted languidly and disbelievingly on 13 June: 'I suppose this may be *put by* till we hear from the parties who consider themselves [sic] aggrieved by the proceedings?' Grey, however, decided to pass the buck completely — let Palmerston handle this one, it looked like trouble.

Foreign Office Priorities

Another factor obscuring an initial awareness of the new situation on the river was the Foreign Office's preoccupation with the territorial implications of the Belgian initiative, which went back to the news of the first Belgian interest in the Nunez from 1847 onwards; it was the sole British focus until the news of the Boké incident started to filter through in August 1849. Palmerston's basic instinct, conveyed to Lord Howard de Walden, and by him to d'Hoffschmidt, the foreign minister, had been to warn the Belgian government against doing anything which might lessen the rights of British traders in general. D'Hoffschmidt was now walking a tightrope with his colleagues; they had already unconstitutionally concealed the expenditure on their expedition, to avoid exposing the project to debate by their cost-conscious *députés*.[80] Now he realized that he had to allay the suspicions of the French and the British that the Belgian proposal would not impact on their nationals trading on the Nunez. The doubts of both Paris and London were eventually — and surprisingly — assuaged through the subtle diplomatic wording of the Belgians' communications. Sylvain Van de Weyer was in due course able to confirm direct to his master in Brussels, before Howard de Walden formally reported, that the British were 'satisfied'. General de la Hitte in Paris was to convey the same surprising but reassuring message to the Belgian ambassador in Paris, Firmin Rogier.[81]

Undoubtedly this concession, with its implication of a lack of

Sketch of the Town of Debucca and its Vicinity — Rio Nunez

J. Martin's drawing of scene of 'The Battle of Dubucca/Dubucka/Boké' endorsed as correct by Captain Lysaght RN showing the Braithwaite and Martin 'House and Store', A.

Cartoon of a jaunty 'Pam', popular 'bottle-holder between the European powers, 6 December 1851, just before his shock 'resignation', with the Palmerstonian 'signature tune' — the straw in the mouth, and holding his celebrated 'Protocols' — the allusions, and the humour, now obscured).

'Winston', an early Low cartoon of 'Winnie', print from supplement of 1 May 1926, with the famous cigar.

ABOVE. Belsize Court/House, Hampstead, nineteenth-century view from the south, family home of Matthew Forster.
BELOW. Captain Van Haverbeke of the *Louise-Marie*.

The Battle of Boké by J.P. Clays, Collections Musée royal de l'Armée, Brussels. The print (in P. Crokaert, *Brialmont*, p 407) identifies the Belgian three-masted barque *Emma* (left) and the French brick *Dorade* (right), 'le plus beau fait d'armes de la Marine royale militaire belge.'

The Belgian 'ally', Lamina Towl, king of the Nalus, Rio Nuñez, displaying the very European symbols of his authority on the river. Drawing
based on that of Ensign Massui (Leconte, 'Ancêtres, p 164).

Bicaise's house, the Franco-Belgian dependant *comptoir*, Ropass, Rio Nuñez. Litho by Jacottet trom Leconte (*Ancêtres*, p.172)

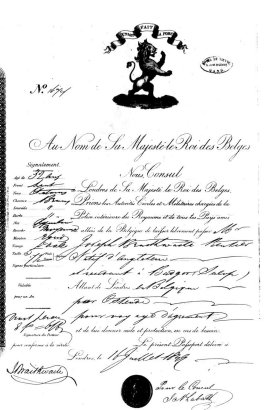

RIGHT. Cartoon from *Punch*, 10 January 1852, after the news of Palmerston's dismissal. The irony of depicting both these constitutionally appointed ministers as merely Victoria's 'servants' would not have been lost on anyone at the time (including the onlooking bust of Mr Punch) – except perhaps the Queen herself.

BELOW. Palmerston replying to the toast in honour of his *civis Romanus* speech, at the public dinner at the Reform Club, Saturday 27 June 1850.

British commitment to the Nunez, emboldened the Belgians in the stance they adopted towards Britain both then and later; it highlights the importance of the construction that can be placed on apparently innocuous diplomatic language. Neither government crosschecked this permissive signal with their naval commanders on the west coast, who had to deal with the situation on the spot. Captain Bouët-Willaumez, although told to cooperate with the Belgians, in practice countermanded that policy; Admiral Hotham, as was apparent when Captain Murray visited the Nunez, was not even told about it.

The final layer of the veils that served to obscure the truth about the incident was the filing by Van Haverbeke of his report with the Belgian Marine Ministry, on his return to Belgium on 17 June. His report must take its place as one more aspect of the political wrangles which were soon to unfold.[82]

The Delcourt Revelations

There was above all one incident within the attack which could well cause both the French and the Belgian commanders some uneasiness: the looting and burning of Braithwaite and Martin's buildings, which they were to deny as being the fault of the Fula people. The truth cannot have been unknown to the attackers, yet it is absent from both their reports, almost certainly by design. It has lain unidentified in the archives: surprisingly, no historian has either discovered it or seen fit to make it public, in the intervening 150 years.

This vital evidence, which throws a totally new light on the scene, was in the 36-page *journal de mer* of the most junior officer of the Belgian force, Aspirant (first-class) Guillaume Delcourt. It was faithfully preserved over the years by his daughter Françoise, at Antwerp, in unconscious parallel with the papers of Joseph Braithwaite in England.[83] This young officer, whilst an admirer of the British colonial manner as he perceived it on his outward journey at Bathurst St Mary, on the Gambia, was nevertheless no supporter of the British traders. Like all the other officers, French or Belgian, he never met them, but accepted the line fed to him by his seniors about their iniquity. His comments are typical of the beliefs that must have inspired the attacking force, and fired its actions: 'Despite the undoubted cooperation of the Englishmen, despite their alliance with Mayoré, nevertheless they had planted the white flag on their building: this treachery really incensed us all.' At a later point, Delcourt repeats the hearsay evidence that 'Majoré had been delivered over to the wicked advice of the Englishmen'.

This memorandum also illuminates much else in the real story. The most crucial section of his account reads as follows:

> We had already set fire to most of the village when as we came down towards the river bank, we reached the house of the Englishmen where the British flag was flying. We were surprised to see that the table was set, there were four fine places laid with silver cutlery; the whiteness of the linen, the transparency of the glasses, and the two bottles of wine standing on the table seemed to be inviting us to sit down and eat the meal so disastrously interrupted, but we could find neither the victuals nor the chef. This room was well furnished in the European style. A large bed still in disorder made us think that we had perhaps intruded upon a happy married couple. We forced open the door of the room next to this, and found a store beautifully equipped with all sorts of furniture, household utensils, cutlery, silverware, materials etc. Our men had enough respect not to take away any of these objects, apart from a few knives, some brushes and pairs of shoes, things of little importance.

Delcourt then offers a critical view of an unpalatable truth about two of his fellow officers, one of them the author of the hitherto accepted account of the actual attack, M. Dufour.

> We appropriated all the guns and gunpowder we could find, and after tearing down the British flag, M. Doriac and M. Dufour with one accord, but without reflection or discussion, gave the order to set it alight. This act was not at all wise, in my opinion, and perhaps in due course we shall have cause to regret having done so. However we could not set fire quite so easily to the building itself before the natives of our party, who had, it must be said, only come running up to join us at the end of the affair, had time to take away whole quantities of things. Many of them pounced on several bottles of rum which we had missed, and became so drunk as to lose all

reason. At last at about midday everyone got back on board ship.[84]

Several facts make Delcourt's testimony amazing. The first is that it demolishes at a stroke (and there is no reason to impute any ulterior motive to his account) much of the case that was subsequently to be built up by the French and Belgian governments about the complete innocence of Van Haverbeke's and de la Tocnaye's forces in the burning and looting of the British establishment. Delcourt himself went on to lead a distinguished career, rising to the rank of *ingénieur en chef*: his word is not to be doubted. As we now know, history pays him a small reward for his honesty. In the Military Museum's 'cabinet of fame', while Van Haverbeke has to content himself with that faded photograph in a dusty corner at the back, Delcourt's final full-dress uniform, and the story of his career, are set prominently in the centre of the display.[85]

Secondly, his account shows that a decision in principle to attack Mayoré, and thus by implication anyone thought to be on his side, was taken before any of the intermediate steps, which purported to offer the opportunity for 'palaber', were entered into. A martial spirit was being engendered among the Belgian forces, who were impatient to fight, as early as 27 February: 'February 27th: Ishmael arrived . . . some blacks had abducted his wife and his child . . . from that moment onwards war was decided . . . we train every day in target-practice.'

Moreover, it is clear from Delcourt's minute observation that, the Britons were certainly not expecting to be attacked themselves that morning in March. They were not manning the warehouse, but were about to have their normal civilized breakfast. The die was cast weeks before they even entered the picture. They evidently had no sense that they were to be co-defendants with Mayoré. They became the 'fall guys'.

By 11 March, Delcourt further reveals that he was seeing Mayoré and his people as enemies, in black and white terms, perhaps both literally and figuratively; yet the ultimatum for war was not issued until 15 March. The news that the Britons had conveyed 30 rifles, with ammunition, to Mayoré the previous night, was highlighted by de la Tocnaye to his men as proof of their complicity; the fact that no prohibition on such a transaction had yet been issued, and that it was therefore within the Britons' trading rights, was not even considered. Braithwaite and Martin produced several independent witnesses, including John Holman, that they refused to trade in arms once the prohibition was received, and Monypenny at least seemed to confirm it.[86]

By the crucial day in March, Sunday the 17th, when the traders were deemed by the French and the Belgians to have been given full warning of what impended, and of the help available to them, Delcourt records his belief, based on what he had been told by his superiors, of what was communicated to them: 'Communication was made to the English traders to withdraw ... on pain of running the risk of seeing their house burned, every transport facility having been provided for their merchandise.' That version is certainly not borne out by the actual messages.

Another inference to be drawn from Delcourt's journal is that, as Bouët-Willaumez was later to judge, the forces did not think they were attacking a superior enemy, but one they could beat: 'One circumstance worthy of note was the confidence with which we approached ever closer to Boké, the contempt which we expressed for the enemies which we were about to fight, indeed the lightness with which we treated the whole expedition. This low opinion of the courage of the Landoumas became more pronounced as we advanced.' This supported the argument presented to Palmerston about the inequality of the battle, and thus the lack of any necessity to extend the firing to their own stores.

One curious phrase in that account deserves a brief examination — Delcourt's discovery of a disordered bed in one of the two bedrooms, and his speculative description of it as perhaps the bed of a 'happy married couple'.

A particular piece of information about the British traders may well not have been known to him at the time, or to any of the junior officers and ratings from either contingent, since clearly the senior officers played things close to the chest. The fact was that both Joseph Braithwaite and George Martin had had attacks of a fever — probably a mild form of the malaria whose antitoxins must by then have been well-established in their systems. By his own account, Joseph may both have been the first to succumb, and also the first to recover: given the 10 to 14-day incubation period, his attack must have passed quickly, as they had only been on the river some 35 days by the time of the assault on 24 March.[87] George Martin on the other hand was still incapacitated by his fever on the very morning of the battle. As Joseph wrote later to Lord Palmerston: 'Martin might have been burnt in his bed.'[88]

It was assuredly Martin's fever-tossed bedclothes in one of the bedrooms that Delcourt observed when Ensign Dufour led his party into the warehouse and carried out the initial acts of pillage and arson. A prurient late-twentieth-century eye might look at two bachelors living far away from creature comforts, and allow in a question about the sexual side of their lives: did they simply practice abstinence for the sake and memory of a loved one back home?[89] Clearly, their business partnership broke up after the disaster, and they were to go their separate, seemingly celibate ways. No more can be surmised of Joseph and his possible feelings about Cousin Susanna, still tucked away minding the Mill in rural Badger.

If, as they were to claim confidently to Lord Palmerston, they had 'resided' on the west coast of Africa for ten years up to 1850, they must presumably have enjoyed the benefits that landlords traditionally offered their adopted strangers, namely the pick of whichever native women or perhaps one of their own wives their landlord chose to offer them during their time on the territory.[90] On the Gambia, as in Senegal to the north, the local women accepted a 'country marriage' with a European settler or trader as a matter of course, realizing equally that that it would end if their European returned to Europe. They might be left 'holding the baby' in more senses than one, but probably well enough provided for to survive, with some share in whatever business had been built up; many had gone on to become traders — and even slavers — in their own right.[91]

Whether or not Joseph and George had had such relationships elsewhere along the coast is unknown: it is almost certain that their budding commercial contact with King Mayoré would not have had time to flower into the full 'landlord and stranger' arrangement during their short, fraught time at Boké, even assuming they were to have had time for such relaxations. There was also the assumption, widely promulgated within the Royal Navy, and so by extension among the commercial community, that 'excesses' of any kind, alcoholic or otherwise, would pre-

dispose vulnerable Europeans to 'the fever'. Although there is
startling new evidence that there are still Bicaises alive in Guinée,
it seems highly improbable that the legacies of any Braithwaite or
Martin genes are still present on the Rio Nunez today: what
Delcourt observed was the extremely unhappy bed of a sick man,
who had only managed to rise from it in time to save his skin, as
the Belgian shells fell around him.[92]

The sole matter of importance is that neither the French nor the
Belgians took the minimum responsibility to find out whether the
two traders, the citizens of a friendly nation, were actually in a
state to decamp from their house at short notice, with or without
their goods. Even a brief first-hand visit would have made
Martin's condition self-evident, and might have shown the French
and Belgians that they were not dealing with another bunch of
tough dyed-in-the-wool 'palm oil ruffians', but simply two rather
prim, precise and peaceable — if also naïve and over-trusting —
English gentlemen.

On 5 April, de la Tocnaye, in the name of France, organized the
inauguration of Tongo as the successor to the apparently defeated
and deposed Mayoré; certain treaties were also drafted by the two
commanders. The French did not know that amidst all the
confusion following the return from Boké, Van Haverbeke would
succeed on that same day in securing from the newly-crowned,
and compliant and grateful king, an extraordinarily disproportionate concession of land rights along the banks of the Nunez;
this 'coup' was to feature prominently in the subsequent political
argumentation. For the price of a mere 5000 francs, Belgium
appeared to have acquired the provisional rights, subject to royal
ratification, on territory amounting to 25 square miles. It was
effected despite the fact that the Franco-Belgian friendship, sealed
in blood, was barely a week old. From a narrow Belgian perspective, this was a triumphant development of her secret colonial
mission, but as a piece of *Realpolitik*, to use that Bismarckian
expression anachronistically, it takes the breath away.[93]

On 24 April, by now returned to Gorée and on their way home,
the Belgians joined their apparent blood brothers to greet Captain
Bouët-Willaumez, who — significantly for the affair — had been
away during the Nunez happenings. He was now just about to
return from his own, and much celebrated expedition to a distant
territory — to be even more celebrated one day for its Albert

Schweitzer connection — the Gabon. Delcourt recalled their earlier 'glacial' reception by him on the outward journey, when he had refused even to meet Van Haverbeke.[94] They at least expected to be congratulated for their valorous achievements, but the events that followed his arrival the next day sadly confounded such expectations, and revived their first impressions of this fearsome commander, with his wider vision of true French interests. He had by now got wind of the official British complaints about the attack on the two Britons. He rounded on his two officers, to their 'consternation'; he had sent them to the Nunez precisely to prevent the Belgians stealing a commercial march over them, as well as to forestall difficulties with the ever-suspicious British. Delcourt and other officers in both camps suspected that he was also jealous of the apparent success of their mission compared with his own, in which, despite commanding forces greatly superior to those available for the Nunez, four French sailors had been killed, two in circumstances reflecting badly on the orders given them: 'Here was a proud and extravagant man, looking for any chance to grab the favours of his government.'

Whatever might be the cynical and understandably resentful comments of the aggrieved Belgians, who like their French fellow officers were getting no thanks from Bouët-Willaumez — he even cut out all reference to their exploits in his official order of the day on 1 May — he had rightly perceived one salient fact. Van Haverbeke had rushed in where 'other angels might have feared to tread'; he had not thought 'politically', and had all but got out of his depth by the time the two French officers arrived and took over. The problem was that, instead of damping down the situation, they had taken the same short-term view that there was only one way to deal with Mayoré. In a phrase that has come ringing down through the years, Delcourt writes: 'He was so angry that he accused the French commanders of having pulled the chestnuts out of the fire for the Belgians.' Braithwaite and Martin learned of this explosion through Richard Lloyd's letter of 16 June.[95]

The most abiding part of Delcourt's evidence of Bouët-Willaumez's initial accusation — that the French had got the Belgians off a hook of their own making — was that it was all unnecessary — that they had ignored a fundamental aspect of the African way of doing things: 'They could equally well have obtained justice through threats and parleying.' The Nunez had become a special ambition, even for the ambitious Bouët-Willaumez. Pushed to the limit by the entreaties of de la Tocnaye, and even of his friend de Kerhallet, to accept their reports, he feared — wrongly as it transpired — that what du Colombier called 'his dream' had been shattered. 'The Belgian commander had taken it from him ... one never forgave a man who had stolen from you something that you considered as your own creation.' In fact, the French commander's great dream was to survive for the next 100 years, as *Guineé*, a huge territory the size of Britain, developed as part of French West Africa, and flourished.

* * *

Meanwhile, on the Nunez, now that Joseph Braithwaite and George Martin had completed the process of gathering evidence, and, for better or worse, had also also given evidence themselves to Captain Monypenny, they could only trust in the wisdom and efficiency of Her Majesty's Colonial Office to support their cause. The main reponsibility for pursuing their rights seemed to be falling on Joseph's shoulders alone: George did not appear to have the stomach for it. They managed to secure a rough passage on the Swedish barque, *Statsraadet Foerhaus*, bound for Ghent from Catougama, and so back to England.

To describe their journey as from Catougama to Worthing is to invite the accusation of bathos, nevertheless that is the strange route they took. On 27 June they found themselves rowing ashore, two sad and quintessentially Dickensian figures, landing forlorn and unwelcomed on the beach of that small and as yet scarcely known Sussex fishing village, together with a bag containing their few belongings: visions of Magwitch come to mind.[96] They were alive, but destitute. They made their way by train to London, where they went their separate ways — Martin to his family at Saltash, in Cornwall, Braithwaite to his brother Charles and his family at Islington in London, although there could be no permanent room for him over the tiny shop at 8 Theberton Street. He made the first approaches to the Forsters in Bishopsgate to bring them up to date with the situation; all they knew was what Richard Lloyd had reported in his last letter. His boyhood friend and cousin William, at the Mill at Badger Heath, in Shropshire, offered him shelter. He took a train to Birmingham and thence a coach to Shifnal, where William and Susannah met him with the pony and trap.[97]

He set about carrying the fight for justice and compensation to its next stage. There were some big gaps. Richard Lloyd had written to them on 17 June at the Gambia, that according to Captain Derecourt of the brig *Nunez*, some of their guns and ammunition had been sold at Bissao.[98] There were even rumours that their merchandise had surfaced in Ghent itself, after the *Louise-Marie* returned to port. All this needed to be corroborated.

The first step was to try to track down where any foreign crew members of the Belgian merchant vessel involved — the *Emma* — could be by now: they might be prepared to testify, having no patriotic axe to grind. He realized that he would need to get over to Antwerp and Ghent to obtain some of the outstanding evidence about the disposal of their merchandise at first hand from any non-Belgian sailors who would be prepared to tell the truth. A special passport was needed from the Belgian authorities.[99] He naturally turned now to Forster & Smith. Matthew Forster MP, the rumbustious but good-hearted old campaigner, and his son John were eager to help. Matthew began forthwith to pull the political strings for which the preceding 35 years had prepared him, and which he understood so well.[100]

Lord Palmerston's only involvements in the Rio Nunez up to now had been first his concern, almost exactly ten years previously, in 1839, for the need to effect 'conventions' with the quarrelling native chiefs of the 'Landemars' and the 'Naloos', to bring about 'the cultivation of friendly intercourse and Commerce, and the Suppression of the Slave Trade'.[101] More recently, within the context of his growing interest in Africa and its commercial potential for Britain, he had raised the broad policy issue which he had instructed his minister at Brussels to investigate — the proposed Belgian settlements, and their impact in principle on the need to maintain free trade for all nations. Suddenly, and fortuitously, here was new ammunition for him to fight with. On 17 July, a clerk by the appropriate name of John Bidwell at the Foreign Office, one of a well-known family of loyal servants to this over-worked department, provided Joseph Braithwaite with a letter of introduction to the consuls at Ghent and Antwerp: fulfilling the promise of his family name, he had been well and

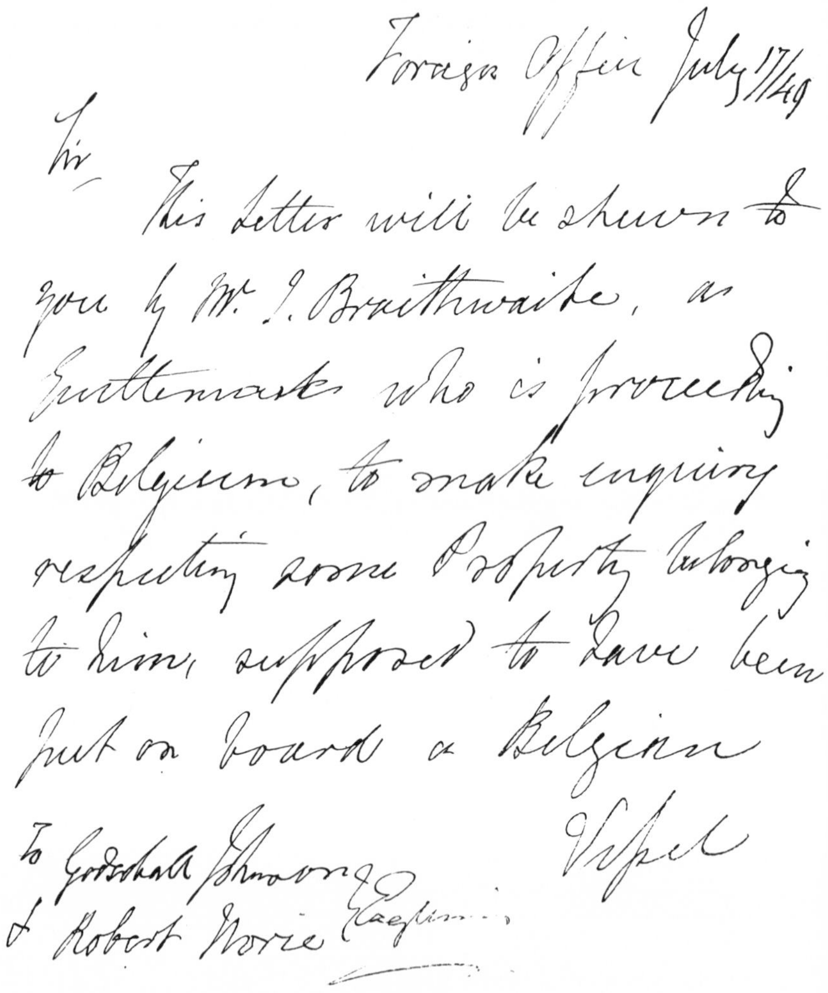

[handwritten letter]

Foreign Office July 17/49

Sir,

This Letter will be shewn to you by Mr. J. Braithwaite, an Guttemaster who is proceeding to Belgium, to make enquiry respecting some Property belonging to him, supposed to have been put on board a Belgian Vessel

To Godschall Johnson Esq.
& Robert Morier

FIGURE 4 Letter on Palmerston's authority, from John Bidwell, senior clerk, Foreign Office, London, to HM Consuls at Ghent and Antwerp, July 1849, author's collection.

expressly bidden to do so, by Lord Palmerston himself, who was now about to enter the chronicles of the Rio Nunez on a much more individual and personally committed basis.[102] The interests of two more of Britain's 'wandering sons', soon to be immortalized in Palmerston's words as representatives of his *cives Britannici*, were at stake.

Notes

1. The facts here and in Chaps 5 and 6 are drawn from the combination of Belgian, French and British diplomatic, colonial and naval archives listed in the Bibliographical Summary. The main PRO source is FO97/198 'France: Messrs Braithwaite & Martin's Claims 1849–1853', source used where no attribution given. Original sources have also been used in conjunction with the Belgian contemporary accounts, particularly the journals of du Colombier and Delcourt, and the accounts (1847–57) of the three Belgian doctors who took part in the eight Belgian voyages to West Africa (see P. Lefevre, 'Les Voyages de la Marine royale belge en Senegal', *Revue belge d'histoire militaire*, vol.21, no.23), as well as with data provided by C. De Wilde. In addition to the known published Belgian, American and British sources, Dr C. Fyfe, and Professor G. Brooks Jnr, have supplied expert advice about the West African trade at that period. See George Brooks Jnr, *Yankee Traders, Old Coasters, African Middlemen* (Boston, 1970), p.202, for ways of bringing ships upstream on the Nunez: 'African seamen were indispensable to vessels trading in the Nunez and Pongo. . . . Ships' boats were chiefly manned by the domestic slaves of the resident traders, Susu from the Pongo . . . Grumetes (domestic or field slaves hired from Bissao) or more frequently, as the years passed, by Kru from the Liberian coast. . . . African pilots were generally employed in the Nunez.' The later accounts of the actual incidents of March 1849 by French and Belgian writers have been largely superseded, in the light of the latest knowledge, as shown especially in Bruce Mouser, 'Trade and Politics in the Nunez and Pongo [*sic*] Rivers, 1790–1865' (Ph.D. thesis, Indiana University, 1971).

2. Few descriptions of the geography are contained in the original SGA/B papers. All the topographical descriptions, and those of the fauna and flora, are taken first from the accounts by Capt. Belcher RN, 'Extracts from Observations on Various Points of the West Coast of Africa Surveyed by HM Ship *Aetna* in 1830–32' (*JRGS*, vol.2, 1832, pp.278–304) during his two explorations, see *infra* n.11, which Forster, who kept himself well informed, would certainly have pointed out to his associates travelling to the Nunez. They also derive from Lefevre, 'Voyages', see n.1. See also topographical data in A. H. Barrow, *Fifty Years in Western Africa* (London, 1900), pp.19–22.

3. W. Rodney, *A History of the Upper Guinea Coast, 1545–1800* (Oxford, 1970), p.157.

4. SGA/B doc. FP 17, 28-page statement by B&M, with skilful assistance from Forster, in London, of January 1851, to P, refuting what they term the 'infamous insinuations' of de Kerhallet's and de la Tocnaye's letters to the French government of the previous summer; it also highlighted the prejudice of de la Hitte's letters to the British government, 'with the exalted ideas he entertains of the dignified feelings which pervade his Countrymen

from the highest to the lowest'. This vital document was fully absorbed by P. For Bicaise, see Brooks, *Yankee*, p.202 *et seq.* 'Some of the most prominent middlemen in the Nunez ... were mulattos, descended from European and American slave traders, who had ... fostered their commerce by inter-marrying with the local chiefly families ... a kind of aristocracy ... outsiders who wished to further their trade found it advantageous to collaborate with the established families. ... John N. Bicaise who came from Trinidad and was probably the most influential trader in the Nunez in the 1840s and 1850s married Mrs Elizabeth Proctor early in 1845' (Lefevre, 'Voyages', p.574). See also Chaps.3 and 5.

5. GL/A docs, see Chap.2.
6. C. Fyfe, *A History of Sierra Leone* (London, 1962), p.125, i.e. 'Oldfieldia Africana'; also Lefevre, 'Voyages'.
7. 'The harmattan ... (the dry wind from the interior) ... blew erratically in November and December ... the dust also contributed to the dark sallow look that marked the African trader'(Brooks, *Yankee*, p.81). See also G. Delcourt, 'Relation du Voyage à la Côte d'Afrique avec la goélette *Louise-Marie* 1848–9', p.13; Lefevre, 'Voyages', who wrote 'Bicaise ... intélligent, très actif ... de caractère jovial et hospitalier, sait se faire aimer par les indigènes ... revéré comme maître et seigneur.'
8. 'We arrived off Ropass the same day and almost the same hour as the *Louise-Marie*' (SGA/B doc. FP17). See also C. Lannoy/T. du Colombier, 'Une Expédition franco-belge en Guinée: La Campagne de la goélette de guerre *Louise-Marie* dans la Colonie belge du Rio-Nunez (1849)', *BESBEC* (Brussels, mai–juin 1920), pp.178–210. Joseph Braithwaite clearly understood French, and translated the various documents into English; the Flemish accent would have been foreign to him. VH spoke English (Lefevre, 'Voyages', vol.22, p.648). Durant records VH's arrival at the Nunez as being on 9 February.
9. C. De Wilde, letter to author, 26 June 1995. See also G. Brooks, *Landlords and Strangers* (Oxford, 1993), pp.124, 136, 181, 195. For Portuguese variant of a term for cabin boy or apprentice seaman (ibid., p.231) cf. Almada 'native assistants'.
10. SGA/B doc. FP 17; also Belcher, 'Extracts', *passim.*
11. For earlier descriptions see Belcher, 'Extracts', *passim.* His spellings differ, i.e. Walkeria, Cassasez, Debucko, Landamahs, Baggas/Baccas/ Barkas, Ka-Koon-dee (for Nunez), Proggot (for Proctor). For references to Kykandy/ Wakaria see CO267/155, 1839. Also Lefevre ('Voyages', pp.574, 655) uses 'Ropace', 'Bancoflette', 'Boucherez'.
12. For contemporary comment on the Simo, the sacred woods, and their druidic blood practices, see Lannoy/Colombier, 'Expédition', pp.187, 205; also Lefevre, 'Voyages', p.569. For a description of '*gris-gris*', see Chap.3 *supra.*
13. The early life of Joseph Braithwaite is conjectured.
14. SGA doc. FP17; also Brooks, *Landlords*, pp.1, 4, 37–9, 137, 182; and R. V. Dorjahn and C. Fyfe, 'Landlords and Strangers, Changes in Tenancy Relations in Sierra Leone', *JAH*, vol.3, no.3, 1962, pp.391–7. Also Lefevre, 'Voyages', pp.572–4.
15. For the French custom of setting up *Chambres de Commerce*, see P. Curtin, *Economic Changes in Pre-Colonial Africa* (Wisconsin, 1975), p.130. SGA/B doc. FP17 claimed at least 500 yards; Moneypenny records '1000' yards. S. D. Ellam was a discharged white soldier, petitioned about a land dispute in 1829 by Eli Ackim, one of the celebrated and ill-fated band of

early settlers in SL, who had been brought over from Nova Scotia. He was brought back from the Nunez to Freetown in 1832 as a suspected slave trader but acquitted. He was also party to an agreement of 27 March 1839 with one of the Nalu chiefs, to which Campbell, 'Becaise', d'Erneville and Laporte were also signatories. I owe this information once more to Dr C. Fyfe (letter, 5 February 1995); cf. SL government archives MP 4248/1895; CO267/114 and /155. Ellam is shown buying rigging in 1839 from an auction of condemned slave ships in a report of the Commissioners of the Court of Mixed Commission (FO 84/269). In the abominable coffle trails, slaves were chained at the neck and made to walk, carrying heavy loads of goods and food, for hundreds of miles in order to get to the barracoons, the 'concentration camps' for slaves, at the coast.

16. CO267/211, 4 October 1848, Quinette to d'Hoffschmidt, in which the Nunez is described as a *'rivière franche'*, open to *'tous les pavillons'*; also on 7 June 1849 P shows his astonishing grasp of matters in Africa with this comment to de Walden. See also Brooks, (*Yankee*, p.4) for an essential overview of what he called the 'symbiotic' relationship between the legitimate trade and the slavers at this time in West Africa. He quotes (p.115) the noted contemporary ex-slaver Theodore Canot [q.v.] in his comments on the 'self-serving defences of the status quo by legitimate traders'.

17. CO267/211, Hotham to Secretary of ADM, 2 December 1849. 'The climate of the Rio Nunez being for four or five months of the year as deadly and pernicious to the constitution of Europeans as that of the Niger.... It is possible that the visits of the French men of war may have been more frequent than ours but it should be borne in mind that ... we have mercantile establishments on every part of the West Coast, with the exception of Senegal.' More from professional naval solidarity than knowledge of the truth, Hotham goes on to imply that the French naval action may not have been so unjustifiable as it clearly looked, and also indicates that Pine would soon be back in London, clearly to elaborate his version to the CO. See Chap.5, *infra*.

18. See Howard Temperley, *White Dreams, Black Africa* (New York, 1991), *passim*.

19. CO368/1, F&S to FO, 20 November 1849; CO267/211, Hotham to ADM, 2 December 1849; ADM to CO, 1 December; CO368/1, Fanshawe to FO, 21 January 1850; CO267/218, CO to ADM, 26 March 1850; CO267/218, 24 April 1850; Merivale to Senior Clerk (later Sir) G. Barrow writes, it is 'unnecessary to transmit this list to [F&S] ... Likely to invite further controversy'; Grey and Merivale, 'put by'. CO267/218, FO to CO, 31 January and 24 April 1850, Fanshawe to Secretary of ADM, purporting to refute the F&S allegations. In fact only three visits were made to the Nunez throughout 1849, by *Favorite* in February, and then two visits occasioned solely by the B&M requests to Freetown — *Sealark* in April and *Phito* in May. Merivale clearly judged that F&S had a point, for the naval presence had been inadequate, by any standards.

20. B/MAE, and CO267/211, Hotham, HMS *Penelope*, SL, via Capt. Murray, HMS *Favorite*, to officer commanding Belgian naval force in the River Nunez, 17 February 1849. 'It is not ... to be presumed that the two governments will approve of a negotiation conducted by a third party (Belgium) whose mercantile connexions [*sic*] with that part of Africa have ... been comparatively insignificant.... Whilst I anxiously await

instructions from my government I protest against your proceedings.' See also n.80 *infra.*

21. For Anglo-French Anti-Slave Trade Convention of 29 May 1845, see Chap.3 *supra*; also n.19 *supra*. For reference to the expiry of the treaty on 6 March 1856, see CO267/272, Hammond (CO) to Sir F. Rogers (FO), 13 March 1861.

22. See n.15, *supra.*

23. SGA/B doc. FP 17, 'Ishmael ... has degraded himself by trafficking in Slaves'; also docs AP 18, 20, B&M to Acting Gov. SL, GA, 2 April, 9 May 1849; doc. AP 21, Deposition T, B&M at Catougama, to Capt. Monypenny, 25 April 1849.

24. SGA/B docs AP 14, 24, Bateman to B&M, 30 March, 5 May.

25. Avril to VH, 4 March 1849.

26. *Procès-verbal*, 26 February 1849, Bicaise and others to VH.

27. The date is from information supplied by C. De Wilde; SGA/B doc. EP6, Joseph Braithwaite at Badger, Shropshire, to J. Forster, New City Chambers, undated draft, but *c.*20 August 1849.

28. SGA/B doc. AP22, Dep 'V', Mayoré to B&M, 27 March 1849.

29. There were many references to support this contention. For example Delcourt, 'Relation du Voyage', p.551.

30. Delcourt, 'Relation du Voyage', pp.31–2; also Chap.3 *supra.*

31. Accounts of the three expeditions to Boké are given by du Colombier and Delcourt, quotation provided by C. De Wilde, VH to the commandant of *La Recherche* from Ropass harbour on 5 March 1849: '*J'ai la certitude ... que vous approuverez les mesures que j'ai présenté dans l'intérêt de tous.*'

32. Capt. J. Denman to George Martin, 19 February 1851. For the Gallinas incident, see Chap.2 *infra*. Also PPSC 1842, Clegg to Q 1662, 'the greatest portion expended for rejoicings and for firing over the graves of the dead'.

33. Delcourt, 'Relation du Voyage', p.18. In fact to everyone's surprise, the gin was not touched until after the battle. By contrast, Joseph Braithwaite would learn in Antwerp that the French and Belgian sailors were constantly drinking rum during the battle: SGA/B, visit to Belgium, July 1849).

34. For descriptions of Cassassa, also of 'Toncko', Mayoré's half-brother, see SGA/B FP 17. Also Brooks, *Yankee*, p.83; D. Robinson, *The Holy War of Umar Tal: The Western Sudan in the Mid-Nineteenth Century* (Oxford, 1985), pp.140–1.

35. 'Bateman and the Landumas ... had organized effective defences' at Boké in 1821 (Mouser, 'Trade and Politics', p.134); also in 1844/5 'well-fortified position' at Boké (p.235); see Chap.3, n.110, *supra*. SGA/B doc. FP17, backed by reasoned assumption based on the available letters of George Martin, from Ipstones, Staffordshire and Saltash, Cornwall, and Joseph Braithwaite from his cousin William's Mill at Badger, Shropshire: SGA/B documents EP, *passim*. In contrast, for evidence of the defensive capabilities of the Landumas at Boké see the revealing evidence of one of the original anti-British observers, '*Le (26), j'allai visiter ... le camp de Tongo. Il l'avait protégé par une forte palissade que l'on travaillait avec ardeur à prolonger*' (Lannoy/Colombier, 'Expédition', p.212). Yet the same commentator reports (p.203) the hearsay evidence that '*Tous les jours on nous rapportait que, sous leur [B&M's] direction, les Landoumas se fortifiaient et faisaient de formidables préparatifs de défense.*'

36. Tocnaye to Pine, 2 April 1849.
37. For drawing of Towle by Ensign Massui, see B/MRA.
38. Lannoy/Colombier, 'Expédition', p.197.
39. The two commanders to B&M, 14 March 1849.
40. The signing of the letters makes it clear that VH was acting on equal terms with the French commander, de la Tocnaye, not as an *auxiliare*, as d'Hoffschmidt was later to argue to the British, see Chap.5.
41. CO267/207, Monypenny, Report to Acting Gov. Pine, 1 May 1849.
42. B&M to Gov. MacDonnell, 9 May 1849.
43. B&M to the two commanders, 15 March 1849.
44. For these traditions see Brooks, *Landlords*, pp.1, 4, 37–9, 137. For Nunez as a frontier see Brooks, *Landlords*, pp.23, 66. 'The area between the Grande and Nunez rivers represents a geographical and linguistic frontier along the Upper Guinea Coast.... Linguists identify this area as the site of separation between the northern and southern branches of the West Atlantic languages' (Brooks, *Yankee*, p.23). Also J. H. Greenberg, 'The Languages of Africa', *International Journal of American Linguistics*, vol.29, no 1, January 1963, p.167; P. Hair, 'Ethnolinguistic Continuity on the Guinea Coast', *JAH*, vol.8, no.2a, 1967, pp.247–68; J. D. Hargreaves, *Prelude to the Partition of West Africa* (London, 1963), p.14. For attributions of 'insolence', see Delcourt, 'Relation du Voyage', p.16. Du Colombier's own term, *hautaine* (lofty) sounds more in B&M's character, with a less aggressive flavour (ibid., p.202).
45. Nowhere is this discrepancy identified in the many published versions of the du Colombier account.
46. Archive of the B/MRA, not reproduced here since they can also be seen as racist, in twentieth-century eyes.
47. F/CAOM 26.e, Tocnaye to B-W, 15 and 28 April 1849.
48. SGA/B doc. FP1; also FO 97/198, de Walden to P, July 1849.
49. FO97/198.
50. P memo to Addington, 20 December 1850, refers to French 'abuse and vituperation ... strong presumption in the wrong'.
51. For Risquons-Tout incident, see Chap.6 *infra*.
52. This paragraph is highlighted here, to underline the colonialist (and racist) attitudes of the time.
53. SGA/B doc. AP17, B&M to Campbell, 30 March 1849.
54. SGA/B doc. FP17 asserts that there were no native deaths, but an estimate of 200–300 deaths is recorded by Derecourt (doc. EP7a, Derecourt to F&S, 21 August 1849).
55. SGA/B doc. FP 17, AP1, 2, 11, 16, 23, Holman's and S. D. Ellam's depositions from Correra and Catougama, 4, 18, 23 April, 1 May. Their offer of shelter is inferred.
56. See Chap.5, *infra*.
57. B&M to Acting Gov. Pine, 2 April 1849.
58. G. Macoir, 'Note sur un Sabre d'Honneur décerné à Capt [VH]', *Bull. des Musées royaux des Arts décoratifs et industriels* (Brussels, 1907). See Chap.3 *supra* reference to the giving of swords; Capt. Lysaght also received one, for his sterling work for the traders on the river, in 1848 (data from C. De Wilde).
59. Tocnaye to Pine, 2 April 1849.
60. F/CAOM, Tocnaye to B-W, 15 and 28 April 1849.
61. F/CAOM 26.e, comments by B-W; see n.47 *supra*.

62. CO267/207, Grey, memo to Merivale, 27 October 1849 speaks of 'so much confidence in [Pine] . . . very efficient'; also CO257/216, 12 December 1850, Grey memo referring to 'so much confidence in his judgement, he must have had some good grounds'.

63. CO267/207, Pine to Grey, CO to FO, 22 June 1849. This was the report on which, again, Barrow languidly commented to his superior, Merivale, 13 June, that 'I suppose this may be put by till we hear from the parties? According to J. Sainty, *Colonial Office Officials* (London, 1976), Sir G. Barrow became chief clerk in 1870.

64. O'Byrne, *A Naval Biographical Dictionary* (London, 1849). In some contexts, Capt. William Backhouse Moneypenny's name is also spelt thus, with an 'e' in the middle, but there is no doubt that this is one and the same person.

65. SGA/B doc. FP 17, 28, Bicaise, deposition to Monypenny, 25 April 1849.

66. F/CAOM 26.e. A long, clearly collusive letter from de Kerhallet to Navy Minister, 27 July 1850, refers to two traders Holman and Miller, and one from Tocnaye to Director of Colonies at Ministère de la Marine et des Colonies, Paris, 15 August 1850 refers to '*deux hommes qui nous aurions eu le droit de fusiller*'. See also Minister to Director of Colonies, 16 February 1850 reference to 'fait de guerre'; SGA/B doc. AP11 Dep.'K', Holman, and AP12 'L', Miller, 18 April 1849.

67. This quotation on *baïonettes* is ascribed to a French journalist Emile de Giradin (1806–81), and is often used in military contexts. Thanks to Dr C. Fyfe for this data.

68. See n.41 *supra*, Monypenny to Pine, 1 May 1849.

69. CO267/218, Addington to P, 7 February 1850.

70. SGA/B doc. FP 17. Twentieth century parallels are all too evident, from the Nazi pretexts for invading Czechoslovakia and Poland, to the intricacies of the 1990s conflict in the former Yugoslavia. In West Africa in the nineteenth century there was another example in the way the African rulers of the Temne people in SL 'assented to treaties they didn't understand and then were blamed for not observing them' (Fyfe, *Leone*, pp.74, 89–90, 96–7; and letter to author, 17 December 1995, which is here gratefully acknowledged).

71. CO267/211, Pine to Grey, 2 May 1849.

72. F/CAOM 26.e, civil servant's note for *le Ministre*, undated, pp.6, 7, cites Consul Guillaumard d'Aragon at Freetown to B-W at Gorée, 23 May 1849. He was later Spanish consul.

73. See Chap.5; CO267/218, Addington to F&S, 7 February 1850, claiming 'fire was justified'.

74. F/CAOM 26.e, note, p.7, refers to '*pas à blamer*'.

75. Ibid., p.6, '*haut fonctionnaire*'.

76. Much of this background picture about the third Earl Grey and the CO is drawn with the kind permission of Professor Peter Burroughs from his paper to the Seminar in Imperial History, Institute of Historical Research, 10 October 1994, and from subsequent discussions and papers generously supplied. Also J. Prest, *Lord John Russell* (London, 1972), Chaps.12, 13, pp.219–302.

77. For Stephen, see *supra*, Chap.2.

78. Dr C. Fyfe, letter to author, 18 September 1994.

79. CO267/211, note on Grey in response to Barrow. See n.63 *supra*.

80. CO267/211, 18 June 1849, d'Hoffschmidt to de Walden states that '*Dès le mois d'Aôut 1848, le ministre* [of GB] *à Londres a fait part de nos intentions.*' See Chap.1 *supra*, n.28; also CO267/205, 16 March 1848, CO to FO stating that 'no information has reached this office' – despite the warnings of F&S to FO of 17 February. R. Massinon, *L'Entreprise du Rio Nunez: Mémoire de Licence inédit ULB* (Brussels, 1965), p.343 and *passim*.

81. B/MAE, 'Correspondance diplomatique', v25, doc. 122b, 27 9bre [*sic*, i.e. novembre], Van de Weyer to Minister.

82. The only extant document that approximates is in B/MRA, VII 159–274.

83. See Chap.3, Delcourt, 'Relation du Voyage', n.50.

84. '*MM. Doriac et Dufour de commun accord mais sans réflexion ni discussion, ordonnèrent d'y* [the *pavillon*] *mettre le feu. Cet acte était peu prudent, à mon avis et peut-être que par la suite on aura à se repenter de l'avoir accompli. Cependant on ne put mettre le feu si bien à la case*' (Delcourt, 'Relation du Voyage', p.24).

85. B/MRA, Brussels.

86. SGA/B, AP 11, 12, depositions, n.66 *supra*.

87. For background, see D. G. Carlson, *African Fever* (New York, 1984), *passim*; Brooks, *Yankee*, p.83.

88. SGA/B doc. FP 17, extract 5, p.11.

89. The relationship is conjectural only, but is a working hypothesis for the purpose of this book. The facts of Joseph's residence at the tiny village of Badger, in Shropshire, in at least 1849/50, lay in the family papers, and were the starting point from which this project developed. The census of 1851 shows him as 'V' (visitor).

90. Brooks, *Landlords*, pp.38–9, gives some of this data.

91. Brooks, *Yankee*, pp.202–3.

92. Carlson, *Fever*, p.7 *et seq.* For evidence of the Bicaise descendants in present-day Guinée, I am indebted to C. De Wilde for sharing with me his *in situ* research, 1995.

93. The term *Realpolitik* ('realistic nationalist policies') is used by later historians to characterize the foreign policy of Otto von Bismarck, the Iron Chancellor of Prussia during the latter part of the nineteenth century. See *supra*, Part I.

94. Delcourt, 'Relation du Voyage', p.30. Albert Schweitzer, the famous French founder of the Leper Colony at Lambaréné, now, like all reputations subject to review. See BBC 2 television programme, October 1994.

95. Richard Lloyd to B&M, 16 June 1849.

96. SGA/B doc. FP 17; additional information provided by C. De Wilde, letter to author, 26 June 1995; research in B/MAE, File 2024/III. R. Lloyd took the brig *Nunez* to Catougama on 8 May, to facilitate departure for England.

97. SGA/B doc. AP20, Joseph Braithwaite to R. G. MacDonnell, governor of the GA, 9 May 1849, 'We have lost all we possessed, having escaped with only the Clothes on our persons'; also SGA/B doc. AP27, R. Lloyd at the Nunez to Joseph Braithwaite, 10 May 1849; also R. Lloyd to B&M, 16 June 1849. Some local colour is imagined here.

98. Derecourt to B&M, 21 August 1849.

99. SGA/B doc. FP 5; see n.95 *supra*.

100. See Chap.1, for Forster's blooding in the arts of lobbying government.

101. CO267/155, FO to CO, 18 November 1839, ADM to FO for Viscount P. A letter from Lt Comdr Hill to Rear Admiral Elliot, 5 April 1839, refers to a 'Quarrel between the Landemars, a tribe owning . . . the upper part of the river, and the Naloos . . . the lower part. . . . I found . . . the Naloo Chief v. well disposed towards the Europeans, his chief object being [for] Chief Boymoddo, the prime adviser of King Saarah of the Landemars [to] leave the country'. See also C. W. Newbury, *British Policy Towards West Africa: Selected Documents* (Oxford, 1965), p.257, CO268/35, LJR to Gov. Doherty, 23 July 1840, Doc 12.
102. The advice of Dr K. Hamilton of the FCO has been invaluable here (letter, 7 March 1996, and enclosure showing signatures in the 1850 FO Derby sweepstake). This was the elder John of the Bidwell 'Foreign Office' family. See Kenneth Bourne, *Palmerston: The Early Years, 1784–1841* (London, 1982), p.423. J. M. Collinge, *Foreign Office Officials* (London, 1979) mentions J. Bidwell, junior clerk from 1843, becoming a senior clerk in 1852.

5. Political Scandals and the Affair: Palmerston versus de la Hitte, d'Hoffschmidt and the Court, 1849–1851

By accepted definition, the Rio Nunez Affair cannot be part of that later period of accelerated partition between the European powers, labelled 'the Scramble for Africa'. Nevertheless the ruthlessness with which first the Belgians, closely followed by the French, not only asserted jurisdiction over an indigenous people in *res nullius*, but also took satisfaction in competing with England, bear all the hallmarks of a phenomenon still lying a quarter of a century in the future. The affair was to become not only part of the 'Prelude to the Partition of West Africa': it could even be seen as a kind of early intimation of the infamous Scramble itself. As Braithwaite and Martin were later to declare dramatically to a willing listener, Palmerston, its purpose was 'to annihilate England completely' in this part of Africa. It was Franco-British rivalry which gave rise to both events — a limited French ascendancy on the Nunez in 1849 contrasting with France's far greater humiliation in Egypt in 1876.[1]

* * *

On the Nunez, it was now the summer of 1849. While the gunpowder stolen from Braithwaite and Martin's stores was reportedly being consumed at the Ghent fête on 21 July, to celebrate the eighteenth anniversary of King Leopold's accession, and Belgian newspapers were full of the patriotic exploits of their navy in foreign waters, the French naval commanders had begun to feel worried. The thought was dawning that they might have gone too far at Boké.[2] They would have had far greater cause for worry if they had known that at that very moment in Britain the affair had already escalated from the naval and colonial level into the diplomatic arena. That concern would have been even more acute if they could have foreseen that their actions were to become associated with four years of political challenge, and indeed scandal at the highest level, involving Britain, France and Belgium. The period from 1849 to 1853, 'the affair within the affair', became the private central core of the wider Rio Nunez story. That public version occupied a decade of conflicting European and African ambition in West Africa, which had started to evolve in 1847; it was to become the subject of over 25 books, theses and articles, by French, Belgian and American historians over the ensuing 150 years.

Its unchronicled 'secret story' encapsulated a critical moment in the evolution of Europe's relations with Africa; in particular it highlighted one facet — and by no means a flattering one — of imperial Britain's relationship with the European nations who were now beginning to challenge her position of colonial supremacy. With the new evidence available, it can be seen today to assume a greater significance than history has accorded it so far.[3]

Over 500 documents — one of them 60 pages long — passed between the three governments before this affair finally died, succumbing, in 1853, to the fate which Bicaise had so breezily predicted for it. After first the French and then the Belgian commanders had filed their initial misleading reports with their governments, in April and June respectively, and wearing his French persona, he wrote to Captain de la Tocnaye on 25 June: 'I do not think that the Braithwaite and Martin affair will cause as much difficulty as you believe'.[4]

Royalty was to touch the affair in different ways. Its outcome dashed the coolly conceived ambitions of one European monarch — Leopold I of the Belgians, and was dramatically affected by the anachronistic prejudices of another — Victoria; it was also to reflect the increasingly grandiose aims of a third, Louis Bonaparte, the future Napoleon III of France. It violently changed the lives of two other 'monarchs' — King Mayoré and King Tongo, who — despite the microscopic size of their disputed kingdoms — were officially treated as fellow sovereigns in the various treaties — or as Palmerston would have it, 'agreements' drawn up with them on behalf of their European counterparts.[5]

That brief, bloodthirsty and unnecessary incident on a remote river on the west coast of Africa — basically decided, even if not completed, in less than four hours — developed over the ensuing four years into a highly sensitive and potentially explosive political affair. It embroiled seven of the world's leading foreign ministers and their staffs, principally Lord Palmerston for Great Britain, in opposition to d'Hoffschmidt de Resteigne for Belgium, and — of prime importance — General de la Hitte for France. In addition, it involved two overworked colonial ministers, five under-resourced and isolated colonial governors, eight consuls — from Sweden, Denmark, France, Belgium and Britain, a detachment of the West India Regiment, 20 naval officers of varying calibre, from admirals to *aspirant*s, and some 200 sailors of various nationalities. Apart from the many hundreds of Landuma warriors whose oral traditions about this incident in the history of their people are now lost for all time, altogether over 100 people from a dozen different territories — high and low, conscientious and lazy, from the patently truthful to the downright mendacious — became witnesses, facilitators and contributors to the inner story of the Rio Nunez Affair: they spawned some 5000 pages of diplomatic documentation. Probably more than 300 men died in its cause; the career of one naval officer was blighted, and one colonial governor retired to obscurity in Taunton, at least in part due to actions and dispatches arising from the affair.[6] One trader, Bicaise, would wax even fatter on its outcome; his 'partner in crime', Abraham Cohen, of Marseilles and Ghent, totally disillusioned and unrewarded for his pains, finally gave up trying to create much needed *comptoir*s for his adopted country. The lives of two others, Braithwaite and Martin, were ruined. A dozen awards for gallantry and other services were to be liberally awarded to celebrate the battle which precipitated the affair, this despite the fact that the senior French naval commander, Captain Bouët-Willaumez, personally regarded the attack not merely as counter-productive to his longer-term strategy for France's interests, but simply a needless and unfair fight. The later Belgian verdict about this attempt to become a colonial power like her two big and dominating brothers to the south and west of her has already surfaced: that this was *'une expédition sans lendemain'*.[7]

Apart from the negativity of so many of its outcomes, or possibly even because of it, a mythology started to grow up around it. The most conspicuous and most enduring — and perhaps the most scandalous — among the legacies to that mythology were the *Sabres d'Honneur* — which would be presented by 1850 to the two commanding officers.[8] Van Haverbeke's sword, a magnificent product of the Belgian royal jeweller's art, depicts the established traders on the river as a beautiful bare-breasted maiden, ensnared, poisoned and all but throttled by a huge Guinean python. This powerful serpent was intended to symbolize the *influence étrangère*, as the *Précourseur d'Anvers* put it on 25 June: an extraordinary capacity for ordering events was attributed to the two British fever-ridden *malhonnêtes trafiquants*, who, as is now clear, had only been on the river for precisely two weeks, before the Belgian commander had decided, in principle, to attack King Mayoré. The melodramatic elements of this design demonstrate just how far the demonization of the victims-turned-perpetrators was allowed to go.

This was not just another unregarded 'scrape' — to use Lord Malmesbury's derisory phrase — of two more of Britain's unwary 'wandering sons' abroad, the epithet with which the MP Roebuck was to dignify the future beneficiaries of Palmerston's protective policies.[9] Although it ran in parallel with several other cases for compensation against both governments, including the better-documented case of Mr Mills's claims from the fledgling Belgian colony in Guatemala, this one was different.[10] Those carefully contrived pages of depositions, dispatches, letters, secret memoranda and civil servants' positioning papers make it clear that, behind the scenes, and with their diplomatic eyes focused on how things might well deteriorate, all three foreign ministries took this incident very seriously indeed.

A number of broad and baffling questions arise. France was to go to extraordinary lengths to try to defeat the British claim; what was the reason for this outlay of time, ingenuity and energy? More inexplicable, and necessarily needing to be viewed in a separate compartment, why did Belgium take the same path of prevarication, evasion, collusion and dissimulation? Why did Britain, who seemed to be putting up such a strong, promising and sustained fight for her two *cives Romani*, decide not to increase the diplomatic 'temperature' to the next accepted level in such disputes — raising it in Parliament? Claims against the French at that time took an inordinate time to settle — a point that Forsters, and Palmerston, knew only too well from experiences at Portendic in the 1830s, as the processes of diplomacy, heavily laced with expediency, took their course. The same was true for Belgium: Britain would later threaten to raise the Mills case to the status of an 'international matter', whereupon a 'satisfactory' arrangement was then reached in less than a month.[11]

Last, why did neither Lord Palmerston — an adept traveller along the path to the doors of newspaper editors — nor indeed Matthew Forster MP, the interlocutor for the two British traders — his 'media' skills having been established in the Madden controversy — take the decision to go to the press? This would surely have increased the diplomatic pressure, thereby strengthening the hand of the British government in its stance with the French and Belgian foreign ministries.[12]

The time factor in analysing these interrelated questions is vital. As far back as 1849, the perennial 'Eastern Question' was certainly starting to affect Britain's thinking, but it did not at that stage influence her attitudes to France and other powers. Diplomatic relationships were in the same groove that they occupied following the year of revolutions, 1848.[13]

Of the two accused nations, France presents a more understandable case. Even in 1850, the memory of Waterloo still rankled, and was overlaid with naval rivalry; there was deep resentment over Britain's — or rather Palmerston's — handling of the Athens and Don Pacifico incident, to the exclusion of France.[14] The brief *entente* was forgotten, and now the newly created prince president was just starting to 'imperialize'. In short, there were at least five good reasons for France to want to keep perfidious Albion at bay, and not to bend the knee to her in any sphere that touched the national pride.

But why should Belgium seek to deceive and outmanœuvre the very country that had helped to create her, like Adam's rib, from the flanks of France and Holland in 1830? How could this small and vulnerable nation fly in the face of the country that had befriended her for 20 years, where diplomatic relations were of the best, with their respective ministers, Lord Howard de Walden at Brussels, and Sylvain Van de Weyer in London, each enjoying an unusually high standing in their capitals of appointment? How could the monarchy that stood so close to the Great Britain of the beloved Queen Victoria appear to be plotting to defy her venerated 'guarantor'? How is it that Lord Palmerston's long and intimate link with the country that many regarded as 'his child', elegantly immortalized in the Avenue Palmerston in Brussels, counted in the end, seemingly, for nothing? And how could Belgium continue, after Palmerston's term of office, to defy Britain on the Braithwaite and Martin claims, when she might yet need Britain's support against the possibility of a renewed aggression by France on her borders?[15]

As a subplot in both situations, could the actual amount of the claim that Braithwaite and Martin were to present be itself part of the problem: the sum of £7592. 11s. 6d., of which only a 'moiety', in Palmerston's phraseology, would eventually be demanded from each government? Even when translated into its contemporary equivalent of over a quarter of a million pounds, surely such a relatively small amount could not even enter into the reckoning?[16]

As to the British failure to have recourse to the media, could Forster's surprising reticence be due to the political opprobrium that might be building up around the circumstances of his election for Berwick?[17] As far as Palmerston is concerned, was it a weapon still held in reserve, awaiting release if all else failed, but which his Prime Minister's intervention on 19 December 1851 suddenly denied him?[18]

A non-nationalistic pursuit of the truth about these four interrelated mysteries demands the kind of forensic dissection of evidence that any one of the celebrated detective creations of the three nations concerned — Hercule Poirot, Sherlock Holmes or even Arsène Lupin, would have enjoyed putting to work: after 150 years of legend that can be the only way to proceed.[19]

Before that process of political analysis can begin, the actual battle of Boké needs to be seen in its historical perspective. If it was, with the long eye of history, a scandalously disproportionate act of aggression against a weaker foe, however provocative, and one more incident in the long debt for which Europe and the West still stand accused by Africa, it was at least a crime of its time. The European attitude towards Africa at that period of the nineteenth century, manifested in the second phase of the Rio Nunez Affair, although generally humane, was also characterized by intermittent exploitive, repressive and punitive incidents. Teaching backward natives '*une rude leçon*' about treating the white man with respect, to use Constant Dossche's phrase from his letter to his brother in the *Journal du Commerce d'Anvers*, was what many Europeans believed they had a right, even a duty, to do, whether the purpose was the defence of their national honour, or their God, or the suppression of the slave trade; or simply in support of their interests, and at the same time as a reprisal for actions that did not suit a European perspective in particular circumstances.[20] The scandals that formed the political climax to the 'affair within the affair' were of a different order. No more blood was spilt; no more battle plans were hatched secretly late at night by French or Belgian captains; no more defensive palisades were built; no more injustice was contemplated or meted out to innocent victims under the guise of the 'rules of war'.[21] What now followed were scandals on the plane of European statecraft, not at a localized Afro-colonial level. They had already embraced a deception by the Belgian government of its democratically elected parliament, and the breaking of one of its key financial laws — Article 68 — and would later contribute to the disbanding of its embryonic navy (and indirectly to the creation of the first German national fleet).[22] The astonishing dereliction of duty by a lax British acting governor against his fellow countrymen, which biased the Colonial Office's approach from the outset, was also now part of the story: this single momentary breach of confidentiality, tantamount to treachery, was radically to alter the whole course of the subsequent proceedings, immeasurably strengthening the diplomatic cards in the hands of the French.

Another disreputable aspect of the proceedings was to be the collusion by Paris and Brussels against London, evident from as early as 26 December 1849.[23] Admittedly, this was at a tricky time in Anglo-French relations: it became one more event in a personal battle waged by the French foreign minister, General de la Hitte, against what must have seemed to him to be his unbearably dominant 'opposite number', Lord Palmerston, then at the height of his influence.[24] This diplomatic duel coincided with the time when the Don Pacifico incident in Athens was coming to a head, in the spring of 1850, with Britain ignoring legitimate French interests in the Near East.

Finally — a wholly extraneous but decisive intervention — in December 1851 there erupted into the course of the affair what was in fact a potential, if purely insular, scandal in its own right: the culmination of a series of acts of questionable constitutionalism by the court of Britain's constitutional monarchy, which led to the sacking of Viscount Palmerston, Britain's popular and successful Secretary of State for Foreign Affairs. With this single act, one of the less well known of those 'foreign affairs' would immediately lose its knowledgeable and most committed champion — the affair of the Rio Nunez.[25]

In the paper battle that flowed from the physical conflict at Boké, it was not lives, but livelihoods that were wasted. The plots that were hatched were not military ones, enhanced by a due measure of martial valour, but mean and unnecessary diplomatic manœuvres — conceived in cool cabinets in daylight, not in humid cabins in the small hours of the morning; the purpose of these plans was ostensibly to protect the reputations of the French and Belgian commanders and their colleagues, and the orders of the Légion d'honneur and of Leopold of the Belgians, with which they were to be publicly decorated, between July 1849 and December 1850.[26] The defences that were constructed were verbal and ministerial, intended to ensure that truth became obfuscated by the passage of time. Injustice was institutionalized, not merely by the acts of the French and Belgians, but also by the negligence of a British ambassador in Paris, Constantine Henry Phipps — Lord Normanby. This was the same diplomat who, disapproving the foreign policy of his superior, Palmerston, became a key but covert element in the ousting from office of that same master in December 1851.[27] He achieved this personal revenge for past reproofs through the machinations of his brother, Colonel Phipps; he happened to be treasurer and private secretary to Prince Albert, the rigidly moralistic German royal consort, who had long been urging Victoria to get rid of her 'immoral one for foreign affairs'.

The inner workings of this subtle process of duplicitous communication, distortion and good old-fashioned bluff have never before seen the light of day. To all outward appearances, the British lion was still able to flick its tail at will outside Europe and win the day; in fact, that famous tail could now be tweaked and pulled, if her opponents were sufficiently determined. The pieces of this jigsaw have lain in the international archives, awaiting detection and reassembly, for nearly a century and a half.

Invoking the Master's Touch

As Joseph Braithwaite landed at Ostend on Wednesday 18 July, he was armed with a much more powerful weapon than simply King Leopold's elegant visa for Belgium, No 1674, his *'laisser librement passer'* of two days previously. He carried with him the letter handed to him the day before at the Foreign Office, on behalf of the Foreign Secretary:

> To Godshall Johnson and Robert Norie ... Her Majesty's Consuls at Antwerp and Ghent:
> This letter will be shewn to you by Mr J. Braithwaite, a Gentleman who is proceeding to Belgium, to make enquiry respecting some Property belonging to him, supposed to have been put on board a Belgian Vessel on the Coast of Africa recently arrived at Ghent or Antwerp: — And I am directed by Viscount Palmerston to instruct you to afford Mr Braithwaite every assistance in your Power to enable him to obtain the Information which he is desirous to obtain.
> I am, Sir, Your most obedient humble Servant,
> John Bidwell.[28]

From this moment, Braithwaite and Martin began to feel the first signs of the potential power of Lord Palmerston himself. He was now, in the year following the overthrow of Metternich, and Guizot — both exiled and passing under his very nose in London — the most feared and as yet undisputed senior statesman in Europe. The further evidence that Joseph was about to gather at Antwerp and Ghent was to be the penultimate link in the chain of events that would bring the 'Palmerston touch' to bear upon the situation. The preliminary sighting shots would soon be completed: the big guns were about to go into action.[29]

A bare three weeks after his abject landing by rowing boat at Worthing, on 27 June, here was the victim of the attack applying himself in the most business-like and resourceful way in another 'corner of a foreign field'. His self-appointed task here was to try to obtain affidavits from members of the crew of the *Emma*, now in port; all depended on the support he could enlist from the British, Swedish and Danish consuls in both cities. He had armed himself with three foolscap pages of questions to put to such seamen, if he should ever find them. Of the 30 draft questions, one sample must suffice: 'Did you hear any and what commands (were) given as to firing at the English factory at Debucca? ... Did you see the English Ensign flying at B&M's stores before and during the action?' Perhaps, after all, Joseph was simply displaying the same worldly virtues of thoroughness and determination, but dressed in different clothes, that had helped him make his way as one of the unsung army of confident Victorian commercial empire builders, in the river valley of the Nunez.

Palmerston was accustomed to being tough with his small but growing army of consuls around the world. He had already complained of the lack of support given by HM Consul at Ostend in 1840 to 'a British Traveller who was friendless and a stranger'; Mr Norie would even be dismissed on 28 May 1851 for a similar neglect.[30] However, in July 1849, Norie performed his task admirably; Joseph commended his 'promptitude and energy' in a letter to his 'friends' and 'agents', Forster & Smith. John Forster, Matthew's son, was now servicing the costs of the investigation; those costs included his eight-night stay at the stylish Hotel de Petit Paris at Antwerp from 18 July, and then for the final two days, 'on my way home', at the equally comfortable Hotel de Vienne at Ghent, once the town's biggest coffee house. Time was of the essence; he and Forster maintained almost daily contact, London mail arriving the next day in Belgium.[31]

That time in Antwerp provided him with a list of the names and, even more important, the provenances of the 12 officers and crew who had returned with the *Emma*.[32] However, in addition to the master, Captain Jacques Witteveen, who had so distinguished himself on the scene of battle at Boké, there were the mate, Leonard Bins, of Ghent, and six other Belgians, none of whom would surely be likely to offer to help, or be allowed to by their compatriots. As Joseph wrote to Forster, 'It is evident ... that the crew of the *Emma* have been and consider themselves guilty of conduct they would rather not divulge and I am convinced that they have been cautioned against saying anything that might tend to implicate any of the Parties concerned in the expedition against Debucca.'

The mission looked like aborting. Joseph then had a brainwave: 'I was almost brought to a standstill when it struck me that there were three of the Crew who did not hail from Antwerp and I discovered that they belonged to places under the Dominion of the

King of Denmark.' They were George Mehrens from Elsfleth on
the Weser, Guillaume Andre Nissen from Sylt, and Peter Umland
from Bromsbuttel Holstein — all apparently still at Antwerp. A
fourth potential witness, Eric Wahlgren, a Swede from Lubo, had
unfortunately just transferred to the schooner *Jeannette*, which
had set sail for Liverpool on 21 July. He then learned that Umland
had joined him. On 25 July Joseph had to report 'ill success', due
to the 'very dilatory and inefficient manner in which the Danish
consul (Mr Nottebohm) has acted.'

On the 26th Joseph decided to travel to Ghent, by one of the
world's earliest railways, to seek out a particular sailor, Nissen.
He found himself 'very well received' by Mr Norie, and by the
Danish consul, 'an intimate friend of his'. Joseph now had another
piece of insight, uncannily conjuring up images of Poirot at his
most persistent:

> I rode in a Second Class Carriage from Antwerp in the hopes
> of falling in and getting into conversation with the man
> about [to be] joining the *Emma* when I found myself in the
> carriage with one, the mate Leonard Bins who left Ghent
> yesterday ... he informed me that there were about 200
> Muskets and other Guns brought on board the *Emma*, one
> Casket of Powder and Four or five Kegs [of] Gunpowder.
> ... He likewise added that the French were all intoxicated
> during the action, taking a dram from a Cask of Brandy each
> time they loaded their Guns.[33]

More hearsay, and not hard evidence producible in court, but was
this another potential witness — and a Belgian? Sadly, no. 'He
told me a great deal respecting the Nunez business that I knew to
be falsehood therefore I would not ask him to furnish me with any
statement.'

A new problem now loomed, yet one more example of the way
that the events of the affair interrelated with the European world
far beyond the Nunez. Another of the celebrated and complex
'questions' of nineteenth century history had arisen — the
Schleswig-Holstein question, which was reputedly only ever
understood by three men, including Lord Palmerston:

> The Danish consul ... informs me that all Danish sailors are

by the orders of his Government bound to return to their own Country in consequence of the wars of which he has no official account of the termination. He can therefore compel his attendance on that ground, and when he appears will take that opportunity of questioning him on my business.[34]

Nissen duly appeared before his consul on the morning of 27 July, who had had to put him under arrest as a deserter in order to get him to attend at all. These circumstances were later to be used by the Belgian government to try to undermine his seemingly very relevant evidence. Nissen was at first uncooperative. Joseph wrote that day to Forster:

He was very impertinent to his consul and was in consequence of that and his being a Deserter given in charge of two Sergeants of Police — probably a little reflection will bring him to his senses and induce him to divulge something and as I shall be present at the Danish Consul's this evening at Six, will be able to know whether he is telling the truth.[35]

Nissen duly deposed. His deposition was, within the month, to enter the voluminous bundle of evidence produced by Forsters for Lord Palmerston's keen eye, as a distraction from the absorbing Danish question. Norie had assured Joseph that Nissen's sworn affidavit would provide the acceptable testimony which he needed. His deposition included these statements:

That several small casks of gunpowder came also on board of the said Belgian ship *Emma*; ... that Captain Witteveen had appropriated some. That a part of this powder had been used here in the Harbour of Ghent, on occasion of the fête last Sunday. ... That he saw an English flag on the English factory ... and that he afterwards saw in the hold ... several pieces of a torn English flag ... that a great number of the Guns ... had been [brought] on shore at ... Rio Nunez or Bissao.

Joseph had done 'all that lay in his power' in Belgium. He returned to England on 28 July. The next destination was Liverpool, where he hoped to intercept the Dane and the Swede who had eluded him.[36] Safe in Shropshire again by 2 August, and onwards to Radleys Hotel in Liverpool, he was able to use the services of the Danish consul, Adolphus Mullens, and an 'Attorney and Solicitor at Law', Charles Bardswell. The evidence of Wahlgren, the Swede, was also no better than hearsay and was disregarded. In his statement of 25 August, Umland confirmed some known facts, but with new additions 'that a French Schooner followed the *Emma* to Debucca ... that [it] belonged to a Merchant of the name of Bicaise. ... After the English factory had been destroyed I saw two Europeans standing on the Beach hailing the *Emma* — no Boat was sent to their assistance — they were left there.'

On 20 August Joseph wrote to Matthew Forster, now directing the political process, expressing his pleasant surprise that his 16-page letter of 16 July had been sent to Lord Palmerston. Joseph also commented on a letter of Richard Lloyd's of 16 May, in which he had told Forsters, with undue optimism, of the information about Bouët-Willaumez: 'I am pleased to hear that the French Commander does not approve of the proceedings and acts of his Officers at the Nunez: this will facilitate the Settlement of your claim for reparation.'[37]

Meanwhile, Forsters had received a significant letter dated 21 August, from another unbiased source, Captain William Derecourt, master of the brig *Nunez*, who had been at Bissao in May, with Richard Lloyd and Thomas Jackson. Although unsworn and thus unusable in any formal context, it further confirmed Braithwaite and Martin's worst suspicions about the unholy partnership between Cohen and Bicaise:

Another person named Cohen or some such name came on board ... and informed me 'that the premises of Messrs Braithwaite and Martin had been destroyed by the French and Belgians ... that some 200 to 300 lives were sacrificed in the affray and that on shore the blood might be bailed up in buckets'. We then proceeded to the Nunez ... where we ascertained ... that Braithwaite and Martin remained on the premises till a shell fell through the roof ... [they] were perfectly harmless in the whole affair ... the fact was that the King did come to Braithwaite and Martin's for Shelter and they immediately turned him out.[38]

The British claim seemed to be shaping well. It was now ready for Matthew Forster to place it formally before Palmerston.

Although the evidence now amassing was encouraging, there were several areas of difficulty ahead. Part of the problem that now confronted the two Britons, and thus anyone who would champion their cause, lay in the fact that although this was a once and for all catastrophe for them, and was in fact an incident unprecedented along the west coast, it could easily fall into a *déjà vu* category from the point of view of every other interested party. For cynical politicians and their staffs, world-weary aristocratic diplomats, remote colonial governors, and under-resourced naval commanders — 'wanton attacks' and even 'gross outrages' were not unusual: they had seen many things that, prima facie, looked just the same as this one.

For example, the case of the schooner *Highlander* had been outstanding since 1840, and was still being pursued against France by Palmerston in August 1849. It would not be settled (for a mere 15,000 francs) until 19 January 1850. Forster & Smith knew the score by now, *vis-à-vis* their supposedly protective government: '*caveat viator*' would have been a good slogan for anyone who associated with them. On the very day that Matthew Forster wrote to Palmerston about the Rio Nunez incident, he was writing a separate letter about yet another 'outrage' on the River Casamance to the north. This outstanding request for compensation against the French government for an attack on British traders at Sedhiou, was still awaiting resolution in 1850, at the time when the Rio Nunez claims of a mere year before were to be processed.[39]

As to the burning of villages, both the French and the British, were more than accustomed to resorting to punitive raids, usually against slave dealers: the Gallinas attack by Captain Denman, in 1840, whatever its motives, was still remembered. King Mayoré was but one more in a long line of chieftains who had been burnt out, in the vain hope of thereby wiping them out. Indeed, so common was the incidence of the burning of villages during warfare that the contents of many of those homes were believed to be kept simple and movable with that ever present contingency in mind.[40] Chief Dibby partially burned his own village at Kacundy, during the latter stages of the battle of Boké, simply to deceive the Belgians and the French; Tongo burned his village too and fled into the forest, rather than face the odds against him.[41]

From a purely military perspective, today's Third World was there to be exploited, and to provide proof of military prowess, the end being more important than the means. De la Tocnaye's exploits in Argentina could be matched by Van Haverbeke's at Canton, where his capacity for 'ruses' tricked the Chinese, and preserved the safety of his ship and his crew.[42] Indeed a kind of informal code seemed to demand that officers stuck together. Once the force commander, de la Tocnaye, had presented his decisions as commensurate with his remit from Captain Bouët-Willaumez, and in France's interests, his next task was to recommend military honours for both parties, in what would hopefully prove to be just another little foreign engagement without any aftermath.

Similarly, Captain Van Haverbeke's first duty as he saw it, apart from protecting his own career prospects, and the purported legitimacy of his actions, was to stand by the officers and men who had risked life and limb to achieve their given objective, the vanquishing of Mayoré's part of the Landuma domains, and the defence of putative Belgian territorial rights. A minor injustice to foreign nationals along the way was not too important.

From the vantage point of an acting governor in Freetown, tucked away in his remote fastness, two to three months removed from any comment, approval or reproof — let alone assistance — that might be issued by Downing Street, the demands on his military and naval resources constantly exceeded his capacity. It was difficult enough to marshall his forces within Sierra Leone, without accounting for two British traders foolhardy enough to seek their profits outside the formal British jurisdiction. Where did his duty start and finish?

The *civis Romanus* may well have already been forming as a real and vital figure in Palmerston's subconscious (if indeed he can ever be said to have enjoyed such a luxury) but his presence had not yet been proclaimed to the world at large.[43] For Benjamin Pine, the supposed rights of British citizenship paled into insignificance in the face of distance and practicality, and the necessity not to cause repercussions in distant London, where his career was judged. He also had a daily need to live in some kind of bearable reciprocity with the French representatives at Freetown — the naval officers who in theory at least were by now sharing the burden of the anti-slave trade patrols with Britain. He also had to coexist with the French consul, Guillaumard d'Aragon — already appearing in the story as one of the crucial background figures. Above all, it must be assumed that the beleaguered cadre of colonial officials at Freetown could still recall the ill-will directed at their local administration during the Madden–Forster controversy six years earlier, and the way that Matthew Forster had used his 'media' skills to castigate publicly both Madden and the Sierra Leone government.[44] Yet here were some kind of representatives of that same forceful merchant, seeking help from the administration so recently abused. It was not exactly calculated to predispose Pine, or Macdonald, in their favour.

Another of the immediate difficulties facing Braithwaite and Martin was that, unknown to them, the British and French governments had already been engaged in an initial paper battle with Belgium over the 1848 expedition of Van Haverbeke to the Nunez. Matthew Forster was continually drawing Palmerston's attention to this threat to British interests, particularly in his note of 7 August 1849: 'For some years past the Belgian government have been ambitious of establishing themselves on the Coast of Africa ... but it is only in the last twelve months that the increase in the trade of Ground Nuts on the Windward Coast appears to have fixed their attention on the Rio Nunez.'[45] The Belgian ambassador to London, the doyen of the diplomatic corps, Jean Sylvain Van de Weyer, believed that he was already on the way to gaining Palmerston's clearance for the Belgian initiatives on the Nunez. The subsequent misunderstandings were a compound of Belgian understatement and British, even Palmerstonian, miscommunication and negligence.[46]

After Captain Murray's mission to Ropass on 17 February, Admiral Sir Charles Hotham had reported to the Admiralty, which duly passed the dispatch on to the Foreign Office, that the Belgians appeared to be infringing the Franco-British Convention of 1845, whereby both countries abjured further acquisitions of territory on the west coast of Africa for a ten-year period; this was to avoid unneccessary disputes between the two superior naval powers on the coast. As he recorded, however, 'Monsieur' Bouët-Willaumez at Gorée seemed to be playing a double game: he doubted the French motives, declining to ally himself with the proposed French line.[47]

* * *

Knowing nothing of these background factors, but with his dili-
gence in seeking out eyewitnesses about to reap rewards, Joseph
Braithwaite was at last in a position on 31 July fully to brief
Matthew Forster, following his letter of 6 July. There was now an
invaluable European element in the building evidence: this was the
real achievement of the Ghent and Antwerp investigations.

Forster had moved into action swiftly and surely, knowing that
the indefatigable Palmerston would still be hard at work at Carlton Gardens during what to most other politicians was the normal
August holiday period. He wrote urgently to him on 7 August,
making the central argument about what, for him, gave this
'extraordinary outrage' its unique character.

> [It was] unprecedented we think in the peaceful intercourse
> of civilized nations, and perpetrated not by Outlaws or
> Pirates, but by the public servants of two European nations
> in amicable relations with this Country. By this calamity
> Messrs Braithwaite and Martin are reduced to beggary, every
> shilling they possessed and more than they possessed, a
> considerable sum belonging to their friends [i.e. Forsters]
> was ... sacrificed.

He sent a second letter the same day forwarding a drawing by
George Martin's brother of the scene, clearly showing the line of
fire, followed by a further letter on 24 August: 'If these outrages
are not redressed ... no English trader can in future attempt to
establish himself beyond the range of the Guns of our own Forts
on the Coast ... it is a system of land Piracy, as iniquitous as
Piracy on the seas.'[48]
On 6 September, he wrote again, enclosing, among other items,
the only letter from a representative of the colonial service which
did something more than passively pass on papers to the Foreign
Office. This was the dispatch from Governor Richard Graves
MacDonnell of The Gambia, of 4 June: 'The conduct of the
French appears to have been of so wanton and outrageous a
character that I can scarcely suppose it not to admit of some
explanation. At the same time it is my duty to state that neither
... have I as yet been informed of any mitigating circumstance.'[49]

Forster undoubtedly knew that the Palmerston touch would bring five principal benefits to their case. It would breathe energy into the cumbersome, unmonitored and often inefficient mechanism of international diplomacy; occasionally Palmerston himself was an inadvertent part of that inefficiency. In December 1849 Palmerston had to apologize to de la Hitte, through Normanby in Paris, for not informing him about the actions of his envoy, Mr Southern, in a matter vitally affecting France on the River Plate, where in theory there was a joint Franco-British force: there had been 'some slight oversight in this office'.[50] Usually he was meticulous in following up initiatives in which he was interested.

Involving Palmerston would at the same time substitute what was presumed to be the positive attitude of the Foreign Office, for the approach manifested by their colonial colleagues, which at the very best was leisurely; no one apart from the French, and Pine himself, knew that it actually embraced an undermining element as well.[51] It should also draw on the benefits that ought to flow from the close ties — 'special relationships' were a twentieth-century phenomenon — between Belgium and what Leopold called her 'guarantor' state. As a subsidiary benefit, it might ensure that Palmerston's well-known views on the duties of Her Majesty's consuls towards Britain's citizens abroad, were brought into action. Lastly, his touch would impose on subsequent events his well-established commitment to the tenets of international law.

International Law and the Queen's Advocate

As well as being an astute politician, Palmerston was also a good bureaucrat and administrator. His many earlier years as 'the organization man' for the army — the Secretary at War — had taught him to build a case on objective criteria. His first reaction in any contentious issue in foreign affairs was to test what the relevant legal authority had to say on the matter, and then to refer it to the 'Queen's Advocate'.[52] Palmerston's belief in and thorough familiarity with the still largely inchoate field of international law, and the way that, for a brief period of the nineteenth century, the little-known office of the Queen's Advocate became a decisive factor in British foreign policy, merit separate analysis.[53] Palmerston was continually driving home the precepts of Vattel and Grotius to his envoys, to strengthen their hand in dealing with recalcitrant foreign ministers. In March 1848 he was 'laying down the law' to

Lord Normanby at the Paris embassy at the time of Lamartine's short-lived French Revolution: 'There is [no] doctrine in the Law of Nations more universally acknowledged or more essential as a Foundation in International Relations than this, namely the Principle that a Nation does not free itself from its treaty engagements by changing the form of its internal Government.'[54]

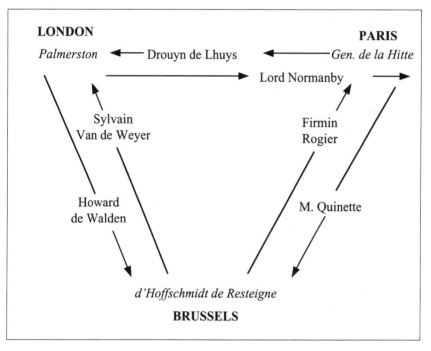

FIGURE 5 The Diplomatic Triangle, London–Paris–Brussels, October 1849–December 1850, by kind permission, the *Revue belge d'histoire militaire.*

In Brussels, in 1841 he had been reminding his minister with regard to some earlier 'wanton outrages', this time by Belgian volunteers against British subjects during a civil disturbance:

Though the laws of a state are conclusive as to a claim made by its own subjects, such laws cannot be pleaded as a ban to the claims made by a Foreign Government on behalf of its

subjects ... founded on the ... principles of International
Law. ... For what does Vattel say in this head, B III cap XVI
#241? It is moreover an acknowledged principle of inter-
national law clearly laid down by Grotius (*de lege: bell et
pac*) 'That whoever is responsible for an act is responsible for
all the consequences of that act'.[55]

As recently as 1848 he was instructing Lord Howard de Walden
at Brussels about aspects of international law as they affected
British citizens' rights after the attack at Risquons-Tout.[56] These
were all markers for later events on the Rio Nunez. The French
and Belgians claimed officially that a Fula mob came on the scene,
as they normally did when there was any disturbance, and that it
was they, not the European naval forces, who were thus responsible for the burning of the British warehouse. On nice Palmerstonian legal logic, the precise reverse was the case: their intervention was a foreseeable 'consequence' of such an attack in Africa,
and thus became, as Palmerston would argue, the unavoidable
legal responsibility of the two civilized governments. With this
process at the forefront of his mind, Palmerston's first action on
receiving the papers from Forster on 8 August was to send them at
once to the Queen's Advocate. This augured well for the next
stage of the British claim for compensation — the battle on paper.

Palmerston's Battle: September 1849–December 1851

In the warp and weft of European diplomacy of that time,
governments blew hot and cold with each other, and favours and
rebuffs alternated with astonishing frequency. Such fluctuations
were exacerbated by the turmoil of the year of revolutions. In the
case of Belgium, 20 years of harmony with Britain seemed about
to be ruffled; for her near neighbour, France, the ambivalence of
attitudes towards the conquerors of Napoleon surfaced anew.

Edouard Drouyn de Lhuys was removed from the role of
French foreign minister in 1849, giving way all too briefly to an
admirer of Britain, Alexis de Tocqueville. De Lhuys moved to
London, where he remained as ambassador until 1850, the critical
year in the diplomacy of the Rio Nunez Affair.[57] Meanwhile, a
new presence was to represent the increasingly assertive Napoleon's foreign policy, General de la Hitte, a conservative patriot of
long military memory, and former aide-de-camp to King Charles

X's brother-in-law, the Duc d'Angoulême. From November 1849 to January 1851, his was to prove the decisive political influence. His first experience of Palmerston had not been auspicious — the unilateral action through Mr Southern over the River Plate.[58] It did not increase his trust of Britain, nor did it help Normanby in his relations at Paris.

A foreign minister instructed his ambassador, who then communicated with his accredited government, noted what he was told, and reported back; he interpreted events when necessary, but much of the time acted simply as a conduit. Not all the messages followed that path: none of France's plotting with Belgium about the Nunez was to go via the French minister plenipotentiary at Brussels, M. Quinette. It all went direct between de la Hitte and the Belgian representatives in Paris, Firmin Rogier and the chargé d'affaires, M. Carolus.[59]

In Britain's case, if the impulse to prevail did not come from Palmerston, it often did not come at all. His ambassadors did not continually advocate and plead causes: they selected the cases, and the times, when such advocacy was worth the effort, balancing it against all the other weighty matters going forward. Much depended too on the personal relationship between Palmerston and his envoys. De Walden was so close to his master that he would go out of his way to intervene to protect Palmerston against himself, as he saw it.[60] Normanby harboured no such protective instincts. The diplomacy of the time was an unsatisfactory process, akin to two barristers lobbing statements at each other, without any judicial presence mediating between them to ensure fair play within the rules. Diplomatic battles proceeded by a series of sporadic but concentrated bursts of argument; each was in due course rebutted by counter-arguments, which were then referred to the originating parties on both sides for comment; activity was interspersed with long periods of silence.

The initial pattern was for Joseph Braithwaite to activate Matthew Forster, who quickly added his personal endorsement to the transmission to Palmerston. Forster was astute, diligent and ubiquitous in this role: even though he once addressed Palmerston erroneously as an 'earl', he knew the ropes of politics, and was a fellow member of the Reform Club. On 24 September 1849 he had again written to the Foreign Secretary from that address, commending him for his swift follow-up to his letter of the 6th: 'I

saw Addington the other day from whom I was happy to learn
that his Lordship has already called upon the Belgian and French
governments for explanations respecting the proceedings at the
Rio Nunez . . . which I cannot doubt will be followed by redress.'

Duly prompted, Palmerston then equally swiftly set out his
thinking in a memorandum in his own hand to Henry Addington,
for him to take the necessary actions with Earl Grey at the
Colonial Office, or with de Walden and Thomas Waller at
Brussels, and Normanby and the Honourable R. Edwardes at
Paris. In such formal communications, if he thought it necessary,
Palmerston's treatment of his diplomatic 'agents' could also be
peremptory. Two years after the appointment of Lord Normanby
to the Paris embassy, his dispatches on the outbreak of the new
French revolution of 1848 were unequivocal, and not best calculated to make Normanby better disposed to his master: 'I have to
instruct Your Excellency to tell the French Govt . . . I have to
instruct you to remain in your Post until you receive further orders
to the contrary and you will send to me daily accounts of the
Events which may be passing.'[61]

Although d'Hoffschmidt was in due course to try to argue that
the Belgian forces merely performed an auxiliary role in the
attack, it is now abundantly clear that after Van Haverbeke initi-
ated the recourse to arms, his smaller force still played a central
part in the battle itself. It was nevertheless the French forces under
de la Tocnaye, reinforced by those of de Kerhallet, who took over
the control of the plan, aiming to reassert French primacy on the
river; they also reassured Van Haverbeke afterwards that they
would answer for its consequences, exonerating Belgium.[62]
Although the British government was to prosecute the Braithwaite
and Martin claims against both governments, it was France that
was always the main protagonist, because that is how all parties
wanted it.

The joint Franco-Belgian case against Mayoré, enunciated
before the attack, had five main elements to it.[63]

- Mayoré was preventing everyone from trading;
- He had broken his word repeatedly, culminating in his refusal
  to return the wife and son of Ishmael;
- The standing of both European nations on the river required
  each of them, in turn, to demonstrate an act of leadership;

- From an early stage, no more negotiation was possible; force alone was the answer; and
- As Mayoré had become their enemy, the rules of war applied.

Once Mayoré was beaten, everyone would have learned their 'lesson', and trade could at last return to normal.

The plausible case against Braithwaite and Martin's position before the battle — constructed and refined *post hoc*, and elaborated over the ensuing years, as a counter-argument against their claims for compensation — had four strands to it:

- The two traders wanted to win all the trade on the river, and to undermine the society formed by the existing 'establishment'; they had thereby betrayed 'the whites' against 'the blacks';
- the Britons had incited Mayoré to resist, they had not remained neutral: thus they had become part of the 'enemy';
- they were the architects of the defences around Boké, which the Landumas could never have conceived on their own; and
- they had conveyed arms to Mayoré after the arms prohibition.

Three other factors related to the events of the attack itself:

- They were deemed to have been given ample warning of the outbreak of war; they had been given sufficient time and the expectation of assistance to get their stores out of the way of the attack; they had insolently refused to act reasonably; they had themselves to blame;
- the stores were fired on because the 'enemy' was hiding there; and
- the burning and the looting of their stores was the work of the Fula mob, whom they themselves had paid to oppose the attack. Even that act was held to be directed against the attackers, rather than a reasonable act of self-defence: the fact that the Fula turned tail, and then later took part in the looting, was one more example of the traders' iniquity!

From the very outset there had even been an insinuation that Braithwaite and Martin themselves, not Mayoré, had actually caused the troubles in the first place. Bicaise had organized on 30

March 1849 a 'protestation' to Palmerston, on behalf of a group he called, in beguiling language which needs to be recorded in the original, the '*négoçiants anglais, français et belges établis dans le Rio Nunez*', accusing them 'of disturbing the peace of the river and its commerce'. Although the two traders later became aware of this and dismissed it as a 'vile fabrication', the French never went so far as to present this accusation openly against the two '*malhonnêtes trafiquants*'.[64] This was just as well: there were no Belgian traders on the Nunez at the relevant time, and the predominant influence among the traders was French.

The British case has already emerged through the events themselves. It was set out laboriously — to be repeated several times — over the heartbreakingly extended period of the next four years. In essence, it was a rebuttal of every one of what can now be fairly described as the joint Franco-Belgian counter charges. It had at its heart the simple legal — and strongly Palmerstonian — concept that, in the circumstances, the forces of France and Belgium could not escape responsibility for both the actual and foreseeable consequences of their acts.

Autumn 1849 to Summer 1850: Attack

In the two years from August 1849 to the autumn of 1851, the paper war had two clear phases. From the outset, the diplomatic battle developed into Palmerston's own personal battle, once his patriotic enthusiasm had been won over to the cause; his commitment became apparent as soon as Matthew Forster wrote to him on 7 August. The initial papers were immediately passed by Palmerston to his Permanent Under-Secretary, Henry Addington, to refer to the Queen's Advocate for a preliminary opinion; this was delivered on 14 September. He now knew that there was a prima facie case. The first battle cry was sounded, in a note in his clear, bold hand, of 16 September:

> Prepare statement of the case to be laid by Lord Normanby before French and by Lord Howard before Belgian Govt claiming compensation for Parties, and pointing out that it cannot with any justice be contended that Messrs B&M are answerable for the Loss because they did not when summoned to do so remove their Property, from the first Place; it was not physically possible for them to do so, and their

Stores were so situated that the Most Extreme Hostilities might have been carried on against the native Chief without any molestation to their Stores, and the Destruction and Plunder of their Stores was an act of wanton aggression on the Part of the French and Belgian Force and this is conclusively proved by the Fact that the Property ... was carried away by the French and Belgian expedition and actually embarked on Bd their ships, and to Belgian Govt it may be said that there is Reason to suppose that the Powder was brought to Belgium and has been used on a late public occasion at Ostend.

Despite all the other European matters pressing upon him at this time, Palmerston had seen fit to master the essentials of this incident. He most certainly cared about the situation in Africa, and now put his decisive imprimatur on the subsequent diplomacy.

The wheels were starting to turn. On 23 October he sent copies of all the Forster and Braithwaite and Martin papers first to the Marquis of Normanby at Paris, who however — significantly — did not acknowledge them, and on 25 October to the Honourable Thomas Waller, the chargé d'affaires at Brussels, for Lord Howard de Walden, who acknowledged receipt by return. On 1 November, Waller, acting on behalf of his minister, represented the British view to d'Hoffschmidt, faithfully echoing Palmerston's trenchant cadences: it was the first salvo in the diplomatic campaign:

I am further instructed to state ... that in the opinion of Her Majesty's Government there seems strong reason to suppose that this act of wanton aggression was caused by commercial jealousy and a desire to drive these British merchants away from the Rio Nunez and that therefore this transaction renders it the more incumbent on Her Majesty's Government to obtain from the Government of the King of the Belgians a distinct and satisfactory answer to the former response to the proposed Belgian settlement on the Rio Nunez ... on 21st July last.

A Vital Ally: Captain Lysaght

While the ponderous diplomatic machinery was getting under way, Joseph had been exploring all the avenues he could find, to help strengthen their case. He discovered that there were two Royal Navy officers who might be in a position to describe the actual scene at Boké, from first-hand knowledge. He wrote both to a Lieutenant Cockcroft, and to Captain Thomas Lysaght who had been on the Nunez with HM steam vessel *Grappler* in January 1848.[65] Cockcroft had been posted by now to the Mediterranean on HMS *Spiteful*, but Lysaght wrote from Adbury Lodge, Newbury, offering a meeting at his club, the 'Army and Navy' (*sic*) in St James's Square. Joseph had written on 10 December, seeking his help in respect of what he condemned, and Lysaght confirmed as 'a most wanton and unjustifiable act'. On 16 December, Lysaght wrote back to Joseph with his endorsement of the drawing that George Martin's brother, also a Joseph, had earlier drawn for Palmerston, and which had been sent to him; it showed clearly that the British warehouse and stores were well outside the line of fire from the *Emma* and the *Dorade* to the Landuma village:

> I am of opinion that the Town might have been destroyed without compromising in any way the safety of your Premises. At the time I was in the Nunez the French officers were evidently endeavouring to obtain in a secret manner an undue influence in the River, altho' they denied any desire to obtain territorial rights, saying that 'it was contrary to our mutual treaties' ... That there are mutual jealousies and rivalries in the River Nunez we are all well aware.

Putting the Claim to Palmerston

The year 1850 saw both a sharpening and a marked personalization of the conflict, on both sides of the diplomatic divide, as Palmerston maintained the pressure. De Walden had replied to Palmerston's instruction on 3 December. Palmerston responded on 3 January, making the clear connection between the current British claims and the general principle of Belgium's colonial intentions in West Africa:

> If within the districts to be ceded there should be any ground

belonging to British subjects ... HM Govt would expect that the properties should be respected and that the owners should remain unmolested. ... HMG does not look with a jealous eye upon an extension of commerce carried on by the Belgian govt. ... Commerce is the best Primer for Civilization ... there is room enough in the vast and prosperous Country [sic] of Africa for the commerce of all civilized Nations of the world ... provided [it is] ... not founded on monopoly, and was not conducted upon an exclusive system.[66]

Brussels had been receiving similar messages from Paris, causing d'Hoffschmidt to write to his ambassador, Firmin Rogier, in February, conveying the news that Britain seemed satisfied with the Belgian explanations.[67]

On 23 February 1850, the Foreign Secretary of the mightiest empire the world had ever known, despite the myriad other matters demanding his time, not least the growing crisis in his own political career, agreed to meet Braithwaite and Martin. What kind of a man was it who went out of his way to receive two unknown gentlemen on a Saturday morning, at his private London residence, Carlton Gardens? What sort of figure did they find awaiting them — or more probably, like so many of his own ambassadors, foreign visitors, and even his own monarch, causing them in fact to wait for him?[68]

He was probably standing at his upright writing table with which he is commemorated for posterity, and where he had already penned a good many encouraging notes on the traders' behalf during the past six months. Joseph Braithwaite and George Martin came face to face — almost certainly for the first time in their lives — with the perfect epitome of an early Victorian statesman at the peak of his powers. The scene cannot have been too different from that described by a celebrated foreign observer only a few years later:

Lord Palmerston did not keep us waiting long. ... He had an aristocratic and elegant figure and the manners of a man who was used to the exercise of power and was well bred at the same time. ... He holds himself very erect, walks with a light step. He has a white face, not too creased, and thin features

... his tightly-closed lips and drooping cheeks expressed a great deal of indifference, superciliousness and stubbornness ... when he laughs, his whole face becomes animated and assumes a gay expression, which is rather rare among the English. According to people who know him, he is very good company. ... Palmerston spoke rather slowly, as though hesitating, searched for words, and in between finding them kept on saying 'Er-Er', accompanying his speech by movements of the right hand, and always found a beautiful and precise ending for his sentences.[69]

Joseph, for all the self-evidently good education which had brought him this far, would not have been able to match the acuteness of that view set down for later ages by one of the worlds's greatest writers, Turgenev; it is nevertheless a pity that neither he nor George Martin do not even appear to have attempted it. They were evidently much too keen to get across the glaring injustice of their plight to him, and to bring out from their now voluminous papers, the fundamental elements of their case. Quite apart from that, it was not in Joseph's nature to sentiment-alize: this was a purely business occasion.

The meeting clearly went well, for thereafter the diplomatic wheels started to move into a much higher gear, and Palmerston was enabled to further energize his representatives both in Brussels, and in Paris, where a new complication had arisen.

* * *

When Palmerston caused instructions to be sent in the previous October to his envoys at Paris and Brussels about the Rio Nunez Affair, he had assumed that events in both capitals were moving in parallel. On 28 March 1850, Addington requested of de Walden 'to report what steps have been taken with reference to Lord Palmerston's No 6 of 25 Oct '49'. A reminder on 30 April elicited a reply by return, dated 2 May, reassuring him that Thomas Waller had immediately transmitted an appropriate note to the Belgian Foreign Office on 1 November 1849. However, a new factor had entered the record:

M. d'Hoffschmidt considering this Claim as much made on

the French Govt as that of Belgium instructed the Belgian minister at Paris to seek from the French Foreign Office all the information possible. [He] tells Lord Howard de Walden that he has three times inquired but that he learns that no similar claim or complaint has been advanced by HMG to that of France, which he could not understand as even in Mr Waller's note a French Force was charged equally with a Belgian force of the commission of a joint outrage. . . . Lord Howard observed that M. d'Hoffschmidt was much annoyed at Mssrs Braithwaite and Martin's claim appearing to be solely pressed upon the Belgian Govt.[70]

From Palmerston's reply on 10 May 1850, his fifth letter in just under six months on this one issue, it is clear that Normanby in Paris had received the same dispatch as de Walden, but had failed to act on it, even when reminded. A pattern of inefficiency and resistance at the Paris embassy had been emerging ever since 1847: in August 1849 Palmerston had had to complain that Normanby had failed to report back on another Forster matter, the Sedhiou incident on the River Casamance.[71]

At the moment when d'Hoffschmidt was now seen to have crosschecked with the French, de la Hitte was right in what he wrote to Firmin Rogier on 19 April. This fact ought to have alerted London as to what was afoot. De la Hitte's note also demonstrated what far-reaching consequences were now flowing from Acting Governor Pine's dereliction of duty in May 1849:

As for the claims of the two English traders, we have so far received no communication from the British Govt on this subject. But the service of the Navy command has provided . . . information which in the light of what the Navy Minister has written leave no doubt on the lack of basis for their demands. Their conduct is even said to have been censured by the Sierra Leone Government.[72]

A month later, on 7 May, Palmerston spelt out to Normanby what he wanted him to do; the language is uncompromising. General de la Hitte would need managing.[73] Within a few short weeks, the mood at Paris momentarily changed. The French suddenly realized that they needed Britain's good offices over a difficulty in the Dominican Republic. De la Hitte had no qualms about changing tack and appealing to Palmerston's humanitarianism. His predecessor and now his ambassador, Drouyn de Lhuys, actually wrote to the Foreign Secretary on 3 April, at Broadlands: 'My dear Minister, forgive me for pursuing you with my letters as far as your country retreat, but it is a question of a work of humanity and in such a case you will customarily allow one to knock at your door.'[74] In a similarly unwonted access of warmth, later that summer, de la Hitte would also be expressing satisfaction at Palmerston's 'language' in relation to the problems over Tahiti.[75]

The 'Civis Romanus' Speech

Meanwhile, the diplomatic corps in London was watching with fascination, and sharing its views, on a far more interesting matter. It believed it was about to witness the imminent fall of the British statesman, who now seemed to have gone too far in his unilateral dealings with Athens and yet another 'affair', that of Signor Don Pacifico. His relations with Queen, party and France were becoming more strained every day.[76] Van de Weyer reported to d'Hoffschmidt on 12 April: 'The English Minister loses ground in the heart of Parliament with every day that passes.'[77] On 20 May, the Belgian ambassador, underestimating Palmerston's political resilience and personal strength of will, reported the French view after a new turn of events: 'They are flattering themselves in Paris and elsewhere with the thought that these new complications will bring about the fall of Lord Palmerston.'

Already on 6 December of the previous year, d'Hoffschmidt had requested from his ambassador a report over the divergences that existed between Palmerston and his colleagues over foreign policy, but Van de Weyer had attributed them mainly to the machinations of the disappointed wife of the former Russian ambassador, the Princesse Lieven, even though returned by then to reopen her salon in Paris, and to her lover Guizot, but still firing off like a loose anti-Palmerston cannon.[78] Now the chickens appeared to be finally coming home to roost. On 24 May Van de Weyer wrote to Brussels: 'Drouyn de Lhuys, on the day before his return to Paris, said that in wounding France to the quick, Lord Palmerston was committing a mistake which could well bring down on England's head a war in which France would take its revenge for Waterloo'.[79]

Even if neither the British court nor de la Hitte, were assuaged by it, the *civis Romanus* speech on 25 June seemed to do wonders for the relationship with Belgium. Van de Weyer called it *'une profonde sensation'*. He cited Palmerston's warm references to Belgium, the country his critics dismissed in the 1830s as his *'petite monarchie expérimentale'*. Most significantly, the Belgian ambassador picked out one particular theme that can only have been inspired by the case then at the forefront of Palmerston's mind, the Rio Nunez claims. He told d'Hoffschmidt that the speech was 'full of concern for the interests of English subjects abroad'.[80]

On 27 June d'Hoffschmidt asked Van de Weyer to thank Palmerston for the way he had spoken of Belgium during the historic debate.[81] Surely this could only lead to a good outcome for Braithwaite and Martin?

* * *

What Palmerston did not know, and what even he, a cynical man of the world, would have scarcely believed, was that from at least as far back as December 1849, his beloved Belgium had been colluding with his *bête-noire*, France, over the Rio Nunez claims.[82] On 10 January, d'Hoffschmidt had written to Firmin Rogier:

> It would appear that it must suffice for France to have the certainty that in the event that Belgium were to form an establishment on the river, French trade would be placed on the same footing of equality as Belgian trade. . . . For the moment what is most important for us is to know what reaction has been given to the claim of Mm Braithwaith [*sic*] and Martin. It will soon be two months since the English Government presented this claim and I cannot put off a reply for much longer: however before doing so, I would very much wish to know what reception the French Government has accorded to the same claim.[83]

De la Hitte wrote again to the Belgian ambassador on 15 June, evidently feeling free to exploit the political temperature in London which was now approaching fever pitch:

You have made me aware ... of the desire of the Belgian Government to concert with France on the subject of the Braithwaite and Martin gentlemen. ... Lord Normanby has just addressed to me the claim of these Gentlemen. ... I would wish to know what reception the Belgian government has given to this affair. ... I have written to the Navy Minister to ask him to pass me the papers which he declares that he has in his hands and I shall not reply to the English ambassador until I have received his reply and yours.[84]

His request to his *'Cher Collègue'*, the navy minister, had one objective: to define 'the assertions which we have to rebut.'[85]

On 29 August de la Hitte wrote to Carolus a letter which was probably the most important piece of documentation in the whole affair, for it revealed just how deep and implacable was his determination not to give way yet again to the man who had so recently humiliated his country over the events in Greece:

M. Rogier has done me the honour of communicating on the twentieth of this month the draft reply with which the Belgian Foreign Minister proposes to counter the claim presented by the English Ambassador. ... The whole of this work seemed to me to be in perfect accord with the note which I am addressing to Lord Normanby and which you will find attached herewith.

De la Hitte picked out one aspect where there still seemed to be a lack of an *'analogie favorable'* between the two 'stories': 'I refer to the burning and pillage of the stores, which the Belgian version would confirm up to a certain point for attribution to all the blacks ... whereas on the contrary the French version identifies as the sole authors of the disaster the Fulas and other natives.'

The foreign minister went on to make clear that the reports of de la Tocnaye and de Kerhallet were designed to absolve the French and Belgian forces from all responsibility to the two Britons; this would avoid casting any shadow over the valour of the men concerned and the decorations agreed for them.[86] These awards had been planned as far back as 7 July 1849; the Order of Leopold would be offered to the two French commanders, if the Légion d'honneur could be bestowed on Captain Witteveen and two Belgian sailors. D'Hoffschmidt had given further point to this action by causing Firmin Rogier to emphasize Leopold's personal interest: contrary to views expressed by other authorities, he was most certainly involved in the Nunez Affair.[87] The king evinced 'a royal satisfaction, and a shining recognition of the courage shown by the sailor in question, Witteveen'.

Van Haverbeke's name was added later; Cohen was not even mentioned. General de la Hitte concluded his note to Carolus by summing up the apparent benefits that would flow to their joint case by these elaborate dissimulations:

> It follows from this ... that none of the men who fought with us contributed to the fire and pillage of the English stores, that the weapons put on board our ships must have been snatched from the pillagers. I wanted ... to respond to the desire expressed by the Belgian Government by pointing out these differences, which would have the awkwardness of leaving some opening to a [counter]claim which the measured and patient conduct of the French and Belgian officers enables us to rebut without reserve.

On the same day, 28 August 1850, de la Hitte delivered to Lord Normanby in Paris a 22-page response to his eventual letters of 29 May and 11 August, presenting the British claims as 'at least very exaggerated'. In this self-styled *'fidèle exposé des faits'*, there is a classical example of 'lexical leakage'. Hitte described the second letter to the two traders, of 15 March 1849: the original French reads: *'Une nouvelle lettre accordant aux traitants un terme "fatal" de 48 heures pour se mettre à l'abri'*. That word revealing the underlying intention is crossed out and replaced by the more concealing word *'final'*.[88]

Knowing nothing of the manœuvres between Paris and Brussels, Palmerston decided to facilitate a meeting between the British traders and a diplomat he thought he could trust, the Belgian Ambassador Van de Weyer. This took place on 19 August, 1850.[89] So far from this meeting transforming their cause, the next event to come out of Brussels was the bold communication by d'Hoffschmidt to de Walden on 9 September that the Belgian government 'declines to indemnify' the two Britons.[90] Although in a continuing state of political crisis, Belgium was nevertheless able to take a decisive stance on the Nunez issue: it had seized on the inconsequential fact that Britain had presented the claim on Belgium but not simultaneously on France.[91]

Instead of immediately demurring from accepting this extraordinarily unfriendly '*démarche*', de Walden had limited his own freedom of action by reaching a quite separate and tangential view about the claims, based according to him on his wide commercial experience: that the value of the merchandise was a major element, not a subsidiary issue. The value of goods could be radically inflated if invoiced prices rather than cost prices were quoted, due to the high profit margins that he believed were obtained in the West African trade. He gave no authority for this view. Earlier that year de Walden had written privately: 'My Dear Palmerston ... Pacifico is more difficult to deal with ... his dubious bona fide nationality ... the exorbitant character of his claims set all against him.'[92]

On 31 August he wrote to Lord Eddisbury, the Under-Secretary at the Foreign Office, that he was highlighting the value of the Braithwaite and Martin claim in order to save his friend and political master from exposing himself again to the same criticisms he had just suffered that summer — the question of an inflationary element in the claims made by Don Pacifico in Athens. Regardless of any question of its inherent justice or injustice, the over loyal envoy wanted to save Britain what he feared to be another humiliating situation '*à la Pacifico*'.[93]

In contrast to her resistance on this front, however, Belgium was having to give ground to Britain on the much more strategically important point of the Rio Nunez treaties. On 7 February the following year, 1851, d'Hoffschmidt would be forced to concede to de Walden that none of Van Haverbeke's new treaties with the Landumas had been ratified by the Belgian parliament: only the treaty of 1848 with Lamina Towl and the Nalus were to be allowed to remain in force. All the effort, the expenditure, the plotting, and the bloodshed had been in vain.[94]

Palmerston Counter-Attacks

The long, detailed but defensive letters from de la Tocnaye and de Kerhallet stand in the British and French archives as a sign of the seriousness with which both governments at this time viewed the outcome of the Rio Nunez claims. They were eventually communicated to London, where they were studied minutely by Palmerston. The only explanation for these papers never previously having seen the light of day, must be the historians' stereotyped 'European' perspective on him.[95]

On 2 September 1850, the records reveal the astonishing grasp Britain's hard-pressed Foreign Secretary had troubled to achieve and continued to apply with regard to the tortuous documentation of the Braithwaite and Martin claims. In a ten-page quarto-size memorandum to Addington, he analysed lucidly, and with scarcely a crossing out, writing as quickly as he thought, the mounting body of obfuscating evidence which was coming at him from Paris and Brussels, following the referral of the papers to the two naval officers, and their responses:

Let Messrs B&M see these Papers and make their answers ... it should be said that the Papers transmitted by the French seem to afford the strongest confirmation of the opinion expressed by me that the outrage of which Messrs B&M will complain was the result of commercial jealousy and of personal ill will, and moreover these Papers explain what that jealousy was founded upon. ...

It appears by the letter of Captain Kerhallet dated Paris 27 July that Mr Bicaise who calls himself a British subject but whose connections and Interests seem altogether foreign had formerly been in the habit of supplying himself with goods for his Trade with the natives, from Messrs Forster ... but that ... Bicaise had lately derived his supplies from Belgium and not from England, and it is clear that ... [he] could no longer with truth be considered as representing English commercial Interests. It seems moreover that Messrs Forster having withdrawn their Employment from Mr Bicaise employed Messrs B&M to carry on for them their Traffic at Debucca. ...

It is manifest from the various Papers sent by the French Govt that this new Establishment ... excited the liveliest commercial jealousy in the minds of the French and Belgian traders, and ... this bad feeling further increased when Messrs B&M ... declined to take part with the French & Belgian traders in the Differences [with] the Debucca Chief. ...

It is not necessary to inquire how far it was owing to the Superior Good Conduct of Messrs B&M that they remained on good terms with him ... the whole Tone and Tenor of these letters from the French and Belgian naval officers breathe that spirit of personal Enmity towards Messrs B&M which would naturally tend to those acts of violence ... of which they complain. ...

It is stated in the French account that Messrs B&M were warned at the End of Fb'y that an attack was likely to be made ... but it is quite clear that they could not be expected to remove in consequence of such a vague and general communication and it seems ... [the communication] only gave them 48 hours, to be counted not from date of Receipt but from the date of Signature ... the French and Belgian Offrs ... knew perfectly well that Messrs B&M had no possible means of removing their goods. ...

But if the Explanation given of the Course of Proceedings before the attack is unsatisfactory, the account of that which followed it is not less so. ... Here Messrs B&M must supply Details as to alleged Firing ... from the ground close to their Factory.

Palmerston then reverted once again to his legal grounding, while at the same time not concealing his racial prejudices:

The statements made by the French Offrs themselves offer the most complete confirmation of the assertion ... that Part of [the] Property was carried off by the French and Belgians, for those Off'rs distinctly acknowledge that a large Quantity of Muskets and Gunpowder was carried on Board their Ships. ... What possible right had the French and Belgians to apply to their own use Property which they knew to belong to British subjects, and did they not by so doing make themselves more culpable than the negro Plunderers in Proportion to their superior Civilization and greater knowledge of Right & wrong, and in Proportion as according to the well known axiom the Receiver of Stolen Property is held to be even more criminal than the Person by whom it was taken?

The British Foreign Secretary added a surprising comment

which gave the lie to the view that he only knew or cared about Europe, and that Africa was of little interest to him:

> The French off'r ... attempts to draw a distinction between Arms and Gunpowder and what he calls *des Marchandises*, but it is well known to all who have been on the West Coast of Africa that Muskets and Gunpowder form a large Portion of the '*Marchandises*' with which the European traders on that coast carry on their Traffic, and that those Muskets and Gunpowder are used not only for Purposes of attack and Defence but for Rejoicings at the periodical negro Festivals, when repeated & long continued firing of blank cartidges from Muskets forms an Essential Part of the Ceremonial.
>
> HM Govt therefore are still more confirmed by the Papers ... that Messrs B&M have suffered a wrong for which they are justly entitled to Compensation, and HM Govt earnestly entrust the French govt to take a candid and impartial Review of the whole case and to give a liberal decision upon the Claims of these British Subjects.
>
> 'P' 2/9–50

The French and Belgians continued to exchange views on tactics, with a further secret communication between Firmin Rogier and de la Hitte on 2 October.[96] Palmerston's view stood firm. None of the feverish counter-attacking to his own counter-attacks seemed to divert him. In a further memorandum to Addington on 20 December 1850, he shrewdly brought into the reckoning his deep instincts about the ways of men: 'This abuse and vituperation which abound in all the French dispatches afford a strong Presumption that the French were in the wrong and therefore compensation is due.'[97]

Two days later, he dropped in a reiteration of his argument against the point with which the French had made much play: that as John Nelson Bicaise claimed British citizenship by virtue of his birth in Trinidad, the French and Belgian attack could be plausibly presented as in the interests of 'the British': Palmerston roundly dismissed such an implication. (See Figure 6.)

In January 1851, Braithwaite and Martin, responding to Palmerston's invitation, produced their 28-page refutation of the arguments of de la Hitte, de la Tocnaye and de Kerhallet.[98]

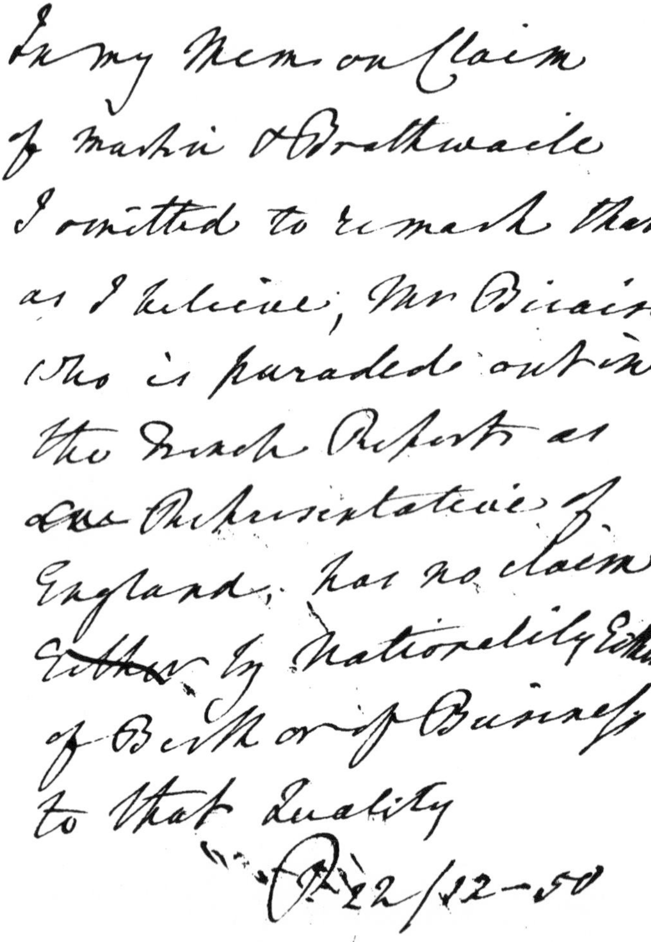
In my Mem. on Claim
of Martin & Braithwaite
I omitted to remark that
as I believe, Mr Bicaise
who is paraded out in
the French Reports as
the Representative of
England, has no claim
~~Either~~ by Nationality Either
of Birth or of Business
to that Quality
P 22/12-50

FIGURE 6 Palmerston's memo on Bicaise's disputed nationality, sequel to his astonishingly detailed ten-page memorandum of 2 September 1850, to his Parliamentary Under-Secretary, Henry Addington, in his characteristically strong hand, and signed with the flowing initial 'P' (FO France 97/198, by kind permission, the Public Record Office and Crown Copyright Unit.

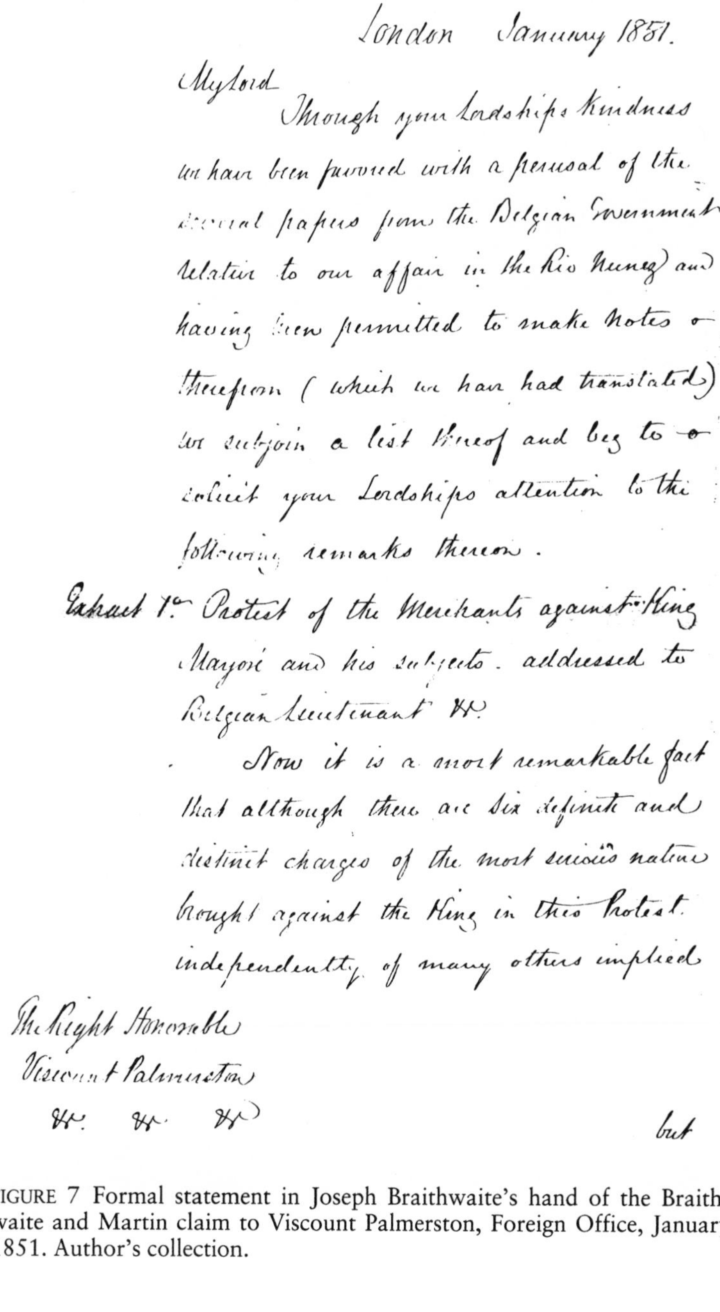

London January 1851.

My Lord

Through your Lordships Kindness we have been favoured with a perusal of the several papers from the Belgian Government relative to our affair in the Rio Nunez and having been permitted to make notes therefrom (which we have had translated) we subjoin a list thereof and beg to solicit your Lordships attention to the following remarks thereon.

Extract 1st Protest of the Merchants against King Mayore and his subjects. addressed to Belgian Lieutenant &c.

Now it is a most remarkable fact that although there are six definite and distinct charges of the most serious nature brought against the King in this Protest independently of many others implied

The Right Honorable
Viscount Palmerston
&c. &c. &c.

but

FIGURE 7 Formal statement in Joseph Braithwaite's hand of the Braithwaite and Martin claim to Viscount Palmerston, Foreign Office, January 1851. Author's collection.

Matthew Forster, in his turn, four months later, while providing another picture of Bicaise's nationality, was to give the first real evidence as to Bicaise's reasons for at least a duality — if not an outright switching — of allegiance, and for the two traders' choice of Boké. He wrote to them:

> He was born we believe in the British West Indies, we knew him first as clerk to the late Mr Procter. . . . On the death of that Gentleman (who, supported by our capital established one of the most successful houses in Africa) the business was continued by Mrs Procter; a woman of Colour of much ability and worth; Mr Bicaise, who was her corresponding and managing clerk, after some years married her; and the business under his control fell into ruin. We found ourselves compelled to withhold further supplies, being, and remaining, Creditors for a large sum, which we have now no means of recovering.
>
> Mr Bicaise was compelled to seek Credit in Countries where he was less known: his wife left him and has since died. He now, we understand, conducts what trade he has, by advances from French and Belgian merchants; the withdrawal of English supplies, and the turbulent state of the River for so many years, have greatly diminished Trade there.

The essential point was, of course, as Palmerston had realized, that it was not Bicaise's nominal citizenship that mattered, but which of the competing commercial interests he was nowadays closest to. Clearly, it had been towards France that he had been turning for some time; the Belgian presence had been in his eyes an expedient and temporary means of excluding Britain, not protecting her or her traders.

During all this time, Palmerston's energy had also been directed towards overcoming the fault in Earl Grey, which he confided to his office in his having 'so much doubt on this matter'.[99] Governor Macdonald, back from leave, was at last cajoled into composing a three-man investigating team, led by Captain P. Prendergast of the 3rd West India Regiment, supported by Assistant Staff Surgeon Watson RN, the ubiquitous Benjamin Campbell JP from the Isles de Los, and Lieutenant Commander Selwyn. In the spring of 1850 they met Lamina Towl, King Tongo, and his now deposed and chastened brother 'Morgery'. Their meeting at Ropass, 'in the presence of 400 to 500 or so armed men', led to a 27-point report. The treaties purported to have been made with Lamina's Nalus in 1848 and with the Landumas in 1849, were now starting to look fragile, 'his own countrymen being dissatisfied at the cession he has made to the Belgians'.

Tongo showed them the treaty made on 5 April 1849 with de la Tocnaye and de Kerhallet, ceding sovereignty at Boké for a 'Fort or Mercantile Establishment'; also the secret treaty made the same day with Van Haverbeke. Prendergast recorded:

> These documents contain stipulations so extraordinary that we deem it necessary to make some observations on them. ... Tongo and his Chiefs ... expressed the greatest astonishment at their contents and declared ... that they had never been translated to them. ... Tongo is made to cede over to the Belgian government for a most paltry consideration 40,000 *Mètres carrés* at Debukkah. As this amounts to nearly 25 Square miles, not a foot of ground would be left to the Landoumahs on that side of the river. ... This document ... has been fairly copied ... with a blank left to fill up the amount of territory to be ceded, and which is filled up in a coarse heavy hand writing, apparently after the Treaty had been signed ... the dates all bear 'Ropass Rio Nunez le 5 avril 1849' ... in the handwriting of a person who it is well known ... was not in the Rio Nunez at that date ... we feel warranted ... in stigmatizing it as a gross deception played off on Tongo and the Landoumahs as well as on the French.
>
> [sec.] 25 ... We believe all the disturbances ... to have arisen from the attempt to create two authorities there ... all that appears necessary is for each government to have a resident agent duly authorized to settle any differences arising between the different traders and with the Natives.[100]

This trickery of an illiterate people certainly amounted to another aspect of the scandals that run through the Rio Nunez Affair. There is no evidence of how often such deceit may have been attempted by Europeans on black Africa. This example certainly does not redound to the credit of the Belgian officer concerned.

Later in the year, 'King Tongo[h], Kicandy' and 'Old Buncheny Chief of the same' wrote a colourful letter to Campbell: 'This river is now settled ... my Kingship is restored to me ... my brother and all the Landumas wishes me to go up to ... Debucca for there is my Father's House.'

Tongo went on to make the point that Prendergast had made: 'The peace was made betwixt ourselves Landumas without the Nallows' invitation ... ; for it was through their misleading Dibbee and my Brother, the war lasted so long amongst us.' Too late for Braithwaite and Martin, Tongo asked Campbell to pass on this appeal to the Sierra Leone governor:

> [L]et us make a treaty supplying us with able Merchants ... their trade is not to be disturbed by any other nation but the English government ... the Nallows are for ever ... deceiving Europeans with their large words, and never pay their debts. ... We will not forget to state that we want no Slave Dealers in this river. ... PS ... the Government are at liberty to build a School House wherever they please up above and civilize our Children.

The British traders were left in ignorance of this development; it could have resolved all their dire problems.[101]

* * *

The months dragged on; the affair merged into its second phase. European politics were extremely tense at this time, with many incidents occupying Palmerston's attention. After much chopping and changing at the French Foreign Office, the Marquis de Turgot took over the reins in the autumn of 1851.[102] By now the will and the arteries were hardening. Precedents were on the record for resisting the British claims; General de la Hitte had left his own dogged legacy, and Turgot was entirely content to fasten on to what his predecessor-but-three had set down as the French policy.[103]

Matthew Forster was still fighting. He had sent a renewed appeal to Palmerston on 14 June 1851: 'The situation of these poor men kept here in suspense is really deplorable.' Once more, the redoubtable champion leapt into the saddle, and charged into the fray. On 9 September 1851 he referred the current papers yet again to the Queen's Advocate. Despite the resistance of both the Belgian and French governments, Palmerston was clearly still determined to continue the pressure on behalf of his two embattled but increasingly desperate compatriots. There are no surviving records of the legal opinions provided by this shadowy legal entity, as a complement to Palmerston's instincts. At least nine references appear to have been made during the period of the Braithwaite and Martin claims.[104] The fact that there is no indication of a similar legalistic approach by France or Belgium, does not rob the British recourse to this mechanism of its potential usefulness: the only problem was that it could only spur on the political will, not replace it if it was lacking in the first place.

The autumn of 1851 became a depressing 'doldrums' for the case. There was much going on politically in the three countries during these months, including demonstrations against the Austrian, General Haynau — 'General Hyena' — in both Brussels and London, on account of his bloody suppression of opposition in the Habsburg domains.[105] Palmerston had plenty on his mind, and the momentum faltered — with fateful consequences, as it transpired, for the Braithwaite and Martin claims, now in their third soul-destroying year.

Coup de Grâce or Coup d'État? December 1851

On 19 December 1851, Queen Victoria finally brought about a technically constitutional action which she had unconstitutionally precipitated. The statesman whom she preferred to think of as 'her' Prime Minister handed over to her the Foreign Secretary's seals of office; he did so in the unexpected absence of that equally — if not in some senses even more — senior statesman whom *The Times* had described as the holder of 'one of the most arduous and important offices not only in this country but in the whole world'. Lord Palmerston's resignation was being 'required' by Lord John Russell; it was formally within the remit of the Prime Minister who had appointed him. He was sacked by a Prime Minister whose own understanding of foreign affairs was slender — not for his failure in keeping Britain at the table of European power, but for his raw success in that increasingly difficult balancing act, with its fulcrum in Vienna. Its immediate cause was Napoleon III's *coup d'état* in Paris: the sacking of Vienna's main opponent,

Palmerston, was attacked as a *coup d'état* in its own right, by those who believed foreign hands were involved — Viennese hands.[106] It certainly delivered a *coup de grâce* for the Nunez Affair.

The young Queen just managed to draw back sufficiently from the brink of direct intervention, to remain on the right side of the constitution; however, there is little doubt among the major published authorities, both biographical and legal, that her thinking, which pushed Russell into this action, was subtly unconstitutional. She had been aided and abetted in this thinking for the preceding ten years by a trio of inputs — the constant but skewed advice of Uncle Leopold, who believed that the reform legislation of 1832 had abolished the very spirit of this ancient British monarchy, which might so easily have become his own; the middle-European conditioning of Albert; and the fundamentally influential but misguided views of the court's *éminence grise* and '*Uitlander* adviser', Baron Stockmar. When fed into the mind of a strong-willed Queen, a merely troublesome trio became a very querulous quartet.[107]

Indeed their thinking was also anachronistic, in terms of the way the unwritten British constitution could be judged to have evolved since Russell's own Reform Act. Her behaviour was castigated at the time not only by Palmerston, in fact a committed British constitutional monarchist, and the 'arch Whig' Russell himself — proud of his seventeenth-century republican ancestry — but also by a courtier, the Earl of Clarendon, at that stage still no acolyte of Palmerston. Always a difficult point for foreigners to understand, what Clarendon termed as 'THEY' were seen to be interfering in a way that was against the trend of the conventions, as opposed to the laws, of that constitution — what Clarendon called 'a habit of inconvenient meddling'.[108] It was a scandal.

In this 'affair' too, in ironic parallel with the Nunez Affair, some could advance an argument that the leading figure 'only had himself to blame'. Nevertheless, the fact is that the weary Russell finally capitulated to months, indeed years, of royal nagging in what was to prove to be the British monarchy's last attempt to exercise one of the Crown's vestigial royal prerogatives — a purported right to dismiss a minister, in this case a man with over 40 years of experience of politics, whom Victoria had earlier described as merely 'one of her public servants'.[109] The *Morning*

Post had weighed in with the warning that 'hitherto ... England has at least been governed by ministers of her own choice, owing responsibility to no sovereign and no country "but their own".'[110]

This thinking was certainly not aimed at benefiting France — or Belgium. It was a cumulative reaction by the court to a succession of actions by Palmerston, notably that autumn in relation to his endorsement of the abuse of Austria's General Haynau in London's streets; the reception given, against the court's wishes, to pro-Kossuth supporters from that hotbed of radicalism, Islington, in Palmerston's home; and finally Palmerston's informal approval of Louis Napoleon's own *coup d'état* of 2 December, despite a British Cabinet decision to be neutral. In the Queen's eyes, the action she so fervently desired was meant to restore royal relationships with other monarchies in Europe, even absolute regimes, where the court had come to believe that Palmerston's conduct was detrimental to smooth working, and 'with whom she professes to be on terms of Peace and Amity'.[111] It was also undoubtedly meant to stem the tide in that inexorable waning of the Crown's constitutional power in relation to the ever-strengthening executive, at that time most colourfully epitomized in her Secretary of State. As the French *Journal des Débats* put it succinctly,[112] '*Lord Palmerston tenait, après et même auprès de Lord John Russell, la première place dans le cabinet.*'[113]

Only Gladstone was later to upstage Palmerston in the populist but royally unpopular assertion of the growing role of the executive *vis-à-vis* the Crown, eschewing, like Palmerston, the softer, less obvious ways of circumventing that mighty royal will, which their respective opponents, Disraeli, and even Russell himself, had so delicately espoused.[114] His justifiable constitutional stand did him even less good in the eyes of his doughtily resistant sovereign than it did Palmerston.[115] This single action — exercised through Russell — the result, as Queen Victoria expressed it in her Journal, of 'our anxiety and worry during the last 5 years & ½', and the outcome of a whole series of foreign policy episodes, had a decisive, if not immediate, effect on the issue of the Rio Nunez Affair.[116]

France was the power that had above all others obsessed Palmerston, not without good reason, ever since the time of the first Napoleon. In the formal statement of outstanding business feverishly prepared by Palmerston's clerks for his successor on 27

December, there is an astonishing testimony to the importance
that Palmerston, and therefore the British Foreign Office, still
clearly attached to the Braithwaite and Martin claims. All
ministerial papers were regarded as the personal property of the
outgoing minister, not of the state. The papers carefully kept by
Palmerston about what he bitterly referred to as 'My removal',
summarized his bequest to those that were to come after him.
Under the heading FRANCE — it is omitted from the Belgian
papers — what can now be better described as the Rio Nunez
Affair is identified as the second most pressing item on the list:

> *State of Current Business.* FRANCE ...
> Messrs Braithwaite & Martin's claim. This claim is
> founded upon the alleged wanton destruction of the Stores of
> Messrs Braithwaite & Martin, British merchants established
> at Debucca in the River Nunez, during an attack on that
> town in 1849 by a French and a Belgian Vessel of War. The
> case has been referred to the Queen's Advocate and he has
> reported that HM's Govt. would be borne out in demanding
> from the French and Belgian Govts compensation for Messrs
> Braithwaite & Martin. The French have, however, withstood
> this Claim, and at present the matter rests with the Queen's
> Adv'te, to whom a second reference was made on the 5th of
> Sept last, to which no answer has yet been returned.[117]

This endorsement was Palmerston's legacy to his successors.

Notes

1. T. Pakenham, *The Scramble for Africa* (London, 1991), pp.185–8, 488, 680, *passim*.
2. For report on Ghent fête on 21/22 July 1849, see BL Add. MS 48,553, de Walden to P, 26 July 1849; also SGA/B doc. BP 9, deposition of sailor Nissen, 28 July 1849.
3. For coverage in British history, see R. C. Braithwaite, 'Palmerston and the Nunez: The Affair Within the Affair, 1849–53', *JICH*, vol.23, no.3, 1995; and Prologue, n.42 *supra*. For portrayal by Belgian and French historians, see Bibliographical Summary.
4. Bicaise to Tocnaye, 25 June 1849.
5. For relevance of Belgian royal involvement, see J. Everaert and C. De Wilde, 'Pindanoten voor de eerste ontluikende industrële revolutie: Een alternative kijk op de Belgische commerciële expansie in West-Afrika, 1844–1861', *BARSOM* (Brussels, 1992), *passim*; also, Chap.3, *supra*; R. Massinon, *L'Entreprise du Rio Nunez: Mémoire de Licence inédit ULB* (Brussels, 1965), pp.326–3, 339, 351–2. For role of HM, see Appendix 2. For impact of

Napoleon III on the affair, see *infra*, Chap.6. See also C. W. Newbury, *British Policy Towards West Africa: Selected Documents* (Oxford, 1965), pp.21, 226, Doc 7P. The ambivalence of P's attitude towards matters African, making his interest in the Nunez Affair even more extraordinary, is well exemplified here: 'Lord Palmerston had forbidden the use of the word "Treaty" in the African context, "to mark the distinction between Agreements with barbarous Chiefs and the international Compact of Civilized States" . . . they were "Second-class Agreements".' By contrast see F/CAOM dossier 26.c, 5 August 1847, '*A Sa Majesté Louis-Philippe, premier Roy des Français: Sire Le nommé Mayoré, Roi des Landoumans*'.

6.   See C. Fyfe, *A History of Sierra Leone* (London, 1962), p.268. 'Some 30 years later . . . an obscure Mr Macdonald was entering his third decade of inglorious retirement at Taunton' (ibid., pp.256–7); see also Epilogue. For estimate of deaths, see n.38 *infra* on Derecourt to F&S.

7.   Apart from the Swords of Honour to VH and de la Tocnaye, Massinon (*Entreprise*, p.334) records 12 mutual awards being given to VH, Ensign Dufour and Maître-Cannonier Rietveldt on 18 July 1849, chevaliers de l'Ordre de Leopold to Captain Witteveen of the *Emma* on 29 August 1849, an award by the French government of the Cross of the Légion d'honneur to VH, Surgeon-Major Durant, Ensigns Dufour and du Colombier, and Cohen on 25 January 1850, chevaliers de l'Ordre de Leopold to Captains de la Tocnaye and de Kerhallet on 12 April 1850 (p.341) and an Ordre de Leopold to Bicaise on 10 December 1850. '*Un arrête du 10 décembre 1850 conféra l'Ordre de Leopold au traitant anglais Bicaise, en récompense de son rôle dans les préliminaires du traité belgo-nalou et de l'appui qu'il fournissait depuis lors tant aux officiers de la Marine royale qu'aux agents des expéditions belges.*' There were no Belgian awards for Cohen.

8.   G. Macoir, 'Note sur un Sabre d'Honneur décerné à Capt [VH]', *Bull. des Musées royaux des Arts décoratifs et industriels* (Brussels, 1907), see Chap.3 *supra*; also Braithwaite, 'Sabre'.

9.   See Part I for Roebuck's speech, Hansard, 25 June 1850; also HRO/M, Malmesbury Papers, Diary, 28 May 1852, in connection with the injury to the son of a Mr Mather, in Florence: 'The Opposition . . . are making capital of this and other freaks of travelling Englishmen abroad . . . who put themselves into scrapes. . . . This conduct . . . is very much due to a blustering speech . . . by Lord Palmerston, declaring that John Bull, wherever he was or whatever he did, was to be as sacred as the ancient *civis Romanus*.'

10.   For Mills, see FO 125/2, Abstr. of Correspondence to Belgium 1836–57, P to de Walden, 9 April 1850, 6 May 1851, Malmesbury to de Walden, 19 April, 9 May 1852. For other cases of *cives Romani*, see J. Ridley, *Lord Palmerston* (London, 1970), p.359 *et seq*. For significance of colonies to Belgium, see Massinon, *Entreprise*, p.311.

11.   FO 125/2, Malmesbury to de Walden, 9 March 1852 on 'if Mills claim not immediately settled, to be made an international matter'. For comparable F&S claims re French actions in Portendic in Senegal in the 1830s, again with P, see R. C. Braithwaite, 'Palmerston and the Nunez'; cf. FO 97/185.

12.   B. Kingsley Martin, *The Triumph of Lord Palmerston: A Study of Public Opinion in England before the Crimean War* (London, 1924, rev. edn, 1963), *passim*. For Forster's experience of press manipulation, see the Madden controversy Chap.2 *supra*, and n.44 *infra*.

13.   See Chap.6 and Appendix 3.

14.   Ridley, *Palmerston*, Chaps.26 and 27, pp.359–91; Donald Southgate, *The Most English Minister: The Policies and Politics of Palmerston* (London,

1966), pp.263–4. One direct parallel with the *civis Romanus* metaphor would not have been lost on P, since it bore directly on the Nunez Affair; it was brought out by Gladstone in the debate (see Part I, *supra*), and is commented on by Kingsley Martin, *Triumph*, p.60, who says that 'There is, as Gladstone pointed out . . . no real analogy between the British subject, travelling in countries which possess their own laws and civilization, and the Roman citizen of the Empire, dwelling among conquered and semi-barbaric peoples whose only law and justice came from their conquerors' — a not inexact picture of the Nunez in 1849.

15. FO 147/35, Malmesbury to de Walden, 30 March 1852; for examination of France/Belgium, see Chap.6.

16. FO 125/2, P to de Walden, 27 August 1850; FO 147/33, P to Normanby, 413, 6 August 1850, despite continuing repercussions from the Athens 'affair'; see n.60 *infra*. Calculation by Bank of England Information Dept.

17. See Chap.2 *supra*.

18. Kenneth Bourne, *Palmerston: The Early Years, 1784–1841* (London, 1982), p.451; see Appendix 2.

19. *Arsène Lupin* (by Maurice Le Blanc); *Poirot* (Agatha Christie); *Sherlock Holmes* (Conan Doyle).

20. *Journal du Commerce d'Anvers*, 6 July 1849; see Chap.4.

21. For too ready recourse to 'rules of war', see Chap.4. Also FO 123/674, another '*exposé des faits*', which d'Hoffschmidt tries to use as pretext in his letter to de Walden of 3 September 1850 stating that '*Les nécessités du combat n'ont pas permis de respecter l'habitation de B&M.*'

22. O. Petitjean, '*Les Tentatives de colonisation faites sous le règne de Leopold Ier*': *La Belgique en 1930* (Brussels, October–November 1930), pp.6–11, with reference to M. Osy to Chambre des Représentants, 26 May 1851, states that '*L'Article 68 est formelle . . . Les traités de commerce et ceux qui pourraient grever l'Etat . . . n'ont d'effet qu'après avoir obtenu l'assentiment des Chambres*'; see also Massinon, *Entreprise*, pp.340–3; Braithwaite, 'Sabre', pp.89, 94; C. Lannoy/T. du Colombier, 'Une Expédition franco-belge en Guinée: La Campagne de la goélette de guerre *Louise-Marie* dans la Colonie belge du Rio-Nunez (1849)', *BESBEC* (Brussels, mai–juin 1920), p.179. All the Belgian officers who volunteered to transfer and found the new German navy in 1850 declined to continue when that service was re-formed as the Prussian fleet a few years later.

23. B/MAE, Correspondance politique, Hitte to Firmin Rogier, letter 19 April 1850, refers to '*Votre note verbale*', Rogier to Hitte of 26 December 1849.

24. See account of the Don Pacifico affair, *infra*.

25. See n.107 *infra*.

26. See n.7 *supra*.

27. Brian Connell, *Regina v. Palmerston* (London, 1962), pp.132–3; cf. RA A 79 17.xii.1851 and RA QJ 11–29.xii.1851; see Appendix 2.

28. SGA/B doc. FP 4, Bidwell to Joseph Braithwaite, 17 July 1849.

29. For considerations of the P 'touch', and even his 'Churchillian touch', see Southgate, *English Minister*, pp.xv–xvi, pp.371–8. For questions of passports, see Ridley, *Palmerston*, p.362. For flight of Louis-Philippe and Guizot to London (after 24 February 1848) and Metternich (after 13 March), see Ridley, *Palmerston*, p.332.

30. SGA/B doc. BP 11, 12. For Norie's later dismissal, see FO 125/2, 9, 28 May 1851, P to de Walden.

31. See SGA/B docs BP 1 to 12, *passim*. Hotel de Vienne, was Le Grand Café de Bruxelles (*Guido Deseyn*, (Antwerp, 1991), p.297). It was at 8 Koorn-markt,

in the town centre; today it has art deco windows, within a tall and narrow frontage, painted cream and white. The owner in 1849 was E. Bourgeois (*Wegwijzer der Stad Gent en Provinciale Almanack van Oost-Vlaenderen voor het jaer des zaligmakers* (Gent, 1849), p.63). C. De Wilde, letters to author of 31 May, 26 June 1995. Also FO 125/2, 28 May 1851.

32. SGA/B doc. BP 1, Joseph Braithwaite to J. Forster, 27 July 1849.

33. SGA/B doc. BP 6 and 7, Joseph Braithwaite to John Forster, 26, 27 July 1849.

34. Ridley, *Palmerston*, pp.356–7, 569–74; Southgate, *English Minister*, p.211. As P told this story after 1861, as one of his few celebrated jokes, the three men were Prince Albert (who had now died), the former head of the German Dept at the FO, (Richard Charles Mellish), who had gone mad, and himself, who now said he had forgotten it. For other references to Mellish, see Bourne, *Early Years*, pp.430, 446, 635.

35. FO 123/69, M. Thader, Danish consul at Ghent, to Joseph Braithwaite, 12 January 1851. He claimed Nissen gave his evidence freely and was released amicably the next day.

36. SGA/B doc. EP1a, Joseph Braithwaite from Badger Heath, Shropshire, to John Forster at New City Chambers, 2 August 1849.

37. SGA/B doc. AP 27, Dep. AA, 10 May 1849, Lloyd to F&S.

38. SGA/B doc. EP7a, Derecourt to F&S, 21 August 1849; FO 97/198.

39. FO 147/35, Normanby to P, 19 January 1850. For early use of term 'wanton outrages', see n.55 *infra*; FO 97/198 BL SPIS.

40. See PPSC 1842.

41. See Chap.4 *supra*.

42. Archives of the B/MRA.

43. See Part I, *supra*, and Appendix 1.

44. See Madden episode, Chap.2 *supra*; see n.99 *infra*, for example of the difficulties faced by colonial governors in their relationships with 'Downing Street'.

45. FO 123/60, 11 June, 21 July 1849, Forster to P, 7 August 1849.

46. See Appendix 3.

47. CO267/211, Hotham to ADM, 1849; ADM to FO, 9 April 1849, stating that M. Bouët's 'idea did not meet my views . . . French eyes are turned to this River'. See also Chap.3.

48. SGA/B docs BP 1 to 12, and Joseph Braithwaite to F&S, 6 July 1849, Forster to P, 7 and 24 August 1849.

49. FO 27/858, Gov. MacDonnell, GA to CO, 4 June 1849, reference to B&M to MacDonnell, 9 May, 'Debucca where we contemplated residing'.

50. For impact on de la Hitte at a time critical to the Nunez Affair of instructions to Southern to ratify peace with General Rosas in Buenos Aires, see FO 147/32, Normanby to P, 568, 2 December 1849. A possible explanation was that this omission was deliberate, not accidental, as P tried to claim. See BL Add. MS 48,557,561, P to Normanby, 4 December, referring to 'some very unusual and therefore . . . avoidable neglect . . . in this Office'.

51. See Chap.4, *supra*.

52. Ridley, *Palmerston*, pp.230, 361, 365.

53. Ridley, *Palmerston*, pp.363–9, 681. However, the Queen's Advocate is not identified in the Index; international law is not listed in the indices of Bourne or Southgate. See Appendix 2.

54. BL Add. MS 48,557, P to Normanby, 26 February 1848; see n.71 *infra*.

55. BL Add. MS 48,499, P to Sir J. Seymour, 19 March 1841, says 'the acts of the Belgian volunteers were wanton outrages'.

56. For those involved, 'Risquons-Tout' lived up to its name. BL Add. MS

48,553, de Walden to P, 18 March, 13 July, 31 August 1848 mentions 17 prisoners being condemned to death and 15 acquitted. This minor clash could be seen as the small kingdom's first call to arms following its foundation in 1831, but the battle of Boké was its first significant military event under its national colours. See Chap.6 *infra*, n.26.

57. FO 147/32, FO, 1 June 1850.

58. See n.50 *supra*; Ridley, *Palmerston*, p.58. Also J. Ridley, *Napoleon III and Eugénie* (London, 1979), pp.262–7, 277. 'de la Hitte' is the signature in F/CAOM and in the FO 368/1, 2, Register/Abstracts of Correspondence. It is shown elsewhere as la Hitte and De la Hitte. He was one of the unelected conservative ministers appointed by Prince-President Louis-Napoleon in October 1849 to offset the perceived threat to the stability of the state from the Red Socialist 'Mountain'. He contested, unsuccessfully, a Paris deputy's vacant seat, although as a minister he had the right of address to the Assembly in any case. His proudest moment in that Assembly was to be able to present the outcome of the Don Pacifico affair as a complete victory for France, As Ridley comments, P did not mind such a 'spin' to events abroad, provided that his image at home was secure, which it clearly was after the debate.

59. F/MAE, *Correspondance politique, Légations*, vols 30, 31, 32.

60. FO 123/62, de Walden to Eddisbury, 31 August 1850. De Walden compares the B&M claims with another pending claim, that of a Mr Britten; (Lord Eddisbury, the Parliamentary Under-Secretary, was the Hon. E. J. Stanley).

61. FO 123/61, P to de Walden, 7 May 1850, enclosing P to Normanby. FO 84/877, Forster to P, 24 September 1849, refers to his meeting with Addington. See Bourne, *Early Years*, p.463, for the early transactions with Normanby (Musgrave); n.73 *infra*.

62. G. Delcourt, 'Relation du Voyage à la Côte d'Afrique avec la goélette *Louise-Marie* 1848–9'; Chap.4 *supra*.

63. This is a summary of the arguments, from all the sources.

64. F/CAOM, de Kerhallet to Ministère de la Marine, 27 July 1850, Bicaise to P, 'Protestation', 30 March 1849.

65. ADM 53/2594, Log of the *Grappler*, 15–30 January 1848.

66. SGA/B doc. FP 19, p.23; also BL Add. MS, 48,553, P to de Walden, 3 January 1850.

67. B/MAE doc. 128, d'Hoffschmidt to Rogier, February (undated) 1850, after de Walden to d'Hoffschmidt, doc. 126, 17 January.

68. Bourne, *Early Years*, pp.361, 431, 496–7, 551.

69. Ridley, *Palmerston*, p.484; cf. D. Magarshack, *Turgenev* (London, 1954), pp.183–5. Turgenev, guest at a public dinner, in London, April 1858, described it in the *Edinburgh Review*.

70. BL Add. MS, 48,553, de Walden to P, 2 May 1850.

71. P had been ill-served by Normanby for some time: see FO 27/775, P to Normanby, 26 May 1847, where P, using his two-month 'follow-up' system, has to remind Normanby of his failure to reply to a dispatch of 26 March about Mr Jenkyn's claims. For reference to the Paris revolution, see BL Add. MS 48,557, P to Normanby, 26 February 1848, stating 'I have to instruct you to remain at your post until you receive further orders to the contrary'; also P to Normanby, 28 June. 'Lord Normanby will read this despatch to M. Bastide and will give him a copy . . . if he should wish it.' For *Highlander* case of 1840, see BL Add. MS 48,557, P to Normanby, 28 August 1849; also FO 27/858, F&S to P, 7 August 1849, refers to £1000 claim due to incident with brigantine *Mary* at R. Lloyd's factory at Sedhiou and to the 'outrage

committed by the French on the property . . . of a Correspondent of ours, Mr R. Lloyd . . . this process appears to be part of a plan adopted by the French . . . to monopolize trade with the Natives.'

72. B/MAE, 19 April 1850, Hitte to Rogier.
73. FO 123/61, P to Normanby, 7 May 1850, states 'I have to instruct Yr Excy to review the report you were instructed to make to the French Govt . . . my despatch of 23 Oct last!'. Also Hitte to Normanby of 29 August 1850. It seems that Normanby still did not make any representations until 29 May and 11 August. See Chap.6.
74. B/MAE, Lhuys to P, 3 April 1850.
75. FO 147/32, Normanby to P, 254, 22 July 1850, reference to Hitte to Normanby, in Normanby to P, 11 April 1850. In dispatch 325, October, Hitte also expressed appreciation for the British attitude over the Albréda problems on the GA, and said that he wanted to reach an 'amicable arrangement'.
76. Ridley, *Palmerston*, pp.380–5; Southgate, *English Minister,* pp.263–4.
77. B/MAE, docs 57, 77, Drouyn/Van de Weyer to d'Hoffschmidt, 12 April, 20 May 1850.
78. B/MAE, doc 162, 6 December 1849, d'Hoffschmidt to Van de Weyer; doc. 166, 11 December, Van de Weyer to d'Hoffschmidt. F. Mount, Umbrella (London, 1994), p.13; Lord Sudley, *The Lieven Palmerston Correspondence: 1828–1856* (London, 1943), pp.292–3; see also P. Zamoyska, *Arch Intriguer* (London, 1957), pp.232–3. From her lodgings in Richmond, Princess Lieven returned to Paris in November 1849.
79. B/MAE doc. 78, Van de Weyer to d'Hoffschmidt, 24 May 1850, speaks of *'une guerre où la France prendrait la revanche de Waterloo'*.
80. B/MAE doc. 104, Van de Weyer to d'Hoffschmidt, 26 June 1850.
81. B/MAE doc. 107, Hoffschmidt to Van de Weyer, 27 June 1850.
82. B/MAE doc. 107, refers to Rogier to Hitte, 26 December 1849.
83. B/MAE, Afrique 2024/3, 2019, ordre 19, d'Hoffschmidt to Rogier, 10 January 1850.
84. B/MAE, Afrique 2024/3, Hitte to Rogier, 15 June 1850.
85. F/CAOM, 15 June 1850, Hitte to Ministère de la Marine, refers to meeting on 11 March: *'telles sont les . . . assertions que nous avons à repousser'*.
86. B/MAE, Afrique 2024/3, Hitte to Carolus, 29 August 1850. The long letters of de la Tocnaye, 15 August 1850, and de Kerhallet, 27 July 1850, are excluded merely for reasons of space: they are to be found in FO 97/198. See Chap.6.
87. Everaert and De Wilde, 'Pindanoten'; see n.7 *supra.*
88. 'Lexical leakage', term used in the counselling process, where the inadvertent use of a particular word reveals the true intent, the inner agenda of the writer.
89. FO 97/198; see n.86 *supra.* Re visit, the B/MAE doc 143, Van de Weyer to d'Hoffschmidt, records this as on 17 August; B&M to P '19 August 1850'. He provides B&M with a letter of introduction to Van de Weyer. Perhaps P, with his characteristic optimism, put too much faith in Van de Weyer, trusting the relationship built up in the 1830s during the long negotiations in London to settle Belgium's future. Significantly, his friend de Walden had earlier, on 15 January 1849, questioned Van de Weyer's reliability 'My dear Palmerston, I cannot help thinking that King Leopold's vanity has led to a communication with *The Times* . . . are you sure of Van de Weyer?' (PBHA GC/HO/ 713/1).
90. FO 125/3, d'Hoffschmidt to de Walden, 3 September, and de Walden to P, 9 September 1850.
91. B/MAE doc. 145b, Carolus to d'Hoffschmidt, 30 August 1850.

92. PBHA, GC/HO/719–739, de Walden to P, 4 February 1850.
93. FO 125/3, de Walden to Eddisbury, 31 August 1850.
94. De Walden to P, 7 February 1851.
95. See Part I *supra*.
96. B/MAE doc. 145b, Hitte to Rogier, 2 October 1850 (many of these letters were burned in a fire at the B/MAE and are difficult to decipher).
97. P to Addington, 20 December 1850.
98. See Chap.4 *supra*.
99. By contrast, CO267/216, Grey memo on Barrow to Merivale refers to Pine, 12 December 1850, saying he had 'so much confidence in his judgement'. On 14 October 1852, Macdonald was to be replaced by Gov. Kennedy, after a witch-hunt from within the comfort of 'Downing Street' by Merivale, for having moved 'Government troops out of the colony [of SL] ...Hawes described it as 'censurable' in CO267/213, 3 May 1850. This underlines the 'catch-22' nature of the problem faced by distant, misunderstood governors. See Chap.2 *supra*.
100. CO267/215, Prendergast and Commissioners to Macdonald, 15 March 1850. Lt-Com. Selwyn also reported at length to Gov. Macdonald. P belatedly appointed a consul for the Nunez, but by then the territory had slipped from Britain's potential grasp.
101. Letter from George Martin to F&S, 9 June 1852, states that he had heard from 'a friend of mine on the Gambia that Mr Braithwaite was well'. He was writing from Llanstephen Cottage, Saltash, a charming thatched cottage which still overlooks the hillsides of the Tamar, the home of his sister, and his brother, an RN paymaster. Data supplied by Saltash Heritage, in author's possession.
102. F/MAE. See Chap.6 *infra*, n.1.
103. FO 147/35, Turgot to Cowley, 24 February 1852, sees 'No reason to change his opinion'. See Chap.6.
104. The nine dates are 8 August and 14 September1849; 5 March and 30 June 1850; 9 September 1851; 19 January, 16 March and 30 October 1852; and 29 July 1853. No records remain in the PRO Treasury 'TS' series (Chancery Lane at time of writing): they must have been 'culled' by a zealous clerk. See Appendix 2.
105. FO 125/3, de Walden to FO, 23 August 1852. Haynau was hooted on the streets of Brussels; see also Ridley, *Palmerston*, p.395; Southgate, *English Minister*, pp.283–4, 310.
106. *The Times*, 24 December 1851. 'The dismissal of Lord P was announced in the *Breslau Gazette*, in a letter dated Vienna Dec 23rd, a week before the news could have reached Austria ... a day after it was known in London ... [it] was a pre-concerted *coup d'état*' (Effingham Wilson, *Letters of W. Coningham* (London, 1854), pp.5–30).
107. For the most comprehensive accounts of this 'resignation', see Southgate, *English Minister*, pp.248–51, Chap.15, pp.279 *et seq*.; Ridley, *Palmerston*, Chap.28, pp.392–405; Connell, *Regina*, Chaps.4 and 5, pp.99–138, who says that 'the wonder is that it did not lead to a constitutional crisis of the first magnitude'. This comment is all the more relevant in the light of the *Breslau Gazette* letter. This important constitutional episode is examined fully in Appendix 2.
108. Southgate, *English Minister*, p.248; cf. Sir H. Maxwell, *The Life and Letters of the Fourth Earl of Clarendon* (London, 1913), vol.1, p.341, Clarendon to G. C. Lewis, 26 December 1851.
109. RA A 79/76, HM to LJR, Windsor Castle, 31 October 1851.

110. *Morning Post*, 25 December 1851.
111. RA C10/28, HM to LJR, Windsor, 20 November 1851.
112. For a contemporary comparison, attended with comparable problems, see appointment of M. Heseltine, June 1995.
113. *Journal des Débats*, 26 December 1851.
114. P. Guedalla (ed.) *Gladstone and Palmerston: Being the Correspondence of Lord Palmerston with Mr Gladstone, 1851–1865* (London, 1928), *passim* and Introduction (source of the book's opening quotation); Ridley, *Palmerston*, pp.392–9. 'When [Disraeli] was asked later . . . the secret of his success with the Queen, he replied: "I never refuse; I never contradict; I sometimes forget".' (André Maurois, *Disraeli: A Picture of the Victorian Age* (Paris and Appleton, 1927), p.241 *et seq.*, 244–5); see n.107.
115. Roy Jenkins, *Gladstone* (London, 1995), pp.232, 296–7, 337–40, 342–7; see also W. E. Gladstone, *Gleanings of Past Years: 1843–78* (London, 1879), *passim*; also Lord H. J. Gladstone, *After Thirty Years: A Defence of W. E. Gladstone* (London, 1928).
116. RA, QVJ, 20 December 1851.
117. PBHA, FOC/3–4, State of Current Business, FO for Earl Granville, 27 December 1851. See Appendix 2 for examination of the little-known role of the Queen's Advocate in P's conduct of foreign policy.

6. The Affair Within the Affair: End-Game, 1852–1853

Over the ensuing 18 months, there were no less than four different pairs of hands on the conduct of foreign policy in both London and Paris.[1] This common instability was to prove inimical to any British hopes of taking the Rio Nunez claims forward. In default of actual understanding, both Foreign Offices fell back on the comfort of precedent. Only Leopold's trusted minister, d'Hoffschmidt, stayed in power.

In Britain's case, the next four Secretaries of State for Foreign Affairs were all either already Earls of the realm, or shortly destined to be elevated to that patrician eminence. The first three in succession, Earl Granville, the Earl of Malmesbury and Lord John Russell, could not exactly be described as pro-Palmerston on their past record, although Granville now held him in healthy regard. Conversely, the fourth, the Earl of Clarendon, was by 1853 both an admirer, and a protégé of Palmerston; yet, ironically, it was during the brief tenures of office of the first three, despite all the other pressing European matters, with the Eastern Question becoming more and more menacing, that some kind of attempt was made to continue the Rio Nunez 'campaign'.

As each new figure appeared on the scene, Matthew Forster's political instinct told him to remind the new incumbent of the outstanding claim. A letter was accordingly sent to Granville early in January 1852; Queen Victoria had recorded in her Journal that already Granville 'had had an interview of nearly 3 hours with Lord Palmerston whom Lord John had desired to give him the usual information, and whom he had found very civil & cordial'.[2] The agenda must have been the 'Current Business' memorandum. The inexperienced Granville, stepping respectfully into his great

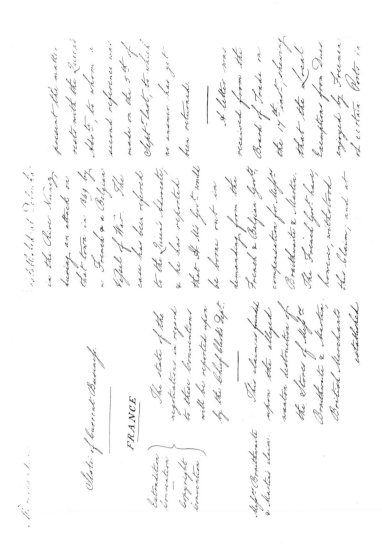

FIGURE 8 Palmerston's State of Current Business (handover) note for Earl Granville, December 1851, showing the high importance still attached to the Nunez Affair by the outgoing Foreign Secretary. By kind permission of the Trustees of the Palmerston Archives, Hartley Library, Southampton University, and the Crown Copyright Unit.

predecessor's shoes, grasped the legacy firmly. Even within the span of his mere two months in office, he boldly relaunched the campaign with Palmerstonian energy. Having instructed Lord Cowley to write to the government of first resort, France, on 29 January, he sent a parallel dispatch to Lord Howard de Walden on 31 January:

> I transmit ... a letter from Messrs Braithwaite and Martin ... and as (these ... appear) ... satisfactorily to refute the statements in question I have to instruct you to represent the matter again to the Belgian Government, and to express the confident hope ... that they will no longer delay to afford ... that equitable compensation which the justice of their cause entitles them to claim.[3]

D'Hoffschmidt replied to de Walden on 23 February. Turgot in Paris, who had now followed on from de la Hitte and his successors, replied to Lord Cowley's parallel request a day later, that 'he had no reason to change his opinion': de la Hitte's view still stood.[4] It was no coincidence.

De Walden reported to Granville on 25 February, but it came three days too late. Russell's Ministry had already been overturned by Palmerston's 'tit-for-tat' motion on 22 February, and the even less experienced Malmesbury was in the hot seat at the Foreign Office, a member for the next nine months of the ineffectual 'Who? Who?' Ministry of Lord Derby.[5] He too got the benefit of Palmerston's advice about 'foreign relations', on 24 February, with or without any mention of the Rio Nunez — the records are silent.[6] His first encounter with Forster & Smith was on 16 March, when he forwarded their letter 'pressing for settlement' of the parallel claim for the destruction of the *Highlander* on the neighbouring River Casamance. It is impossible to discern whether this concurrent pressure militated against the prospects of the Rio Nunez claims; it cannot have enhanced them, given the irritation factor in such situations.[7] He was written to again by Matthew Forster, this time on behalf of Braithwaite and Martin, on 11 May, and he in turn, belatedly, went through the motions of communicating with his two envoys, Cowley and de Walden, on 17 August, referring to Granville's notes of 31 January 'urging a reply'. He did so without enthusiasm. He confessed to not having 'any liking for the stormy life' and the Foreign Office's ten-hour working day; his constant concern was to try to cope with his workload, which he found increasingly injurious to his health, 'from the anxiety and fatigue of such a laborious place'. On 28 May his sentiments emerged when he was caught up in a comparable incident about what he called 'freaks of travelling Englishmen who get themselves into scrapes'.[8] Nevertheless, despite his obvious prejudices, Malmesbury allowed Palmerston's long arm to reach out and cause him also to enter the lists on Braithwaite and Martin's behalf, even if their case was in no way due to Palmerston's John Bullish encouragement — the factor that he was later to impute to his eminent predecessor.

* * *

By now however, a new orientation was discernible at both Brussels and Paris. From the communications of d'Hoffschmidt as well as Turgot, an abrasive and confident refusal to accept any legitimacy in these British claims was starting to emerge. They seemed to sense that the tide had turned, that they were dealing with a weaker administration. The erstwhile champion's influence was waning with every month that passed; they only had to 'withstand', and to hang on to their *version*s. This stance was further strengthened on 6 September 1852, by the 26-page 'observations' of Van Haverbeke. This long and all too successful attempt at self-justification built on the letters of two years previously, from de Kerhallet and de la Tocnaye to the French Ministère de la Marine; in it the British rebuttals were in their turn, roundly if speciously, rebutted.

Whatever the genial picture of the later Van Haverbeke might be, relating naval anecdotes to his cronies well into his nineties, this particular piece of mid-career storytelling does not enhance his reputation.[9] The most charitable explanation is that he was acting under ministerial instructions to build what d'Hoffschmidt could then claim to be an *examen approfondi*. He certainly declared his hand at the start: this was to be a piece of self-defence against the calumnies he asserted to have been made against him in the 57-page Braithwaite and Martin statements of 1851 and 1852: 'I will destroy the framework which they have so laboriously built up against me.'[10] Some of his points do have a plausibility: he might well have believed, in his ignorance of African matters, that Bicaise 'owned' some land at Cassassa, having bought outright, in European terms, what in fact could only be, in African eyes, the 'leasehold' from M. Valentin in 1837; Bicaise, however, would have known very well that the ultimate title to the land could never be 'his'.[11] The precise boundaries of the plot were, as in so much else, vague. There is also no doubt that Mayoré had gone too far, and that some kind of action was rightly called for. Van Haverbeke was very conscious of the six complaints that needed to be addressed. He added one more — 'Seventh complaint . . . the way I was received at Debouka.'

This was on his first expedition on 26 February, when he portrayed himself as nobly representing white civilized Europe, personified in the French and the British interests on the river — but with no mention at all of any Belgian plans: 'it is a question of maintaining the dominance of European influence.' The overriding purpose was evidently to remove himself, now well decorated for his pains, from any responsibility for what he openly described at the outset as 'our aggression against the Landumas'. The blame was placed firmly on the French: 'the superior commander was . . . de la Tocnaye'. Cohen, Witteveen and the Belgian colonial mission were not mentioned once. No one would know from this document alone that it was Van Haverbeke who controlled the mortar so ferociously and single-handedly that morning in 1849; that it was one of his own ensigns who first set fire to the English warehouse; let alone that it was Van Haverbeke who broke all known precedents — his recourse to a military solution against two legitimate traders representing a friendly European power.

Most of the Belgian's 'Observations' are so full of non sequiturs (to put it generously) that it is hard to represent fully their real flavour. One example must serve, a purported disavowal of the evidence of the foreign crew of the *Emma*, which Joseph Braithwaite had so painstakingly gathered at Antwerp and Ghent in the summer of 1849, and which was still valid in terms of what they witnessed going on: 'The declarations of the crew of the *Emma* do not merit the slightest credence — no one disembarked at Deboqué'. He constantly resorted to hearsay to support his view of the two traders, and their supposed influence on the Landumas, despite what he admitted to be merely a week's residence: 'It is public knowledge in the Rio Nunez that if [they] had not employed all kinds of means whereby Mayoré refused our demands, he would have given in to them instantly.' Van Haverbeke seemed to wear his heart permanently on his sleeve. On the second expedition he claimed that a yacht, belonging to M. Salcedo, not Bicaise, was brought along with a sole purpose, which no one bothered to tell the traders about. It was 'to put it at their disposition'. He later asserted that 'M. Bicaise is English by birth ... it is in this capacity that we protected him.'

Although Van Haverbeke went up to meet Mayoré in his stronghold, with undoubted courage, face to face, he never bothered to meet these two Englishmen: he sent a messenger instead. This strategem at least enabled him to preserve the extraordinarily melodramatic and bloodthirsty picture he had built up about them: 'They would have advised the Landumas to fall on us and exterminate us all.'

It would not have needed a barrister, let alone a clerk, to demonstrate the defects in most of these comments, with their none too subtle overlay of professed humanitarian principles. However, the point is that they succeed. The case did not fit easily into some 'wider picture', the time-honoured preferred pretext for Foreign Office action. There was no political advocate left to plead the British case. No one could be bothered to analyse the continuing holes in the Franco-Belgian arguments: despite reassurances otherwise, the clerks may not even have referred back to all the counter-arguments. On 14 October d'Hoffschmidt riposted with the Van Haverbeke 'Observations' to the British minister, who reported to the Foreign Office on 18 October. Damagingly, de Walden's earlier comments of 31 August 1850 to Lord Eddisbury, designed to save Palmerston from himself, about the pricing of such claims, were still on the files.[12] Malmesbury grasped eagerly at this flimsy pretext for washing his hands of the whole business, disregarding all the matters of substance, and on 22 November he caused Henry Addington to write to Braithwaite and Martin, purporting once and for all to dismiss the claim.[13]

On the fall of the Derby administration in December 1852 Lord Aberdeen brought back Lord Russell, temporarily holding the fort at the Foreign Office, to pave the way for the succession of the Earl of Clarendon, now a fervent if sorely pressed advocate of Palmerston's policies. Russell made no input to the Rio Nunez issue: there were no hand-over notes in the files about the affair, either to him from Malmesbury, or onwards to Clarendon. It appeared at last, three and a half years later, to be fulfilling John Nelson Bicaise's prediction of 'dying a natural death'.

By this time Joseph Braithwaite had sailed out again to the Gambia, resuming business to offset his debts. He was playing once more the role of a respected, if impoverished, member of what Governor O'Connor called 'our little community', and had been appointed a Commissioner of the Court of Requests. George Martin had by now found a roof over his head in the West Country, and was living with his brother's family. From Llanstephen Cottage, he had written to Forsters, reporting that he had heard that Mr Braithwaite was in good health, and trading again.[14] This absence caused them some delay in recontacting the Foreign Office, which they still devoutly hoped was pursuing their interests without the need for any further evidence. Patience was the only virtue they believed they needed while the wheels slowly ground onwards. On 29 May 1853, four years on, Braithwaite and Martin made their first and, as it transpired, last appeal in an 11-page letter to Clarendon. They were in danger of running out of things to say, other than to point out the 'very imperfect perusal of the Papers' in Malmesbury's handling of the evidence. They cited his dismissive, even callous remark 'that our statements rest on our assertion alone without any corroborative evidence'.

As they said, 'the strength of their position consisted in the possession of numerous documents from disinterested parties.' They went on to draw from written evidence provided by 'a gentleman conducting the business on the Coast of Africa of an extensive establishment in the US to the effect that he always paid anchorage [dues] at the Nunez'. This had been another negative point raised by Malmesbury. The letter concluded bravely, but forlornly: 'We venture to claim ... you will feel convinced that our case is one which demands speedy [sic] redress from our Aggressors.' This letter was sent on 1 June, covered with five pages from the sturdy if prejudiced old fighter, Matthew Forster, in 'utter consternation' at Malmesbury's earlier letter:

As Agents for those gentlemen and authorized in their absence to open all communications addressed to them from the Foreign Office, we lost no time ... in entreating his Lordship to reconsider [his decision]. ... They were the less

prepared for such an issue ... from the considerable attention ... which Lord Palmerston (by whom all the essential
negotiations ... had been conducted) had uniformly paid to
their representations ... and from which they indulged a
natural hope that the outrages ... would not be suffered by
the British government to be explained away ... by the mis-
representations and sheer recklessness of those responsible
for them. ... We forebear therefore from ... enlarging on ...
the injurious effects which such acts must ... have on the
developement [*sic*] of British commerce amongst the barbarous tribes of Western Africa.[15]

Even at this late stage there was what proved to be the last of
the nine references of the papers to the Queen's Advocate, on 29
July, before Clarendon, like Turgot, bowed to the precedent
conveniently provided by his predecessor. He commanded Henry
Addington to signal the Foreign Office's lily-livered capitulation to
the French and Belgian position in a sad letter of 25 August 1853;
the two Englishmen did not receive this until two months later, 26
October. All their hopes were now finally and absolutely dashed.
The virtues required to confront the import of this letter needed to
be of a higher order than mere patience:

Messrs Braithwaite & Martin

Gentlemen,
    I am directed by the Earl of Clarendon to acknowledge the
receipt of your letter of the 29th May last renewing your
claim upon the French and Belgian Governments for compensation of your property at Debuka in the river Nunez in
the year 1849. In reply I am directed to inform you that your
case has been again fully considered, and that as no new
point is raised in your letter upon which the representations
of Her Majesty's Goverment to the Governments of France
and Belgium could be renewed with any prospect of a
successful result, the Earl of Clarendon considers it useless to
reopen the case, and regrets therefore that he must adhere to
the decision already come to by Her Majesty's Government
not to take any further steps in the matter.

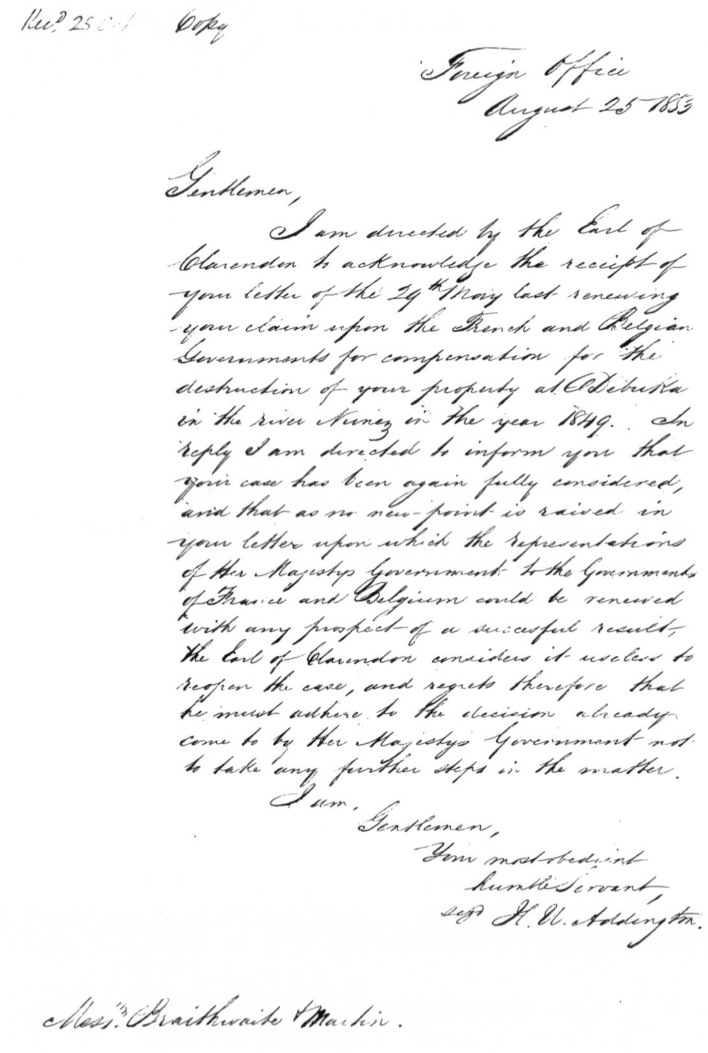

Recd 25 [...] Copy

Foreign Office
August 25 1853

Gentlemen,

I am directed by the Earl of
Clarendon to acknowledge the receipt of
your letter of the 29th May last renewing
your claim upon the French and Belgian
Governments for compensation for the
destruction of your property at Obibuka
in the river Nunez in the year 1849. In
reply I am directed to inform you that
your case has been again fully considered,
and that as no new point is raised in
your letter upon which the representations
of Her Majestys Government to the Governments
of France and Belgium could be renewed
with any prospect of a successful result,
the Earl of Clarendon considers it useless to
reopen the case, and regrets therefore that
he must adhere to the decision already
come to by Her Majestys Government not
to take any further steps in the matter.

I am,
Gentlemen,
Your most obedient
humble Servant,
sgd H. U. Addington.

Messrs. Braithwaite & Martin.

FIGURE 9 Final letter on behalf of the then Foreign Secretary, the Earl of
Clarendon, to Braithwaite and Martin, August 1853. Author's collection.

This is the penultimate document in the British government's official summary of 'the affair within the affair'. It was not the last word in the events that had erupted at Boké on 24 March 1849.[16]

Conclusions

What were the determining points? Weariness and boredom with such an isolated piece of injustice, however unprecedented, with no obvious connections to a wider Foreign Office 'issue'? The language of priorities, as Tsar Nicholas loomed ever larger in the Cabinets of Paris and London, and Britain's consequent need for a strong friend once again? Forster's decline in influence, perhaps not unconnected with his subsequent fall from grace in his career as Berwick's MP? Or the sheer passage of time? All or any of these factors could explain why Britain threw in the towel. As to Belgium, her importance was disproportionate to her size or even to Leopold's ambitions for her power-broking role: she was then, as again in the Europe of the 1990s, a vital intelligence centre. Palmerston understood this well, writing to de Walden that 'Brussels is a place where much may sometimes be heard about things that are going on elsewhere.'[17]

The actual nature of the balance of evidence was not by now uppermost in the official mind; there was no sign of the bluffing instinct of the Palmerston of the Pacifico or Mehmet Ali crises — that if Britain stood her ground, the French and in this case the Belgians also would cease to 'withstand'. The most plausible explanation seems to be the simple one that none of Palmerston's three successors were up to the job as he had created it. It was a succession problem. As Russell conceded (unnecessarily in Victoria's eyes), he had 'a capacity for business which has never been surpassed'.[18]

Either by virtue of their less determined characters, or through inexperience, or through the impact of the increasingly ominous Russian threat to the route to India, they each failed in their duty to their two citizens in need. With Palmerston still at the helm, somehow Britain would have wrung some concession out of a reluctant Belgium or even an antagonistic France; whatever the merits of the calculation of the claim, regardless of de Walden's argument, some compromise would have been, at long last, arrived at by the 'master of bluffs'.[19]

The actions of Queen Victoria, Albert, King Leopold, Baron

Stockmar, Lord John Russell, Lord and Lady Normanby, Colonel
Phipps — with Prince Schwarzenberg in Vienna exercising his own
influence at a distance, had a strategic outcome; for seven members of that disparate group it was also an objective — to oust
Palmerston. They also had a short-term and catastrophic — albeit
quite unintended — effect on one of the lesser causes patriotically
espoused by that embodiment of John Bull's pugnacity — the
claims at the core of the Rio Nunez Affair.[20]

* * *

France's attitude is explicable. Before the Eastern Question — '*la
grande question du jour*', as Lord Stratford de Redcliffe described
it to Rashid Pasha — had brought France and Britain together,
they were moving further and further apart.[21] Matters in Greece
had brought resentment to the point where threats of 'another
Waterloo' were in the air. The French ambassador in Brussels,
Quinette, refused to participate in the minimal diplomatic cour-
tesies of attending de Walden's reception to celebrate the birth of a
son to Queen Victoria.[22] Despite Palmerston's earlier hopes of
diminishing the rivalry, French pride had resurfaced to the point
where de la Hitte could now see no wrong in the actions of his
French officers: 'The feelings of dignity which inspire the lowliest
officer of the French Navy and the general spirit which dominates
their orders are at such a complete variance with the reports ...
that I have not hesitated in ... regarding the complaints as at least
very exaggerated.'[23]

On the west coast of Africa, France's policy with regard to
Britain's hegemony was relentless and ruthless. The French navy
minister was reported as having told his commander to 'do what
you want, only ... it must have the appearance of being lawful.'[24]

There remains the mystery of Belgium's dogged refusal to
accede to a request which, it must have known, was actually
grounded in justice. Was it the fact that honours and decorations
had been awarded to the combatants and across national boundaries, envisaged from as early as the summer of 1849? National
honour was if anything even more important to the Belgians than
to the French: to admit that the action against the two British
traders was unjustified would itself bring into question the validity
of the attack on Mayoré and the Landumas; and there was that

comment of Bouët-Willaumez's to his two commanders about it all being unnecessary.

Of course for Belgium, apart from the incidents on the Belgian-French border at Risquons-Tout in the spring of 1848, there had been up to then a complete lack of opportunity for military glory of any kind in its history: the so-called battle of Boké represented a disproportionately high point of potential self-esteem in Belgium's short existence as a nation. It desperately needed a symbolic and if necessary colonial victory, somewhere, hence all the huge efforts in Guatemala. Even if the problem with the two chambers of its legislature over the legitimacy of the Nunez expedition meant that the colonizing undertow of the battle had to be foregone, the purely military aspects, the valour and the challenge, had to be supported. It was in fact the last Belgian call to arms, despite Bismarck's threats in the 1870s, before the disaster of the second Great War, in 1914.[25]

Could there have been here a Belgian extension of the French sense of Palmerston's personal attitude towards France, her wounded pride, and their consequent vendetta against his blusteringly exclusive tactics? The effusiveness of the praise that flowed between Palmerston and Belgium over the maintenance of its national identity during Europe's troubles in 1848 paralleled with Van de Weyer's praise for Palmerston's *civis Romanus sum* speech in June 1850, suggest that this was not the case; d'Hoffschmidt warmly endorsed these messages.

The only explanation that fits the extraordinary stance that Belgium took was her historic fear of invasion — not then from Germany but from France. Under Leopold's deft hand, Belgium had succeeded in occupying the pivotal position astride the seesaw of Anglo-French relations. A lurch to one side would upset the tenuous diplomatic balance. Belgium could not forget that in the spring of 1848, in the wake of France's third Parisian revolution in half a century, Ledru Rollin had worked up a significant ground swell for Belgium's reannexation.[26] With a Napoleon once more in power from 1850 onwards, Belgium's press freedom was proving increasingly irritating to him. While Palmerston was still in the Russell cabinet, Lord John had pointed out the dangers of 'the triumph of democracy', namely that 'a Red Republic in France would probably attack Belgium, which we are bound to defend.'[27] A mere week after Palmerston's 'resignation', Lord John Russell told Granville: 'The Belgians must be defended by us and by Prussia. Belgium is threatened by France ... Van de Weyer reports correctly Palmerston's uniform language on this subject.'[28]

Leopold reflected these anxieties graphically in his weekly correspondence with Victoria, through and beyond the time of the dismissal of Palmerston (which he appeared to welcome, primarily because it seemed to strengthen the monarchical position). His arguments have a strangely Palmerstonian ring to them:

> [A] purely military France must and will go to war. ... France is the nearest and sincerest enemy of England. ... France must be considered like a tiger kept on terms of kindness in a house, one must not for a moment forget that it is a tiger. ... We are to[o] exposed, to[o] near Paris ... we are now in the awkward position of persons in hot climates who find themselves in company ... for instance in their beds, with a snake, they *must not move because that irritates* the creature, but they can hardly remain as they are, without a fair chance of being bitten.[29]

Rumours increased to the point where, by 30 March 1852, Britain was seriously considering with Belgium and the Great Powers 'the course it would be expedient to take' in the event of a French aggression against the tiny monarchy. Even if the rumours of wars had dissipated by the time of the final decision on the Braithwaite and Martin claims in 1853, nevertheless, a vestigial French resentment towards Belgium was still apparent in the remark that Count Walewski made to Lord Clarendon in London, which he duly passed on to Lord Cowley in Paris and de Walden in Brussels: 'the lesser state ... should exhibit deference to its more powerful Neighbour.'[30] Another French invasion under a second Napoleon in the summer of 1852 or 1853 was a far greater evil to be feared than the temporary undermining of the support that Belgium still needed from Britain; if it played its cards carefully — and Leopold was always credited with doing exactly that — Belgium could come through this diplomatic crisis without too much damage.

Although Malmesbury made no mention of the Nunez in his statement of affairs on 22 December, Belgium was prominent: 'The principal matter is the danger of an aggression on the part of

France ... the Invasion of Belgium would not be an isolated Act but ... would lead to an European War.'[31] Only this strategic consideration can explain the tactical collusion that took place between Belgium and France throughout the central part of this period: the striving for '*une analogie favorable*', to use General de la Hitte's phrase, between the two apparently unrelated smoke-screens proffered to Britain.

Britain was certainly now overstretched, both in resources and in the calibre of her political leadership. This was to be demonstrated across the whole range of her overseas commitments; its most glaring manifestation was that within two years, Lord Aberdeen's 'Chamberlainesque' vacillation as Prime Minister, and the lack of Palmerston's sure hand on the Foreign Office tiller, allowed the Eastern Question to slide into the débâcle of the Crimean War.[32]

On the coast of West Africa, Britain allowed herself to be outwitted by France and Belgium: with Palmerston gone, the assertiveness of Britain's position evaporated. In parallel with her capitulation on the Nunez claims, Britain stuck to her status quo policy for not extending British influence at that stage beyond the rough boundaries already in existence around the Gambia, Sierra Leone, and the Cape Coast Castle settlement, which then became the colony of the Gold Coast.

If this incident marked a further moment in the imperceptible but continuous shifting of the balance of power in Europe, could it also be seen as an early whisper of Britain's long-term decline in global terms? Historians continue to debate the question of the decline of Britain, with important distinctions being drawn between her absolute and agonizing decline in political power (at the heart of late twentieth-century arguments about Europe) and her relative decline in economic competitiveness, compared with other states such as the United States and Germany.[33]

There are those who see Palmerston's last period as a statesman, the nine years of his premiership, leading up to his death in 1865, as evidence of 'the first political leader who had to grapple even in the Victorian heyday with the early premonition of Britain's national decline'.[34] Others, defining power primarily in industrial terms in relation to Britain's membership of the world economy, see the evidence of the 'British disease' as lying at least as far back as the 1880s, or even earlier. 'Britain has now been in

decline for a hundred years ... the height of Britain's industrial
domination of the world was reached in the middle decades of the
nineteenth century ... since 1850 Britain's position in the world
economy has been precarious and vulnerable.'[35] Significantly, the
author of *Britain in Decline* nevertheless goes on to emphasize the
growth of the role of capital and the City of London: 'this further
increased the importance and the influence of Britain and the
City ... they came to supply a great part of (the world's) financial,
shipping and insurance needs.'[36] The historiography of decline
continues. Among recent commentators, both M. Daunton and N.
Crafts have underlined how complex were the roots of the initial
rise to economic power, and have demonstrated that industrial
decline has been 'relative rather than absolute'; it is arguable that
Britain's real dominance continued well into the twentieth
century.[37]

* * *

None of these retrospective speculations alter the strange facts of
the Rio Nunez Affair: that in the early 1850s, when Britain —
under any definition — was at the height of her power, she was
either unwilling, or possibly no longer able, to carry the day in a
small diplomatic battle on behalf of two of her wronged citizens,
against two other European powers of lesser current political,
military or economic strength. One of the earliest writers about
Palmerston's glorious doctrine asserted that he 'would move the
whole force of the British Empire in order that this Brown or
Jones — *Civis Romanus* — might not be defrauded of his
Worcester sauce amid the ice of Siberia, or of his pale ale in the
Mountains of the Moon'.[38]

By any reckoning, incipient decline or no, it still seems, at the
distance of 150 years, that the battle of these particular 'Brown or
Jones' — Braithwaite and Martin — was one that the British
Empire could, and should, have fought and won. If Russell had
stood up to Victoria one more time, if he had actually bothered to
see Palmerston in person, enabling his great Secretary of State to
survive in office, and thus to continue to champion the case and
the cause of his *cives Britannici*, it assuredly would have been. If
only ...

Notes

1. For France, Archives of the F/MAE, Quai d'Orsay, Paris. The sequence from 1849 to 1853 was Drouyn de Lhuys (1849), De Tocqueville (March 1849), General de la Hitte (October 1849), De Lhuys (17 January 1851), Brenier (2 February 1851), Baroche (19 April 1851), Turgot (October 1851), De Lhuys (2 August 1852). For Britain P (1846–51), Granville (19 December 1851–22 February 1852), Malmesbury (1852), LJR (December 1852–20 February 1853), Clarendon (1853–5).
2. RA QVJ, Windsor Castle, 29 December 1851.
3. FO 123/69, Granville to Lord Cowley, 29 January 1852, and to de Walden, 31 January. Other dispatches at this time from Granville and Malmesbury, with Paris and Brussels, are in FO 97/198.
4. Turgot to Cowley, 24 February 1852.
5. For the best expositions of the 'tit-for-tat' episode, see J. Ridley, *Lord Palmerston* (London, 1970), p.401; cf. Palmerston to his brother William: 'I have had my tit-for-tat with John Russell, and I turned him out on Friday last.' Also Donald Southgate, *The Most English Minister: The Policies and Politics of Palmerston* (London, 1966), Chap.16. For 'Who? Who?' story, see E. Longford, *Wellington: Pillar of State* (Panther edn, London, 1972), pp.484–5; also André Maurois, *Disraeli: A Picture of the Victorian Age* (Paris and Appleton, 1927), pp.211, 218. Wellington had never heard of any of the names of the new Derby ministry, including that of Malmesbury, the grandson of an eminent statesman, who was Palmerston's guardian and the means of his initial introduction into politics. As each new name was read out, the by now very deaf Wellington called out in increasing frustration, 'Who? Who?'.
6. J. Harris, *Earl of Malmesbury: Memoirs of an ex-Minister* (London, 1885), I, p.305; see *supra* Part I, n.78.
7. HRO/M 9M73/25, Letter Book to France, 16 March 1852, Malmesbury to Cowley, re payment due to F&S.
8. Harris, *Malmesbury*, vol.2, p.108 and (I, p.335) re the offer of the FO by Lord Derby: 'I am unwilling to do so, as it will keep me in London the whole year'.
9. G. Macoir, 'Note sur un Sabre d'Honneur décerné à Capt [VH]', *Bull. des Musées royaux des Arts décoratifs et industriels* (Brussels, 1907) states '*à 95* [VH] *reste un infatigable et charmant causeur*'; Sub-Lt. Collignon, 'A la Découverte de Van Haverbeke', *La Gazette du Soldat* (Brussels, December 1956), p.6.
10. VH to Hoffschmidt, 6 September 1852. The month is written in the archaic form '7bre'.
11. For authority on paying rent for land, see G. Brooks, *Landlords and Strangers* (Oxford, 1993), pp.38–9, 189–90; also D. Robinson, *The Holy War of Umar Tal: The Western Sudan in the Mid-Nineteenth Century* (Oxford, 1985), pp.140–1, writes 'while the whites were seen as the masters of the water, the blacks remained the masters of the land.' Also C. Fyfe's letter to author, 5 February 1995, and C. Fyfe, *A History of Sierra Leone* (London, 1962), pp.4–5, 8, 74.
12. De Walden to Eddisbury, 31 August 1850; see *supra*, Part I, n.67 re amounts claimed by Pacifico, 'the exorbitant nature of his claims'.
13. Malmesbury to B&M, 22 November 1852; also FO 123/69.
14. In CO 90/26–8, CO 87/57, and CO 401/10, Joseph Braithwaite was one of some 200 white members of the colony's population, out of *c.*6000. He was appointed 13 October 1852. Fellow merchants and commissioners were A.

Pierre and C. Boocock JP, later to join the Legislative Council, who, with W. H. Selby JP, were to become administrators of his bankrupt estate, on his death in 1854; also T. Chown JP. See Chap.1 *supra*, n.40. See FO 97/198 and FO 123/73, B&M at Saltash to Clarendon, 29 May 1853 on 'delay . . . due to Mr [Braithwaite] being out of England'.

15. Forster to Clarendon, 1 June 1853.

16. Clarendon to B&M, 25 August 1853. The last paper is a note of the transmission of a copy of this letter to Paris. For Turgot's reliance on the precedent established by de la Hitte, see Turgot to Cowley, 24 February 1852.

17. PBHA, GC/HO/849–866, P to de Walden, 2 November 1847.

18. RA A 79/133, LJR to P, 17 December 1851.

19. M. E. Chamberlain, *Lord Palmerston* (K. Morgan (ed.), Political Portraits series, Swansea, 1987), p.121; cf. H. W. V. Temperley, *England and The Near East: The Crimea* (Cambridge, 1936, repr. 1964), pp.59–60. P 'excelled in calling "bluffs" and in making them. It was not the highest statesmanship but it often served.'

20. PBHA, de Walden to P, 14 November 1851; GC/HO/ 740/1: 'Most private . . . Seckendorff, the Austrian ambassador to Brussels, told de Walden, of Schwarzenberg, "that he is determined to effect your overthrow".' For a summary of the still unclear constitutional issues in P's removal, see Part III, Appendix 2, *infra*. Even if they were critical of his way of proceeding, only Stockmar and Leopold could not be said to have actively sought to bring about the removal of 'Pilgerstein', the name by which P was paranoically referred to within the royal — and German-speaking — network of the House of Hanover, ('Pilger' being an unholy literal translation of the holy role of a 'palmer'). M. Partridge, *Lord Palmerston 1784–1865: A Bibliography* (Greenwood, 1994), p.2 says 'he personified Britain's pugnacity'.

21. FO 123/73, Dispatches to and from Brussels, 20 June 1853. Lord Stratford de Redcliffe was British ambassador to the 'Sublime Porte', the Turkish court and Rashid Pasha was the Sultan's foreign minister. For an account of the rediscovery of the Anglo-French *entente* before the Crimean War, see J. Ridley, *Napoleon III and Eugénie* (London, 1979), Chap.28, p.366.

22. F/MAE, Quinette to de la Hitte, May 1852.

23. Hitte to Normanby, Paris, 29 August 1850, reference to Normanby to Hitte, 2 May 1850.

24. CO267/211, Ministère de la Marine to B-W, quote by Hotham to ADM, 17 February 1849, '*Faites ce que vous voudrez, seulement, il faut avoir l'apparence du droit*'.

25. 'In 1875 when Bismarck menaced Belgium and then threatened France, Disraeli wrote . . . that Bismarck was really another old Bonaparte and had to be bridled. Bismarck beat a retreat. England's return into European politics had been triumphant' (Maurois, *Disraeli*, p.285).

26. BL Add. MS, 48,553, de Walden to Palmerston, 18 May 1848; also '*Avec l'affaire de Risquons-Tout en février 1848, le combat de Debocca fut, en effet, la seule occasion où, avant les jours tragiques d'août 1914, les Belges se battèrent sous le drapeau tricolore largement déployé*' (A. Duchesne, 'Un Centenaire oublié: Le Combat de Debocca (Rio Nunez) 24 mars 1849', *Carnet de la Fourragère*, vol.8, no.7, (Brussels, 1949), p.416). For further background on Rollin, see also Ridley, *Napoleon III*, pp.203–11, 254–5.

27. RA A 79/95, LJR address to Cabinet, 3 November 1851.

28. RA A80/76, LJR to Granville, 31 December 1851.

29. RA Y 77/36, Leopold to Victoria, 26 December 1851 (first three quotations); Y 77/37, 2 January 1852; Y 77/47, 5 March 1852; see also E. Corti, *Leopold*

I: *Oracle politique de l'Europe* (Brussels, 1927), p.125, who claims 'Leopold was always between two fires'; also re Nunez, 'the Chambers showed themselves unwilling to continue their support', see J. Richardson, *My Dearest Uncle: A Life of Leopold, First King of the Belgians* (London, 1961), pp.167, 221.

30. FO 123/73, Clarendon to Cowley, 13 September 1853, quotes Walewski to Clarendon, 3 September, with copy to de Walden.

31. HRO, Malmesbury Papers, 9M73/431/6, 22 December 1852. Jasper Ridley has pointed out to the author that there is no evidence that Napoleon III ever actually contemplated aggression against Belgium, notwithstanding that profound perception in both Brussels and London. See Appendix 3.

32. See Southgate, *English Minister*, p.328 for development of the Aberdeen/Chamberlain and Palmerston/Churchill analogies. He argues that 'He (Lord Aberdeen) had not Neville Chamberlain's excuse for appeasement, that it was popular, but he had all his temperamental and personal aversion to the Churchillian mode.' See Part III, Appendix 3 for a summary of the impact of the Eastern Question on British political institutions at this time.

33. For two thoroughly argued views about the paradox of the timing of Britain's long-term decline, see P. J. Cain and A. G. Hopkins, *British Imperialism* (London, 1993), vol.1, Chaps.1, 3, 6, 11, vol.2, pp.1–7. Also introduction to Andrew Gamble, *Britain in Decline: Political Strategy and the British State* (London, 1985). At another level, possession of colonies was seen as a measure of greatness, see Southgate, *English Minister*, p.555.

34. See Foreword by Dr K. Morgan to Chamberlain, *Ld Palm* (p.ix) for freshly revived views of the achievements of Britain's empire; see also Professor P. Marshall's talk, 'Imperial Britain', at University of London's Creighton annual lecture, 7 November 1994, in *JICH*, vol.23, 3 September 1995.

35. Gamble, *Decline*, pp.xiv, xv, 56.

36. Gamble, *Decline*, p.57.

37. See features in *History Today* (vol.44, no.5, June 1994) on 'The Rise and Fall of Industrial Britain? 1700–2000', particularly Martin Daunton, 'The Entrepreneurial State: 1700–1914' (pp.11–16) and Nick Crafts, 'Managing Decline? 1870–1990' (pp.37–42). See also Cain and Hopkins's argument (*Imperialism*, vols 1 and 2) that 'relative decline must also be dated at least as far back as 1870 and probably before', p.113.

38. Southgate, *English Minister*, p.272; cf. E. Walford, *Memoir of Rt Honourable Viscount Palmerston* (London, 1865), p.34. This is one of many books appearing at the time of P's death, explaining something of the 'halo effect' Walford was trying to evoke.

7. Epilogue

Was it all worth the effort? Were the bloodshed, the destruction, the disruption, the cost, the deviation from other potential goals — the whole episode on that distant West African river a century and a half ago really justified? Was Palmerston wasting his time with those many diplomatic encounters on behalf of Braithwaite and Martin? Would Forster & Smith have been better advised to cut its losses both financially and morally, on its beleaguered associates, and concentrate on new markets elsewhere?

These are not necessarily historians' questions. Hindsight is not part of the process. Yet they are clearly questions that a serious consideration of those events and that era does raise. Would King Mayoré and his Landumas, and all the millions of African peoples in a similar relationship to their white 'exploiters', have been better off in the long run if Europe and the Americas had stayed at home?

The Nunez story also poses questions of particular interest to Britain at the turn of the twentieth century, as she looks back to the apparent certainties of her past, in order to try to deal with an increasingly uncertain future, the imminent return of the territory acquired through those distant Opium Wars which gave birth to the *civis Romanus* concept — Hong Kong — serving to dramatize that process of uncomfortable change: in Europe, the needle of the British compass continues to waver between the desire for isolation, and the knowledge that it is impossible.

All great empires find the contemplation of their greatness the subject of endless fascination; however, time is needed for any perspective to be correct. The British Empire was, at its greatest, at that midpoint in the nineteenth century, arguably greater, relative to its rivals, than either of the two apparently dominant empires of that successor century which is now drawing to its close — the Soviet Union, and the USA. Given the inevitability of ascendancy and decline in the growth of states, debates about the apogee of such a curve are easier and more palatable to consider, than the more awkward questions on when that decline first started to show — the moment of truth. That difficulty is all the greater because, by definition, the signs will be small and scattered, and coexistent with manifestations of the continuation of greatness.

So it was for Great Britain in the 1850s, even if her eventual decline, in terms of the various criteria by which greatness may be measured — political, economic, financial, or military — might only become fully apparent a century later, after the ravages and upheavals of the Second World War. Notwithstanding the subsequent 'Scramble for Africa' of the 1880s, Britain was already engaged in withdrawal both from overseas commitments, and also from pan-European involvements: the metaphors of colonial 'millstones' and 'splendid isolation' became common currency, at the very time when the empire was at its zenith.

The Nunez story brings out certain truths which have some bearing on the wider issues that this ambivalent period of British history presents to us. Palmerston may well have been racially prejudiced about the 'barbarous tribes of Africa', in late twentieth century terms, but his attitude towards the peoples of that continent was in many respects one of understanding, as judged by his writings and speeches. In his eyes, and those of many of his contemporaries, the continent needed to be opened up to the benefits of Western civilization, and Britain's historic role was seen as the appointed bringer of those benefits: this was one of Palmerston's implicit assumptions. Matthew Forster, as judged by what he said and wrote, particularly to Buxton and his fellow reformers, typified many, if not necessarily all, those merchants who believed that their slowly expanding lawful trade was the best, most organically sound and evolutionary way of bringing Africa alongside Europe; he constantly propounded the view that the only way to proceed in Africa was to work within her rich and varied indigenous cultures. He also described the legitimate trade as one way of beginning to pay the 'debt' owed to Africa, although there might well have been a degree of sophistry about such sentiments. At the individual level, the two British 'strangers', whose lives were ruined by the events on the Nunez, again as judged by their writings, were doing what they could to work equably with their 'landlord', trading peacefully and dealing honourably for the achievement of ongoing relationships, not exploiting for short-term gain and dominance, or for a fast uncaring exit. At its moment of greatness, the British record was by no means unworthy, and certainly did not seem so at the time. There was a job to be done — politically, and commercially; British naval power was there as a safeguard for the accomplishment of that job, not for territorial aggrandisement, and not as an end in itself. The exchange was two-way, by definition.

That philosophy may well have been of small immediate comfort to many of those concerned in the Nunez incident. Joseph Braithwaite died of a fever, at Bathurst, The Gambia — alone, bankrupt and destitute, on 18 August 1854. His business partner, George Martin, ceased to contest the African trade, his subsequent life being shrouded in mystery. The future career of Governor Macdonald at Freetown was in no way enhanced by the reverberations of the Nunez Affair: he finished his days in obscure retirement in Taunton, whilst his deputy, Benjamin Pine, for whose actions he had had to bear overall responsibilty, ended his career in relative glory, with several other governorships and a knighthood to show for it. Although a British consul was belatedly appointed with responsibility for overseeing the Nunez region, that territory remained *res nullius* for Britain, until it eventually evolved into a French domain, and part of French West Africa. According to the Belgian records, King Mayoré became the proud recipient of a golden armchair, costing 200 francs, on the occasion of the next visit by Van Haverbeke, before he finally made way for his brother Tongo; he fell ill, and died without honour, in obscurity. John Nelson Bicaise merely received two lanterns for his pains, on the same Belgian naval visit, although in the aftermath of the affair seeming to gain a new lease of life as a French official, a consul and a *commandant de cercle* at Boké. Nevertheless, he also ended his life in poverty, in 1878. The Belgian captain, Joseph Van Haverbeke, in many ways the instigator of the unhappy happenings on that sultry morning in March 1849, alone of all those directly involved, lived on to witness the next century; he died of an extreme but untroubled old age, on 7 September 1907, in his beloved and native Antwerp: his military record lay unquestioned until the new researches on the Nunez incident at last showed those Swords of Honour to be capable of bearing a very different interpretation.

One other figure, an unknowing and at best indirect character in this little drama, also lived on to greet the new century — the great Queen herself, the embodiment, at its greatest, of all that British effort, ambition and achievement. The enigmatic Baron Stockmar, the real source of the misleading constitutional ideas which so influenced Prince Albert, had long since died: at long last, some 40 years after the death of that beloved consort — whose counsels at the time of Good Old Pam's apparent downfall had diverted Victoria from the ways of the British constitution — the 65 years of her reign came to their end.

At that moment, the great statesman himself had been lying at rest, after an anything but restful life, in his honourable place in Westminster Abbey for almost the same length of time. One of the Palmerston writers, Donald Southgate, imagines his ghost laughing good-humouredly about the imperial legacy which Disraeli and others built upon, in the opening phase of that very different world that was to succeed his own. It may not be too fanciful to think of that same strong spirit remembering the Nunez Affair as a not unworthy battle in the wider awakening of Africa, one of the battles that he sought to win peacefully for Britain, and for two of his *cives Britannici*. It was not one which he was allowed to bring to the normally successful John Bullish conclusion which was his patriotic trademark.

Part III

Appendices

Appendix 1
'Pam' and 'Winnie'
A Comparison

Notwithstanding many fine biographies, Palmerston has become somewhat obscured for late twentieth century eyes, both by the enduring Disraeli–Gladstone confrontation, which outshone his own more spasmodic conflict with Russell, and also, despite the necessary corrections of writers such as Denis Judd and Muriel Chamberlain, by the all too ready epithet of 'gunboat diplomacy', which appears out of tune with Britain's role today. The associations that, as Palmerston's recent bibliographers have pointed out, ought to apply, such as 'Palmerston and the Crimean War', or 'Palmerston and the Slave Trade' do not spring to mind.[1] It is still too easy to treat him superficially as a more distant regency — even an eighteenth century — man, than a true Victorian.[2]

Yet in the mid-nineteenth century, and indeed long after his death, he was as familiar, and beloved, a figure to ordinary men and women as Winston Churchill has been for the greater part of the current century. Ensor has retailed for generations of history students the story of how a Somerset man was seeking to illustrate the pride of place that a local farmer held in the minds of the surrounding community, and chose as his political yardstick of popularity, not Gladstone or Disraeli, but Palmerston: 'As late as 1900 an old village worker wished to convey to the present writer his sense of the eminence of a local worthy. "He held", he said, "a position in the neighbourhood like that which the late Lord Palmerston used to hold in this country". Palmerston had been dead thirty-five years.'[3]

In the interests both of bringing into sharper focus the Palmerston of the Rio Nunez Affair, and also of re-presenting him to a wider audience, a limited comparison between these two great popular statesmen of their respective eras is offered here. In contrast to the general perception today, Palmerston is counted by most writers, even those most critical of his policies, as among the major four or five most outstanding Foreign Secretaries of the past two centuries. Just as Churchill remains the dominant figure of Britain's mid-twentieth century, so does Palmerston emerge as the central British statesman of the middle of the fast-receding and preceding century, of that very period when the English nation, still bathing in the afterglow of the triumph of Waterloo, was very much Great Britain, and at her most influential — often at her most infuriating, able to assert British rights when she, and he, wished to, against other countries, great and small.

Other writers have considered the Palmerston–Churchill parallel, but none of the Palmerstonian biographies have yet sought to assert it, nor have any of the distinguished army of 'eminent Churchillians' looked back to parallels in Palmerston.[4] There are a few references in the literature, first of all in Kingsley Martin's revised *The Triumph of Lord Palmerston*: 'It is tempting to compare Palmerston, the tough traditional John Bull, with Winston Churchill, who also took charge when appeasement failed.' Donald Southgate in his *The Most English Minister* conjectures how Palmerston's 'Churchillian touch' might have coped with the Berlin blockade or the Cuban missile crises of the twentieth century (see Chapter. 7). There is a shrewd but glancing note in the only major comprehensive contemporary biography, where the author, Jasper Ridley, compares Palmerston's loyal but half-hearted Commons defence of the Aberdeen government's conduct of the Crimean War in the debate of 25 January 1855: 'Palmerston was in the same position as Churchill was during the debate on Norway in May 1940: the House, by voting against his arguments, was voting to make him Prime Minister.'[5]

In Churchill's own writings, there were some comments by Churchill himself, but even then Churchill was only thinking of his and Palmerston's common experiences in managing administrations on wafer-thin majorities.[6] A. J. P. Taylor at least wrote in his introduction to Judd's *Palmerston*: he was 'a sort of nineteenth century Churchill' — but neither he nor that author developed the idea.[7] On the dust cover to Bourne's *Palmerston: The Early Years*, his publisher does venture the comparison with Palmerston's

length of time as an MP — only Lloyd George and Churchill having served longer in the House.[8] Sir Robert Rhodes James makes a
surprisingly complimentary comparison in his *Churchill: A Study
in Failure, 1900–1939*, where in a concluding chapter he develops
an argument about Churchill's intellectual ability: 'Churchill had
much imagination and he was always fertile with ideas and
projects. But compared with Gladstone, Disraeli, Salisbury, or
even [*sic*] Palmerston, there is a certain absence of political depth,
comprehension and wisdom. ... He marched magnificently on the
surface of affairs.'[9] That comparison is all the more interesting in
that this eminent biographer of both centuries includes the view
expressed by Leo Amery about the period that characterized the
'set' of Churchill's mind, and which would appear in this context
to bring him closer to Palmerston:

> But in Churchill's case it is a striking fact of his political
> character that it had altered so little ... at the end of this
> process we behold essentially the same man that we glimpsed
> taking his seat in the House of Commons for the first time in
> February 1901, and it is this fact that prompted Amery's
> comment in 1929 that: 'the key to Winston is to realize that
> he is a mid-Victorian ... and unable to get to the modern
> point of view'.[10]

Sir Robert goes on to place the comment in a wider setting: 'It was
Churchill's greatest deficiency that in the 1930s he was
unchanged; it was to be his greatest strength in the ordeal that
began on 3rd September 1939.'[11] That judgement accords with the
one which the main Churchill writers enduringly present, notwithstanding later attempted reconstructions.[12]
      A. J. P. Taylor made a further limited comparison with Palmer-
ston in a tentative comment about their respective roles as critics
of the initial management of the two great wars in which they
were each to lead their country, the Crimean War of 1854–56,
and the Second World War: 'Called to power during the Crimean
War as the saviour of his country, [he] duly carried it to victory, as
Chatham had done before him and Lloyd George and Churchill
... after him.'[13]
      There are of course many obvious moral, temperamental,
chronological and policy differences. While Palmerston was no

author, he was at the centre of power for half a century. Churchill
was never titular Foreign Secretary, and had two great periods of
major office, separated by what one writer has called, despite his
many other political roles during that time, the years of 'failure' —
(embracing the 'wilderness years') — from 1929 to 1935.[14]
Alcohol was never a Palmerstonian weakness; Churchill's extraordinary ability to sustain it is well chronicled. Palmerston, the
breezy extrovert opimist, compares sadly with the recurrent 'black
dogs' of the sensitive Churchill's depressions.[15]

There are nevertheless some striking points of reference, both
major and minor, which may help to place Palmerston before a
new audience as a member of Guedalla's 'living shifting world'. In
this general cause, the latest of the biographers, whilst not seeking
any overt parallel, still makes the comparison that 'even Palmerston usually preferred jaw-jaw to war-war, to adopt Churchill's
phrase'.[16] There is also another aspect of Churchill. 'He had
survived . . . he had demonstrated one of the most rare of political
qualities, that of bounce.'[17] That same metaphor is picked up
elsewhere, with a slightly different inflection, apropos the Palmerstons' visit to Paris in 1846, an attempt to repair the bad image
formed about him there: 'The French formed a mixed impression
of Palmerston. Some of them were a little taken aback by his
bounce.'[18]

Both men evolved from the level of national politicians to
become, at their peak, internationally acclaimed statesmen,
respected, or feared, by their diplomatic foes as well as their
friends: thus Talleyrand, ambassador of France and one of his
favourite earlier protagonists, pronounced upon him, 'Lord
Palmerston is certainly one of, if not quite the ablest statesmen I
have ever met in my entire career'.[19] The judgement of another
French opponent, Thiers, in 1846, was recorded as saying that 'he
had no reason to be a friend to Palmerston by whom he had been
worsted . . . that did not prevent him from regarding him as the
first statesman of this age and perhaps of any other.'[20] Palmerston,
like Churchill, covered an immense canvas of Britain's history.
Herbert Bell, the American writer of the longest, two-volume,
biography, wrote:

He was born before the American constitution saw the light,
yet survived the Civil War. He was a minister five years

before Napoleon laid down his power at Fontainebleau, a minister for three years after Bismarck came to power at Berlin, and a minister for all but about ten of the years that lay between. During those years his attitude was a factor in almost every political issue of real importance which sought solution in England.[21]

Significantly, both statesmen achieved that highest of offices to which they openly aspired only at a very late stage in their careers, at a time of supreme national crisis. Yet both these great statesmen fell into what may be called the 'Cromwellian fault': both Palmerston and Churchill were so conditioned by a traditional enemy whose shadow darkened their childhood, that they did not initially see the further enemy emerging behind it. In Palmerston's case, he grew up as a young man in fear of an ever revolutionary and unstable France — exemplified by his family's first-hand experience in Paris in the period preceding 'The Terror'. First his fear of Napoleon, then later of Russia, and then once more, after the Crimean War, his obsession with France again — these preoccupations concealed the slowly emergent and greater long-term danger of Prussia's Bismarck, although he was certainly not unmindful of the growing strength of the country of which Bismarck was later to become the mastermind. In 1844, visiting Berlin, 'he came to the conclusion that Prussia would be a more important power in the future than she had been in the past'.[22] A reference by Charmley presents Churchill's similar dilemma, with regard to the emergence by 1943 of Stalin's Russia as something quite other than simply the heroic fellow resister against Hitler. Thinking about Cromwell, Churchill brooded one evening in Cairo — to quote Harold Macmillan, 'He had made one terrible mistake. Obsessed in his youth by the fear of Spain, he failed to observe the rise of France. Will that be said of me?'[23]

There are factual similarities too. Both men went to the Harrow of their day: 'the Harrow Boys', as Queen Victoria was amused to call both Palmerston and Lord Aberdeen, whose earliest encounter had been their celebrated pillow-fight at school. Both were centres of a loyal political circle — albeit of different magnitude. Churchill's small group of embattled acolytes gathered at Chartwell between the two world wars; invitations to the Palmerstons' London houses, first at Carlton Gardens, and later at 110

Piccadilly, now The Naval and Military Club, the 'In and Out', became the most coveted addresses on every politician's list.[24] Both men's mental energy and practical sense of what was important led them at appropriate moments in their careers to study military technology and weaponry in great detail: only one of the major Palmerstonian biographers picks this up, writing not of his time as Secretary at War, but, more interestingly, of the period following his return to the Foreign Office in 1846. 'He became keenly interested in all kinds of military matters, learning all the technical details about muskets, heavy guns, and armour casing for forts.'[25] Many of those defensive constructions against the old enemy, France, such as that on the Tamar, are still known locally as 'Palmerston's forts'. Churchill's curiosity about all new weapons is legendary.

As another parallel, highlighted by Southgate in his dedication, both men were invited into the select international band of wardens of the Cinque Ports at Walmer, on the Channel, alongside Pitt and Wellington. Both were *bons viveurs*, yet physically adventurous to a late stage in their lives, the legendary Churchillian energy and addiction to a punishing work rate being more than matched by Palmerston, who sometimes rode, or walked to and from Parliament, and took his horse through Hyde Park every day as a matter of principle. The editor of the Political Portraits series highlights the tale of how even at the age of 80 he was 'capable of bounding up the stairs to the Ladies Gallery of the Commons'.[26]

Each could be accused of bullying, insensitivity, arrogance and hauteur, yet each showed great kindnesses to individuals, and manifested strong 'liberal' humanitarian instincts. Churchill's abhorrence of the Amritsar massacre, and of the butchery in the Zulu wars has recently been brought back into focus; Palmerston's sentiments were most publicly in evidence in what evolved as his profound hatred of negro slavery and his passionate leadership of the international fight against the slave trade: both that sentiment, and his concern for the individual, were background factors in the Nunez situation. It was also a facet of this instinct in each of them that Palmerston evinced a strong sympathy with Jewish aspirations to a homeland in Turkish Palestine, just as did Churchill.[27] Each was a deep believer in the British constitutional monarchy, although their beliefs differed in nature. Palmerston's was pragmatic and intellectual, Churchill's so emotional, even mystical, that it could lead him to support the lost cause of Edward VIII at a time when, as a current BBC television feature, *The Traitor King*, has demonstrated, sensible opinion clearly pointed the other way.[28]

Both these scions of wealthy aristocratic Tory backgrounds turned out to be unconventional mavericks in their political careers, defying neat labels. Each moved from right to left, and back again, along the political spectrum, at times being seen as radically left of centre, according to the ebb and flow of events. Both were natural 'media men' ahead of their respective times, with Palmerston utilizing to the full his sense of what the growing radical electorate and his wider audience wanted, and needed, to hear; this he achieved through his early articles in the *Morning Chronicle*, and more notably later on in the *Morning Post*. This power to communicate was common to both Churchill and Palmerston, of whom it has been said that 'his pen and voice influenced a remarkable number of developments in five continents'.[29] Although Palmerston's pen was in his own way as busy as Churchill's, his oratory was less sustained, though each continued to pitch it in the familiar limelight of the lower House: Churchill, who might have had the choice, eschewing the 'House of Peers', to the very end of his life; Palmerston, being technically an Irish peer, could only sit in the Commons anyway, and declined to be 'kicked upstairs' on more than one occasion. Both men could make dull speeches, and as that acute observer, Turgenev, bore witness, Palmerston, like Churchill, had a slight peculiarity of expression;[30] for one of Palmerston's more critical contemporaries in the early days of the 1830s, he was even 'an indifferent speaker ... he often stutters and stammers'.[31] Nevertheless, each was to develop an instinct for the great occasion, and for the great phrase that would touch the national consciousness at such moments. Palmerston's *civis Romanus sum* doctrine, a central element in the Nunez story, has already been cited here.

The most significant parallel, however, is that both these aristocratic leaders became 'popular' men. Palmerston has been well described as representing 'the unarticulated assumptions and prejudices of his people'.[32] Although both were compared with the very masculine John Bull legend, there remains the simple and surprising fact that 'Pam' and 'Winnie' are the only leading

politicians of either century to have become known to the man in
the street — Palmerston's 'man on the omnibus' — by affectionate
feminine diminutives of their names — ('Gladdy', for Gladstone,
not really counting). It is even arguable that the epithet 'Pam' was
better known in his day, as Ensor seems to suggest, than the
nickname 'Winnie' is today for Churchill — indeed many people,
30 years on, are now quite unaware of it. As a subset of this
phenomenon, both caused countless dog owners to borrow these
nicknames: one of the 'Pams' for example was a famous large
black Newfoundland, the pet of a member of his Foreign Office
staff, who used to roam the older offices at will, opening doors
and jumping up to take people's hats off. Bulldog 'Winnies' were a
proud commonplace during and after the Second World War.[33]

Moreover, both men lived in the context of that decidedly
modern, post-1832 age in which it became increasingly important,
as Kenneth Baker has recently illustrated, that leaders of the
people could be instantly recognized in the 'public prints'.[34] Both
had faces that were 'well lived-in', unlike other premiers, such as
Rosebery or James Callaghan, whose physiognomies defied the
popularizing urge of contemporary cartoonists.[35] Within the set of
their respective and rapidly familiar features, each became
endowed with a unique visual 'signature tune', which endeared
them to their electorates. Winnie was rarely depicted by Low
without his famously defiant cigar: the jaunty Pam, with his well-
known love of racing and the world of the stables, was given a
straw to chew by one of the early cartoonists — possibly Leech or
Doyle — and Sir John Tenniel then confirmed and immortalized
this debonair version of the great man in the pages of *Punch*.[36]

There are two further reasons why comparisons across the
centuries have up to now proved difficult for historians to deal
with. The first lay in the institutional differences of their two eras:
'A mid-nineteenth-century Palmerston had not the power acquired
by a Lloyd George or a Churchill.' Thus Palmerston's resolution
of the Crimean War may not compare in depth or 'creativity' — to
use Taylor's phrase — with the great twentieth-century 'saviour of
the nation' — Churchill. Secondly, by the time of his accession to
the greatest office of state, and the final decade of his life and
career, by which he has been disproportionately judged, 'he was
after all older than Chatham had ever been, and as old as Winston
Churchill was at the end of the 1939–45 war.'[37]

However, it is perhaps in the simple central point that South-gate almost throws away that the abiding case for a comparison between Palmerston and Churchill must surely lie: he found no justification 'for comparing him with the elder Pitt, or Churchill, except in spirit'.[38] That is surely an overriding exception. It is that magnificent 'Churchillian' spirit of Palmerston that lives through his actions and his speeches, and indeed in all his communications: a spirit instinctive to both statesmen, and which might well have carried the day in that distant affair on the Nunez: a very patriotic, historically rooted, deeply felt English spirit, the spirit indeed of one of England's 'most English' ministers of any age.

Conclusion

The points of difference between Palmerston and Churchill have caused some writers to refrain from the comparison; those views deserve respect.[39] All historical parallels are contentious, and this comparison of two national heroes may well not equate to others in every single area (for instance that drawn massively and in detail, although not without its critics, by Alan Bullock, between two international villains, Hitler and Stalin).[40]

Nevertheless, the points of comparison between 'Pam' and 'Winnie' are there in the record. They at least deserve to be reviewed here, in that they help in some measure to bring into fresh relief the Palmerston who became so personally, and surprisingly, involved in the Rio Nunez Affair.

Notes

1. See n.4 *infra*. For a later perspective on 'gunboat diplomacy', see R. Howell, *The Royal Navy and the Slave Trade* (London, 1987), p.222, quoting as a definition, 'The use of warships in peacetime to further a nation's diplomatic and political aims'; A. Preston and J. Major, *Send a Gunboat! A Study of the Gunboat and its Role in British Policy, 1854–1904* (London, 1967), p.3; Donald Southgate, *The Most English Minister: The Policies and Politics of Palmerston* (London, 1966), p.xvi; M. S. Partridge and K. E. Partridge, *Lord Palmerston 1784–1865: A Bibliography* (Greenwood, 1994), p.viii.
2. See, for example Lord David Cecil, *Lord M* (London, 1954); cf. Part I *supra*, n.42; also Roy Jenkins, *Gladstone* (London, 1995), p.xiii.
3. R. C. K. Ensor, *England 1870–1914* (Oxford, 1936), pp.1–2.
4. The Palmerston biographies cited here are those by J. Ridley, *Lord Palmerston* (London, 1970); Kenneth Bourne, *Palmerston: The Early Years, 1784–1841* (London, 1982); H. Bell, *Lord Palmerston* (London, 1936); Southgate, *English Minister*; B. Kingsley Martin, *The Triumph of Lord Palmerston: A Study of Public Opinion in England before the Crimean War* (London, 1924, rev. ed. edn, 1963); Denis Judd, *Palmerston* (London, 1970); and M. E.

Chamberlain, *Lord Palmerston* (Swansea, 1987). The Churchill writers consulted are Sir Martin Gilbert, *Churchill: A Life* (London, 1991); Sir Robert Rhodes James, *Churchill: A Study in Failure, 1900–1939* (London, 1970); Lord Blake and W. R. Louis (eds) *Churchill: A Major New Assessment of his Life in Peace and War* (Oxford, 1993); and A. Roberts, *Eminent Churchillians* (London, 1994).

5. Southgate, *English Minister,* pp.xv, 371–8; Ridley, *Palmerston,* p.432; Kingsley Martin, *Triumph* (rev. edn. 1963), pp.25, 26.
6. I am indebted to Churchill's biographer, Sir Martin Gilbert, for pointing out this reference to me. See early volumes, especially *Winston S. Churchill* (vol.2) by Randolph Churchill (London, 1967), pp.429, 437, 566–7.
7. A. J. P. Taylor's Introduction to Judd, *Palm,* p.vii.
8. Bourne, *Early Years,* cover page.
9. See Rhodes James, *Failure* (London, 1970), Part 7, 'The Return from Exile', pp.346, 348.
10. Rhodes James, *Failure,* pp.186, 348. For a skewed view of P's policies, see leader, *Guardian,* 22 September 1995, 'Exorcising Palmerston's Ghost'.
11. Rhodes James, *Failure,* p.349.
12. This is not the place to assess the Churchill Revisionists. See Roberts, *Churchillians;* also R. Gott, 'V for Vilification', *Guardian,* 4 May 1994; also Philip Ziegler, *The Late Show,* BBC 2 TV, 9 May 1994; see D. Charmley, *Churchill: The End of Glory* (London, 1993).
13. Taylor, Introduction to Judd, *Palm,* p.vii.
14. Rhodes James, *Failure, passim;* also BBC TV series, 1970–80.
15. Anthony Storr, *Churchill's Black Dog and Other Phenomena of the Human Mind* (London, 1991), pp.3–51; see Rhodes James, *Failure,* p.14, on the early Churchill seen as 'brash, assertive'.
16. Chamberlain, *Ld Palm,* p.ix.
17. Rhodes James, *Failure,* p.186. On P (1841–60), 'Palmerston became ... a master of the telling-phrase, many of which displayed the flippancy and bounce that he ... exemplified', see David Wetzel, *Crimean War: A Diplomatic History* (New York, 1985), p.60
18. Ridley, *Palmerston,* p.302, on visit to Paris, 1846.
19. Bell, *Lord P,* vol.1, pp.197, 333, cites Prince de Talleyrand, *Mémoires* (Paris, 1891), pp.281–2.
20. Ridley, *Palmerston,* p.590 cites Thiers to Beauvale, in Beauvale to Lady P, 5 January 1846; Lady Airlie, *Lady Palmerston and her Times* (London, 1922), p.105.
21. Bell, *Lord P,* vol.1, p.vii.
22. Ridley, *Palmerston,* p.298, P to Temple, 1844.
23. Charmley, *Glory,* pp.467, 649.
24. L. Mitchell, *Holland House* (London, 1980), *passim.*
25. Ridley, *Palmerston,* p.300
26. Chamberlain, *Ld Palm,* p.ix, 119.
27. *Guardian,* 4 May 1994; Ridley, *Palmerston,* p.292; Gilbert, *Churchill: A Life,* pp.432–5, 448.
28. BBC 2 television programme, November 1995.
29. Bell, *Lord P,* vol.1, p.vii.
30. D. Magarshack, *Turgenev* (London, 1954), cited by Ridley, *Palmerston,* p.483.
31. J. Grant, *Random Recollections of the House of Commons 1830–1835, by One of No Party* (London, 1836), p.218.
32. Southgate, *English Minister,* p.555, xxviii, xxiv (Trollope's view).

33. Sir E. Hertslet, *Recollections of the Old Foreign Office* (London, 1901), p.184.
34. Rt Hon. K. Baker CH MP, *The Prime Ministers* (London, 1995) *passim*, and for much appreciated advice to the author, letter of 17 January 1966.
35. Sir R. Rhodes James, *Rosebery: A Biography* (London, 1963), p.75.
36. H. W. Lucy, *Peeps at Parliament* (London, 1903), p.226.
37. Southgate, *English Minister*, p.375.
38. Southgate, *English Minister*.
39. The author has valued the views, expressed in correspondence and discussion, 1994–5, of Jasper Ridley, Sir Robert Rhodes James and Sir Martin Gilbert in this context, whilst not seeking here to imply any endorsement of the limited analogy here advanced.
40. Alan Bullock, *Hitler and Stalin: Parallel Lives* (London, 1991), *passim*.

Appendix 2
Constitutional and Legal Aspects

This Appendix summarizes three areas of British constitutional and international law and convention which underlay the story of the Rio Nunez incident and the Braithwaite and Martin claims.

The Evolution of the Relationship Between the British Crown and the Executive: The Interface Between Law and Convention, and the Understanding Existing in 1851

From 1832 onwards, the tide of the constitution had begun to flow towards the supremacy of Parliament, with gathering momentum. A century and a half ago, the British monarchy made its two final attempts to stem that tide. The first attempt, in 1834, a very direct, clear cut affair, was, from a short-term point of view, successful: Victoria's uncle, William IV, did succeed in sacking the elected Prime Minister of the day, Grey, letting in Lord Melbourne; however, the longer-term constitutional repercussions of that act rendered it a Pyrrhic victory. The second attempt came in 1851, with the sacking of Palmerston: it was by contrast a more subtle, indirect and complicated business.

The commentaries of the historians and biographers of Victoria, Albert, Palmerston, Russell, and indeed Baron Stockmar, with regard to Palmerston's dismissal in December 1851, are contradictory. None of them draws explicitly from one of the best authorities on British constitutional law and convention, although the first edition of I. Jennings's *Cabinet Government* had been available since 1936.[1] Jasper Ridley, the only barrister to write about Palmerston, clearly knew his legal authorities, although this source is not referred to.

The available analyses mix theory with personality. Some writers appear to argue that one or other of the court circle was justified in his or her assertion of the state of the royal prerogative at that time; others that this was not a constitutional issue at all, merely a matter of personalities and practical power politics. Some pick up the role of Stockmar, others ignore it completely. Most identify two influences, first of King Leopold, and then, increasingly, of Albert over Victoria from 1841 to 1852; few discern the ambiguity of Victoria's deeper views with regard to Palmerston's policies, as opposed to her feelings about his personality and behaviour towards her personally, which she found insulting. Even fewer of the writers pick out Lord John Russell's central constitutional role and responsibility towards Palmerston, concentrating rather on the party politics and the personal aspects of his tortuous function as the 'shock absorber' between sovereign and Foreign Secretary. There is common ground in realizing that the events of 1851 cannot be seen in isolation from what went before, nor from the international pressure on the court. Even then there is no unanimity about the interaction between the two evolutionary processes involved: the 'court's' view of the royal prerogative, and Palmerston's view of the British government's political need — rather than its constitutional right — to 'intermeddle', short of war, during a turbulent and fluctuating decade of European politics — the 1840s. No one at that period could actually say with finality what the true constitutional position was. The threads need unravelling.

The views of Jennings form a critical starting point. In what is still relegated, even in the context of the third edition of his standard work, to the status of a footnote, not a main part of the text, Jennings comments that 'The views of Baron Stockmar on British constitutional questions are of no value, except as indicating what the Queen and Prince Albert believed to be the constitutional position'.[2] (Jennings would appear not to have realized that the court's beliefs substantially derived from, and did not merely reflect, or unhappily coincide with, Stockmar's inputs). That footnote was related to his paragraph about the dismissal itself: 'The classic precedent for the dismissal of a minister occurred in 1851. As early as 1848 Queen Victoria was anxious for the removal of Lord Palmerston from the Foreign Office to some other department because of her fundamental disagreement with his policy.'[3] Earlier, Jennings makes explicit the nature of the right of dismissal: 'According to law, the minister holds his office at the pleasure of the Crown. He can, therefore, be dismissed, according to law, at any moment; and this prerogative is exercised solely on the advice of the Prime Minister. ... A Minister always holds his office "at the disposal of" the Prime Minister.'[4]

Jennings goes on to highlight the practical political consequences of the misuse or ill-considered use of the Prime Minister's right to require a resignation: 'Such advice would be required only in the most extreme cases. ... A dismissal is a declaration of weakness which necessarily has repercussions in the House of Commons. ... The minister dismissed may have support in the House, or even in the Cabinet.'[5] This was precisely why Russell resisted exercising his constitutional right of advising the dismissal of Palmerston at any of the earlier stages when prompted by the court to do so, in 1848, 1849 and 1850; and it was due to his ultimate political misjudgement, even in December 1851, that the adverse 'tit-for-tat' vote in the House succeeded in February 1852.[6] To use the language of Gladstone in 1872, it was not 'a case of which the sufficiency can be made intelligible and palpable [to] the world'.[7]

Jennings, and Ridley, also bring out a fourth point which has escaped many of the biographers: that even Palmerston himself seemed partially to concede the constitutionality of the court's pressure on him, by itself, to step down: 'Palmerston retorted ... "If the Queen or [sic] the Cabinet were dissatisfied with his management of the Foreign Affairs, they had a right to demand his resignation, and he would give it".'[8] Later in 1852, after his dismissal, there is some indication that Palmerston 'would have liked to return to the Foreign Office, had it been possible; but he knew [sic] that the Queen had decided [sic] that he should never again be Foreign Secretary'.[9]

Given that apparent concession by one of the protagonists, it is perhaps pardonable that most of the writers have not sought to present the conflict in the strict light of constitutional legality. For example one of the major biographers of Victoria contents herself with this initial judgement: 'The Queen told Lord John Russell that she might soon be unable to "put up with Lord Palmerston any longer which would be very disagreeable and awkward". ... Not only would it be awkward, it would also be unconstitutional. The Sovereign had no more right to dismiss her Minister for failure to consult her than the Minister had to treat her with discourtesy. Constitutionally, both sides were sailing near the wind.'[10] They were, but perhaps not quite in the way that the famous biographer implied.

There are five further constitutional points to be made here:

(i) Even as early as 1851, the sovereign had no right, on any ground, to dismiss a minister: 'The notion that the Sovereign could, without the consent of the Prime Minister, dismiss a minister, is without foundation ... the idea is probably the product of Baron Stockmar's unqualified statement of the previous year.'[11]

(ii) Discourtesy has nothing to do with constitutionalism — the two points were suggested in order to provide a convenient balance of responsibility. (Anyway, Palmerston's discourtesies were nothing compared with those forced by the Queen's later behaviour out of her Prime Minister of the 1880s, Gladstone, when, for example, he said he 'does not presume to estimate the means of judgement possessed by your Majesty'.)[12]

(iii) It would appear that even Palmerston himself did not totally understand, or at least choose to assert, his full constitutional right to be dismissed solely by a Prime Minister backed by Cabinet support.

(iv) Two final points concern the Prime Minister himself. For all his liberal sympathies, which kept him very closely behind Palmerston's line and principles, Lord John always seemed to impute a greater prerogative to the Crown than would appear to be justified constitutionally. He writes to Palmerston on 1 November 1851, apropos the visit of the Islington delegation to Carlton Gardens, and a few weeks before finally caving in to the court's pressure, 'I do not see how it is possible for you either in your private home or elsewhere to be other than the organ of the Queen towards all foreign powers.'[13]

(v) He nevertheless also asserted the important balancing role of evolutionary practice, reflecting the will of the people: 'He admitted it was the prerogative of the Crown to dismiss and appoint Ministers, and to dissolve Parliament. But the people also possessed their privileges which on fit occasions were to be exercised' and, although King William IV's dismissal of

Grey 'was consistent with the principles, it was opposed to the practice of the English constitution'.[14]

The explanation of Palmerston's concession derived partly from his sincere convictions about the value of the constitutional monarchy, and his sense of how he, as a gentleman, should behave towards his sovereign lady. However, his views were also bound up with his own image, as much as with the possible constitutionality of his position: 'they could not wish him to lower himself in public estimation.'[15] As Jennings remarks, even that apparent plea to consider his political reputation was somewhat disingenuous, and suggests a fine calculation as to how far he could push things: 'As Palmerston had just defended his foreign policy triumphantly in the House of Commons, this was the last thing Lord John wanted.'[16] Longford makes the same point in her conclusion: 'the reason must be that the brinkmanship of the four major actors [which she defines only as Victoria, Albert, Palmerston and Russell, omitting Leopold and Stockmar] was deliberately geared to something less than catastrophe.'[17]

The Basis of the Views of 1851
How was the position understood at the time, and on what published authorities were such views based? At the time of the 1851 conflict, there was no Jennings, no Anson, no Maitland, no Bagehot, or a St John-Stevas to interpret Bagehot to the mid-Victorian world. The first serious post-1832 attempt at a constitutional history was not destined to appear until a quarter of a century later, in 1875, when Taswell-Langmead, the first holder of a chair in constitutional law and history, published his *English Constitutional History*. Even in Plucknett's revised tenth edition published in 1946, there is still a leaning towards a stronger interpretation of the royal prerogative than is evident in Jennings, for example, with the attribution to the sovereign of words such as 'executive administration', 'share of business', and 'controlling'.[18] Plucknett goes on to say that

[T]he personal influence of the sovereign in the executive administration has steadily declined. It has, however, been asserted at intervals with effect. ... [I]n controlling one minister the sovereign still acts upon the advice and responsibility of another — her first minister — to whom copies of despatches and other information are also communicated in order to enable him to give such advice effectively'.[19]

Bagehot, starting to write in the *Fortnightly Review* a mere 14 years after these events, only intended to 'show the actual workings of the constitution between the first and second Reform Acts — a glance behind the veil at the realities of power as they existed at the end of the 35-year period'.[20] The trenchant views he expressed about the famous three residual rights — 'the right to be consulted, the right to encourage, the right to warn' — must, however, have had their roots well back in the 1851 era: the extract in Costin and Watson, *The Law and Working of the Constitution*, includes the key elements:

> The popular theory of the English Constitution involves two errors as to the sovereign. First ... it considers him an 'Estate of the Realm', a separate coordinating authority with the House of Lords and the House of Commons. This and much else the sovereign once was, but this he is no longer. ... It is a fiction of the past to ascribe to her [the Queen] legislative power. She has long since ceased to have any. Secondly, the ancient theory holds that the Queen is the executive. ... The defining characteristic of ... [British Cabinet government] is the choice of the executive ruler by the legislative assembly.[21]

The fact that Bagehot did not examine the 1851 conflict in his essays suggests that it was still too recent even for him to feel able to do so. However, the radical bias of the thinking he would have brought to that task, writing four years after Prince Albert's death in 1861, is unmistakable: 'It is nice to trace how the actions of a retired widow and an unemployed youth [the Prince of Wales] become of such importance.'[22]

Victoria's own views about her prerogative were formed from more than half a dozen different sources. First in time came her book learning under the notorious 'Kensington system' of Conroy and Lehzen. This included, every morning, in addition to studies of Racine and Paley, reading from the original 1768 four-volume writings of Blackstone about the law and the constitution.[23] These were 'the traditional lawyer's views', which, according to Maitland writing in 1888, 'still maintain a certain orthodoxy'.[24] This was reinforced by the enduring effect of the counsels of King Leopold: 'For the first 15 months of her reign he left Stockmar in England as his alter ego, contenting himself in sending her advice. Much of it influenced the Queen as long as she lived.'[25] Melbourne's genial but in many ways misleading teaching leant towards a party-political interpretation of the position of the monarch, but also towards a dominant role for the Prime Minister of the day: 'Take care that Melbourne is not King', was the caveat of Victoria's mother, the Duchess of Kent.[26] Counteracting this was the steadily growing influence of Prince Albert.[27] This was coupled with the lessons Victoria believed she had herself finally learned through her own experience from the Melbourne and Peel crises of 1839 and 1840. By the time of the fall of Peel in 1846, 'she congratulated herself on her spotless constitutionalism and fairness of her behaviour this time compared with 1839.'[28]

Two concluding points: the effects of the appeasing weakness of Lord Aberdeen in the sphere of foreign policy between 1841 and 1846 reinforced the trend taking place in Albert's own thinking: 'In foreign politics, encouraged by Stockmar and Lord Aberdeen, they [the royal couple] intended henceforward to assume special responsibilities in foreign affairs; their happy family life would keep the country morally safe.'[29] Of all the influences, Stockmar's was the most pervasive, and the least detectable. He was able partly to set in motion views about the sovereign's rights which were unfounded, partly to provide chapter and verse — a handy *post hoc* rationalization — for the way that Victoria's 'vein of iron' wanted to run anyway: 'When the court had reached an impasse Stockmar usually helped them out with a masterly analysis. The Don Pacifico affair was no exception.'[30] Gladstone later said that 'his constitutional knowledge was, after all, only an English top-dressing on a German soil'.[31]

Given all these influences, both intrinsic and extrinsic, the behaviour of the court in 1851, whilst now recognizable as being subtly unconstitutional, is also not too surprising: the conditioning was deep and strong, and there was also a sense in Victoria that the democratic waves unleashed in 1832 both could and should be kept back, to keep the country 'safe'. With the shocks of 1848, the year of revolutions, these views had gathered pace. Following the non-event of the Chartist march on Kennington Common — 'our revolution' as Victoria put it, much relieved — and the Queen's temporary enforced evacuation to Osborne, Victoria was able to start arguing with Russell on astonishingly anachronistic grounds — the language reeks of Stockmar: 'Obedience to the laws and the Sovereign is obedience to a higher Power, divinely instituted for the good of the people, and not of the Sovereign, who has equally duties and obligations.'[32] Longford adds: 'We do not know what thoughts occurred to the pugnacious little Whig as he listened to this Victorian version of the divine right of Kings.'[33] Perhaps they were not quite so incredulous as the biographer was implying. This emphasizes a further compounding factor: that in the crucial period from 1846 to 1851, the monarch had a very complicated and unpredictable Prime Minister whom, for all his moral strength — 'he was ignorant of moral fear' — she did not ultimately respect;[34] she and Albert undoubtedly, therefore, manipulated him. He did not ever dare to take a stand on the constitutional position that he, the author of the 1832 Reform Act, could see more clearly than anyone, even Palmerston: 'he had a greater constitutional knowledge, perhaps, than any other member of the House.'[35] In default of gentle Melbournian correction, the royal thought process took on its own momentum.

In this grey area, where conditioning, constitutional theory, political calculation, ignorance, personality and the sheer coincidence of events, all played their shadowy part, perhaps some non-constitutional criticism does lie after all with Palmerston. He was clever enough to have been able to follow his wife's pleadings to 'manage' the royal couple more creatively: 'Lady Palmerston was asking her husband to "ménager" the English court just as the Queen had desired Palmerston to "ménager" foreign monarchs.'[36] He could have bent the knee even more than he in fact did, after the various flare-ups; Lord John even believed that he could have made Palmerston apologize once again, at the eleventh hour, in December 1851: 'I think I could, without difficulty, have induced him to make a proper submission to Her Majesty's wishes.'[37] Palmerston had the constitution on his side, and he had the added justification that he was putting his time where it mattered — on foreign affairs, and not in acting the courtier like the Foreign Secretaries who preceded and succeeded him — Aberdeen, and Granville. In the end, both he and his monarch allowed their temperaments to master their judgements.

There were four further factors that Palmerston, with all his astuteness, might have better appreciated about Victoria at that time. First, that at heart Victoria's instincts about the need for a patriotic assertion of Britain's rights were converging more on those of Palmerston himself than they were on any of the other influences around her — Leopold, Aberdeen or Albert — let alone Stockmar: 'As sometimes happened she was gradually coming round to Palmerston's view though not to his person.'[38] Moreover, she had always had a decided respect for his ability, and at the formation of the Russell ministry in 1846, Lord John was able to reassure the antagonistic Earl Grey that 'she was, in short, convinced that I was right in wishing to retain Palmerston at the Foreign Office'.[39] This view held firm. For example, when deliberating with Russell as to who should take his place in 1851, she asked, 'Who could succeed Lord Palmerston? Russell proposed his father-in-law, Lord Minto. "Not able enough after Palmerston", retorted the Queen.'[40] This covert partiality was to mature later in the light of Palmerston's energetic resolution of the Crimean War débâcle. Further, Jennings makes the suggestion that if Palmerston had chosen to push his claims to the Foreign Office during any of the subsequent ministries after 1851, despite his refusal to throw down the gauntlet to his Queen, the court might have given way: 'Probably the Queen would have acquiesced if the political situation had warranted the proposal, or Lord Palmerston had been less good-humoured.'[41] Palmerston had, however, decided that enough was enough.[42] Finally, Palmerston might have stopped to think more deeply about what can now be seen as the psychological basis for Victoria's assertion of her position, and thus her continuing need, understood intuitively by Disraeli, to find potential paternal surrogates — in Leopold, Melbourne, Peel, Aberdeen, and even the Duke of Wellington.[43]

Both Russell and Stockmar looked back on the events between December 1851 and February 1852 with regret, realizing that an injustice had been visited on the Foreign Secretary. In old age Lord John wrote: 'Baron Stockmar ... seems to have acquiesced in the opinion that my conduct upon that occasion was dilatory and undecided. My own judgement upon it is that it was hasty and precipitate. I ought to have seen Lord Palmerston.'[44] Palmerston certainly forgave Russell, and his political career did not suffer — quite the contrary. By her later behaviour Victoria became more or less reconciled with Palmerston, but there is no evidence that she ever properly appreciated the real nature of the constitutional crisis that nearly befell her. Perhaps the most generous view of the stance that the Queen took comes from the pen of the one Prime Minister whom she never came to terms with — Gladstone. This was the long-serving Liberal leader who had to fight Disraeli's strong Conservative presence in the House of Commons, and at the same time to counteract his beguiling influence with the Queen in private. In 'Comments on Royal Office: The Drawbacks 1880–90', he wrote:

> Who can blame the Queen? Prince Albert and Lord Beaconsfield alike had made her believe that continuity of high reponsibility gave her knowledge and experience to which no passing minister could attain. This she firmly and honestly believed. But in fact this continuity on the heights cut her off from all opportunity of personal contact with the ideas of the people, and relieved her from the necessity of ever going to the roots of big questions by reason and argument. Politicians had to fight these things out in principle and detail on the platform, in the press, and in the House of Commons. They were in the continuity, not of the Throne, but of arduous public life. ... Discussion and inquiry produced stages in their minds and in the minds of the people, which were steps to progress.[45]

* * *

International Law: The Rights of British Subjects Abroad

There were many aspects to Palmerston's approach at the Foreign Office to matters of international law, as they affected the rights of British subjects abroad; the connecting thread was the protection to be derived for British citizenship by virtue of the British constitution. They are detailed with particular care by Ridley, citing examples across the whole period of Palmerston's influence over foreign affairs, from 1831 through to 1865, both as Foreign Secretary and as Prime Minister.[46] The only internationally accessible source for the determination of international law at that time was an 1839 edition of the three-volume textbook of a continental

jurist, Emmerich de Vattel, *Le Droit des Gens*; the English translation was by J. Chitty, of 1834, and was part of the library of
every embassy. Vattel wrote in the middle of the eighteenth century, basing it on the classic work of Grotius.[47] Palmerston
demonstrated a detailed knowledge of Vattel in his dispatches to
his ambassadors abroad, and assumed equal familiarity on their
part. Thus, for example, in his dispatch of 19 March 1841 to Sir
John Seymour, the minister at Brussels, on the subject of the damage caused by Belgian volunteers in the actions against the Dutch
at Antwerp, Palmerston laid down the law, and also quoted from
it, along lines that anticipated the events of 1849–50.[48]

> The Belgian government in its opinion quotes certain pro-
> visions of the French and Belgian Codes [of law] which
> declare that sufferers by civil contest shall not receive recom-
> pense of their losses. ... But though the laws of a state are
> conclusive as to claims made by one of its own subjects, such
> laws cannot be pleaded as a bar to the claims made by a
> foreign government on behalf of its subjects and founded on
> the general principles of international law. ... The Acts [*sic*]
> of the Belgian Volunteers ... were wanton outrages. ... For
> what does Vattel say on this head, BIII cap XVI 241: 'It is
> moreover an acknowledged principle of international law
> clearly laid down by Grotius (*de lege: bell et pac*) — That
> whoever is responsible for an act is responsible for all the
> consequences of that act'.

This example has relevance for the subsequent Braithwaite and
Martin claims; it is also of note that a characteristic Palmerstonian
phrase in such situations — 'wanton outrage' — here sees the light
of day.

There had grown up, in effect, over the two decades prior to the
Rio Nunez incident, a consistent body of precept, precedent and
practice whereby such claims by individuals were — or were not
— dealt with. A dozen elements in that evolving Palmerstonian
doctrine — and therefore by extension that of the Foreign Office
that he dominated — can be identified:

(i)   Unwavering pursuit of the principle that states should
       observe 'international law', in so far as the then published

sources clarified the situation; above all, emphasis on the strict fulfilment of treaty rights accorded under it, and insistence that its provisions be adhered to by other nations and their servants. The lack of clarity about international law was well illustrated in 1838 where the Queen's Advocate (Sir John Dodson QC) — and consequently Palmerston — espoused one line of thinking, 'but were opposed by the sympathizers of King "Bomba" of Naples, who retained the advice of Sir Frederick Pollock, a former "Advocate General", and Dr Phillimore, a leading English lawyer'.[49]

(ii) Basic respect for the inviolability of the jurisdiction of states within their borders, or under their control in time of blockade or war, provided that Palmerston judged that their judiciary was as constitutionally independent of the executive, as was the case in Britain, (for example with regard to France, as opposed to Palmerston's attitude towards Venezuela).[50]

(iii) Insistence that British-born subjects first pursued their claims through the judicial system of the country under whose flag the action giving rise to it had been executed; this was not possible in the *res nullius* of the Nunez.

(iv) Determination that any British representative on the spot should be censured if he did not do all in his power to assist an aggrieved British subject in the pursuance of a claim to justice, short of interfering with due judicial process, (for example Belgium and the case of an English traveller, Miller, and Fauche, the British consul at Ghent, in 1840).[51]

(v)   This case also emphasized the peculiarly personal nature of Palmerston's commitment to individuals, regardless of other priorities facing him: 'Palmerston heard about it at the most critical time in the Middle East crisis, but he found time to give the case his personal attention.'[52] This was reinforced by his patience and assiduity in monitoring that process as it took its traditional course through courts and governments, often over the passage of many years.

(vi) Nevertheless, an acceptance that some judicial systems had features that were more brutal than Palmerston persuaded himself was the case under the British system, and thus within that to limit any intervention to a plea for excess to be avoided in their implementation (for example the consul at

Alexandria, and the use of the bastinado on a British subject).[53]

(vii) A realization that *in extremis*, the inaccessibility of a given territory and/or the liability to involvement by another competing state — with consequential harm to the 'balance of power' in that region — might render British support of the otherwise inviolable rights of its citizens impracticable (for example the case of the imprisonment of Colonels Stoddart and Connolly, and their later beheading, by the Emir of Bokhara, and the Foreign Office's abstention from action, in the light of the possibility of Russian intervention, between 1838 and 1842).[54]

(viii) Commitment to the pursuit of justice as a principle, regardless of whether the offending country was currently seen as friendly or unfriendly to Britain (for example *supra*, where Belgium's case was opposed to Holland in 1841).

(ix) In parallel, a personal avowal by Palmerston at least, to pursue such claims regardless of the size and importance of the state concerned, albeit that his actions differed as to degree, where, for example, the offender was a major power with influence to be currently wooed (for example Russia or Austria).

(x) Reflex referral of contentious points of international law to the advice of the 'law officers', and invariable, although not automatic, acceptance of the advice offered; that advice was sought at that period in the nineteenth century from a now defunct Law Office known as the King's — or Queen's — Advocate;

(xi) Notwithstanding such advice, a preparedness to bring sanctions to bear upon a country where there was a sustained refusal over time to deal justly with a claim or a series of claims: such sanctions could range from the use of extremely undiplomatic language, to actual military force, characteristically by the Royal Navy. The outstanding example was the series of incidents in relation to the then corrupt Greek government and system of justice of King Otho, over the years 1846 to 1850; these are frequently ignored in reference to their culmination in the Don Pacifico actions of 1850. 'Gunboats' were not 'ever-ready';[55] for Palmerston they were a calculated last resort, not an immediate 'knee-jerk' reaction.

(xii) Even for the legalistic Palmerston, the pragmatic position of last resort was nevertheless one of crude expediency, if nothing more could be done, as evidenced in Palmerston's own 'Circular' of 1848 to his embassies.[56]

* * *

The Role of the Queen's Advocate
in the Management of the Foreign Office

Ministers were there to obtain and take advice when appropriate; one such adviser was the shadowy figure of the Queen's Advocate. This function had grown up from 1608, to be abolished in 1867. It was part of the structure of the old ecclesiastical courts, responding to the Archbishop of Canterbury, and became over time the repository for all kinds of non-ecclesiastical matters, until finally 'jurisdiction in all testamentary matters was transferred to the newly established Court of Probate. The advocates who practised before the Ecclesiastical Courts were Doctors of Civil Law, and the Crown was represented by a King's advocate.'[57] Clearly, a variety of strictly legal matters were customarily referred to his office, which was a very senior one; its incumbent from 1834 to 1852 was Sir John Dodson, who had also been for the preceding five years — significantly for matters out on the coast of Africa — the Admiralty Advocate. The appointment carried an automatic knighthood, Sir John becoming thus honoured 11 days after his gazetting, on 29 October 1834. He was in addition a member of the Judicial Committee of the Privy Council from 1852, who later took on the further obscure office of the 'Dean of the Arches', the Court of Arches being the appellate court in such matters. His successor, on 5 March 1852, until 1867, was almost as distinguished — John Dorney Harding QC, who was in his turn knighted on 24 March.

This role was also referred to by some writers, incorrectly, as that of 'The Lord Advocate'.[58] As is shown in the 'List of English Law Officers', the title was also termed the 'Advocate General'; all three were in use until the mid-century, after which time cases started to be handled by the Solicitor General or the Attorney General.

The records of the opinions of the King's (or Queen's) Advocate are in the Treasury series at the PRO (TS25/25 v3 and 25/26, v4 1845–59). Seemingly, the documents were culled at an intervening time, to highlight those where major principles seemed to be at stake, presumably at the time when a certain clerk marks himself down for posterity with the words: 'This book finished and written by Edward Robson, Easter Tuesday 22.4.1851'.[59] There are three points to make about this series:

- They cover a wide range of contentious legal issues, predominantly with a maritime flavour — piracy, distressed seamen, blockade, martial law, courts martial, the slave trade: they also included wills and probate, reflecting the historical origins in the Prerogative Court of Canterbury.
- They embrace the work of two separate law officers — the Queen's Advocate and the Admiralty Advocate, and bring in under their aegis the opinions of junior counsel in their chambers: the Admiralty counsel is R. B. Crowder from 1849 to 1854, and N. Atherton by 1859. There was a normal but not invariable promotional path from Admiralty Advocate to Queen's Advocate.
- Titles were used very loosely; thus the Queen's Advocate is referred to variously as 'HM Advocate', 'HM's Advocate', 'HM Advocate General' (27 July 1849, the 'Charlotte'), and 'The Queen's Admiralty Advocate' (14 June 1848 and 16 July 1849, 'Pirate Bounties').

Palmerston constantly referred cases to the Queen's Advocate. For example, in the case of King Bomba, 'having been assured by the Queen's Advocate that his position was justified in international law, he became more and more threatening.'[60] This policy of referrals also included the case of the Braithwaite and Martin international claims. Another case that came under the wing of this function under its alternate title of Lord Advocate — although it occurred in 1855, outside the time frame of the Rio Nunez incident — is nevertheless instructive. This was the case of a referral for legal opinion of the case of Stephan Tuerr.[61] It demonstrated that Clarendon too, among the long array of foreign ministers, could, when he chose, put time aside for minimal individual matters, in the same way as his recent mentor and role model, Palmerston. Sadly, he chose, or was so constrained by the impact of the business arising from the 'Eastern Question', not to extend that same consideration to the case of Braithwaite and Martin; eventually he washed his hands of the case of Stephen Türr, a reaction that had an unhappy precedent in the Rio Nunez Affair.

Notes

1. I. Jennings, *Cabinet Government* (Cambridge, 1959), *passim*; J. Ridley, *Lord Palmerston* (London, 1970), *passim*.
2. Jennings, *Cabinet*, p.208.
3. Jennings, *Cabinet*, p.208. For the classic account of the relationships between the Queen and her Secretary of State, 1837–65, see Brian Connell, *Regina v. Palmerston* (London, 1962), Chap.4, pp.99–134, who states that 'The triangular conflict must be without parallel in British ministerial annals, certainly in the last two centuries, and the wonder is that it did not lead to a constitutional crisis of the first magnitude'; See n.17 *infra*.
4. Jennings, *Cabinet*, pp.207–8. For later comment, see Harold Wilson, *The Governance of Britain* (London, 1976), p.51.
5. Jennings, *Cabinet*, p.208.
6. S. Walpole, *Life of Lord John Russell* (London, 1889), vol.2, p.18; Ridley, *Palmerston*, pp.385, 393, 399, 400. See Chap.6 *supra*.
7. Jennings, *Cabinet*, p.211; cf. G. E. Buckle, *Letters of Queen Victoria*, vol.2 (London, 1926–8), p.225.
8. Jennings, *Cabinet*, p.208.
9. Ridley, *Palmerston*, p.405.
10. E. Longford, *Victoria RI* (London, 1964), p.199.
11. Jennings, *Cabinet*, p.211.
12. Jennings, *Cabinet*. p.343; cf. Buckle, *Letters*, vol.3, p.603.
13. Walpole, *LJR*, vol.1, p.134, LJR, at Pembroke Lodge, to P, 1 November 1851.
14. Walpole, *LJR*, vol.1, p.173. As early as 9 February 1834, LJR was here beginning to assert the implications of the 1832 Reform Act, while still mentally in thrall to the principle of the royal prerogative; also W. Anson, *The Law and Custom of the Constitution* (Oxford, 1896), vol.2, pp.55–6.
15. Jennings, *Cabinet*, pp.208–9.
16. Jennings, *Cabinet*, p.208.
17. Longford, *RI*, p.209.
18. T. F. T. Plucknett, *English Constitutional History, by T. P. Taswell-Langmead* (London, 1875, 10ᵗʰ edn. 1946), p.723; also E. Freeman, *The Growth of the English Constitution* (London, 1876), quoted in G. Marshall, *Constitutional Conventions: The Rules and Forms of Political Accountability* (Oxford, 1984).
19. Plucknett, *Taswell-Langmead*, pp.722–3.
20. Lord N. St John-Stevas, *The Collected Works of Walter Bagehot* (London, 1965), p.67.
21. W. C. Costin and J. S. Watson, *The Law and the Working of the Constitution: Documents vol.2: 1784–1914* (London, 1952); also H. G. Nicolson, *King George the Fifth* (London, 1952), Chap.8, pp.110–14.
22. St John-Stevas, *Bagehot*, p.226. 'The Queen undoubtedly took the title of "Her Majesty's" Ministers not as fiction but as fact, failing to perceive that the Cabinet no longer rested on royal but on popular approval' (ibid., p.75).
23. Longford, *RI*, pp.51–5; Cecil Woodham-Smith, *Queen Victoria: Her Life and*

      Times, 1819–1861 (London, 1972), vol.1, p.110; Jennings, *Cabinet*, p.343.
24.   Costin and Watson, *Law and Working*, p.444; cf. F. W. Maitland, *The Constitutional History of England* (Cambridge, 1908), p.415.
25.   Longford, *RI*, pp.50–61; Ridley, *Palmerston*, p.392.
26.   Woodham-Smith, *Life and Times*, p.142.
27.   Longford, *RI*, p.184; 'the Queen not unnaturally listened to her husband on subjects which after all, as a European [sic] himself, he must know more about than Palmerston' (ibid., p.199); also Woodham-Smith, *Life and Times*, p.220.
28.   Longford, *RI*, p.182.
29.   Longford, *RI*, p.184.
30.   M. Charlot, *Victoria: The Young Queen* (Oxford, 1991), p.162. 'Stockmar dreamed of . . . a unity of purpose . . . between Germany and England. For him, Albert was . . . above all, a means to an end. . . . 'There was, as Lady Lyttelton noted, a "vein of iron running through her character".' (ibid., p.189); cf. H. Bolitho, *Albert the Good* (London, 1932), p.164. 'Stockmar had drawn up . . . the Belgian constitution . . . unaware that [the British] resembled in no way the logical, synthetic constitution of Belgium' (Longford, *RI*, p.65); also 'Prince Albert's hidden streak was of wax' (ibid., p.149); also ibid., p.202. See also 'the sagacious Stockmar' was 'for some time partially insane' (R. W. Seton Watson, *Britain in Europe 1789–1914: A Survey of Foreign Policy* (Cambridge, 1937), p.291); see Baron F. von Stockmar, *Denkwuerdigkeiten aus den Papieren des Freiherrn Christian Friedrich von Stockmar* (Brunswick, 1872), p.642. 'In 1856 he left England . . . for ever . . . [he] had been consulted by the Prince in every crisis' (Woodham-Smith, *Life and Times*, p.400). See also p.37, for the prophetic comment quoted in the Epilogue that 'Britain is of Europe, and yet not of it. The desire for isolation, the knowledge that it is impossible – these are the two poles between which the needle of the British compass continues to waver'.
31.   Jennings, *Cabinet*, p.344; cf. W. E. Gladstone, *Gleanings of Past Years: 1843–78* (London, 1879), p.84.
32.   Longford, *RI*, pp.197–8, Victoria to Albert at Osborne; Victoria to LJR, 6 August 1848.
33.   Longford, *RI*, p.198.
34.   Walpole, *LJR*, vol.1 p.173, comment by Sidney Smith.
35.   J. Prest, *Lord John Russell* (London, 1972), p.209; cf. HM's remark to Leopold, 23 December 1845, that 'Lord John I am sure never can be Prime Minister for he has not a shadow of Authority' (RA Y92, 36); Walpole, *LJR*, vol.2, p.172.
36.   Longford, *RI*, p.208; also Seton-Watson, *Britain*, p.287; cf. Lady P to P, 1848, saying 'You always think you can convince people by Arguments, and she has not reflection or sense to feel the force of them' (Lady Airlie, *Lady Palmerston and her Times* (London, 1922), vol.2, p.122).
37.   Walpole, *LJR*, p.142.
38.   Longford, *RI*, p.203.
39.   Walpole, *LJR*, vol.1, p.416.
40.   Longford, *RI*, p.201, reference to QVJ, 2 March 1850; for comment of Victoria on P, reference to the Crimean War, see Woodham-Smith, *Life and Times*, p.371.
41.   Jennings, *Cabinet*, p.66.
42.   Denis Judd, *Palmerston* (London, 1970), p.104. P's reaction was '"J'y ai été", as the Frenchman said of foxhunting'. And, as P said to his brother William on 3 April 1853, 'I really would not . . . undertake again an office so unceas-

ingly laborious every day of the year as that of Foreign Affairs. . . . I am very glad that Clarendon got the Foreign Office.' (E. Ashley (ed.) *The Life of Henry Temple, Viscount Palmerston by Sir Henry Lytton Bulwer (Lord Dalling)* (London, 1870–4), vol.2, p.36).

43. 'One who was ever a father to me' (Charlot, *Young Queen*, p.245); also Queen to Leopold, 14 September 1852, 'we shall soon stand sadly alone. Aberdeen is almost the only personal friend of that kind [*sic*] we have left, Melbourne, Peel, Liverpool, now the Duke — all gone' (Longford, *RI*, p.231).
44. Walpole, *LJR*, vol.2, p.142, writing in 1875.
45. Jennings, *Cabinet*, 342; cf. Lord H. J. Gladstone, *After Thirty Years: A Defence of W. E. Gladstone* (London, 1928), p.375; Costin and Watson, *Law and Working*, p.448.
46. Ridley, *Palmerston*, Chaps.22, 26, pp.359, 361. For the comparative inexperience of Granville and Malmesbury — 'amateurs in diplomacy' — and the superior knowledge of international law displayed by their opponents in Vienna and St Petersburg, see P. W. Schroeder, *Austria, Great Britain and the Crimean War: The Destruction of the European Concert* (Cornell, 1972), p.11.
47. Emerich de Vattel, *Traite sur le Droit des Gens* (Brussels, 1758, English translation, J. Chitty, London, 1834).
48. BL Add. MS 48,499, Palmerston Letter-Books 1835–41, P to Seymour, 19 March 1841; Ridley, *Palmerston*, p.361.
49. Ridley, *Palmerston*, pp.354, 363.
50. Ridley, ibid., p.363.
51. Ridley, ibid., p.360.
52. Ibid.
53. Ibid., p.364.
54. Ibid., p.365–6.
55. See Longford, *RI*, p.201; cf. Judd, *Palm*; Ridley, *Palmerston*, p.125.
56. P's 'famous Circular' to 'HM's Representatives in Foreign States, January 1848, in the year preceding the Nunez Affair, [albeit in the context of financial transactions in civilized states]: whilst on the one hand "there can be no doubt . . . of the . . . right which every Govt . . . possesses to take up . . . any well-founded complaint which . . . its subjects may prefer against the Govt of another country"; nevertheless 'The British govt has considered that the losses of imprudent men who have placed mistaken confidence in the good faith of foreign Govts would provide a salutary warning to others.' (D. C. M. Platt, *Finance, Trade and Politics in British Foreign Policy: 1815–1914* (Oxford, 1968), p.398).
57. In the *civis Romanus* debate itself, P refers to 'the distinguished individual who holds the office of Queen's Advocate . . . that meritorious office' (Hansard CXII, 3rd ser P 380, Tuesday 25 June 1850). See Joseph Haydn, *The Book of Dignities* (London, 1894, repr. Baltimore, 1970), pp.349, 360, 418–23, 1009; Sir J. Sainty, *A List of English Law Officers, King's Counsel, and Holders of Patents of Preference* (London, Selden Society, 1987), p.77; W. S. Holdsworth, *A History of English Law* (London, 1903), vol.12, pp.6–8; J. Tilley and S. Gaselee, *The Foreign Office* (London, 1933), pp.115–6. 'Later in the nineteenth century, the Foreign Office only stepped in when British subjects had a claim against a foreign government for denial of justice, or when their legal remedies had been exhausted.' (Ridley, *Palmerston*, p.365).
58. Schroeder, *Destruction*, p.432; Costin and Watson, *Law and Working*, pp.88, 92, 331–3.
59. PRO TS Series 25/25 v3, 25/26 v4, 1845–59 (Chancery Lane).

60. Ridley, *Palmerston*, p.354.
61. Schroeder, *Destruction*, App C, The Tuerr case, pp.432–4, the 'British Lord
     Advocate . . . stated that Britain had no legal grounds to demand Tuerr's
     release'.

Appendix 3
Foreign Office Pressures: 1851–1853

T his Appendix brings together evidence that the British Foreign Office was unable, as opposed to merely unwilling, to prosecute further such cases of individual claims as those of Braithwaite and Martin. The hypothesis is that the Foreign Office's capability, although judged to be among the more 'efficient' departments after Palmerston's first period of office in the 1830s, was thrown off-balance during the period leading up to the Crimean War.[1] This assertion has a bearing on an understanding of the Nunez Affair; the hypothesis rests on four initial propositions.

Effects of 1848
The political changes that erupted in Europe's first year of revolutions were even more profound than those of its twentieth-century equivalent, 1989. Leading on, over six increasingly threatening years, to the Crimean War they would have been enough to test the Foreign Office of any one of the members of the Concert of Europe, however well equipped and staffed. The 'press of business' was heavy.[2] The stresses induced by the changes in the international pecking order were a massive challenge to Britain and its accustomed position of leadership. They were not made any easier by the fact that Britain was 'now the only great power in Europe in which a parliamentary system is in active operation'. By the end of the Crimean War, to a foreign observer, 'the brief two years of fighting seemed to have fully justified his suspicions that a constitutional state of traders and manufacturers could never be a first-rate military power'.[3] From that period onwards the 'British compass' swung back to insular reaction once again,

and the concept of 'splendid isolation' started to hold sway. 'The old Europe was visibly dying, the new not ready to be born.'[4]

Staffing levels

The evolution of the Foreign Office was still very recent, from the early days under Fox at the end of the eighteenth century, the term 'Foreign Department' having been officially superseded only in 1807; the title 'Foreign Office' was still used *pari passu* with the 'Department for Foreign Affairs'. Confronted by a sea change in international affairs, the British did not value highly enough the 'moral and intellectual' capacities of this major office of state and took its staffing less seriously than some of its rivals. At the time of Nicholas's accession to the Russian imperial throne, in 1825, the total Foreign Office staff was 28, as compared with France's 55, and Russia's highly bureaucratized equivalent, over 300: Palmerston and his successors were not supported by the kind of Chancellery enjoyed by some other powers.[5]

The *Records of the Foreign Office: 1782–1939* show an overall figure of 30 for the year 1822; however, this reduces to 26 when such supernumerary functions as a door porter, two office keepers and a printer are discounted. There was one chief clerk, aided by a supplementary clerk, four first-class or senior clerks, six second-class clerks, another six junior clerks, and three assistant junior clerks, all backed up by a librarian, a sublibrarian, a translator, a précis writer, and one 'private secretary', (parliamentary, not shorthand).[6] When Palmerston first entered the office, in 1830, the staff was still only about 30, and the office 'was a shambles of two former private houses and their annexes in Downing Street';[7] they were not pulled down until 1861. The 'library' was 'scattered all over the place', there was an upstairs room called 'the nursery' where the clerks could go and try to relax, and working away in another attic was the elderly and one and only translator.[8]

There were other improvements in the establishment by 1839, but they were not enough. 'There was a further increase in 1849, but Palmerston continued to create more work than clerks to handle it.' The workload led to absences due to illness. There were endemic Treasury pressures on the budget; early in Palmerston's time at the Foreign Office, the Foreign Secretary's own salary had been cut from £6000 to £5000 per annum.[9] Thus, by the end of the period of time in which the Rio Nunez Affair was decided,

1854, a quarter of an increasingly busy century after the first comparison, the overall figure of 30 had merely doubled, to 63, of whom 53 now covered the executive and 'back-room' functions, although the library (research) team had gone up from two to seven, and there was in addition a specific superintendent for the treaty department. At the top there was still only one chief clerk, but with seven senior clerks at his side; still only one translator, one précis writer, and one private secretary. Quality would of course modify quantity, but bodies were vital for both drafting by hand and for research into treaties and other documents. Given that the ages of some of these clerks, although averaging 20, might well have been no more than 16 or 17, or even younger, the question of quality is relevant.[10] With no open competition the say-so of the Secretary of State, or one of his senior clerks, were the sole criterion; the subjects looked for were 'Handwriting, Dictation, Précis, and French, and the standards were not high'. 'British government departments were a haven for mediocrities with influential patrons.'[11] The Secretary of State 'was perpetually assailed by all the influential relations of half the blockheads in the kingdom'.[12]

'The scope for foreign policy was extending yearly, the business of the foreign office rising dramatically. Despatches poured in and instructions poured out. In 1830 there were 11,546 despatches: in 1850, 30,725' — a threefold increase, not reflected in the staffing ratio.[13] The countries that were the object of this activity were still few, and odd, by any comparison that would be recognized today, although there are some states that no longer survive, such as Saxony, Hanover, Württemberg, and Bavaria; those figures had not changed greatly during this period, whatever the greater degree of complexity there might be in the time required to deal with them. From 1852 onwards, the diplomatic side of the office's work was reallocated between its four then existing 'departments'; the first included France, while Belgium was handled by the second, a fact that may well have hampered the coordination of the Nunez claims.[14]

France

A third and critical element that skewed the picture was the nature of the relationship with France. The advice and readings coming up from that first department regarding France during this period must have been tortuous in the extreme as she veered between suspicion and relieved, if reluctant, partnership. Fears of invasion were real enough. One small indicator was that a fifth division was added in 1854; it must have been overdue.[15]

Palmerston's personal impact

The fourth element, and the most important, turns on an evaluation of Palmerston's own capacity for the work of the monolithic department he had in effect recreated since 1830, compared with the capacity of his successors in office after December 1851. As is clear even in the relatively minor matter of the Rio Nunez Affair, the Secretary of State made the decisions, determined the policy line, directed the relationships with the key foreign governments, read and dictated or wrote by hand most of the dispatches, called for research, and monitored what vestigial 'bring-forward' system there was.

Under his reign, there were factors that offset the inherent trend to inefficiency. Although he appeared not to care overmuch about his team, it is on record that when he first left office, in 1834, he sent the clerks a message commending them for 'the sense of indefatigable zeal and unwearied cheerfulness with which they have ... gone though the unusual labour ... arising out of the extraordinary pressure of public business'. There is some indication that this belated compliment did not go down too well. Only right at the end of his political career, and after the pressured period of the 1850s, is there tangible evidence that underneath the tough exterior, he at least, of all the Secretaries of State, did have a real concern for the motivation of his team, *vide* his celebrated letter to Gladstone of 23 August 1865.[16] One complication, at least, was beginning to diminish, that of the specially-constituted 'Slave Department' within the office, where James Bandinel was superintendent from 1819 onwards, and then a senior clerk, until he retired in 1845.[17]

Leadership came into the reckoning. Palmerston effected dramatic improvements to the way the department worked when he first entered it in 1830, bringing with him the concern for detail that he had had to perfect over his many years in the heavily administrative office of Secretary at War; 'he had brought dogged perseverance and bureaucratic bustle ... he had most certainly proved himself a very able administrator.' He drove his clerks hard, insisting on clear quill-penmanship and spelling, and often infuriating them by sending a paper back repeatedly until it was exactly to his liking.[18] There are some celebrated quips: 'Iron Railings leaning out of the Perpendicular', letters sloping backwards 'like the raking masts of an American schooner'; reading the hand of another was 'like running Penknives into one's Eyes'. As Palmerston left the Foreign Office after his first four-year stint, 'his clerks unashamedly rejoiced that their hard taskmaster had gone'.

The comment has been made that 'a great deal of Palmerston's success can be attributed to the fact that he always did his homework very thoroughly indeed.'[19] It should be said rather that Palmerston certainly knew what doing his 'homework' meant, and practised it most of the time, aided by his innate 'bluffing' skill. Karl Marx in an otherwise suspect essay (with roots in the ravings of the notorious Urquhart), presents Palmerston thus: 'When unable to master a subject he knows how to play with it'.[20] To offset this criticism, there is one further point with regard to the quality of work performed by the office and its 'hardened cynics'. 'Only Palmerston felt at home with the professional members of the Foreign Office. The others looked at diplomatists with distrust.'[21]

The workload of the Secretary of State

This study has already recorded that Palmerston was a man with an outstanding application and an ability to cut through quickly to the heart of the matter. 'Unlike Castlereagh, or Malmesbury's grandson as Foreign Secretaries, Palmerston was hardly, if ever, accused of ambiguity.'[22] In one of his brushes with the court, Palmerston omitted from his list of activities the time which he devoted to the private briefing of the press, one of his most skilful attributes as Foreign Secretary.[23] There is a dramatic estimate of his long hours:

His daily desk-work required eight hours work, then there was attendance at the House of Commons or at official functions. He tried never to go to bed later than one o'clock in the morning, and never to rise after seven o'clock. Even when he had been obliged to sit late in the Commons, he still got up at seven o'clock, took some exercise (riding when he

was in London), read some despatches, and then took breakfast.

One picture presents Palmerston often arriving late at the office,
and leaving even later; another overall comment is that 'he arrived
at the Foreign Office at 10.00 a.m., and worked solidly through
till the early afternoon; instead of a midday meal he ate an orange;
Cabinet meetings were held in the afternoon, but were generally
over by 5.00 p.m.; between five o'clock and 6.30 he was available
to ambassadors and other callers on business.'[24] The implication
of this is clear: under Palmerston, the Foreign Office 'worked', in
both senses of the word, due to his character, his standards, and
his experience, and despite the pressures of the world outside it.

The Permanent Under-Secretary

The role of the Permanent Under-Secretary, one of the two
notional deputies to the Secretary of State, was of course also
crucial. For most of the time with which we are concerned, that
office was held by Henry Unwin Addington, a nephew of
Sidmouth's, 'a plain reactionary', a Tory appointee by Lord
Aberdeen, and formerly minister to Spain. The received view has
been hitherto that having been responsible to Palmerston in his
first stint at the Office from 1830 to 1833, he was removed from
the diplomatic service 'as being too stupid and too ill-willed'. He
was appointed to take on the senior in-house role in 1842, which
he held until 1854. Palmerston is said to have disliked both him
and his then chief clerk, and 'must have been glad when
Addington at last surrendered his place'.[25] However, there is now
contrary evidence, not previously published, that his personal
relationship with Palmerston would appear to have been close and
cordial, for on Palmerston's sudden 'removal', we find Addington
immediately writing to him with much solicitude, and appreciation, on 27 December 1851:

> My dear Lord, I will not allow this opportunity to escape
> without expressing to your Lordship my sincere regret at
> your very unexpected retirement, and at the same time beg-
> ging you to accept my (hearty) thanks for the invariable
> courtesy with which you treated me during the whole time
> that I served under you at this office. I will do myself the

honour of calling tomorrow in Carlton Gardens in the
chance of finding you at home.

This is perhaps yet another instance of the difference between
Pam's public and private persona.[26]

A Scurry of Secretaries

What is to be made then of the Foreign Office's ability to cope
under the rapid succession of members of the British aristocracy
who followed on Palmerston's heels in the 14 months between
December 1851 and February 1853? An admirable understatement refers to the early 1850s as 'a strange time in British politics'.
This echoes another judgement, the 'particularly ambiguous
character' of this period.[27] For the Foreign Office, there now
ensued the most chaotic period of dislocation over the whole 150
years since the records were presented in 1790.[28] The nearest in
terms of such anarchy was a three-year period at the time of the
Napoleonic Wars, when there were six Secretaries of State
between 1804 and 1807. This was echoed at the level of the other,
political, Under-Secretary: there were four different office holders
between 1851 and 1852.

In February 1853, the fourth peer, George Villiers, the fourth
Earl of Clarendon, took over the Foreign Office, leaving Russell to
concentrate on the role of leader of the lower House, whilst the
premier, Aberdeen, spoke in the Lords. Much is known about
Clarendon, from his own papers, and also from the voluminous
correspondence with his fellow Cabinet member and nominal
Home Secretary, Palmerston; these show Clarendon in a state of
constant pressure and uncertainty, and in need of continuing
reassurance from his senior confidant, sometimes expressed with
almost pathetic gratitude. Thus to Palmerston he writes in May
1853, 'I am always obliged for any suggestion of yours'; and again
in August, at the time of a sticky note from the Austrian government: 'your letter has done more to put my mind at ease than
anything that has occurred since I have been at the Foreign
Office.'[29] Many historians have written unkindly of him, for
example he was 'the vanished Victorian', 'a meticulous house-
maid', 'Clarendon often whirled about like a weathercock in a
tornado'.[30] He was typified as an exemplar of the 'spontaneous
dishonesty of weakness'.[31] In the context of the antagonisms

within the Aberdeen coalition, as the Crimean situation worsened, he was also likened to a 'referee in boxing ring', not as one of the protagonists.[32]

'Clarendon had a considerable reputation as an unscrupulous adventurer and a regular intriguer.'[33] He had also built up a certain attitude to the workings of the Foreign Office, complaining about 'the old women of Downing Street' and the neglect of his dispatches in that 'Temple of Procrastination'. This then was the last in the parade of incumbents, for perhaps the most crucial office in the country, more so in some ways even than that of the Prime Minister, given the salience of foreign affairs during the period leading up to the outbreak of the war, and the uneasy state of the Cabinet.

From 1852 onwards, and with Palmerston's four inadequate successors, the British Cabinet lurched onwards down an unhappy path, trying to impart assistance across Europe and Asia Minor, without realizing that it also needed help: with it lurched the Foreign Office.[34] It was not a framework likely to give more than minimal time to the claims of two British traders in a non-European theatre, against the very country where Britain now needed a diplomatic and military ally in the Eastern Question, the France of Napoleon III.

Conclusion
When the devil drove, and despite the weight of other matters before it and the inadequacy of its resources, the office could exert itself for individual cases, if policy required. However, the *civis Romanus sum* doctrine depended on the vitality of its creator. The evidence suggests that without Palmerston at the helm, the main thrust of affairs made such care for individual cases for compensation or redress, regardless of the actual merit of the situation, the exception rather than the rule. This certainly seemed to apply to the case of Braithwaite and Martin, who were unfortunate enough finally to coincide with Clarendon's fraught time in office.

Notes
1.   I am grateful to Dr Eva Haraszti-Taylor, through many conversations 1993–5; Dr David Wetzel, Columbia University (letters to author, 27 September 1993, 1 January 1994); Dr Keith Hamilton, FCO Library and Records Dept and editor of *Documents on British Policy Overseas* (letter to author, 26 September and discussion 9 October 1995); and lastly to Dr Ray Jones of

Carleton University, Ottawa (letter to author, 19 October 1995), for guidance here, particularly on the salient point that the staff at the FO had no real executive functions at this period (making the role of P that much more crucial). For references to FO being thrown off balance, see Sir E. Hertslet, *Recollections of the Old Foreign Office* (London, 1901), *passim*; and Kenneth Bourne, *Palmerston: The Early Years, 1784–1841* (London, 1982), pp.409, 416. For the significance in twentieth-century terms of the Crimean War, the battles of Balaclava and Sebastopol, and the 'images' of Florence Nightingale, today remembered more for their countless suburban street names, see David Wetzel, *Crimean War: A Diplomatic History* (New York, 1985), p.116, who claims that 'No military engagement until Dunkirk so moved the British people.'

2. This was the excuse offered by the man whom the Queen held up as a model courtier, for sometimes failing to show her the drafts of FO dispatches before they were sent off, during his time as Foreign Secretary, 1841–6 — the very reason P himself would give but which the court could not understand or accept; by the end of the century, this omission became common constitutional practice.

3. *Edinburgh Review*, October 1852. See Olive Anderson, *A Liberal State at War: English Politics and Economics during the Crimean War* (New York, 1967), pp.275, 277.

4. P. W. Schroeder, *Austria, Great Britain and the Crimean War: The Destruction of the European Concert* (Cornell, 1972), p.22. See also R. W. Seton Watson, *Britain in Europe 1789–1914: A Survey of Foreign Policy* (Cambridge, 1937) in Appendix 2, n.30 *supra*.

5. Wetzel, *Diplomatic History*, pp.27–8; Patricia Kennedy Grimsted, *The Foreign Ministers of Alexander I* (Berkeley, 1969), pp.26–7; Donald Southgate, *The Most English Minister: The Policies and Politics of Palmerston* (London, 1966), p.37. Compared with Paris or Vienna, 'the FO was a crude machine', see Bourne, *Early Years*, pp.409, 416.

6. PRO/HMSO, The Records of the FO 1782–1939 (London, 1969).

7. Bourne, *Early Years*, p.408.

8. Ibid., p.408; also see Part I *supra*.

9. Ibid., pp.416, 438.

10. J. Tilley and S. Gaselee, *The Foreign Office* (London, 1933), Chap.3, pp.50–71 and (on P's reforms), pp.60–4; also Bourne, *Early Years*, pp.416, 422.

11. Anderson, *State*, p.110; HMSO Records; also Bourne, *Early Years*, pp.424, 452–3.

12. Bourne, *Early Years*, pp.449–50.

13. Wetzel, *Diplomatic History*, pp.18, 27–8; Sir H. Maxwell, *The Life and Letters of the Fourth Earl of Clarendon* (London, 1913), vol.2, p.11 on Clarendon's Journal of 19 July 1853.

14. Bourne, *Early Years*, p.426.

15. 'The French were always wont to discern the familiar features of perfidious Albion beneath the new look of their unaccustomed British allies' (Anderson, *State*, p.79). See Henri Contamine, *Diplomatie et Diplomates sous la Restauration 1814–1830*, (Paris, 1970); F. A. Wellesley, *The Paris Embassy during the Second Empire: Selections from the Papers of the 1ˢᵗ Earl Cowley, Ambassador at Paris, 1852–1867* (London, 1928), pp.2–3. 'Fear of France continued to haunt the corridors of British diplomats right down to the spring of 1853. Indeed, belief that Belgium not Turkey, was uppermost in the calculations of British diplomats was the central factor which led Nicholas into the crisis of 1853.' (Wetzel, *Diplomatic History*, p.18.) The last word on this mis-

reading of the Europe of the 1850s, that 'The Second Empire claimed to be Wagner and turned out to be Offenbach', must rest with the master of epigram, A. J. P. Taylor, *The Man of December* (London, 1952), p.27. See Chap.6.

16. E. Hertslet, *Old Foreign Office*, p.64; Bourne, *Early Years*, pp.417, 430. P also thanked the Office on leaving in December 1851.

17. Tilley and Gaselee, *The Foreign Office*, pp.217, 225; Bourne, *Early Years*, p.416; see Chap.2 *supra*.

18. V. Cromwell and Z. S. Skinner 'The FO before 1914: A Study in Resistance', in G. Sutherland (ed.), *Studies in the Growth of Nineteenth Century Government* (London, 1972), pp.172–3. They also quote (p.175) FO 366/760 recording that P 'shaped the office' by 'constant badgering'; also Bourne, *Early Years*, pp.422, 433.

19. Judd, *Palm,* pp.55, 9; Chamberlain, *Ld Palm*, pp.3, 27.

20. Robert Payne's chapter on 'The Unknown Karl Marx', *The Story of the Life of Palmerston* (New York, 1971), pp.148–202; Ann P. Saab, *The Origins of the Crimean Alliance* (Virginia, 1977), p.3.

21. Wetzel, *Diplomatic History*, pp.37, 63.

22. Bourne, *Early Years*, p.28.

23. Anderson, *State*, pp.70–120; B. Kingsley Martin, *The Triumph of Lord Palmerston: A Study of Public Opinion in England before the Crimean War* (London, 1924, rev. edn, 1963), *passim*.

24. Denis Judd, *Palmerston* (London, 1970), p.42; Bourne, *Early Years*, p.431; but see Sir J. Simon's Introduction to Tilley and Gaselee, *The Foreign Office*, p.vii.

25. Addington had other problems at the FO — the antagonism of the chief clerk, G. L. Coyningham; see FO Librarians Department, Correspondence and Memoranda, 1848–1905, v3A. I owe this insight to Dr K. Hamilton, for access to records not usually available. Stratford Canning praised Addington's 'cheerful spirit and ever-ready intelligence' (Tilley and Gaselee, *The Foreign Office*, p.69); Bourne, *Early Years*, pp.409, 418, 473. Addington's conservatism did not assist the Nunez Affair (see Jones's letter, *supra*) and Addington 'was not a very capable Under-Secretary'.

26. PBHA, FO/E/1–19, Addington's letter to P, 27 December 1851.

27. Chamberlain, *Ld Palm*, p.77; Anderson, *State*, p.282.

28. HMSO, *Records*.

29. PBHA, GC/CL/500–514, 515–28, Clarendon to P, 24 May, 1 August 1853. On 30 August, at the time when Clarendon finally washes his hands of the B&M affair, he is writing to P that 'Eastern affairs are critical'. See also Maxwell, *Clarendon*, vol.2, p.89 and vol.1 p.363. Clarendon later described work at the FO as 'penal servitude'.

30. Schroeder, *Destruction*, p.412 also quotes Sir Richard Pares on Clarendon.

31. Wetzel, *Diplomatic History*, pp.88–9.

32. Bourne, *Early Years*, pp.473–4, 590; yet see Maxwell, *Clarendon*, vol.2, pp.298–300. 'Long before their parting as old comrades, P had dismissed all . . . suspicions of Clarendon as an intriguing rival.'

33. Bourne, *Early Years*, p.416.

34. Eva Haraszti-Taylor, *Kossuth as an English Journalist* (Budapest, 1990), p.172, quotes Kossuth having written an article in *The Albion*, 25 May 1855, in which he says 'Alas! England stands more in need of assistance than she is able to impart.'

Appendix 4
The Road to Debucca

This study was waiting to be written for nearly 150 years. Without the discovery of those tattered tightly bound papers in a battered old black tin box, unread by the two Edwardian aunts who preserved them, it might never have met the light of day. My parents' interest had been limited to the information about the family crest on the gold watch and cane; these were Joseph Braithwaite's sole surviving effects, sent back to his brother Charles, the author's great-great grandfather, by the thoughtful administrators of his bankrupt estate in 1854. Those long depositions to Viscount Palmerston — the blue ink still remarkably fresh, their hand evidently well educated, and their content impressively lucid — and their references to an unknown river Nunez, and to Forster and Smith, King 'Moyra', Fumpenny of Debucca, and Nebbo, a 'Krooman Grumetta' — all this began to take on the nature of an irresistible challenge.

A long lunch at Palmerston's own — and Matthew Forster's and the author's club — the Reform, with the late Professor Kenneth Bourne of the LSE, in the autumn of 1992, was the key that unlocked the meaning of those agonized Braithwaite and Martin letters. By 4.30 that afternoon, his vast storehouse of knowledge about Palmerston had guided me towards Rhodes House in Oxford, the Public Record Office at Kew, the Royal Commonwealth Society library, and the School of Oriental and African Studies. From those introductions evolved all the other discussions with historians, archivists and authors, in the USA, Canada, France and Belgium — not to mention Scotland, Wales, Ulster and England — whose generous and valued help I have been happy to acknowledge. The fact that he said that he would now include this episode in the second volume of his life of Palmerston was an added incentive. Sadly, that hope was cut off by his death two months later, my letter to update him about the results of his inspired guidance arriving only on 12 December. The Palmerston bibliographer, Partridge, remarks on the jinx that seems to deprive the world of further writings about Palmerston: the loss of Kenneth Bourne's second volume must rank high among them. Perhaps the greatest single breakthrough in the research came 20 minutes before closing time, one Friday afternoon, at the Broadlands Archive at Southampton, when the real commitment of Palmerston to his two *cives Britannici*, and the impact of Queen Victoria's engineered 'removal' of him, at last came into focus, through hitherto unrecorded papers.

I trust that the true account of all these inputs and insights is worthy of so much expert knowledge about Palmerston and Africa. 'The Road to Debucca' should become more properly 'the Road to Boké', as it became evident that at least in this corner of the predominantly red-coloured globe, Britain had given way to her then arch rival, France: the journey of discovery down that road has been the most exciting I have ever made. I hope I may have succeeded in sharing something of that excitement with my readers.

Dramatis Personae

These are the principal figures who influenced, directly or indirectly, the Nunez Affair. Dates only given where relevant to the story: for further biographical detail, see Index.

BRITAIN

The Court
Queen Victoria and Prince Albert; Baron Stockmar; Colonel Phipps

Politicians and Civil Servants
Secretaries of State for Foreign Affairs: Viscount Palmerston (1830–4, 1835–41, 1846–December 1851); Earl Granville (December 1851–February 1852); Earl of Malmesbury (February–December 1852); Lord John, later Earl Russell (December 1852–February 1853); Earl of Clarendon (February 1853–8)
Under-Secretary: Lord Eddisbury
Permanent Under-Secretary for Foreign Affairs: Henry Unwin Addington (1842–54)
Secretaries of State for War and the Colonies: Lord Bathurst; Viscount Goderich; Earl Grey (1846–52)
Permanent Under-Secretaries for War and the Colonies: James Stephen (1836–48); Herman Merivale (1848–60)
Under-Secretary for Colonies: Sir Benjamin Hawes (1846–51)
Senior Clerk: Sir George Barrow

Foreign, Colonial and Consular Services
Ambassadors to Paris: Constantine Henry Phipps, Marquis of Normanby (1846–52); Baron Cowley (1852–67)
Chargé d'Affaires: Honourable Richard Edwardes
Minister to Brussels: Lord Howard de Walden (1846–68); (Sir) Thomas Wathen Waller, Secretary of Legation (1837–58)
HM Consuls: Robert Norie (Ghent); Godshall Johnson (Antwerp)
Sierra Leone: Norman W. Macdonald (Governor, 1847–52); (Sir) Benjamin Pine (Acting Governor, 1842–51)
Gambia: Sir Richard Graves MacDonnell (Governor)
Gold Coast: Governor John Maclean (Cape Coast Castle)

Royal Navy, Merchant Navy, Army
Admiral Sir Charles Hotham; Captain Murray (HMS *La Favorite*); Lieutenant Commander Selwyn (HMS *Teazer*); Captain Belcher (HMS *Aetna*); Captain Monypenny RN (HMS *Sealark*); Lieutenant Commander Thomas Lysaght RN (HM Steam Vessel *Grappler*); Captain Thomas Venn (SS *Princess Royal*); Captain William Derecourt (Brig *Nunez*); Captain Thomas Jackson; Captain P. Prendergast (Representative of Governor Macdonald, 1850).

FRANCE
Heads of State
King Louis-Philippe (1830–48); Louis Napoleon (Prince-President, 1848–52), Emperor Napoleon III (1852–70)

Politicians and Civil Servants
Ministers for Foreign Affairs: Alexis de Tocqueville (1848); Edmond Drouyn de Lhuys (1848, 1851, 1852–5, 1862–6); General de la Hitte (19 November 1849–January 1851); Brenier (February–April 1851); Baroche (April–October 1851); Marquis de Turgot (October 1851–August 1852)

Foreign, Colonial and Consular Service
Ambassadors to Great Britain: Drouyn de Lhuys (1849–December 1851); Count Walewski (1851+)
Ambassadors to Brussels: M. Quinette (1849–52); Duc Bassano (1852–3)
French Consul, Freetown, Sierra Leone: Guillaumard d'Aragon

Navy: La Royale
Admiral Edouard Bouët-Willaumez (from Captain); Captain Fleuriot de Langle; Captain Ducrest de Villeneuve; Captain de Kerhallet (*La Prudente*); Captain de la Tocnaye (*La Recherche*)

BELGIUM
The Court
King Leopold I of the Belgians (1831–65)

Politicians
Constant d'Hoffschmidt de Resteigne (1847+)

Foreign and Consular Service
Ambassador to London: Sylvain Van de Weyer (1831–67); *Ambassador to Paris*: Firmin Rogier; M. Carolus (Chargé d'Affaires)

Royal Belgian Navy and Merchant Navy
Captain Joseph Van Haverbeke (*Louise-Marie*); Lieutenant Witteveen (*Emma*); Lieutenant Themistocle du Colombier; Ensign Dufour; Ensign-Aspirant (later Inspecteur) G. Delcourt

Traders and Entrepreneurs based in Belgium
Abraham Cohen; Constant Dossche

THE LANDUMAS
King S'ahara; King Tongo, elder son of S'ahara; King Mayoré, younger son of S'ahara, half-brother of Tongo; Chief Dibby; Chief Bonchevy

THE NALUS
Towls: Lamina; Youra; Carimon

THE FULA OF FUTA JALLON
Governor Mahdi

MERCHANTS AND TRADERS TO AND IN WEST AFRICA
West Coast to Lagos: *Forster & Smith*: Matthew Forster MP; John Forster MP; William Forster; Richard Lloyd; J. and C. Boocock; T. Chown

GAMBIA AND THE NUNEZ
Braithwaite & Martin: Joseph Braithwaite; George Martin; Samuel D. Ellam; Billy Ellam (with John Farmer; Samuel Johnson; Fumpenny; Nibbo)
The Nunez: John Nelson Bicaise (trader and domestic slave-owner) with Cubely, his messenger; Ishmael Tay, (Senegalese trader and slaver) with Massounkong, one of his wives, sister of Mayoré
British traders not party to the Chambre de Commerce: J. Holman; J. Bateman; Benjamin Campbell JP.
Michael Proctor; Elizabeth Proctor (later Mrs Bicaise);
French traders: M. Avril, M. Santon, M. d'Erneville, M. Salcedo
Later at Ropass: M. Bols (Belgium). Mrs Skelton (at Victoria)

OTHER CONSULS
In Belgium (Danish); M. Thader (Ghent); M. Nottebohm (Antwerp)

Bibliographical Summary

This summary provides a short introduction to the Sources and Bibliography, highlighting published sources which support the six interwoven threads of the Nunez story; detailed references are in the chapter notes. Sources for other 'background' themes are covered in the Appendices. See notes to appendices for Palmerston and Churchill; the constitutionality of Palmerston's dismissal; Palmerston and International Law; Palmerston and the Queen's Advocate; and Pressures on the Foreign Office.

1. Palmerston
(i) Involvement with Africa
The main source for Palmerston's focus on Africa are R. J. Gavin's Ph.D. thesis, 'Palmerston's Policy Towards East and West Africa 1830–1865'; C. W. Newbury's *British Policy Towards West Africa: Selected Documents*; also Kenneth Bourne's *Palmerston: The Early Years, 1784–1841*. Lynn, and Cain and Hopkins, have drawn attention to this neglected area.

(ii) Involvement with the Rio Nunez Affair
The main sources are archival: the Palmerston archive, PRO FO97/198, and the BL Add. MSS. These are supported by other Foreign Office and Colonial Office documents.

(iii) Background to the civis Romanus sum *doctrine*
Overview: M. S. Partridge, and K. E. Partridge, *Lord Palmerston 1784–1865: A Bibliography*. The three main works consulted were J. Ridley, *Lord Palmerston*; Donald Southgate, *The Most English Minister: The Policies and Politics of Palmerston*; and Kenneth Bourne, *Palmerston: The Early Years, 1784–1841*. Ridley offers the most complete recent coverage, in particular the first access to the Palmerston Papers in the BL Add. MS, although at that time no one apart from Bourne was allowed access to the Palmerston archive. Southgate's work deliberately focuses on 'policies and politics', and is excellent on Don Pacifico, and the 1851 'resignation'. Bourne provides the most comprehensive recent account of the years to 1841, including the formation of Palmerston's character. H. Bell's 1936 two-volume *Lord Palmerston* is the longest of all the twentieth-century biographies, although deprived of the sources used in later biographies. He is good on the *civis Romanus* debate. Of other works, Guedalla gives a nice early impressonistic picture; Kingsley Martin highlights Palmer-

ston's populist 'media' role; Pemberton, Judd, and Chamberlain have all provided good shorter biographies, each bringing some new insights to bear. Of the earlier nineteenth-century work, what Ridley calls 'Dalling and Ashley' needs to be consulted. Additional insights appear in the two main works about the elusive Lord John Russell — Spencer Walpole, and Prest.

2. Forster & Smith and British Policy in West Africa

Overview: C. W. Newbury, *British Policy Towards West Africa: Selected Documents*, is also a valuable source for Forster & Smith activity up to 1869. The best though by no means a total picture comes in F. J. Pedler, *The Lion and the Unicorn in Africa*. The classic 'territorial' works embrace relevant Forster & Smith references: C. Fyfe's massive *A History of Sierra Leone*; J. M. Gray, *A History of The Gambia*, also G. Metcalfe, *Maclean of the Gold Coast*. George Brooks's *Yankee Traders, Old Coasters, African Middlemen* also provides many examples of Forster & Smith activity. Other data are in the unpublished Joan Heddle Papers (JH/ML); in Rhodes House; the Unilever Archive (UL/A) and the Guildhall Library (GL/A). The British Library (BL) Newspaper Library at Colindale and the Berwick Record Office Library provide additional Matthew Forster material through various media. B. Schnapper, *La politique et le commerce français dans le Golfe de Guinée de 1838 à 1871* also provides interesting mentions. See the author's articles in the *Camden History Review*, and the *Journal of Imperial and Commonwealth History*.

3. Belgian Development on the Nunez

Overview: Patricia Carson, *Materials for West African History in the Archives of Belgium and Holland*; and A. Duchesne's 1958, 'Bibliographie: Rio Nunez', *BARSOM*, pp.783–5. The best 'postwar' source is R. Massinon, *L'Entreprise du Rio Nunez: Mémoire de Licence inédit ULB*, although he does not draw from sources used by Bruce Mouser in his thesis, 'Trade and Politics in the Nunez and Pongo Rivers, 1790–1865', and in the *BARSOM* article, and could not have access to the latest Belgian view in Everaert and de Wilde's, 'Pindanoten'. The interwar works by A. Demougeot ('Histoire du Nunez', *Bulletin du Comité d'Etudes historiques et scientifiques*) and Monheim's *L'Affaire du Rio-Nunez* need to be read, but are incomplete and too determinedly patriotic. For the complete picture, aiming off for understandable bias, essential reading are the eyewitness accounts of G. Delcourt, 'Relation du Voyage à la Côte d'Afrique avec la goélette *Louise-Marie* 1848–9', and C. Lannoy/ T. du Colombier, 'Une Expédition franco-belge en Guinée: La Campagne de la goélette de guerre *Louise-Marie* dans la Colonie belge du Rio-Nunez (1849)'. For Leopold I, see E. Corti, *Leopold I: Oracle politique de l'Europe*, J. Richardson, *My Dearest Uncle: A Life of Leopold, First King of the Belgians*, and E. Cammaerts, *The Keystone of Europe: History of the Belgian Dynasty, 1830–1939*. For an updated chronology of international coverage of the wider affair see the author's article in *Revue belge d'histoire militaire*, no. 66.

4. French Development on the Nunez

Overviews: G. D. Westfall, *French Colonial Africa: A Guide to Official Sources*; and J. D. Hargreaves, *France and West Africa: An Anthology of Historical Documents*. Apart from the archival source at the Centre des archives d'outre-mer, Aix-en-Provence, essential reading about the Nunez includes: C. Schefer, *Instructions aux Gouverneurs*; Schnapper's *Golfe de Guinée*; also the earlier and again patriotically biased A. Arcin's *Histoire de la Guinée française*. Anglo-French rivalry is well treated in P. Gifford and W. R. Louis, *France and Britain in Africa: Imperial Rivalry and Colonial Rule*, and its naval aspects in C. I. Hamilton, *Anglo-French Naval Rivalry: 1840–1870*. Wider perspectives are in J. D. Hargreaves, *Prelude to the Partition of West Africa*; J. Martin, *L'Aventure coloniale de la France: L'Empire renaissant, 1789–1871*; W. B. Cohen, *The French Encounter with Africans: White Response to Blacks, 1530–1880*; and R. Aldrich and J. Connell, *France's Overseas Frontier*. The European political setting of the Anglo-French relationship is also well covered by J. Ridley's, *Lord Palmerston*, also his *Napoleon III and Eugénie*. See also the author's article in *Revue française d'histoire d'outre-mer*, no.311.

5. The Peoples of the Nunez

Overviews: N. Matthews, *Materials for West African History in the Archives of the United Kingdom*, and IDC, *Sources de l'Histoire de l'Afrique au Sud du Sahara*. Essential reading includes: W. Rodney, *A History of the Upper Guinea Coast, 1545–1800*; R. Oliver and J. D. Fage, *A Short History of Africa*; A. J. Ajayi and M. Crowder, *History of West Africa*; and A. G. Hopkins, *An Economic History of West Africa*. There are three excellent theses: Bruce Mouser's 'Trade and Politics'; Thierno Diallo's 'Les Institutions Politiques du Fouta Djalon au XIXème Siècle'; and W. F. McGowan's 'The Development of European Relations with Fouta Jallon and the Foundations of French Colonial Rule: 1794–1897'.

6. Braithwaite and Martin

The main source is archival: PRO FO97/198, supplemented by the CO267 series (Sierra Leone) and the Foreign Office Letterbooks series for France and Belgium, which contain some papers not included in the Foreign Office claims' ledger. The main papers are in the Society of Genealogists Archive.

Sources and Bibliography

MANUSCRIPT SOURCES

Great Britain
Royal Archives, Windsor
Correspondence of HM Queen Victoria with Lord Palmerston, Lord John Russell, and Leopold of the Belgians (1850–1).

Public Record Office, Kew
BT 31 series. FO97/198 *France*: Messrs Braithwaite & Martin's Claims (1849–53), supplemented by other main files (Abstracts/Registers of Correspondence: France: FO147/32–4, 36; FO 27/775, 816, 858, also 84/768, 777; 360/, 606/ series); *Belgium*: FO 125/1–4; Diplomatic Correspondence: FO 123/ 60–75. CO267 (Sierra Leone)/205–236: 38, 78, 146, 196; 272; CO96/40, 58 (Gold Coast); 368/1, 2; CO87 series (The Gambia). Admiralty series: incl. 53/313, 2594; 1/5591

Public Record Office (Chancery Lane, until end 1996)
Treasury 'TS' series.

Bodleian Library
Oxford Russell Papers (MS Eng. lett. d269)

British Library
(i) Palmerston Letterbooks (BL Add. MSS 48,553; 48,584; 48,499; 48,581); (ii) Lamb Papers, Letters of Lady Palmerston (BL Add. MSS 45,911, 45,553); (iii) Letters of Afzelius, BL Add. MS 12, 131; (iv) SPIS (Parliamentary Papers)

Broadlands Papers, Hartley Library, Southampton University
Palmerston Papers

Hampshire County Record Office
Malmesbury Papers

Heddle Papers
Collection of the papers of Joan Heddle, reference to the Forster family, by kind permission of Dr M. Lynn

Maclean Family Papers, Elgin
Correspondence of George Maclean with M. Forster

Rhodes House Library, Oxford
Papers of Sir Thomas Fowell Buxton (Mss. Brit. Emp. s. 444), especially volumes 17, 27, 29, 30, 31, 32, 33). Also houses the Monheim and Demougeot works, q.v.

Aix
Centre des archives d'outre-mer (F/CAOM)
Series on Sénégal et Dépendances, dossiers 26, a–e.

Brussels
(i) Ministère des Affaires Etrangères, Rue Quatre Bras
Correspondance Politique/Légations: Grande Bretagne 1850

(ii) Archives du musée royal de l'Armée
Journals of T. du Colombier and G. Delcourt; other valuable data.

(iii) Bibliothèque royale Albert Ier
See Bibliographical Summary, *supra*, for works housed there.

Paris
Quai d'Orsay
Correspondance politique sous-série, belgique, vs 30–33, 1848–53.

Vincennes
Service Historique de la Marine.

PRINTED PRIMARY SOURCES

(i) BL Newspaper Library: Colindale
Berwick Advertiser/Berwick and Kelso Warder; Customs Bills of Entry; United Service Gazette; Leeds Mercury and Intelligencer; The Freeman's Journal; Morning Chronicle; Morning Herald; The Times.

(ii) Theses
These are included within subject sections.

(iii) Contemporary Books and articles
See subject sections.

PRINTED SECONDARY SOURCES:
BOOKS, ARTICLES, THESES

British imperial economic background
Cain, P. J. and A. G. Hopkins, *British Imperialism*, 2 vols (London, 1993)

Crafts, N., 'Managing Decline? 1870–1990', *History Today*, vol.44, no.6, June 1994

Daunton, M., 'The Entrepreneurial State, 1700–1914', *History Today*, vol.44, no.6, June 1994

Eldridge, C. C., *Victorian Imperialism* (London, 1978)

Fay, C. R., *Imperial Economy and its Place in the Free Trade Economic Doctrine 1600–1932* (Oxford, 1934)

Fisher, H. A. L., *A History of Europe* (London, 1936, repr. 1952)

Gallagher, J. and R. E. Robinson, 'The Imperialism of Free Trade', *Economic History Review*, 2nd series, vol.1 (1953)

Gamble, A., *Britain in Decline: Polical Strategy and the British State* (London, 1985)

Howe, A. C., 'Free Trade, and the City of London, 1820–1870', *History*, vol.77, October 1992, pp.391–410

Hyam, R., *Britain's Imperial Century: 1815–1914* (London, 1976)

Lynn, M., 'The Imperialism of Free Trade and the Case of West Africa c.1830–c.1870', *JICH*, vol.15, no.1, January 1986/7, pp.22–40

Malchow, H. L., *Gentleman Capitalists: The Social and Political World of the Victorian Businessman* (Manchester, 1991)

Marshall, P. J., 'Imperial Britain', Creighton 1994 Lecture, *JICH*, vol.23, no.3, 1995

Porter, A. N., 'Gentlemanly Capitalism and Empire: The British Experience from 1750', *JICH*, vol.18, no.3, October 1990, pp.265–95

Seton Watson, R. W., *Britain in Europe 1789–1914: A Survey of Foreign Policy* (Cambridge, 1937)

Taylor, A. J. P., *The Struggle for Mastery in Europe 1848–1918* (Oxford, 1954, repr. 1957)

British political background: Nineteenth Century

Airlie, Lady, *Lady Palmerston and her Times* (London, 1922)

Ashley, E. (ed.) *The Life of Henry Temple, Viscount Palmerston by Sir Henry Lytton Bulwer (Lord Dalling)* (London, 1870–4)

Baker, K.W., *The Prime Ministers* (London, 1995)

Bell, H., *Lord Palmerston* (London, 1936), 2 vols

Benson, A. C. and Viscount Esher (eds) *The Letters of Queen Victoria* (London, 1907), first series, 2 vols

Billy, G. J., *Palmerston's Foreign Policy 1848* (New York, 1993)

Bolitho, H. H., *Albert the Good* (London, 1932)

Bourne, Kenneth, *Palmerston: The Early Years, 1784–1841* (London, 1982)

Bullen, R., *Palmerston, Guizot and the Collapse of the Entente Cordiale* (London, 1974)

— *The Foreign Office 1782–1982* (Maryland, 1984)

Burnet, Bishop, *History of My Own Time* (1724, repr. 1833), James I to 1660, vol.1

Cecil, A., *Queen Victoria and her Prime Ministers* (London, 1953)

Cecil, Lord D., *Lord M* (London, 1954)

Chamberlain, M. E., *Lord Palmerston* (Swansea, 1987)

— *Lord Aberdeen: A Political Biography* (London, 1983)

Charlot, M., *Victoria: The Young Queen* (Oxford, 1991)

Collinge, J. M., *Foreign Office Officials* (London, 1979)

Coningham, W., *Lord Palmerston and Prince Albert* (London, repr. 1954)

Connell, Brian, *Regina v. Palmerston: The Correspondence between Queen Victoria and Her Foreign and Prime Minister 1837–1865* (London, 1962)

Crabites, P., *Victoria's Guardian Angel, Baron Stockmar* (London, 1937)

Czartoryski, A., *Memoirs of Prince Adam Czartoryski* (London, 1888), edited by A. Gielgud

Edwards, O. D., *Macaulay* (London, 1988)

Ensor, R. C. K., *England 1870–1914* (Oxford, 1936)

Fitzmaurice, E., *Life of Granville George Leveson Gower, Second Earl Granville 1815–1891*, 2 vols (London, 1905)

Gladstone, Lord H. J., *After Thirty Years: A Defence of W. E. Gladstone* (London, 1928)

Gladstone, W. E., *Single Works, Gleanings of Past Years: 1843–78* (London, 1879)

Gleason, J. H., *The Genesis of Russophobia in Great Britain: A Study of the Interaction of Policy and Opinion* (Cambridge, Mass., 1950)

Grant, J., *Random Recollections of the House of Commons 1830–1835, by One of No Party* (London, 1836)

Grimsted, Patricia Kennedy, *The Foreign Ministers of Alexander I* (Berkeley, 1969) (FO staffing comparisons)

Guedalla, P. (ed.) *Gladstone and Palmerston: Being the Correspondence of Lord Palmerston with Mr Gladstone, 1851–1865* (London, 1928)

Hamer, F. E. (ed.) *The Personal Papers of Lord Rendel* (London, 1931), containing his unpublished conversations with Mr Gladstone

Harris, J., *Earl of Malmesbury: Memoirs of an ex-Minister* (London, 1885)

HMSO, *The Records of the British Foreign Office 1782–1939* (HMSO, 1969)

Hertslet, Sir E., *Recollections of the Old Foreign Office* (London, 1901)

Hibbert, C., *Queen Victoria in her Letters and Journals* (London, 1984)

Hollis, P., *Pressure from Without in Early Victorian England* (London, 1974)

Jenkins, Roy, *Gladstone* (London, 1995)

Jones, R., *The British Diplomatic Service 1815–1914* (Gerrards Cross, 1983)

Judd, Denis, *Palmerston* (London, 1970)

Kingsley Martin, B., *The Triumph of Lord Palmerston: A Study of Public Opinion in England before the Crimean War* (London, 1924, rev. edn, 1963)

Lever, T. (ed.) *Letters of Lady Palmerston* (London, 1957)

Longford, E., *Victoria RI* (London, 1964)

— *Wellington*, vol.2, *Pillar of State* (London, 1972, Panther edn. 1975)

Lytton Strachey, G., *Queen Victoria* (London, 1921, revd. edn, 1969)

Lucy, H. W., *Peeps at Parliament* (London, 1903)

Magarshack, D., *Turgenev* (London, 1954)

Maurois, André, *Disraeli: A Picture of the Victorian Age* (Paris and Appleton, 1927)

Maxwell, Sir H., *The Life and Letters of the Fourth Earl of Clarendon* (London, 1913)

Minto, Countess of, *Life and Letters of Sir Gilbert Elliot, 1ˢᵗ Earl of Minto* (London, 1874),

Mitchell, L., *Holland House* (London, 1980)

Mount, F., *Umbrella* (London, 1994), a novella on Lord Aberdeen

Normanby, Lord (Constantine Henry Phipps), *A Year of Revolution* (London, 1857)

Parry, J., The *Rise and Fall of Liberal Government in Victorian Britain* (New Haven, 1993)

Partridge, M., *Lord Palmerston 1784–1865: A Bibliography* (Greenwood, 1994)

Pemberton, W. B., *Lord Palmerston* (London, 1954)

Platt, D. C. M., *Finance, Trade and Politics in British Foreign Policy 1815–1914* (Oxford, 1968)

Prest, J., *Lord John Russell* (London, 1972)

Preston, A. and J. Major, *Send a Gunboat! A study of the Gunboat and its Role in British Policy: 1854–1904* (London, 1967)

Reeve, H. (ed.) *The Greville Memoirs: A Journal of the Reigns of King George IV and King William IV* (London, 1875)

Rhodes James, Sir Robert, *An Introduction to the House of Commons* (London, 1961)

— *Rosebery: A Biography, The Fifth Earl* (London, 1963)

— *Albert: Prince Consort* (London, 1983)

Ridley, Jasper, *Lord Palmerston* (London, 1970)

— *Napoleon III and Eugénie* (London, 1979)

Rolo, P. J. V., *Entente Cordiale* (London, 1969)

Sainty, J., *Colonial Office Officials* (London, 1976)

Southgate, Donald, *The Most English Minister: The Policies and Politics of Palmerston* (London, 1966)

Stockmar, Baron F. von, *Denkwürdigkeiten aus den Papieren des Freiherrn Christian Friedrich von Stockmar* (Brunswick, 1872)

Sudley, Lord, *The Lieven-Palmerston Correspondence: 1828–1856* (London, 1943) (Lady Palmerston and Princess Lieven)

Sutherland, G. (ed.) *Studies in the Growth of Nineteenth Century Government* (London, 1972)

Talleyrand, Prince de, *Mémoires* (Paris, 1891)

Taylor, A. J. P., *The Man of December* (London, 1952)

Tilley, J. and S. Gaselee, *The Foreign Office* (London, 1933)

Walpole, Spencer, *Life of Lord John Russell* (London, 1889)

Webster, Sir C., *The Foreign Policy of Palmerston: 1830–1841* (London, 1951) 2 vols

Wellesley, F. A., *The Paris Embassy during the Second Empire: Selections from the Papers of the 1ˢᵗ Earl Cowley, Ambassador at Paris, 1852–1867* (London, 1928)

Wilson, Effingham, *Letters by W. Coningham* (London, 1854)

Wilson, K.M. (ed.) *British Foreign Secretaries and Foreign Policy: From the Crimean War to the First World War* (London, 1987)

Woodbridge, G., *The Reform Club 1836–1978* (privately published, 1978)

Woodham-Smith, Cecil, *Queen Victoria, Her Life and Times 1819–1861* (London, 1972)

Ziegler, Philip, *Melbourne: A Biography of William Lamb 2nd Viscount Melbourne* (London, 1976)

Constitutional Law and History

Anson, W., *The Law and Custom of the Constitution* (Oxford, 1896)

Bagehot, Walter, *Biographical Studies* (London, 1881)

Costin, W. C. and J. S. Watson, *The Law and the Working of the Constitution: Documents vol.2: 1784–1914* (London, 1952)

Dicey, A.V., *An Introduction to the Study of the Law of the Constitution* (London, 1885)

Freeman, E., *The Growth of the English Constitution* (London, 1876)

Haydn, Joseph, *The Book of Dignities* (London, 1894), preface by H. Ockerby (ed. of series) (repr. Baltimore, 1970)

Holdsworth, W. S., *A History of English Law* (London, 1903)

Jennings, Sir I., *Cabinet Government* (Cambridge, 1959)

Maitland, F. W., *The Constitutional History of England* (Cambridge, 1908)

Marshall, G., *Constitutional Conventions: The Rules and Forms of Political Accountability* (Oxford, 1984)

Nicolson, H. G., *King George the Fifth* (London, 1952)

Plucknett, T. F. T., *English Constitutional History, by T. P. Taswell-Langmead* (London, 1875, 10th edn. 1946)

St John-Stevas, Lord N., *The Collected Works of Walter Bagehot* (London, 1965)

Sainty, Sir J., *A List of English Law Officers, King's Counsel, and Holders of Patents of Preference* (London, 1987)

Emerich de Vattel, *Traite sur le Droit des Gens* (trans J. Chitty, London, 1834)

Wilson, Harold, *The Governance of Britain* (London, 1976)

Churchill/Palmerston

Blake, Lord and W. R. Louis (eds) *Churchill: A Major New Assessment of his Life in Peace and War* (Oxford, 1993)

Charmley, J., *Churchill: The End of Glory* (London, 1993)

Gilbert, Sir Martin, *Churchill: A Life* (London, 1991)

— *Winston S. Churchill*, vols 1–8; vols 1 and 2 by Randolph Churchill

— *Winston Churchill: The Wilderness Years* (London, 1981)

— *The Prophet of Truth: Winston S. Churchill, 1922–1939* (London, 1976)

Rhodes James, Sir Robert, *Churchill: A Study in Failure, 1900–1939* (London, 1970)

Roberts, A., *Eminent Churchillians* (London, 1994)

Storr, A., *Churchill's Black Dog and Other Phenomena of the Human Mind* (London, 1991)

African, Imperial and Business History: Books, Articles, Theses

Ajayi, A. J. and Crowder, M., *History of West Africa* (London, 1971)

Bandinel, J., *Some Account of the Trade in Slaves from Africa* (London, 1842)

Barron, T. J., 'James Stephen, the Black Race, and British Colonial Administration 1813–47', *JICH*, vol.5, No 2, January 1977

Barrow, A. H., *Fifty Years in Western Africa* (London, 1900)

Belcher RN, Captain, 'Extracts from Observations on Various Points of the West Coast of Africa Surveyed by HM Ship *Aetna* in 1830–32', *JRGS*, II, 1832

Bennett, N. R. and G. Brooks, *New England Merchants: African History Through Documents* (Boston, 1965)

Blackburn, R., *The Overthrow of Colonial Slavery 1776–1848* (London, 1988)

Boahen, A. A., *Britain, the Sahara and the Western Sudan: 1788–1961* (Oxford, 1964)

Bosman, W., *Guinea: A New and Accurate Description of the Coast of Guinea* (London, 1704, repr. 1967)

Braithwaite, R. C., 'Palmerston and the Nunez: The Affair Within the Affair, 1849–53', *JICH*, vol.23, no.3, 1995

— 'The Nunez: Sabre d'Honneur?', *RBHM*, vol.31, nos 1/2, mars–juin 1995

— 'The Rio Nunez Affair: New Perspectives on a Significant Event in Nineteenth-Century Franco-British Colonial Rivalry', *RFHOM*, vol.83, no.311, pp.23–44, 1996

— 'Matthew Forster of Bellsise: Entrepreneurial Optimist of the Early Victorian Heyday', *CHR* 19, 1995

Brooks, George, Jnr, *Yankee Traders, Old Coasters, African Middlemen* (Boston, 1970)

— *Big Men, Traders and Chiefs* (Harvard, 1972)

— *Landlords and Strangers, Ecology, Society and Trade in Western Africa 1000–1630* (USA/Oxford, 1993)

Burroughs, P., 'Liberal, Paternalist or Cassandra? Earl Grey as a Critic of Colonial Self-Government', *JICH*, vol.18, no.1, January 1990, pp.33–60

Buxton, Sir T. F., *The African Slave Trade and its Remedy* (London, 1840)

Canot, T., *Twenty Years of an African Slaver* (New York, 1854)

Carlson, D. G., *African Fever* (New York, 1984)

Carson, E., 'The Customs Bills of Entry', *JMH*, 1971

Clarence Smith, W.G., 'Business Empires in Equatorial Africa', African Economic History, vol.12, 1983

Coupland, R., *The British Anti-Slavery Movement* (London, repr. 1964)

Crowder, M., *West Africa under Colonial Rule* (London, 1968)

Curtin, P., *The Atlantic Slave Trade: A Census* (Wisconsin, 1969)

322 SOURCES AND BIBLIOGRAPHY

— *The Image of Africa: British Ideas and Action 1780–1850* (London, 1965)
— *Economic Change in Pre-Colonial Africa* (Wisconsin, 1975)
Daniels, W. C. E., 'English Law in West Africa: The Limits of its Application' (Ph.D. thesis, London University, 1962)
Dorjahn, R. V. and C. Fyfe, 'Landlords and Strangers: Changes in Tenancy Relations in Sierra Leone', *JAH*, vol.3, no.3, (1962)
Dunn, R., *Sugar and Slavery 1624–1713* (Carolina, 1972)
Fieldhouse, D. K., *Unilever Overseas: The Anatomy of a Multinational 1895–1965* (London, 1978)
Flint, J., *Cambridge History of Africa* (Cambridge, 1976)
Fyfe, C., *A History of Sierra Leone* (London, 1962)
Gallagher, J., R. E. Robinson, and A. Denny, *Africa and the Victorians: The Official Mind of Imperialism* (Cambridge, 1961)
Gavin, R. J., 'Palmerston's Policy Towards East and West Africa 1830–1865' (Ph.D. thesis, Cambridge University, 1959)
Gertzel, C., 'John Holt: A British Merchant in West Africa in the Era of Imperialism' (D.Phil thesis, Oxford University, 1959)
Gordon, J., 'The Development of the Legal System in the Colony of Lagos 1862–1905' (Ph.D. thesis, London University, 1967)
Grace, J., *Domestic Slavery in West Africa during the Nineteenth Century* (London, 1975)
Gray, J. M., *A History of The Gambia* (Cambridge, 1940)
Grey, Earl *The Colonial Policy of Lord John Russell's Administration* (London, 1853)
Hall, H. L., *The Colonial Office: A History* (London, 1937)
Hamilton, C. I., *Anglo-French Naval Rivalry: 1840–1870* (Oxford, 1993)
Hargreaves, J. D., *Prelude to the Partition of West Africa* (London, 1963)
— *France and West Africa: An Anthology of Historical Documents* (London, 1969)
Harris, J. M., *Annexations to Sierra Leone and their Influence on British Trade in West Africa* (Freetown, 1883)
Hopkins, A. G., *An Economic History of West Africa* (London, 1973)
Howard, T., *Eye-Witness Accounts of the Atlantic Slave Trade* (Boston, 1971), Equiano, 'Black Voyage'
Howell, R., *The Royal Navy and the Slave Trade* (London, 1987)
Ingram, Governor, 'Expedition up the Gambia', *JRGS*, vol.27, 1847
Lloyd, C., *The Navy and the Slave Trade* (London, 1968)
Lovejoy, P. E., *Transformations in Slavery: A History of Slavery in Africa* (Cambridge, 1983)
Lovejoy, P. E. and J. S. Hogendorn, *Slow Death of Slavery: The Course of Abolition in Northern Nigeria, 1897–1936* (Cambridge, 1993)
Lynn, M., 'British Business Archives and the History of Business in Nineteenth Century West Africa', *Business Archives*, vol.7, no.62, 1991
— 'From Sail to Steam: The Impact of Steamship Services on the British Palm Oil Trade in West Africa 1850–1890', *JAH*, no.30, 1989
McCall, D., N. R. Bennett and J. Butler (eds) *West African History* (New York, 1969)

Macgregor, D. R., *Merchant Sailing Ships 1815–1850* (Conway, 1984)

McPhee, A., *The Economic Revolution in British West Africa* (London, 1926, repr. 1971)

Madden, R. R., *The Memoirs 1798–1886* (edited by his son, London, 1891)

Manning, P., *Slavery and African Life* (Cambridge, 1990)

Martin, E., *The British West African Settlements: A Study in Local Administration, 1750–1821* (London, 1927)

Matthews, N., *Materials for West African History in the Archives of the United Kingdom* (London, 1973)

Melville, E., *A Residence at Sierra Leone* (London, 1849)

Merivale, H., *Lectures on Colonies and Colonization* (Oxford, 1841)

Metcalfe, G., *Maclean of the Gold Coast* (London, 1962)

Miers, S., *Britain and the Ending of the Slave Trade* (London, 1975)

Morrell, W. P., *British Colonial Policy in the Age of Peel and Russell* (London, 1930, repr. 1966)

Mouser, Bruce, 'The Nunez Affair', *BARSOM* (Brussels, 1973)

Newbury, C. W., *British Policy Towards West Africa: Selected Documents* (Oxford, 1965)

— *The Western Slave Coast and its Rulers* (Oxford, 1966)

Northrup, D., *Trade without Rulers, Pre-colonial Economic Development in South-Eastern Nigeria* (Oxford, 1978)

O'Byrne, *A Naval Biographical Dictionary* (London, 1849)

Oliver, R., *The African Experience* (London, 1991)

Oliver, R. and J. D. Fage, *A Short History of Africa* (London, 1974)

Pakenham, T., *The Scramble for Africa: 1876–1912* (London, 1991)

Pedler, F. J., *The Lion and the Unicorn in Africa* (London, 1973)

Platt, D. C. M., *The Cinderella Service: British Consuls since 1825* (London, 1971)

Priestley, M., *West African Trade and Coast Society* (London, 1969)

Pudney, John, *London's Docks* (London, 1975)

Robinson, D., *The Holy War of Umar Tal: The Western Sudan in the Mid-Nineteenth Century* (Oxford, 1985)

Rodney, W., *A History of the Upper Guinea Coast, 1545–1800* (Oxford, 1970)

Scotter, W. H., 'International Rivalry in the Bights of Benin and Biafra, 1815–1885', (Ph.D. thesis, London University, 1933)

Stilliard, N. H., *The Rise and Development of Legitimate Trade in Palm Oil in West Africa* (Birmingham, 1938)

Temperley, Howard, *White Dreams, Black Africa* (New York, 1991)

— *British Anti-Slavery 1833–1870* (London, 1972)

Thornton, P., *Africa and Africans in the Making of the Atlantic World* (Cambridge, 1992)

Tindall, P., 'Race Relations in West Africa in the Slave Trade Era', *Central African History Association* (Salisbury, 1975)

Walvin, J., *England, Slaves and Freedom: 1666–1838* (London, 1986)

— *Slaves and Slavery: The British Colonial Experience* (Manchester, 1992)

Walvin, J., M. Craton and D. Wright, *Slavery, Abolition and Emancipation: Black Slaves and the British Empire* (London, 1976)
Ward, W. E. F., *The Royal Navy and the Slavers* (London, 1969)
— *A History of the Gold Coast* (London, 1949)
White, A., *Joseph Conrad and the Adventure Tradition*, (Cambridge, 1993)
Wilson, C., *The History of Unilever* (London, 1954)
Wolfson, F., 'British Relations with the Gold Coast', (Ph.D. thesis, London University, 1950)
Young, D. M., *The Colonial Office in the Early Nineteenth Century* (London, 1961)

French General and Colonial History: Books, Articles, Theses
Aldrich, R. and J. Connell, *France's Overseas Frontier* (Cambridge, 1992)
Appia, B., 'Notes sur le Génie des Eaux en Guinée', *Journal de la Société des Africains*, vols 14–17 (Paris, 1944–7)
Arcin, A., *Histoire de la Guinée française* (Paris, 1911)
Barrows, Leland, 'The Merchants and General Faidherbe: Aspects of French Expansion in Senegal in the 1850s', *RFHOM* (Paris, 1974)
Bouët-Willaumez, E., *Commerce et traite des noirs aux Côtes occidentales d'Afrique* (Paris, 1848, repr. 1978)
Caillié, R., *Travels through Central Africa to Timbuctoo: 1824–1828* (London, repr. 1992)
Cohen, W. B., *The French Encounter with Africans: White Response to Blacks, 1530–1880* (Indiana, 1986)
Contamine, Henri, *Diplomatie et Diplomates sous la Restauration 1814–1830* (Paris, 1970)
Diallo, T., 'Les Institutions Politiques du Fouta Djalon au XIXème Siècle' (Ph.D. thesis, University of Paris, 1924)
Faidherbe, L., *Le Sénégal: La France dans l'Afrique occidentale* (Paris, 1889)
Furet, F., *Revolutionary France: 1770–1880* (Oxford, 1992)
Gifford, P. and W. R. Louis, *France and Britain in Africa: Imperial Rivalry and Colonial Rule* (Yale, 1971)
Goerg, O., *Commerce et Colonisation en Guinée 1850–1913* (Paris, 1986)
Hardy, G., *La mise en valeur du Sénégal de 1817 à 54* (Paris, 1921)
Henege, D. P., *Colonial Governors from the Fifteenth Century to the Present* (Madison, 1970)
IDC, *Guide des Sources de l'Histoire de l'Afrique au Sud du Sahara: Archives et Bibliothèques Françaises* (Zug, 1970), 8 vols
Jennings, L. *France and Europe in 1848: A Study of French Foreign Affairs in Time of Crisis* (Oxford, 1973)
Marfaing, L., *L'Evolution du commerce au Sénégal, 1830–1930* (Paris, 1991)
Marty, P., 'Le Comptoir français d'Albréda en Gambie, 1817–1826', *Revue de l'Histoire des colonies françaises*, vol.17, Paris, 1942

Martin, J., *L'Aventure coloniale de la France: L'Empire renaissant, 1789–1871* (Paris, 1987)

Pasquier, R., 'A Propos de l'Emancipation des Esclaves au Sénégal en 1848', *RFHOM*, vol.54, 1967

Priestley, H., *France Overseas: A Study of Modern Imperialism* (American Historical Association, Harvard, 1938)

Raffinel, M. Anne, *Nouveau Voyage dans les Pays des Nègres* (Paris, 1846)

Schefer, C., *Sénégal et Dépendances: Instructions aux Gouverneurs, 1831–1854* (Paris, 1927), 2 vols

Schnapper, B., *La politique et le commerce français dans le Golfe de Guinée de 1838 à 1871* (Paris, 1962)

Taillemitte, E., *Dictionnaire de la Marine* (Paris, 1962)

Tramond, J. and A. Reussner, *Eléments d'histoire maritime et coloniale contemporaine* (Paris, 1947)

Vigny, A. de (trans, M. Barnett) *The Military Condition* (London, 1964)
— (ed. J. Cruickshank) *Servitude et Grandeur militaires* (London, 1966)

Westfall, Gloria D., *French Colonial Africa: A Guide to Official Sources* (London, 1992)

Belgium: General Political History/Biography

Cammaerts, E., *The Keystone of Europe: History of the Belgian Dynasty, 1830–1939* (London, 1939)

Corti, E. C., *Leopold I: Oracle politique de l'Europe* (Brussels, 1927)

Richardson, J., *My Dearest Uncle: A Life of Leopold, First King of the Belgians* (London, 1961)

Belgian Colonial Development

Carson, Patricia, *Materials for West African History in the Archives of Belgium and Holland* (London, 1968), pp.17, 57–9, 109–13, 189–95, B/MAE dossiers A.f.6.A, A.f.7, 2024

Collignon, Lieutenant, 'A la Découverte de Van Haverbeke', *La Gazette du Soldat* (Brussels, December 1956)

Delcourt, G., 'Relation du Voyage à la Côte d'Afrique avec la Goélette *Louise-Marie* 1848–9', unpublished archive of the MRA, Brussels

Demougeot, A., 'Histoire du Nunez', *Bulletin du Comité d'Etudes historiques et scientifiques* (Paris, 1938)

de Vos, H., 'Petite Histoire de la Marine royale', *Annales de l'Académie de Marine de Belgique*, vol.9 (Antwerp, 1955)

de Vos, L., P. Lefevre, R. Boijen, *J'Avais 20 Ans en 1945*(Brussels, 1995)

Duchesne, A., 'Un Centenaire oublié: Le Combat de Debocca (Rio Nunez) 24 mars 1849', *Carnet de la Fourragère*, vol.8, no.7, (Brussels, September, 1949)
— 'Des Tentatives de colonisation et de l'expansion belge sous le règne de Leopold I', *BARSOM* (Brussels, 1958), no.68, new series vol.4, no.2, pp.783–5

Dumont, Georges-H., *150 Ans d'Expansion et de Colonisation* (Brussels, 1956)

Everaert, J. and C. De Wilde, 'Pindanoten voor de eerste ontluikende industrële revolutie. Een alternative kijk op de Belgische commerciële expansie in West-Afrika: 1844–1861', *BARSOM*, Brussels, 1992

Lannoy, C./T. du Colombier, 'Une Expédition franco-belge en Guinée: La Campagne de la goélette de guerre *Louise-Marie* dans la Colonie belge du Rio-Nunez (1849)', *BESBEC*, Brussels, mai–juin 1920

Leconte, L., 'La Marine de guerre belge: Lamentable histoire de petits bateaux', *Bull. du Touring Club de Belgique*, no.15, Brussels, 1920

Lefevre, P., 'Voyages de la marine royale belge au Sénégal, en Gambie et en basse Guinée. Récits des médicins qui accompagnèrent les navires de guerre belges *Louise-Marie* et *Duc de Brabant* (1847–1856) dans le cadre de la tentative de colonisation au Rio Nunez', *RBHM*, vols 22–3, 1978/9

Macoir, G., 'Note sur un Sabre d'Honneur décerné à Capt [VH]', *Bull. des Musées royaux des Arts décoratifs et industriels* (Brussels, 1907)

Massinon, R., *L'Entreprise du Rio Nunez: Mémoire de Licence inédit ULB*, Brussels, 1962

Monheim, C., *Notre histoire coloniale: L'Affaire du Rio Nunez, 1848–1858* (Louvain, 1931)

— 'Le Rio Nunez: Une Colonie pour 5000 francs', *Communications de l'Académie de Marine de Belgique* (Antwerp, 1950)

Petitjean, O., 'Les Tentatives de colonisation faites sous le règne de Leopold Ier': *La Belgique en 1930* (Brussels, October–November 1930)

Crimean War

Anderson, Olive, *A Liberal State at War: English Politics and Economics during the Crimean War* (New York, 1967)

de Guichen, Comte, *La Guerre de Crimée* (Paris, 1936)

Haraszti-Taylor, E. H., *Kossuth: Hungarian Patriot in Britain* (London and Budapest, private edition, 1994)

— *Kossuth as an English Journalist* (Budapest, 1990)

Judd, D., *The Crimean War* (London, 1975)

Saab, Ann P., *The Origins of the Crimean Alliance* (Virginia. 1977)

Schroeder, P. W., *Austria, Great Britain, and the Crimean War: The Destruction of the European Concert* (Cornell, 1972)

Temperley, H. W. V., *England and The Near East: The Crimea* (Cambridge, 1936, repr. 1964)

Wetzel, D., *The Crimean War: A Diplomatic History* (New York, 1985)

Modern Guinea

Davidson, B., 'Guinea Past and Present', *History Today*, vol.9, no.6, June, 1959

Fröhlich, G., *Guinea nach der Regenzeit* (Leipzig, 1961)

Nelson, H. D. (ed.) *Guinea* (American University of Washington's series of Area Handbooks, 1975)

O'Brien, D. C., J. Dunn and R. Rathbone (eds) *Contemporary West African States* (Cambridge, 1989)

O'Toole, Thomas, *Historical Dictionary of Guinea* (New York and London, 1978)
Rivière, C., *Mutations sociales en Guinée* (Paris, 1971)
Suret-Canale, J., *La République de Guinée* (Paris, 1970)

European History, General

Adenauer, K. (trans B. Buhm von Oppen) *Memoirs: 1945–53* (London, 1966)
Bullock, A., *Hitler and Stalin: Parallel Lives* (London, 1991)
Eckert, W., *Kurland unter dem Einfluss des Merkantilismus: 1551–1682* (Riga, 1927)
Zamoyska, P., *Arch Intriguer: A Biography of Dorothea de Lieven* (London, 1957)

Index

Rolla, HMS, 90, 100n
Roman republic, 26, 29
Romsey, 15

Ropass/Rospas, 2, 125–6, 128, 140–3, 146–7, 149, 151–2, 155–6, 160, 162–3, 166–7, 204, 229
Rosas, General, 237
Rosebery, Archibald Philip Primrose (1847–1929, 5th Earl, PM 1894–5), 13, 274
Rotherhithe, *see* London
Rouen, 68
Royal African Company, 47, 78–9
Royal Army History Museum, Brussels, 113
Royal Navy, 6, 69, 83, 88–9, 146, 175, 214, 290, 310; *see also* navy (British)
royal prerogative, *see* Constitution, British (prerogative)
rules of war, 195, 211
rum, role in trade, 65; *see also* United States of America
rumour, *see* hearsay
Russell, Lord John (1792–1878, 1st Earl 1861, leader HoC 1835–41, Colonial Secretary 1839–41, PM 1846–52, 1865–6, leader 1852–3), 5, 14, 16, 18–22, 27, 30–5, 81, 86, 89, 98, 169, 231–3, 242, 244, 247, 251–3, 256, 278–80, 282, 285–6, 303, 309; *see also* select committee of House of Commons on West Africa; slave trade
Africa, 81, 89
ambition, 21
comparison with P, 19, 21, 31–5, 232, 251
military-mindedness, lack of, 18
Minto, 20
relations with P, 14, 16, 19, 20, 21–2, 30–5, 89, 231–3, 251, 253, 267; Queen Victoria, 18, 19, 34–5, 251, 256, 285
Whig families, 22, 86, 232
Russia, 298; *see also* Nesselrode; Nicholas I; threats to routes to India
Britain's relations with, 12, 261, 290
dock, *see* London
Lieven, Princess, 18
Russophobia, 104 131n; *see also* phobias

Soviet Union, 260
Stalin, 271, 275

S'ahara/Sarah, King (of Landumas, father of Tongo, Mayoré and Massounkong, d.1844), 51n, 129, 130n, 153, 311
St Aubyn, Giles (author), 38n
St Helena, 21
St Herbert, Madame (mistress of Leopold I), 118
St James's Park, *see* London
St Katharine's Dock, *see* London
St Louis, Senegal, 63, 69, 73, 101, 109
St Mary Axe, *see* London
St Thomas, island of, 88
sacred woods, *see* Simo secret society
Sahara desert, 63
Salcedo, M. (French trader), 247, 311
Salisbury, Lord, 269
Salop, *see* Shropshire
salt, role in trading, 69
Saltash, Cornwall, 51, 178, 240n
Sandon, Viscount Dudley Ryder (1798–1882, later 2nd Earl of Harrowby, entered HoC 1819, chairman of HoC Select Committee 1842), 82
Santon, M. (French trader), 140, 147
Sarah, King, *see* S'ahara/Sarah, King
Saxe-Coburg-[Gotha], House of, 116; *see also* Albert of Saxe-Coburg-Gotha, Prince Consort; Ernst of Saxe-Coburg; Leopold II, King
Saxon, HMS, 33
Saxony, 299
scandals, political, over Rio Nunez Affair, 34, 54, 189–234
Schleswig-Holstein, Denmark 'Question' of, 20, 199
war with Prussia, 199–10
Schmalz, General, 73
Schoelcher, Victor, 131n
schooners, 45–9, 149, 202
Schwarzenberg, Prince (1800–52, Austrian Chancellor), 35, 252
Schweitzer, Albert, 176–7, 187n
Scramble for Africa, 189, 261
Sealark, HMS, 166, 183n, 310
seasoning, *see* disease
Sebastopol, 305n
Seckendorff, Ambassador, 35, 258n
Sedhiou, 52, 202, 217, 238–9n

BOKÉ, RIO NUNEZ, March 24 1849

(Based on a sketch by Lt. de Kerhallet 1849, Centre des Archives d'Outre-Mer, Aix.)

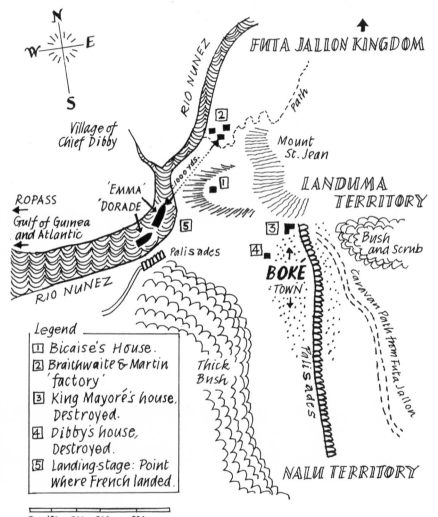

FUTA JALLON KINGDOM

Path

RIO NUNEZ

Village of Chief Dibby

Mount St. Jean

LANDUMA TERRITORY

'EMMA' 'DORADE'

ROPASS

Gulf of Guinea and Atlantic

RIO NUNEZ

Palisades

Bush and Scrub

Caravan Path from Futa Jallon

BOKÉ TOWN

Palisades

Thick Bush

NALU TERRITORY

1000 yds.

Legend
1. Bicaise's House.
2. Braithwaite & Martin 'factory'.
3. King Mayoré's house, Destroyed.
4. Dibby's house, Destroyed.
5. Landing-stage: Point where French landed.

0   100   200   300   500
scale in metres

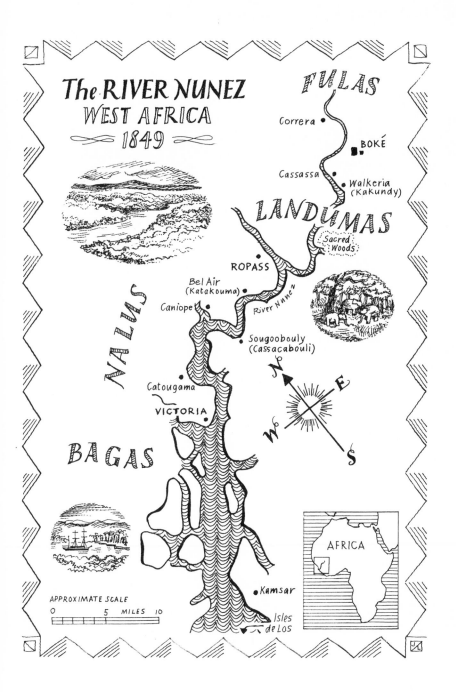

The RIVER NUNEZ
WEST AFRICA
~ 1849 ~

FULAS

Correra •

BOKÉ ■

Cassassa •

• Walkeria
(Kakundy)

LANDUMAS

Sacred
Woods

ROPASS •

Bel Air
(Katakouma) •

Caniope •

River Nunez

Sougoobouly
(Cassacabouli) •

NALUS

Catougama •

VICTORIA •

N

E

W

S

BAGAS

AFRICA

• Kamsar

Isles
de Los

APPROXIMATE SCALE

0   5   MILES   10